François Lenormant

The Book of Genesis

A translation from the Hebrew

François Lenormant

The Book of Genesis
A translation from the Hebrew

ISBN/EAN: 9783337316853

Printed in Europe, USA, Canada, Australia, Japan

Cover: Foto ©Lupo / pixelio.de

More available books at **www.hansebooks.com**

THE
BOOK OF GENESIS

THE

BOOK OF GENESIS

A TRANSLATION FROM THE HEBREW

IN WHICH THE

CONSTITUENT ELEMENTS OF THE TEXT ARE SEPARATED

TO WHICH IS ADDED

AN ATTEMPTED RESTORATION OF THE ORIGINAL DOCUMENTS

USED BY THE LATEST REVISER

BY

FRANÇOIS LENORMANT

MEMBER OF THE INSTITUTE

Translated from the French

WITH AN INTRODUCTION AND NOTES BY THE AUTHOR OF
'MANKIND, THEIR ORIGIN AND DESTINY'

LONDON
LONGMANS, GREEN, AND CO.
1886

CONTENTS.

	PAGE
INTRODUCTION	vii

PART I.

THE MASSORETIC TEXT OF GENESIS IN ITS PRESENT STATE ... 1

PART II.

THE BOOK OF ORIGINS, OR JEHOVISTIC DOCUMENT.

1. THE CREATION OF MAN AND WOMAN	167
2. THE FIRST SIN	169
3. QAÎN AND HÂBEL	172
4. THE TWO LINES OF ÂDÂM'S POSTERITY	174
5. THE SONS OF GOD AND THE DAUGHTERS OF MEN	175
6. THE DELUGE	176
7. THE CURSE UPON KENÂ'AN	179
8. THE LINEAGE OF THE SONS OF NÔA'H	180
9. THE TOWER OF BÂBEL	181
10. THE CALL OF ABRÂHÂM	182
11. ABRÂHÂM IN EGYPT	183
12. ABRÂHÂM AND LÔT SEPARATE	184
13. RESCUE OF LÔT BY ABRÂHÂM, AND BLESSING OF ABRÂHÂM BY MALKÎ'ÇEDEQ	186
14. COVENANT BETWEEN YAHVEH AND ABRÂHÂM	188
15. BIRTH OF YISHMÂ'ÊL	191
16. YIÇE'HÂQ'S BIRTH PROMISED	192
17. ABRÂHÂM INTERVENES ON BEHALF OF SEDÔM	194
18. DESTRUCTION OF SEDÔM AND 'AMÔRÂH	196
19. LÔT AND HIS DAUGHTERS	200
20. BIRTH OF YIÇE'HÂQ	201
21. THE SACRIFICE OF ABRÂHÂM	202

CONTENTS.

	PAGE
22. THE CHILDREN OF NÂ'HÔR . . .	204
23. THE MARRIAGE OF YIÇE'HÂQ AND RIBQÂH	205
24. YA'AQÔB AND 'ÊSÂV	212
25. YIÇE'HÂQ AND ABÎMELECH AT GERÂR . . .	214
26. YA'AQÔB OBTAINS HIS FATHER'S BLESSING BY STRATAGEM	217
27. THE VISION OF YA'AQÔB	222
28. LÂBÂN ENTERTAINS YA'AQÔB .	224
29. YA'AQÔB LEAVES LÂBÂN . . .	231
30. YA'AQÔB PREPARES TO MEET HIS BROTHER	237
31. YA'AQÔB WRESTLES WITH ELÔHÎM . .	239
32. MEETING OF YA'AQÔB AND 'ÊSÂV	240
33. THE SONS OF YA'AQÔB AND THE INHABITANTS OF SHECHEM	242
34. BÊTH-ÊL RECONSECRATED . . .	245
35. DEATH OF RÂ'HÊL . .	246
36. YÔSÊPH AND HIS BRETHREN	247
37. YEHÛDÂH AND TÂMÂR . . .	249
38. YÔSÊPH IN PÔTIPHAR'S HOUSE .	252
39. YÔSÊPH IS ADVANCED IN MIÇRÂÎM	255
40. FIRST MEETING OF YÔSÊPH AND HIS BRETHREN . . .	256
41. SECOND MEETING OF YÔSÊPH AND HIS BRETHREN. YÔSÊPH MAKES HIMSELF KNOWN TO THEM . .	256
42. THE FAMILY OF YA'AQÔB SETTLES IN MIÇRÂÎM	265
43. BLESSING OF THE SONS OF YÔSÊPH . .	267
44. BLESSING OF THE SONS OF YA'AQÔB . .	270
45. DEATH AND FUNERALS OF YA'AQÔB AND YÔSÊPH .	273

PART III.

THE BOOK OF GENEALOGIES, OR ELOHISTIC DOCUMENT.

1. THE GENEALOGIES OF THE HEAVEN AND OF THE EARTH	279
2. THE GENEALOGIES OF ÂDÂM . . .	283
3. THE GENEALOGIES OF NÔA'H . .	285
4. THE GENEALOGIES OF THE SONS OF NÔA'H	291
5. THE GENEALOGIES OF SHÊM .	293
6. THE GENEALOGIES OF TERA'H .	294
7. THE GENEALOGIES OF ABRÂHÂM	295
8. THE GENEALOGIES OF YISHMÂ'ÊL	303
9. THE GENEALOGIES OF YIÇE'HÂQ	304
10. THE GENEALOGIES OF 'ÊSÂV	310
11. THE GENEALOGIES OF YA'AQÔB	314

INTRODUCTION.

In the year 1753 Jean Astruc, a celebrated physician, published a work called 'Conjectures sur les mémoires originaux qui ont servi à Moïse pour écrire la Genèse.' Leclerc ('Diss. Ill. de Scriptore Pentateuchi') and R. Simon ('Hist. critique du Vieux Testament,' livr. i. ch. 7) had previously pointed out the existence of two distinct documents in Genesis.

M. Lenormant observes that while every verse of the Pentateuch has been discussed minutely and word by word with the view of determining its origin, the details of this necessary labour have become so complicated that only a professional critic can obtain a general view of its results. This induced him to undertake the present work, in order that the conclusions of the specialists might become more generally known, and, if his lamented death had not interrupted the project, he intended to analyse the other books of the Pentateuch in the same manner. He says :—

'Many attempts have been made to invalidate the conclusions of criticism, but, to select a few instances, no one has ever been able to explain how it is that man and animals are created by Yahveh in chap. ii. after having been created by Elohim in chap. i.; how it is that the name of Yahveh is said in Gen. iv. 26 to have been known to men ever since a period before the Deluge, when in Ex. vi. 3 it is said to have been unknown to the patriarchs; how it is that in Gen. vi. 5 it is Yahveh, and in verse 12 it is Elohim who sees that the world is corrupt; and, lastly, how it is that while in Gen. vi. 13 Elohim orders Noah to make the ark, it is Yahveh in chap. vii. 1 who commands him to enter it, and how it is that in doing so Noah obeys Elohim according to verse 5, and Yahveh according to verse 9.

Dean Stanley, speaking of 'the gifted seer, whoever he was, that wrote that first chapter of the Book of Genesis,' remarks ('Sermons on Special Occasions,' p. 201) :—

'It is well known that when the science of Geology first arose, it was involved in endless schemes of attempted reconciliation with the letter of Scripture. There were, there are perhaps still, two modes of reconciliation of Scripture and science, which have been each in their day attempted, and have each totally and deservedly failed. One is the endeavour to wrest the words of the Bible from their natural meaning, and force them to speak the language of science. Of this, the earliest and perhaps the most memorable example was set by the Greek translators in the time of the Ptolemies—the Seventy, as they are called. They came, in the course of their translation, to that verse of Leviticus containing the well-known stumbling-block, which they probably were the first to discern, which speaks of the hare as one of the animals which chew the cud. In the old world, before the birth of accurate observation, that which had the appearance of rumination was mistaken for the reality, and was so described. But by the time that the Greek translation of the Bible was undertaken, the greatest naturalist of antiquity, the world-famous Aristotle, had already devoted his sagacious mind to the study of the habits of animals, and through his writings the true state of the case had been made known. The venerable scholars who were at work on the translation were too conscientious to reject the clear evidence of science: but they were too timid to allow the contradiction to appear, and therefore, with the usual rashness of fear, they boldly interpolated the word "NOT" into the sacred text, and thus, as they thought, reconciled it to science by making the whole passage mean exactly the reverse of that which was intended. This is the earliest instance of the falsification of Scripture to meet the demands of science; and it has been followed in later times by the various efforts which have been made to twist the earlier chapters of Genesis into apparent agreement with the last results of Geology

—representing days not to be days, morning and evening not to be morning and evening, the deluge not to be the deluge, and the ark not to be the ark.' (Sermon on the death of Sir Charles Lyell.)

Wellhausen in his 'History of Israel' observes that the language of the Elohist differs considerably from that of the pre-exilic historical books, and that the author makes use of a whole series of characteristic expressions which are not in use before the exile, but gradually emerge and come into use after it. Neither narrative, however, he considers, can be regarded as other than complex products, alongside of which occur hybrid or posthumous elements which do not admit of being simply referred to one or the other formation.

Almost every nation in antiquity had its cosmogony. There are two cosmogonies in Genesis: the Jehovistic one contained in Gen. ii. 4 b-7, and the Elohistic one in Gen. i.–ii. 4 a. The following is a literal translation of the earlier or Jehovistic cosmogony, and the narrative which follows up to the expulsion of Adam and Eve from the garden of Eden, with some extracts from the Targums of Onkelos, Jonathan ben Uzziel and others. The Targum of Onkelos is held to be of equal authority with the Mosaic text, and he is said merely to have committed to writing what had been handed down by tradition from Mount Sinai. Zunz says that 'Onkelos, somewhere about the time of Philo, translated the Pentateuch, and that Jonathan ben Uzziel, the paraphrast on the prophetical books, was a scholar of Hillel.'

[It was all a dry waste][1] when Yahveh made earth and heaven.[2] And no bush of the field and no green herb of the field had yet

---

[1] Wellhausen points out that this first sentence has been cut off by the reviser.

[2] In *Tr. Haghiga*, ii. 1, there is a detailed account of the dispute between the schools of Shammaï and Hillel respecting the creation. The disciples of Shammaï said that heaven was created first and the earth afterwards; the disciples of Hillel held the opposite opinion. The Shammaïtes founded their belief on Gen. i. 1, 'In the beginning God created the heaven and the earth.' This, they said, resembled the act of that king who, after having built up a throne, formed the pedestal (ὑποπόδιον) of it, according to the

sprouted forth, [1] for Yahveh Elôhîm had not caused it to rain upon the earth, and there was not a man (an Âdâm) to till the ground (hâ'adâmâh).[2] And an exhalation went up from the earth, and watered the whole face of the ground. And Yahveh Elôhîm formed the man of the dust of the ground, and breathed into his nostrils the breath of lives, and the man became a living creature.[3]

Here the cosmogony, strictly speaking, ends, but the work of creation is not completed till the end of the chapter. Up to the present time we have an arid earth. Schrader points out the resemblance to the Babylonian creation story, line 6, '... a sprout had not yet sprung forth,' in the representation of the condition of the earth. Yahveh formed the man of the dust of the ground: that is, he fashioned him as a potter does clay. Conf. Job x. 9, 'Remember, I beseech thee, that thou hast fashioned me as clay; and wilt thou bring me into dust again?' Josephus says man was called 'adâm,' red, because he was made of virgin and true earth. See Cant. v. 10. For 'dust' we should probably read 'dry earth' (*trockene Erde*), as in Gen. xxvi. 15; Josh. vii. 6; Job ii. 11 (Ges.).

'And he breathed into his nostrils the breath of lives.' The words (Is. lxvi. 1) 'The heaven is my throne, and the earth is my footstool.' The Hillelites relied on Gen. ii. 4, 'in the day that the Everlasting God made earth and the heavens.' Such, they held, was the custom in regal buildings, to lay the foundation first, and afterwards the superstructure, according to Is. xlviii. 13, 'Yea, mine hand hath laid the foundation of the earth, and my right hand hath spread out the heavens.'

[1] Onkelos, 'And all trees of the field were not yet in the earth, and every herb of the field had not yet sprung up.'

[2] Jonathan, 'Because the Lord God had not made it to rain upon the earth, and man was not to cultivate the ground. But a cloud of glory descended from the throne of glory, and was filled with waters from the ocean, and afterwards went up from the earth, and gave rain to come down and water all the face of the ground.'

[3] O., 'And the Lord God created Adam from dust of the ground, and breathed upon his face the breath of lives, and it became in Adam a Discoursing Spirit.'

J., 'And the Lord God created man in two formations; and took dust from the house of the sanctuary [Mount Moriah], and from the four winds of the world, and created him red, black, and white: and breathed into his nostrils the inspiration of a speaking spirit unto the illumination of the eyes and the hearing of the ears.'

INTRODUCTION xi

Hebrew '*ayyim* is in the plural, and is correctly translated 'lives' by Onkelos. Josephus says that God inserted into man a spirit and a soul, and it was the universal belief, not only among the Jews, but among the ancients generally, that man consisted of spirit, soul and body. In 'Ant.' iii. 1, § 2, Josephus says that the blood of animals was forbidden to be eaten because it had in it soul and spirit. In 1 Thess. v. 23 (conf. 1 Cor. xv. 44, 45), Paul speaks of πνευμα and ψυχη as distinct from σωμα. The Greeks had three sorts of souls—ψυχη the soul of the senses; πνευμα, corresponding to *spiritus*, spirit, or breath, which gives life and movement to the body, and νους, or intellect. The Fathers believed the soul to be material. Irenæus says the soul is only incorporeal in comparison with the body. Tertullian calls the flesh the body of the soul, and the soul the body of the spirit, and mentions the vision of a holy woman who had seen a very brilliant soul which was of the same colour as the air.

And Yahveh Elôhim planted a garden eastward in Êden [1]; and there he put the man whom he had formed. And out of the ground made Yahveh Elôhim to sprout forth every tree that is pleasant to the sight, and good for food ; the tree of lives also in the midst of the garden, and the tree of knowledge of good and evil.[2] And a river flowed forth from Êden to water the garden ; and from thence it was divided and became four heads.[3] The name of the first is Pishôn : that is it which compasseth the whole land of Havilâh, where there *is* gold ; and the gold of that land *is* good [4] : there is the

[1] O., 'The Lord God planted a garden in a region of pleasantness' (Samaritan version, 'paradise,') ' in the time of the beginning.'
J., ' And a garden from the Eden of the just was planted by the Word of the Lord God before the creation of the world.'
[2] O., ' The Tree of Life (Lives), and the Tree of whose fruit they who eat know between good and evil.'
J., ' The Tree of Life in the midst of the garden, whose height was a journey of five hundred years, and the tree of whose fruit they who ate would distinguish between good and evil.'
[3] O., ' And a river went forth from Eden to water the garden ' (Sam. ' islands ').
[4] Sam., ' Phison-kadoph.' J., ' The name of the first is Phishon : that is it which compasseth all the land of Hindiki, where there is gold. And the gold of that land is choice.'

bedóla'h and the shôham stone.[1] And the name of the second river is Qî'hôn[2]: the same is it that compasseth the whole land of Kûsh.[3] And the name of the third river is Hiddeqel[4]: that is it which goeth east of Asshûr.[5] And the fourth river is the Phrâth.

Eden is the region, of which the gan or garden (Deut. xi. 10) is a portion. The rabbis say that the tree of life represents the sixtieth part of the garden, and the garden the sixtieth part of Eden, and that the expression 'A river went out of Eden to water the garden' shows that the latter is only a portion of Eden.

The Aryan Paradise, like the Hebrew one, had four rivers, which the Brahmans named the Sita, the Alakananda, the Vakshu, and the Bhadro, which, according to Wilson, are respectively the Hoang-ho, the Ganges, the Oxus, and the Oby. The Buddhists called them the Ganges, the Indus, the Oxus, and the Sita, and said they all flowed from a great central lake in the plateau of Pamîr called A-neou-ta, that is the Kara-kul or Sarik-kul (Yellow Lake), which, however, they do not. The Mohammedans call the Oxus Jaihîm—that is, the Gihon of the Hebrew Paradise. The Pamîr plateau is called Bâm-i-dunyâ, or the Roof of the World, and is identical with the northern Imaös of Ptolemy (Sansk. *hima*, cold), and Mêru, the primeval Aryan Paradise and the centre from which their migrations took place. Ewald considers the Pison and the Gihon to be identical with the Indus and the Ganges.

Josephus says the garden was watered by one river, which ran about the whole earth, and was parted into four parts, viz. Phison (which he identifies with the Ganges), the Euphrates and Tigris, which run into the Red Sea, and the Geon, which runs through Egypt, and denotes what arises from the east, which the Greeks call Nile. There was nothing surprising in this to the ancients. In Greece the Delians had a stream which they

---

[1] O., 'Bedalcha and burilla-stones.'
J., 'There is the bedilcha, and the precious stones of byrils.'
[2] O., 'Gichon'; Sam., 'Askoph.'
[3] Sam., 'Chophin.'
[4] O., 'Diqelath'; Sam., 'Kephlosah.'
[5] O., 'East of Athur;' Sam., 'Kingdom of Hatsphu.'

said was a branch of the Nile. Pausanias (II. v. 2) says the Nile was identical with the Euphrates, which lost itself in a lake, and reappeared in Upper Ethiopia. Alexander thought that he had found the sources of the Nile when he discovered crocodiles in the Indus. Diodorus says (i. 12; xix. 26) that an ocean stream flowed round the earth; and the Hebrews held that Yahveh 'founded the earth upon the seas, and established it upon the floods' (Ps. xxiv. 2), and again, in Ps. cxxxvi. he is said to have 'spread forth the earth above the waters.' The abyss (Gen. i. 1), or 'the deep that cometh beneath' (Gen. xlix. 25), is the source of the rivers, and even the sea, as in Job xxxviii. 8, 'when it brake forth, and issued out of the womb.' Upon this abyss the earth floated: thus in Eccl. i. 7, 'All the rivers run into the sea, yet the sea is not full; unto the place whither the rivers go, thither they go again.'

The obvious situation for the Hebrew garden of Eden is the cradle of the Noachid races. M. Halévy ('Mélanges de critique et d'histoire relatifs aux peuples Sémitiques') places it in the Semitic territory, bounded on the east and north by the Tigris and the Euphrates, while on the other two sides the country inhabited by the Semites and Kushites in common is watered by the Erythræan Sea, which surrounds the whole land of Kush, or the Arabian peninsula. He identifies the Phison with the Wadi Houdayfa, which flows round the present Khaoulân, where gold dust is still found. The Hebrew author may well have imagined that the Phison was in communication subterraneously with the Euphrates, which would thus have formed the line of demarcation between the Semites and the Western Cushites. There is a tradition to this effect in the country, and Pliny (vi. 28) says, 'Murranimal juxta flumen, per quod Euphratem emergere putant.' M. Halévy finds the name Pishôn, which is unknown to any other Semitic country and to the later Bible writers, in his Sabean texts (Har. 11, 19) as the name of a river: 'the Phison having overflowed, the famine came to an end.' The Hebrew geographer takes as the starting-point of his description, not the sources of the Euphrates and Tigris, nor even their upper courses, which traverse non-Semitic countries, but the Chatti-el-Arab, which is formed by their junction. His description, therefore, indicates only the boundary of the Semitic countries, and has no reference to the current of the rivers, for Hebrew antiquity considered that the sources of rivers in general came from the sea by subterranean communication, whence *the-homoth* (αβυσσοι, LXX). The Schatt is the river which proceeds from the two extremities of the Syrian province of Eden (Ezek. xxvii. 23) to bifurcate afterwards into four branches, two on each side. Paradise itself was situated near the confines of Eden on the Arabian side.

And Yahveh Elôhim took the man, and placed him in the garden of Éden to till it and to keep it.[1] And Yahveh Elôhim commanded the man, saying, Of every tree of the garden thou mayest freely eat : and from the tree of the knowledge of good and evil thou shalt not eat from it : for in the day of thy eating from it dying thou shalt die. And Yahveh Elôhim said, *It is* not good that the man should be alone ; I will make for him a helper corresponding to him.[2] And Yahveh Elôhim formed out of the ground every beast of the field, and every fowl of the air ; and he brought them unto the man to see what he will call it : and everything which the man called every living creature, that was its name. And the man gave names to all the cattle and to the fowl of the air, and to every beast of the field : but for man he found not a helper corresponding to him. And Yahveh Elôhim caused a deep sleep to fall upon the man, and he slept ; and he took one from his ribs, and he closed the flesh instead of it. And Yahveh Elôhim formed the rib[3] which he took from the man into a woman, and he brought her unto the man. And the man said, This *is* now [4] bone from my bones, and flesh from my flesh : she shall be called woman (*isshâh*) because she was taken from man (*ish*). Therefore shall a man leave his father and his mother,[5] and

[1] J., 'And the Lord God took the man from the mountain of worship, where he had been created, and made him dwell in the garden of Eden, to do service in the law, and to keep its commandments.'

[2] J., 'And the Lord God said, It is not right that Adam should be sleeping alone: I will make unto him a wife who may be a helper before him.'

[3] O., 'Builded the rib.' J., 'He took one of his ribs—it was the thirteenth rib of the right side—and closed it up with flesh.'

[4] O., 'Adam said, This now (this time).' J., 'Adam said, This time, and not again, is woman created from man.'

[5] O., 'Therefore shall a man forsake the sleeping-house (*beth mishkeb*).'

shall cleave to his wife, and they shall be one flesh. And they were both of them naked, the man and his wife, and they were not ashamed.

The creation of animals is quite different from that in the first chapter. There is no creation of fish or of reptiles. The birds which, like the fish, were formed out of water in chap. i. 20 *sqq.*, are here made out of the ground. These animals must have been useless to Adam for either food or clothing. They were frugivorous like himself, and death was as yet unknown. The idea of Yahveh bringing them to Adam to see if he could find a helper among them is apparently an attempt to account for their otherwise useless creation. In the prophecy of the restoration of Israel in Is. xi. 6-9, this Paradisiacal state is renewed, the wolf will lie down with the lamb, the cow and the bear will feed and their young ones will lie down together, and the lion will eat straw like the ox. In Deutero-Isaiah lxv. 25, where this passage is partially repeated, it is added that 'dust shall be the serpent's meat.' In Gen. i. 30 also the green herb alone is given for food ' to every beast of the earth, and to every fowl of the air, and to every thing that creepeth upon the earth wherein there is the breath of life.' According to the Hebrew writers, therefore, there were no carnivora in Paradise.

And the serpent was crafty above every beast of the field,[1] which Yahveh Elôhîm made. And he said unto the woman, Yea surely Elôhîm said, Ye shall not eat of any tree of the garden. And the woman said unto the serpent, Of the fruit of the tree of the garden we shall eat. And of the fruit of the tree which *is* in the midst of the garden, Elôhîm said, Ye shall not eat of it, and ye shall not touch it, lest ye die.[2] And the serpent said unto the woman, Not to die shall ye die. For Elôhîm knows that in the day of your eating of it your eyes shall be opened, and ye shall be like Elôhîm knowing

---

J., ' Therefore a man shall leave and be separate from the house of the bed of his father and of his mother, and shall consociate with his wife, and both of them shall be one flesh. And both of them were wise, Adam and his wife, but they were not truthful in their glory.

[1] O., ' The serpent (*chivja*) was more crafty than all the beasts of the field.' J., ' And the serpent was wiser unto evil.'

[2] Sam., ' Lest ye be consumed.'

good and evil.¹ And the woman saw that the tree *was* good for food and that it *was* a desire for the eyes, and the tree *was* to be desired to cause to understand, and she took of its fruit, and she ate,² and she gave also to her husband with her, and he ate. And the eyes of them both were opened, and they knew that they *were* naked; and they sewed leaf of fig tree together, and they made themselves girdles.³

The LXX translate 'crafty' by φρονιμωτατος, 'the most intelligent.' This serpent is no supernatural being, but a 'beast of the field,' who is able to walk and to speak the same language as the protoplasts. Augustine ('De Civ. Dei,' xiv. 26) says that man as originally created might have lived for ever. If he was hungry there was plenty of food, if he was thirsty there was plenty to drink, and the tree of life prevented him from getting old. He could have no pain or sickness, and could meet with no accidents. His body was perfectly healthy, and his mind was quite tranquil. He would have known his wife with an entire tranquillity of mind and body, and without her virginity being touched.

It is evident that if Adam and Eve had had children the garden of Eden would soon have been unable to contain the increasing family. The command given by Elohim in chap. i. 28, 'Be fruitful and multiply, and replenish the earth,' is given to beings who were to inhabit the earth.

Mr. Samuel Sharpe says in his history of the Hebrew nation, 'The garden of Eden, which was watered from heaven

---

¹ O., 'Not to die will you die, for it is manifest before the Lord that in the day in which you eat of it your eyes will be opened, and you will be as the Great-ones, knowing good and evil.' J., 'In that hour the serpent spake accusation against his Creator, and said to the woman, Dying you will not die: for every artificer hateth the son of his art: for it is manifest before the Lord, that in the day that you eat of it, you will be as the Great Angels, who are wise to know between good and evil.'

² O., 'She took of its fruitage (*aiba*) and ate.' J., 'And the woman beheld Sammaël, the angel of death, and was afraid; yet she knew that the tree was good to eat, and that it was medicine for the enlightenment of the eyes, and a desirable tree by means of which to understand.'

³ J., 'And the eyes of both were enlightened, and they knew that they were naked, divested of the purple robe in which they had been created. And they saw the sight of their shame, and sewed to themselves the leaves of figs, and made to them cinctures.'

without rain, the sacred tree of knowledge, the serpent, the author of sin, which speaks and walks upright before it does wrong, but creeps on its belly when cursed, are all of Egyptian origin. Moreover, the whole aim of the allegory is foreign to the Hebrew mind. The Hebrew writers never inquire into the origin of sin and evil. Again, by the forbidden fruit the writer means marriage, which he thus blames: and the first pair have no children till they have fallen from their state of innocence. It was among the Egyptians, but not among the Jews, that celibacy was thought more holy than marriage.'

What was the fruit of the tree of knowledge of which Adam and Eve partook? The Church of Rome says it was an apple. They have the following hymn:

>De parentis protoplasti
>Fraude factus condolens
>Quando pomi noxialis
>Morsu in necem corruit;
>Ipse lignum tunc notavit
>Damna ligni ut solveret.

In many theological systems the serpent is said to have led women away with autumnal fruits. Sometimes apples, sometimes the juice of the grape is the instrument employed. It was the period of the year when fruit hung temptingly on the trees, when snakes and scorpions abounded, and when the serpent, whom Ahriman had made and who assaulted the creation of Ahura-mazda, begins the reign of evil under Libra, when men begin to gather apples. Under the Scorpion cold appears; under Sagittarius, snow; under Capricorn, ice and fogs, darkness and long nights; under Aquarius, rain and hoar-frost; under Pisces, gales of wind.

Sappho gives another version of these legends when she represents the youthful maiden as resembling a desirable apple, which, so long as it hangs on the tree, is longed for by everyone, but which, when it has fallen from the tree, and has therefore become damaged, is no longer wished for by any one; οιον το γλυκυ μαλον ερευθεται κ.τ.λ. ('Philologus,' iii. 242).

The apple, however, is a native of Europe, not of Asia, and its area was confined to Central Europe. Hence it has no individual name in Greek or Latin. Μαλον, Lat. *malum*, merely meant a large tree or fruit in general, and *pomum* had the same meaning.

Schrader observes that the statement respecting fig-leaves cannot have sprung up on Babylonian soil, for Herodotus (i. 193) says that neither the fig-tree, the vine, nor the olive grows in Babylonia. It was undoubtedly a native of Syria and Palestine, and in very ancient times it was known as far west as the Canary Islands. The Egyptians called the fig *teb*, the Arabs *tin* (Lagarde, 'Rev. Critiq. de l'Histoire,' says this name is very ancient), and the Hebrews, &c., *énah*. The fig-tree is a well-known symbol of fertility and procreation. The *Ficus ruminalis*, under which Romulus and Remus were said to have been suckled by the she-wolf, derived its name from Jupiter Ruminus, and the Diva Rumina, who were so called from *ruma* = mamma. On the Cephisus a wild fig-tree, ερινεος, marked the spot where Pluto, the serpent of winter, descended with the ravished Proserpine, whose name in the sphere signifies *præ-serpens*, she who precedes the serpent, just as Procyon, which precedes Sirius, is called *præ-canis* (Hygin. ii. 36). Gesenius thinks the Indian fig or *Musa paradisiaca* with large leaves, which the Germans call *Paradiesfeigenbaum*, is meant. This agrees with the Hebrew, in which 'leaf' is in the singular. Milton has the same idea :—

> So counsell'd he, and both together went
> Into the thickest wood. There soon they chose
> The fig-tree; not that kind for fruit renown'd,
> But such as, at this day, to Indians known,
> In Malabar or Decan, spreads her arms
> Branching so broad and long that in the ground
> The bended twigs take root, and daughters grow
> About the mother tree, a pillar'd shade
> High over-arch'd, and echoing walks between.
> . . . . . . These leaves
> They gather'd, broad as Amazonian targe,
> And, with what skill they had, together sew'd,
> To gird their waist: vain covering, if to hide
> Their guilt and dreaded shame !
>
> *Paradise Lost*, ix. 1099

Allusion is made in the note on p. 11 to the Jewish idea that the fall of man was the result of the jealousy of the angels. While the celestial Sanhedrim were discussing the question whether or not man should be created, God created him, and said to the angels, 'Why dispute any longer? Man is already created.' This led the angels to conspire to lead him into sin so as to accomplish his ruin. Sammaël and his angels undertook to bring this about. Sammaël was superior to the other princes of angels, for he had twice the number of wings the seraphim and the living creatures had. Abulchassen ('Kirch. Œd.' vol. ii. part 1) says that God ordered the upper part of the waters to ascend, and formed the substance of the heavens out of them. The angels who dwelt in the heavens had wings like birds. The name Sammaël is formed from Shâmayim, the heavens. In the Arabian sphere Sammaël and the angels in the form of birds dwell in the first or emerald heaven (Cælum smaragdinum, seu Tarphia). Sammaël, taking his angels with him, selected the serpent—which at that time was not only able to speak, but had hands and feet, and resembled a camel in stature and appearance—as a fit instrument for his design. This is an allusion to the constellation Serpentarius, close to which there was on the Arabian celestial sphere a camel with its trappings, and hence arose the idea of a camelomorphic monster. Maimonides ('Mor. Nevoch. ii. 3) says: 'It is related that the serpent who deceived Eve resembled a camel, on which Sammaël (which is the name of the Prince of the genii of darkness, or of the devil) rode.'

And they heard the voice of Yahveh Elóhím walking in the garden in the breeze of the day,[1] and the man and his wife hid themselves from the presence of Yahveh Elóhím in the midst of the trees of the garden. And Yahveh Elóhím called unto the man, and said unto him, Where *art* thou? And he said, I heard thy voice in the garden,[2] and I was afraid, because I *am* naked, and I hid myself.

---

[1] O., 'And they heard the voice of the Word of the Lord God walking in the 'garden in the evening of the day.' Sam., 'Calling them in Paradise in the breathing of the day.'

[2] O., 'The voice of Thy Word heard I in the garden.'

And he said, Who told thee that thou art naked? Hast thou eaten from the tree which I commanded thee not to eat of? And the man said, The woman whom thou gavest with me, she gave to me of the tree, and I ate.

And Yahveh Elôhîm said to the woman, What is this thou hast done? And the woman said, The serpent beguiled me, and I ate. And Yahveh Elôhîm said unto the serpent, Because thou hast done this, cursed *art* thou above all the cattle, and above all beast of the field; upon thy belly thou shalt go, and earth shalt thou eat all the days of thy life. And I will put enmity between thee and between the woman, and between thy seed and between her seed; she shall lie in wait for thy head, and thou shalt lie in wait for his heel.[1]

Unto the woman he said, I will multiply thy pain and thy conception, in pain shalt thou bear children; and thy desire (*shall be*) unto thy husband, and he shall rule over thee. And to the man he said, Because thou hast hearkened unto the voice of thy wife, and hast eaten of the tree which I commanded thee, saying, Thou shalt not eat from it, cursed *is* the ground on thy account; with pain shalt thou eat *of* it all the days of thy life. And thorn and bramble shall it cause to grow to thee, and thou shalt eat the herb of the field. With sweat of thy face shalt thou eat food until thou return unto the ground; for out of it wast thou taken; because earth thou art and unto earth shalt thou return. And the man called the name of his wife 'Ḥavvâh, because she was mother of all living. And Yahveh Elôhîm made to the man and to his wife tunics of hide, and clothed them.

And Yahveh Elôhîm said, Lo, the man has been as one of us, to know good and evil; and now lest he shall put forth his hand, and take also of the tree of [*the*] lives, and eat, and live for ever, Yahveh Elôhîm sent him from the garden of Éden to till the ground from whence he was taken.[2] And he drove out the man, and he

---

[1] O., 'I will put enmity between thee and the woman, and between thy son and her son. He will remember thee what thou didst to him (at) from the beginning, and thou shalt be observant unto him at the end.'

J., 'Upon thy belly shalt thou go, and thy feet shall be cut off, and thy skin thou shalt cast away once in seven years, and the poison of death shall be in thy mouth, and dust shalt thou eat all the days of thy life. And I will put enmity between thee and the woman, and between the seed of thy son and the seed of her sons; and it shall be when the sons of the woman keep the commandments of the law, thou wilt be ready to wound them in their heel.'

[2] O., 'And the Lord God made for Adam and for his wife vestments of honour upon the skin of their flesh, and clothed them. And the Lord God

caused to dwell at the east of the garden of Êden the Kerubim, and the flame of the sword which turned every way to keep the way of the tree of [the] lives.¹

The sentence pronounced by Yahveh on the three culprits is in accordance with their different degrees of guilt. The serpent had not only tempted Eve to disobedience, but had told her that Yahveh had deceived them, and that she and her husband would not die from eating the fruit; and the result proved that he was right. Adam and Eve were created mortal, or the tree of life would have been unnecessary, but Adam lived to be nine hundred and thirty years old. The heaviest sentence, therefore,

---

said, Behold, man is become singular' (or 'alone'; Sam., 'as a branch') ' in the world by himself, knowing good and evil; and now, lest he stretch forth his hand, and take also of the Tree of Life, and eat, and live for ever . . . and the Lord God sent him forth from the garden of Eden to till the ground from whence he had been created. And He drove out the man, and before the garden of Eden he caused to dwell the Kerubaya, and the sharp sword which revolved to keep the way of the Tree of Life.'

J., 'And the Lord God made to Adam and to his wife vestures of honour from the skin of the serpent, which he had cast from him, upon the skin of their flesh, instead of that adornment which had been cast away; and He clothed them.

'And the Lord God said to the angels who ministered before Him, Behold, Adam is sole on the earth, as I am sole in the heavens above: and it will be that they will arise from him who will know how to discern between good and evil. Had he kept the commandments which I appointed to him, he would have lived and subsisted on the Tree of Life for ever. But now, because he hath not kept that which I prescribed, it is decreed against him that we keep him from the garden of Eden. . . . And the Lord God removed him from the garden of Eden, and he went and dwelt on Mount Moriah, to cultivate the ground from which he had been created.'

¹ O., 'And He drave out the man from thence where He had made to dwell the glory of His Shechinah at the first between the two Kerubaya Before He had created the world, He created the law; He prepared the garden of Eden for the righteous, that they may eat and delight themselves with the fruit of the tree, because they would have practised in their lives the doctrine of the law in this world, and have maintained the commandments; (but) He prepared Gehinnom for the wicked, which is like the sharp consuming sword of two edges; in the midst of it He hath prepared flakes of fire and burning coals for the judgment of the wicked who rebelled in their life against the doctrine of the law. To serve the law is better than to eat of the fruit of the Tree of Life (the law).'

is pronounced upon the serpent. Eve is sentenced to the pains of childbirth, though she pleads that the serpent had been allowed to beguile her. Adam is not cursed at all, but the ground is cursed for his sake; it is to bring forth thorns and brambles, which were therefore a new creation, and his food is limited to the herb of the field. To this is added the sentence of physical death, 'with sweat of thy face shalt thou eat food until thou return to the ground; because earth thou art, and and unto earth shalt thou return,' thus excluding any idea of immortality hereafter.

The origin of these serpent myths, so various in their form, is probably the tendency shewn in the Veda to personify the phenomena of nature. In primitive religions physical evil is first noticed, and the Aryan Ahi or Vritra, who menaces heaven and earth with ruin, and against whom beings, protectors of mankind, are ever near Indra as auxiliaries in his contest with him, usually signifies the clouds, which, covering the sky, keep the fertilising rain from the arid earth in their dark recesses as in a cave (*apân bilam*). Ahi is also called Dâsa, the enemy, the destroyer. In the Avesta the same character is attributed to him, only Aji, as he is called in Zend, is no longer the author of physical, but of moral, evil. This serpent, Dahâka—that is, who wounds and destroys—was created by Ahriman to destroy moral purity, and is a wicked deceiver (*aghem gaêthavyô*.)

The Naassim or Ophites held that the serpent raised Adam and Eve to the knowledge of the existence of higher beings than the Demiurge of the present world, and that by inducing Eve to procreate he was the preserver of the species, which would otherwise have died out.

All the gross anthropomorphisms, such as Yahveh walking in the garden, making garments for Adam and his wife, coming down from heaven to see whether the guilt of the cities of the plain had been accurately reported to him, wrestling with Ya'aqob, and so forth, belong to the Jehovist. Maimonides (More Nev. part i. 31) energetically protested against these descriptions when taken in a literal sense. In the Elohist the patriarchs are decorous, if colourless, abstractions. In the Jehovist not only do they repeatedly sin against the laws of ordinary morality, but the vengeance of Yahveh is frequently directed, not against the sinner, but against unconscious offenders. Centuries later we find the same idea in Josephus, who says ('Ant.' xii. 2) that Jehovah punished Theopompus the historian for giving an account of the Jewish creed by making him lose his senses for thirty days. As in the case of Abimelech he was told the cause of his malady in a dream, viz. that he had spread the knowledge of divine things among profane men. Theodectes the tragedian also put some passages of Scripture into one of his tragedies, and was struck with blindness for it, but being made sensible of his fault, and having atoned to Jehovah for it, his sight was restored.

Professor Sayce ('Modern Review,' for October 1882) thinks that Yahveh was a Hittite god. The Hittites are brought into special connection with Abraham in the south of Palestine in Genesis, and David, who reigned at Hebron before he reigned at Jerusalem, while making war on the Semitic Arameans of Damascus and Zobah, was in alliance with the Hittite king of Hamath. 'The alliance lasted long, and when in later days a panic fell upon the Syrians, they at once concluded that "the king of Israel hath hired against us the kings of the Hittites" (2 Kings xii. 6). Tou or Toi—itself a non-Semitic name—was the king of Hamath, who sent his son Joram to form a league with David, and that Yahu is the first element in the name of Joram seems evident from the form Hadoram, which takes its place in 1 Chron. xviii. 10. I have tried to shew elsewhere that Hadad was the Semitised form of Dadis or Attis, the Hittite god of the air, and that when Macrobius makes Adad the supreme god of the Syrians, and says that the word means "one," he is referring not to the Semitic Syrians, but to the people of Hierapolis and its neighbourhood, the White Syrians of Strabo. However this may be, a later king of Hamath, in the time of Sargon, when the city appears to have passed into the hands of the Semites, is called by the Assyrians Yahu-bidi in one place, and Hu-bihdi in another, and since Hu is the Hebrew El, "god," it would seem that Yahu must have been as much the supreme deity of

Hamath as he was of Judah. It is therefore significant that the Hittite captain in David's army was named Uriah. Outside Hamath and Israel the inscriptions, neither of Assyria nor of Egypt, reveal any names of which Yahu forms part.'

After the return from captivity the strictest monotheism prevailed. Even the heretical Samaritans preferred the singular El to the plural Elohim as proclaiming more distinctly the unity of God (Ges. ' De Pent. Sam.' p. 50 *sqq.*). Maimonides (, More Nev.' part i. 50, 53) will not allow any attributes of the Deity to be enumerated, for he considers God and his attributes to be identical. Passages may be found in the Apocrypha which tend to modify the rude expressions of the Hebrew text, and make the people understand that these expressions were types, not realities, but it is in the Targums of Onkelos and Jonathan that these modifications are prominently brought forward. Both these Targums interpret the tree of life to mean the Law.[1] When God is represented as speaking with men, the Word of God (the Memra [2]), or the Glory of God (the Shechina, the dwelling, or the Abiding Presence), is always substituted. Is. i. 15, ' I will hide mine eyes,' is paraphrased ' The visage of the majesty of Jehovah.' Gen. xv. 1, is paraphrased ' After these things came the pithgama (word) of Jehovah unto Abram in prophecy, saying, Fear not, Abram; my Memra shall be thy strength, and thy very great reward.' In Gen. iv. 27 it is the Shechina of God that dwells in the tents of Shem. The Samaritan poets (Ges. ' Carm. Samarit.,' Lipsiae, 1824) have the same idea. They say, ' God has spoken, yet he has no mouth; he sustains the world, yet he has no hands.' ' He has created the world, and is not fatigued, and has rested on the seventh day, and is not wearied.' In general there has been since the return from captivity a slow, though often retarded, progress in Judaism, not only to more spiritual views,

[1] The Targum of Jonathan says that the creation of the Law and the preparation of the garden of Eden and of Gehinnom took place two thousand years before the creation of the world.

[2] The Alexandrian Jews translated Memra by the Greek word λογος, which it did not represent, any more than it signified the Messiah, for which a different word is used.

but to reform of ancient institutions. In 'Jer. Talmud Sanhedrin,' 80, a rabbi declares that if the law were regarded as absolutely completed it could have no stability; and in 'Tr. Baba Meziah,' f. 30, another rabbi teaches: 'The destruction of Jerusalem took place because the judges judged (without consulting the spirit) according to the letter of the law.'

The early religion of the Hebrews, as represented in Genesis, was, like most religions in their infancy, one of extreme simplicity. Spencer ('De Leg. Hebr.' III. iv. 1) has shown that the sacrifices in the Old Testament were not ordered by God, but were voluntary offerings of whatever was best and most precious. In animal sacrifices it was the usual practice to lay the blood and fat upon the altar, while the people consumed the flesh. In Is. i. 12, Yahveh says of the sacrifices, 'Who hath required this at your hand?' In Jer. vii. 12, he says, 'I spake not unto your fathers . . . concerning burnt offerings and sacrifices.' In 'Constit. Apost.' Abel, Noah, and Abraham are said to have brought victims of their own accord. Justin Martyr (or whoever was the author) also says ('Respons. ad quæst.' 38) that God never ordered any sacrifice for his own pleasure, and Chrysostom ('Hom. 12. ad pop. Antiochen.') says the same thing. Vicarious atonement was contrary to the spirit of Mosaism. In Ex. xxxii. 33, Yahveh says to Moses, 'Whosoever hath sinned against me, him will I blot out of my book,' and in Deut. xxiv. 16, it is said, 'The fathers shall not be put to death for the children, neither shall the children be put to death for the fathers; every man shall be put to death for his own sin.' In Gen. xxviii. 18 Ya'aqob takes the stone which he had placed under his head and sets it up as a pillar and pours oil on the top of it, and calls the place Bêth-Êl, the house of God. It is curious to observe that in the primitive Aryan religion also, the head of the family, who was also the worshipper or priest, used to erect in the open air a stone which was wide at its basis (*grâva-prituhudnah*), which made the place where it was set up sacred. This altar was consecrated by the Aryan shepherd by being anointed with liquid butter (*gritaprishṭam*). On his knees, or standing, with his hands extended towards heaven, he invoked the Deity, and sang improvised prayers. Wood was placed on the altar, and fire being obtained by the rapid rubbing together of two sticks (arâni) and the juice of the sôma plant (indu) thrown upon it, the flame consumed the oblation, which might be butter, curdled milk, or victims taken from the flocks. Unlike many other nations in which religious rites are numerous and complicated, the Hebrews had at this time neither marriage ceremonies nor funeral rites. Marriage was a purely social institution among the Aryans also, and there is no trace in the hymns of any religious ceremony accompanying it ; only in a hymn addressed to the Aditis it is said, 'Preserve me from evil, as from an illegitimate child,' which shows that the institution had a sacred character. In the Gâthâs (Yaç. liii. st. 5.) there is an exhortation to those who marry to be sincere to one another. There is no trace of funeral rites in Genesis until the deaths of Ya'aqob and Yoseph, but they take place in Egypt. Abraham mourns and weeps for Sarah, and purchases the cave Machpelah (where the Jews say that Adam is buried), that he may bury his dead out of his sight ; but neither on this nor any other occasion is there any mention of funeral ceremonies. The Aryans in ancient times had no funeral ceremonies either, but they prayed over their dead until the burial was finished, and these prayers show that their ideas of another world had become developed. 'Go,' they said, 'set forth for those ancient paths which our ancestors have trodden ! Thou wilt see the two kings, Yama and the god Varuna, who take pleasure in oblations. Go, with the ancestors, with Yama, with the happiness thou hast deserved, to the highest heaven.' When the dead was about to be consigned to earth, they said, 'Draw near to our mother earth, that wide-spreading and ample dispenser of happiness, that virgin soft as wool for those that follow the right path ; may she keep thee from the brink of calamity.' And when the dead person is deposited in the grave and the earth is thrown upon him, some such words as the following were sung ; 'Raise thyself, O earth ! do him no harm ; receive him kindly. Cover him, O earth, as the mother embraces her offspring.'

Maimonides ('Mishnah Torah,' Hil. Mel. viii. 10) gives a list of the Noachid laws which, the rabbis held, should be the ground work of missionary efforts :—' The first man was commanded concerning six things : idolatry, blasphemy, shedding of blood, incest, robbery, and administration of justice. Although we have all these things as a tradition from Moses, our master, and reason inclines to them, yet, from the general tenor of the law, it appears that he was commanded concerning these things. Noah received an additional command concerning the limb of living animal (not to be eaten), as it is said, " But flesh in the life thereof, which is the blood thereof, ye shall not eat " (Gen. ix. 4.). Here are the seven commandments, and thus the matter was in all the world until Abraham.'

Upon the apologue, or philosophical disquisition, as Josephus calls it, of the garden of Eden the Greek and Roman Catholic Churches have founded the doctrine of the eternal damnation of every unbaptised person. The General Council of Africa, held in A.D. 418 upon Pelagianism, excommunicated those who held that Adam was subject to death when he was born. The council held that he only became mortal after his fall, and that all the children of men who came into the world shared in the crime committed by their first parent : a crime which could only be effaced by baptism. Fulgentius (' De Fide,' § 76) says of original sin : 'Hold thou most firmly, nor do thou in any respect doubt, that infants whether in their mothers' wombs they begin to live and there die, or when after their mothers have given birth to them they pass from this life without the sacrament of holy baptism, will be punished with the everlasting punishment of eternal fire.' The Council of Trent defines as of faith, that Adam lost original justice, not only for himself, but also for us; that he ' poured sin, which is the death of the soul, into the whole human race,' and that this sin comes, not by imitation of Adam's transgression, but by propagation from him.

Augustine was compelled to acknowledge that unbaptised infants had better not have been born, but denies emphatically that a separate place (Limbo) is assigned to them, and in a sermon against the Pelagians distinctly declares that they

descend into everlasting fire. When these doctrines became
formulated, the terror among mothers was so great that they
took every precaution they could think of to protect their
children. Baptismal water was sprinkled on the womb, still-
born children were baptised, the mother would receive the Host
or obtain absolution, and apply them to the benefit of the child;
but the priests anathematised all these attempts. (See Lecky,
'History of Rationalism.') In the Greek Church, not only the
unbaptised child, but its parents also are damned. Exorcism
is retained in both Churches, and until this ceremony is completed the devil is said to be in possession of the child.

The doctrine of Original Sin is entirely unknown to
Judaism. The Talmud teaches that the evil desire or impulse
was created by God, and in several passages it is said that he
repented having done so on seeing the consequences. Everyone,
however, can overcome sin by study and works, and obtain
righteousness. In Is. xlv. 7, Yahveh says, 'I make peace and
create evil.' Job (ii. 10) says 'What? shall we receive good
at the hand of God, and shall we not receive evil?' In Lam.
iii. 38, it is said, 'Ont of the mouth of Elyon cometh there not
evil and good?' And in Ezek. xviii. 19, Yahveh says, 'Yet say
ye, Wherefore doth not the son bear the iniquity of the father?
When the son hath done that which is lawful and right, and
hath kept all my statutes, and hath done them, he shall surely
live. The soul that sinneth, it shall die: the son shall not bear
the iniquity of the father, neither shall the father bear the
iniquity of the son; the righteousness of the righteous shall be
upon him, and the wickedness of the wicked shall be upon him.'

In the apocryphal book of Enoch, which, however, is quoted
as Scripture in Jude, verse 14, it is said (xxxviii. 2, first
parable): 'When righteousness shall be manifested in the
presence of the righteous themselves, *who will be elected for their
good works duly weighed by the lord of spirits;* and when the light
of the righteous and the elect who dwell on earth shall be
manifested, where will the habitation of sinners be? and where
the place of rest for those who have rejected the lord of spirits?
It would have been better for them had they never been born.'

The Jewish hell is much more merciful than the Christian one. Souls come out of hell on Friday evening, and only return on Saturday when the prayer is finished. Menasseh ('Chajim,' f. 39, c. 1) says, 'Even the wicked, of whom it is said that they descend into hell, and ascend not into heaven, enjoy rest on the Sabbath.'

The Rabbis held that all souls were created on the first day of creation. The angels wished to prostrate themselves with reverence before the first man ('Ber. Rab.' c. 8), for a virtuous man is above the highest angels ('Sanh.' 93 a). In 'Nidda' it is said that the soul of man, the Divine Light, is by its nature pure, stainless, and moral in the highest degree. All pre-existing souls are in a place called Guf (body) ('Abod. Sar.' 65 a, 'Nidda ' 13 b, ' Jebam,' 63 b). Raschi in his Commentary says that Guf is the space between the Shechina and the dwelling-place of the angels; the spirits and souls which were created during the first days of creation, and which will one day inhabit human bodies are all there ('Jebam,' a, a, O). R. Jose says the Messiah will not come till there are no more souls in the Guf. The Talmud ('Chag.' 12, 6) places the Guf at the summit of heaven, in the seventh heaven (Arabot), where justice and virtue, peace and benedictions, in a word all the souls that are to be created, exist. In some Jewish prayer-books in use among the Spanish and Portuguese Jews, part of the morning service is, ' My God! the soul which thou hast given me is pure; thou hast created, formed, and breathed it into me; thou dost also carefully guard it within me; thou wilt hereafter take it from me, and restore it unto me in futurity.'

A learned rabbi quoted by Hoornbeck ('Contra Jud.' iv. 2, p. 356) says: 'The Jews deny original sin, and that for the most weighty reasons. For the seat of sin is exclusively in the soul, and all souls derive their origin, not from Adam, but from God the creator; whence it follows that the descendants of Adam could not have sinned. That sin is seated in the soul is evident, for that vice or delinquency is seated in the soul or intellect. And the Scripture expressly declares "That soul shall utterly be cut off: his iniquity shall be upon him," or *in it*. Hence, then, it may be clearly perceived that sin is seated in the soul. In like manner, that souls are created by God, without the mediation of any instrument, is testified by Isaiah: "The spirit should fail before me, and the souls which I have made." Ezekiel confirms this same, when he represents God as saying, "All souls are mine: as the soul of the father, so the soul of the son is mine: the soul that sinneth, it shall die." Hence, then, it clearly and certainly follows, that the souls of Adam's posterity could not have sinned in him, and that all mankind are born obnoxious to the punishment due to the sin of Adam, which, as they are all corporeal, affects the bodies of all his children, inasmuch as they are his children with respect to their bodies: just as, if a man be brought into a state of slavery, all his children become slaves also in consequence of being the offspring of an enslaved parent.'

In an article on the Talmud by Emmanuel Deutsch in the 'Quarterly Review' (vol. cxxiii. p. 458) it is stated that 'there is no death without individual sin, no pain without individual transgression. That same spirit that dictated in the Pentateuch, "And parents shall not die for their children, nor the children for their parents," has ordained that no one shall be punished for another's transgressions.' The article goes on to say that in the judgment of sin the *animus* is considered. The desire to commit sin is more wicked than the sin itself. 'Everything is in God's hand except the fear of God' ('Ber.' c. 5), so every human being can carry out a virtuous existence; only the help of God is requisite for it. The righteous are to rise by the mystic power of the 'Dew of Life,' in Jerusalem; the Targums add, on Mount Olivet. There is no everlasting damnation. Even for the worst sinners, idolaters, apostates, traitors, there is only temporary punishment, though it may last generations upon generations. But the sinner has only to repent sincerely, and he is forgiven. No human being of whatever creed or nation is excluded from the world to come. The notion of Elijah or Moses having ascended to heaven is utterly repudiated.

At the Reformation the doctrine of original sin became, like other doctrines of the Church, the subject of discussion. Luther described the teaching of Paul as to the derivation of human

sin from Adam as a 'laughable doctrine.' He asks what can
be more ridiculous than that the fact that Adam took a bite of
an apple should have the tremendous result of putting all men,
to the very end of the world, into the power of death? 'For,'
he says, 'he had committed neither murder nor adultery; he
had robbed no one, nor blasphemed God, nor committed any of
the horrible sins of which the world is now full; but only eaten
the apple, over-persuaded and deceived by the devil, through
the woman. Must we, then, says reason, make this single
apple of so much account that the whole world must pay for it,
and so many fine, excellent, wise folk, yea, God's Son himself,
with all prophets, fathers, and saints, must die?' ('Werke,' viii.
1240, 1241. Auslegung 1 Cor. xv. 136). He speaks afterwards of faith strangling reason, but as he made use of reason
in so many other instances (as in his rejection of the Apocalypse,
the preface to which had to be suppressed), it is not clear why
he did not employ it in this instance also. Zuinglius held that
original sin was nothing more than a malady or evil tendency,
and did not, in any way, involve guilt. Erasmus distinguished
between those who received the sacrament of baptism without
accompanying grace and those who answered to it with newness of
life, and says of hell, 'There is no other flame in which the sinner
is plagued, and no other punishment of hell, than the perpetual
anguish of mind which accompanies habitual sin.' Jeremy
Taylor said on this subject: 'That every man is inclined to evil,
some more, some less, but all in some instances, is very true;
and it is an effect or condition of nature, but no sin properly:
1, because that which is unavoidable is not a sin; 2, because it
is accidental to nature, not intrinsecal and essential; 3, it is
superinduced to nature, and is after it.' Locke, in his 'Commonplace Book,' has laid down the golden rule on these subjects.
'No one should believe any proposition that is contrary to
reason, on the authority of either inspiration or miracle, for the
reality of the inspiration or miracle can only be established by
reason.'

The chronology of Genesis is obviously limited by the dates
assigned for the Creation and Deluge. The modern Jewish

chronology makes the Creation to have taken place on September 10th, B.C. 3761. This date was fixed in A.D. 360 by R. Hillel, when the cycle of Meton was finally adopted, and they say that this form of the year is to continue till the coming of the Messiah. According to this chronology, the Deluge took place in B.C. 2104; Babel was built B.C. 1969; Abraham was born B.C. 1812; the confusion of tongues took place B.C. 1764; the descent to Egypt was in B.C. 1522; and the Exodus took place B.C. 1312. Josephus, however, who had in his possession the Temple copy of the Old Testament which was in use at the fall of Jerusalem (' I had also the holy books by Titus's concession '), and must therefore have had the actual numbers before him, places the Creation in B.C. 5688, or, as corrected by Dr. Hales, in B.C. 5411; while R. Lipman places that event as late as B.C. 3616. There is thus a difference of some two thousand years between the different Jewish calculations.

In modern times the longest period was that introduced on astronomical grounds by Alfonso X. King of Leon and Castile (1252–1284). He fixed the date of the Creation at B.C. 6984, but the astronomical system followed by him was, like the cosmological system adopted by all the Fathers and by Milton, the Ptolemaic, according to which the earth was the centre of the universe. Other opinions, too numerous to mention, vary from that of the Œcumenical Council held at Constantinople in A.D. 381, which adopted the year B.C. 5509 as the date of the Creation, to that of Jerome who fixes it in B.C. 3941. In this country the received chronology has long been that of Archbishop Ussher, according to whom the world was created in B.C. 4004, and the Deluge took place in B.C. 2349. About fifty years ago Dr. Hales adopted the longer chronology of Josephus, which he reduced to a system which gave the year of the Creation as B.C. 5411, and that of the Deluge as B.C. 3155. In this system Noah and his sons are transported somehow from Armenia to Egypt, where they reign from B.C. 3155 to B.C. 2612 (543 years), after which they are succeeded by Misraim and his successors. Ussher's dates are now again assumed as the approximate ones, and we are informed that in the year B.C. 2350 or thereabouts the whole of the then known world was destroyed, and that it is absolutely certain that the whole human race, except eight persons, had perished. Well may Bunsen say, 'It ought long ago to have been a settled point that our present popular and school chronology is a fable strung together by ignorance and fraud, and persisted in out of superstition and a want of intellectual energy.'

The Jewish conception of the universe is that it was created expressly for them. In 'Yalkut,' § 2, it is said that God created the world on account of Israel, and for their merit, preparing for them as a king does who foresees the birth of his son. Adam and his wife spoke the language which Yahveh conversed with them in, and which was Hebrew. They considered this the fountain-head of all the languages in the world. Josephus tells us that all living creatures had but one language, and both the names which Adam gives to Eve are Hebrew. The seed of Abraham, 'the chosen ones' (Ps. cv. 6), was under the special care of Yahveh. 'As for the other people, which also come of Adam, thou hast said that they are nothing, but be like unto spittle: and hast likened the abundance of them unto a drop that falleth from a vessel' (2 Esd. vi. 56). With such ideas the legend of a deluge in which all mankind perished with the exception of Noah (who according to the Talmud married Naamah, the daughter of Enoch) and his family seemed perfectly natural.

The following is the Chaldean account of the Deluge in an abbreviated form. Chasisadra (Xisuthros) relates the story of his deliverance to Iztubar, an ancient Babylonian hero, as follows :—

The gods Anu, the warrior Bel, the throne-bearer Adar, I'nuggi, the prince, and I'a, the lord of inscrutable wisdom, had assembled in the ancient city Surippak, on the Euphrates, and had resolved to bring about a flood. I'a-Aos announced this determination to Chasisadra, and ordered him to build a ship of certain prescribed dimensions, and to take refuge in it with his family and servants. Everything necessary for subsistence was to be stored within the ship, and cattle and wild animals of the field were to be brought beneath its shelter in order to preserve 'seed of life of every kind' (conf. Gen. vii. 3). During six days and seven nights storm, flood and tempest roam abroad, and 'cast down to the ground.' On the seventh day the tempest subsides, the sea retires, and the evil wind and flood cease. Chasisadra traverses the sea, which bears along on its surface corpses like the stems of trees. He opens the roof-window of the vessel; light streams over his countenance and tears flow down it. Wheresoever he directs his gaze no land is to be seen. The ship speeds to the land Niṣir. The mountain of the land Niṣir holds the vessel fast, and there Chasisadra waits till the earth becomes dry. Then he offers there a sacrifice to the gods.

In the Jehovist Noah and his family are ordered to go into the ark and take with him seven pairs of clean and two of unclean animals and birds. This distinction is not found either in the cuneiform legend or in the Elohist. The deluge is forty days upon the earth and all living things are destroyed, but nothing is said about the waters rising over the tops of the mountains. The whole narrative resembles the account of an inundation rather than of a deluge. The sending forth of the birds and the erection of an altar to Yahveh are also peculiar to this account, which is inconsistent with that of the Elohist, for if Noah had only taken two of every sort of animal, the species which he offered as burnt offerings would have been destroyed.

The deluge is brought about in the Elohist in quite a different manner, and with more detail. Not only are the floodgates of heaven opened, but the fountains of the great deep are broken up, and thus the waters under the earth combine with the waters above to bring about the catastrophe. In the cuneiform legend the Anunnaki (the gods of the subterranean water) bring floods. When the deluge is at its greatest height it is fifteen cubits above the highest mountain under the whole heaven. Wellhausen remarks that the legend is spoiled by Noah's heaving the lead, and marking the date of the highest flood in his log-book. He also misses the poetical incident of the birds and the broken-off olive leaf: but this was inevitable, for not even Jewish credulity could suppose that any vegetation would be left after the whole earth had been a twelvemonth under water. According to Onkelos, the ark rested on the mountains of Kardu; according to the Samaritan version, Al teborah Sarnedib, 'Upon the mountains Sarnedib.' The covenant with Noah and his sons is made voluntarily by Elohim, and the setting of the bow in the cloud recalls the approach of the goddess Istar, who rears aloft 'the great bow which Anu had created' in the cuneiform account.

When the Semites, the Kasdim of Scripture, first came into contact with the civilised Accadians, they were a nomad race, living in tents, and quite uncivilised. They borrowed the rudiments of their civilisation and mythology from Accad, and even the words in which these were expressed. M. Burnouf says that the myths they have adopted, such as the deluge, the creation, the garden of Eden, and the fall of man, have been taken by them from nations which preceded them in civilisation, and which appear to be connected, at least in part, with Aryan mythology, only they have converted myths into history ('Science des Religions,' p. 66). Josephus holds Thelassar, the Arrapachitis of Ptolemy, to have been the native land of the Kasdim or Chaldeans. Arrapachitis is a mountain canton of South Armenia, situated between Lake Van and Lake Urumiah at an elevation of more than 6,000 feet, at the source of the Great Zab, which flows through it. It is from this district that the Semitic tribe, or a portion of it—which afterwards became known as the Hebrews or men from beyond the Euphrates—is supposed to have emigrated, and after settling at Ur, on the Lower Euphrates, a portion of the emigrants appear to have ascended the Euphrates to Haran, whence the Abrahamites wandered to the deserts bordering on Canaan.

'Anthropology,' says M. Burnouf (*ib.* p. 231), 'places the Semites between the Aryans and the yellow races; not that their distinctive characteristics are a middle term between our race and that of the Eastern Asiatics, but because, while eminently superior to the yellow race, they manifest as regards ourselves differences which do not admit of their being classed with the

Indo-European race. The true Semite has flat hair, in consequence of which the hair of his head presents a crisped appearance; his nose is extremely hooked; his lips are projecting and fleshy; his extremities are large, his calf small, and he is flat-footed. What is of more consequence is that he belongs to the occipital races—that is, to those races in which the posterior part of the head is more developed than the anterior or frontal portion. His growth is very rapid: at fifteen or sixteen years of age it has ceased. At the latter age the anterior portions of his skull, which contain the organs of intellect, are firmly brought together, and frequently even cemented to one another. The result is that there can be no further development of the brain, and especially none of the grey matter.'

The Semites are unknown to history till a period between 3000 and 2000 B.C., when they gradually conquered the primitive and highly civilised populations of Babylonia.

In the following pages M. Lenormant's notes to the first Part are distinguished by the letter L. In the second and third Parts the notes are all by him.

I.
THE BOOK OF GENESIS

THE MASSORETIC TEXT IN ITS PRESENT STATE

CHAPTER I.

1 In the beginning Elôhim created the heaven and the earth.

2 And the earth was waste and void; and darkness was upon the face of the deep: and the spirit of Elôhim moved upon the face of the waters.

3 And Elôhim said, Let there be light: and there was light.

4 And Elôhim saw the light, that it was good: and Elôhim divided the light from the darkness.

5 And Elôhim called the light Day, and the darkness he called Night. And there was evening and there was morning, one day.

6 And Elôhim said, Let there be a firmament in the midst of the waters, and let it divide the waters from the waters. [And it was so.[1]]

7 And Elôhim made the firmament, and divided the waters which were under the firmament from the waters which were above the firmament. [And Elôhim saw the firmament, that it was good.[2]]

[1] These words are at the end of verse 7, but they are out of their proper place, and they have been inserted here in accordance with the unvarying parallelism of the recital of the other creations, and in conformity with the Septuagint version, which inserts them here.—L.

[2] The LXX retains this sentence, which is necessary to the progress of the narrative. It has been allowed to lapse in the Hebrew text, in which it has been replaced by the sentence which originally formed the conclusion of verse 6.—L.

8 And Elôhim called the firmament Heaven. And there was evening and there was morning, a second day.

9 And Elôhim said, Let the waters under the heaven be gathered together unto one place, and let the dry land appear. And it was so.[1]

10 And Elôhim called the dry land Earth; and the gathering together of the waters called he Seas: and Elôhim saw that it was good.

11 And Elôhim said, Let the earth put forth grass, herb yielding seed, and fruit-tree bearing fruit after its kind, wherein is the seed thereof, upon the earth: and it was so.

12 And the earth brought forth grass, herb yielding seed after its kind, and tree bearing fruit, wherein is the seed thereof, after its kind: and Elôhim saw that it was good.

13 And there was evening and there was morning, a third day.

14 And Elôhim said, Let there be lights in the firmament of the heaven[2] to divide the day from the night; and let them be for signs and for seasons, and for days and years:

15 And let them be for lights in the firmament of the heaven to give light upon the earth: and it was so.

16 And Elôhim made the two great lights; the

---

[1] The LXX adds, 'And the water which was under the heaven was collected into its places, and the dry land appeared.'

[2] The LXX and Samaritan insert here 'to give light upon the earth.' This light differs from the light in verse 3, which is light in general, diffused light, ôr, while mâ-ôr signifies a luminary, and is used of the sun and moon (verse 16). See also Ps. lxxiv. 16.

greater light to rule the day, and the lesser light to rule the night: he made the stars also.

17 And Elôhim set them in the firmament of the heaven to give light upon the earth,

18 And to rule over the day and over the night, and to divide the light from the darkness: and Elôhim saw that it was good.

19 And there was evening and there was morning, a fourth day.

20 And Elôhim said, Let the waters swarm with a living pullulation, and let fowl fly above the earth towards the face of the firmament of heaven: [and it was so.[1]]

21 And Elôhim created the great sea-monsters,[2] and all the living and creeping things with which the waters swarm, after their kinds, and every winged fowl after its kind: and Elôhim saw that it was good.

22 And Elôhim blessed them, saying, Be fruitful, and multiply, and fill the waters in the seas, and let fowl multiply in the earth.

23 And there was evening and there was morning, a fifth day.

24 And Elôhim said, Let the earth bring forth the living creature after its kind, cattle, and creeping thing, and beast of the earth after its kind: and it was so.

25 And Elôhim made the beast of the earth after its kind, and the cattle after their kind, and everything that creepeth upon the ground after its kind: and Elôhim saw that it was good.

[1] This sentence is omitted in the Hebrew, but retained in the LXX.—L.
[2] Τα κητη τα μεγαλα.—LXX. Whales existed in the Mediterranean as late as the Roman period.

26 And Elôhîm said, Let us make man[1] in our image, after our likeness[2]: and let them have dominion over the fish of the sea, and over the fowl of the air, and over the cattle, and over [every beast of[3]] the earth, and over every creeping thing that creepeth upon the earth.

27 And Elôhîm created man in his own image, in the image of Elôhîm created he him; male and female created he them.

28 And Elôhîm blessed them; and Elôhîm said unto them, Be fruitful and multiply, and replenish the earth, and subdue it; and have dominion over the fish of the sea, and over the fowl of the air, and over every living thing that moveth upon the earth.

29 And Elôhîm said, Behold, I have given you every herb yielding seed, which is upon the face of all the earth, and every tree, in the which is the fruit of a tree yielding seed; to you it shall be for meat:

30 And to every beast of the earth, and to every fowl of the air, and to every thing that creepeth upon the earth, wherein there is the breath of life,[4] I have given every green herb for meat: and it was so.

[1] Heb. Âdâm, and so wherever man is mentioned.
[2] 'According to our image and likeness.'—LXX. Tzelem means a shadow (Ps. xxxix. 6), hence an image, from its shadowing forth. In 2 Kings xi. 18, Ezek. xxiii. 14, &c., it means idols. Demûth is likeness, likeness in form: it occurs again in this sense in Ps. lviii. 4, Ezek. i. 26. Maimonides explains this to refer, not to any corporeal resemblance, but to the Divine Intellect (philosophically the Active as distinguished from the Passive Intellect) which has been imparted to man.
[3] These words are not in the text, but the mention of them in verse 24 implies their insertion here. L.
[4] Nephesh 'ayyâh, ψυχην ζωης.—LXX. Nephesh is a word the primary meaning of which is the vital principle common to all living beings (Maim. Mor. Neb. Part I. c. 41). It means here 'breath of life' (conf. Job

31 And Elôhim saw everything that he had made, and, behold, it was very good. And there was evening and there was morning, the sixth day.

CHAPTER II.

1 And the heaven and the earth were finished, and all the host[1] of them.

2 And on the seventh day Elôhim finished his work which he had made ; and he rested on the seventh day from all his work which he had made.

3 And Elôhim blessed the seventh day, and hallowed it ; because that in it he rested from all his work which Elôhim had created and made.[2]

4 These are the genealogies of the heaven and of the earth when they were created.[3]

---

xli. 21). 'Ayyâh (living, to live) is said of all beings which have the power of feeding themselves, and which live, as in Gen. ix. 13. It is never used of plants.

[1] Κοσμος, order, LXX, which adds ' and God finished on the sixth day his works which he made.'

[2] Ων ηρξατο ο Θεος ποιησαι, ' which God began to do.'—LXX.

[3] This portion of the verse gives us the invariable form in which the titles of every section of the book of genealogies constituting the Elohistic document begin. It ought to have preceded the history of the creation which forms the first chapter in the present state of the text, but the editor who finally combined the Elohistic and Jehovistic documents has placed it at the end. It is evident that he wished to begin the sacred book by affirming the doctrine of the creation *ex nihilo* contained in chap. i. 1, in opposition to the doctrines of emanation which were held by the Pagan nations by whom the Israelites were surrounded.—L.

Philo, however, and the Alexandrian Jews saw nothing in the Mosaic cosmogony inconsistent with the pre-existence of matter. Philo (*On the Incorruptibility of the World*, § 2) says,—

' As nothing is generated out of nothing, so neither can anything which

In the day that Yahveh Elôhîm [1] made earth and heaven
5 No bush of the field was yet in the earth, and no herb of the field had yet sprung up: for Yahveh Elôhîm had not caused it to rain upon the earth, and there was not a man to till the ground;
6 But there went up a mist [2] from the earth, and watered the whole face of the ground.
7 And Yahveh Elôhîm formed man [3] of the dust of the ground, and breathed into his nostrils the breath of life; and man became a living soul.
8 And Yahveh Elôhîm planted a garden eastward in Êden [4]; and there he put the man whom he had formed.
9 And out of the ground made Yahveh Elôhîm to grow every tree that is pleasant to the sight, and good for food; the tree of life also in the midst of the garden, and the tree of the knowledge of good and evil.
10 And a river went out of Êden to water the garden; and from thence it was parted, and became four heads.

exists be destroyed, so as to become non-existence. For it is impossible that anything should be generated of that which has no existence anywhere, and equally so that what does exist should be so utterly destroyed as never to be mentioned or heard of again. And indeed, in this spirit the tragedian says:—

" Nought that e'er has been
Completely dies, but things combined
Before another union find;
Quitting their former company,
And so again in other forms are seen." '

Euripides, *Chrysippus*.

[1] Yahveh Elôhîm is translated Κυριος ο Θεος, 'the Lord God' by the LXX, and they continue this expression for several chapters, so that the Deluge, for instance, is brought about not by Yahveh, but by Yahveh Elôhîm, in chap. vi. 3, 5, &c.
[2] Πηγη, a fountain.—LXX.
[3] Heb. hû 'Âdâm, '*the* man.'
[4] Our translation says that 'Yahveh Elôhîm planted a garden *eastward* in Êden,' but Onkelos holds that *qedem* should be translated 'in ancient times,' 'formerly,' as in Ps. xliv. 2, Isa. xxiii. 7. The word Êden really signifies 'field,' or 'plain,' Assyr. *idinu* (*edinu*), and Delitzsch considers it to be a primitive non-Semitic word which afterwards passed into the Semitic.

11 The name of the first is Pishôn: that is it which compasseth the whole land of 'Havîlâh, where there is gold;
12 And the gold of that land is good: there is the bedôla'h and the shôham stone.
13 And the name of the second river is Gî'hôn: the same is it that compasseth the whole land of Kûsh.
14 And the name of the third river is 'Hîddeqel: that is it which goeth in front of Asshûr. And the fourth river is the Phrâth.
15 And Yahveh Elôhîm took the man, and put him into the garden of Êden to dress it and to keep it.
16 And Yahveh Elôhîm commanded the man, saying, Of every tree of the garden thou mayest freely eat:
17 But of the tree of the knowledge of good and evil, thou shalt not eat of it: for in the day that thou eatest thereof, thou shalt surely die.
18 And Yahveh Elôhîm said, It is not good that the man should be alone; I will make him an help answering to him.
19 And out of the ground Yahveh Elôhîm formed every beast of the field, and every fowl of the air; and brought them unto the man to see what he would call them: and whatsoever the man called every living creature, that was the name thereof.
20 And the man gave names to all cattle, and to the fowl of the air, and to every beast of the field: but for man there was not found an help meet for him.
21 And Yahveh Elôhîm caused a deep sleep to fall upon the man, and he slept: and he took one of his ribs, and closed up the flesh instead thereof;
22 And the rib, which Yahveh Elôhîm had taken from the man, made he a woman, and brought her unto the man.
23 And the man said, This is now bone of my bones, and flesh of my flesh: she shall be called woman (*isshâh*) because she was taken out of man (*ish*).
24 Therefore shall a man leave his father and his mother, and shall cleave unto his wife, and they shall be one flesh.
25 And they were both naked, the man and his wife, and were not ashamed.

CHAPTER III.

1 Now the serpent was more subtil than any beast of the field which Yahveh Elôhîm had made. And he said unto the woman, Yea, hath Elôhîm said, Ye shall not eat of any tree of the garden?

2 And the woman said unto the serpent, Of the fruit of the trees of the garden we may eat:

3 But of the fruit of the tree which is in the midst of the garden, Elôhîm hath said, Ye shall not eat of it, neither shall ye touch it, lest ye die.

4 And the serpent said unto the woman, Ye shall not surely die:

5 For Elôhîm doth know that in the day ye eat thereof, then your eyes shall be opened, and ye shall be as Elôhîm, knowing good and evil.

6 And when the woman saw that the tree was good for food, and that it was a delight to the eyes, and that the tree was to be desired to make one wise, she took of the fruit thereof, and did eat; and she gave also to her husband with her, and he did eat.

7 And the eyes of both of them were opened, and they knew that they were naked: and they sewed fig leaves together, and made themselves girdles.

8 And they heard the voice of Yahveh Elôhîm in the breeze of the evening: and the man and his wife hid themselves from the presence of Yahveh Elôhîm amongst the trees of the garden.

9 And Yahveh Elôhîm called unto the man, and said unto him, Where art thou?

10 And he said, I heard thy voice in the garden, and I was afraid, because I was naked; and I hid myself.

11 And he said, Who told thee that thou wast naked? Hast thou eaten of the tree, whereof I commanded thee that thou shouldest not eat?

12 And the man said, 'The woman whom thou gavest to be with me, she gave me of the tree, and I did eat.

13 And Yahveh Elôhîm said unto the woman, What is this that thou hast done? And the woman said, The serpent beguiled me, and I did eat.

14 And Yahveh Elôhîm said unto the serpent, Because thou hast done this, cursed art thou from among all cattle, and from among every beast of the field: upon thy belly[1] shalt thou go, and dust shalt thou eat all the days of thy life.

15 And I will put enmity between thee and the woman, and between thy seed and her seed: it shall bruise thy head, and thou shalt bruise his heel.[2]

---

[1] 'Upon thy breast and belly.'—LXX.

[2] Τηρησει, LXX, 'he shall keep (watch against) thy head, and thou shalt keep his heel.' No serpent could bruise a person's head. Josephus (*Ant.* i. § 4) says that all living creatures at this time were able to speak, and had one language. He attributes the fall to the serpent's envy of the happiness of Adam and Eve. God, he says, deprived the serpent of speech, and put poison under his tongue; not knowing that out of some 1,300 varieties of serpents perhaps one half are not poisonous. Certain land snakes use the tongue to bring into the mouth stones, sand, &c., which they swallow to promote digestion, which has been mistaken for eating dust. Professor Owen has shown in his description of the Ophidia, in allusion to the text 'Upon thy belly shalt thou go,' that serpents have not been degraded from a higher type, and that no animal has its parts more exquisitely adapted to its necessities. M. Lenormant observes (*Origines de l'Histoire*, t. i. p. 106, note) that 'the serpent has been assuredly a symbol of life for the Chaldæo-Assyrians. One of its generic names in the Semitic Assyrian language is *hawou*, in Arabic *hiyah*, both from the root *hâvah*, to live.' The brazen serpent of Numbers xxi. 5-9, which Yahveh himself ordered Moses to make, was an emblem of Yahveh as a healing deity. This serpent continued to be an object of popular worship until the time of Hezekiah, who broke it in pieces because the Israelites burnt incense to it up to that time, and he called it *ne'hushtan*—that is, brazen. Reuss has observed that there is a pun here, for serpent is called *na'hash*, and brass *ne'hôsheth*. There is no mention of the devil in connection with the serpent until the Apocryphal Book of Wisdom, which is of later date than the Septuagint. Even this seems to be figurative. In Eccl. xiv. 17 it is said, 'The covenant from the beginning is, Thou shalt die the death,' and in Eccl. xxi. 27, it is said, 'When the ungodly curseth Satan, he curseth his own soul.' Lenormant (*Origines*, i. p. 552, note) says, 'One of the images of Malak-Baal, the third person of the Phœnician triad, is the neboushtân, the saviour serpent, whose image Moses set up in the desert.' The Rabbis attributed Adam's

16 Unto the woman he said, I will greatly multiply thy sorrow and thy conception; in sorrow shalt thou bring forth children; and thy desire shall be to thy husband, and he shall rule over thee.

17 And unto the man he said, Because thou hast hearkened unto the voice of thy wife, and hast eaten of the tree, of which I commanded thee, saying, Thou shalt not eat of it: cursed is the ground for thy sake; in toil shalt thou eat of it all the days of thy life.

18 Thorns also and thistles shall it bring forth to thee; and thou shalt eat the herb of the field;

19 In the sweat of thy face shalt thou eat bread, till thou return unto the ground; for out of it wast thou taken: for dust thou art, and unto dust shalt thou return.

20 And the man called his wife's name Havvâh, because she was the mother of all living (*haiy*).[1]

21 And Yahveh Elôhîm made for the man and for his wife tunics of skins, and clothed them.

22 And Yahveh Elôhîm said, Behold, the man is become as one of us, to know good and evil: and now, lest he put forth his hand, and take also of the tree of life, and eat, and live for ever:

fall to the envy of the angels, who, having in vain tried to prevent the creation of man, led him into sin by means of Sammaël and his angels, who was superior to them, and who employed the serpent as his instrument. If Adam had not sinned he would have lived for ever according to some. The immediate consequence of Adam's sin was that the Shechinah was withdrawn from earth to the first heaven, and subsequent sins caused it to be removed to the seventh heaven. The Shechinah was a light created expressly in order to represent the Divine Majesty. The Talmud says that God 'originally offered the Law to all Gentile nations, but they having refused to submit, Israel took the Law on themselves at Mount Sinai, and were literally as Ps. lxxxii. 6 describes: 'I said, Ye are Elôhîm, and all of you sons of 'Elyôn' (the Most High). If it had not been for the golden calf, which put an end to this state of bliss, that generation would have seen the end of Israel.' Dr. Donaldson has a dissertation on this verse, in which he shows from Jer. xiii. 22 and Nahum iii. 5 the real meaning of the word translated 'heel.'—Conf. Hos. xii. 4.

[1] LXX, Ζωη, Eva, conf. Evaιος, Josh. xi. 3, Judges iii. 3, &c. In Phœnician Havâth.

23 Therefore Yahveh Elôhîm sent him forth from the garden of Eden to till the ground from whence he was taken.
24 So he drove out the man, and he placed at the east of the garden of Éden the Kerubîm, and the flame of a sword which turned every way, to keep the way of the tree of life.[1]

CHAPTER IV.

1 And the man knew 'Havvâh his wife; and she conceived, and bare Qaîn, and said, I have gotten (*qânîthy*) a man with the help of Yahveh.
2 And again she bare his brother Hâbel. And Hâbel was a keeper of sheep, but Qaîn was a tiller of the ground.[2]

---

[1] The same word is used for the tree of life that is used in chaps. i. ii. &c. for fruit-bearing and other trees in general. The idea of a tree of life is common to many nations, and everywhere it is the increase of vital energy given by the intoxicating powers of the fruit which has made semi-barbarous nations believe in a promise of immortality conveyed by it. In Arya we have the Soma (*Asclepias acidula?*), in Babylonia the palm, and the Accadian inscriptions show us that that ancient people gave the name Ges-tin, 'tree of life,' to the vine. R. Meir taught that the tree Adam partook of was the vine, for nothing entices man so much as wine, of which it is said (Gen. ix. 21), 'And he drank of the wine, and was drunken' (*Tr. Syhedr.* fol. 70). In the LXX this verse is, 'And he cast out Adam and caused him to dwell over against the Garden of Delight, and stationed the cherubs and the fiery sword that turns about to keep the way of the tree of life.' There seems to be no doubt that the Kerubim are of Babylonian origin, and identical with the winged colossal bulls. M. Lenormant says that upon an unedited parallel inscription in the possession of M. le Clerc in Paris, the legend (AN) ki-ru-bu damku, 'exalted cherub,' appears. In Ezek. i. 10 the Kerubim have the face of a bull (shór). Ezekiel represents them in chap. i. 6, as having four faces, but in chap. xli. 18 this number is reduced to two. Philo and Clemens Alexandrinus said that they represented the two hemispheres, and their wings the rapid movement of the firmament and of time circulating in the Zodiac, for Philo, speaking of the wings of the Kerubim, says the heavens fly.

[2] Josephus says Adam and Eve had two sons and daughters. The Talmud says they had three daughters, one of whom Cain must have married.

3 And in process of time it came to pass, that Qaîn brought of the fruit of the ground an offering [1] unto Yahveh.

4 And Hâbel, he also brought of the firstlings of his flock, and of the fat thereof. And Yahveh had respect unto Hâbel, and to his offering:

5 But unto Qaîn and to his offering he had not respect. And Qaîn was very wroth, and his countenance fell.

6 And Yahveh said unto Qaîn, Why art thou wroth? and why is thy countenance fallen?

7 If thou doest well, shall it not be lifted up? and if thou doest not well, sin coucheth at the door; and unto thee shall be his desire, and thou shalt rule over him.[2]

8 And Qaîn said unto Hâbel his brother [Let us go out into the plain [3]]. And it came to pass, when they were in the plain, that Qaîn rose up against Hâbel his brother, and slew him.

9 And Yahveh said unto Qaîn, Where is Hâbel thy brother? And he said, I know not: am I my brother's keeper?

10 And he said, What hast thou done? the voice of thy brother's blood crieth unto me from the ground.

11 And now, cursed art thou from the ground, which hath opened her mouth to receive thy brother's blood from thy hand;

12 When thou tillest the ground, it shall not henceforth yield unto thee her strength; a fugitive and a wanderer shalt thou be in the earth.

13 And Qaîn said unto Yahveh, Mine iniquity is greater than I can bear.

14 Behold, thou hast driven me out this day from the face of the ground [4]; and from thy face shall I be hid; and I shall be

---

[1] Heb. Min'âh, an offering without blood, conf. Lev. ii. 1. The reason it was rejected appears to be that the earth was still under a curse, which was only removed when the covenant was made with Noah (viii. 21), after which Noah became himself an agriculturist.

[2] In the LXX this verse is 'Hast thou not sinned if thou hast brought it rightly, but not rightly divided it? be still, to thee shall be his submission, and thou shalt rule over him.'

[3] The LXX and the Samaritan text have retained these words. They have been omitted from the Hebrew text, and leave a blank there. St. Jerome replaced them from the Greek version.—L.

[4] The word adâmâh, 'ground,' is evidently used here to indicate the

a fugitive and a wanderer in the earth; and it shall come to pass, that whosoever findeth me shall slay me.

15 And Yahveh said unto him, Therefore whosoever slayeth Qaîn, vengeance shall be taken on him sevenfold. And Yahveh appointed a sign for Qaîn, lest any finding him should smite him.

16 And Qaîn went out from the presence of Yahveh, and dwelt in the land of Nôd (exile) on the east of Éden.

17 And Qaîn knew his wife; and she conceived, and bare 'Hanôch [1]: and he builded a city, and called the name of the city, after the name of his son, 'Hanôch.

18 And unto 'Hanôch was born Yirâd: and Yirâd begat Me'hûyâêl, and Me'hûyâêl begat Methûshâêl [2]: and Methûshâêl begat Lâmech.

19 And Lâmech took unto him two wives: the name of the one was 'Adâh,[3] and the name of the other Çillâh.[4]

20 And 'Adâh bare Yâbâl: he was the father of such as dwell in tents and have cattle.[5]

21 And his brother's name was Yûbâl: he was the father of all such as handle the kinnôr and the 'ûgâr.[6]

22 And Çillâh, she also bare Tûbal-qayin,[7] the forger of every cutting instrument of brass and iron: and the sister of Tûbal-qayin was Na'amâh.[8]

23 And Lâmech said unto his wives:

'Adâh and Çillâh, hear my voice;
Ye wives of Lâmech, hearken unto my speech:
For I have slain a man to my wounding,
And a young man to my hurt.

cultivated and cultivable ground, the Adamic ground, in opposition to âreç, 'the earth,' in its widest signification.—L.

[1] 'Initiated.'   [2] 'Man of God.'   [3] 'Ornament, or beauty.'
[4] 'Shadow.'
[5] M. Lenormant remarks elsewhere (*Prem. Civilis.* t. i. p. 138) that this genealogy of Cain's family is quite inconsistent with the destruction of the whole human race with the exception of Noah's family by the Deluge, for the construction of this verse about Yâbâl implies the present time, 'those who dwell in tents and have cattle' at the period the author wrote.

[6] LXX, ψαλτηριον και κιθαραν. Engel thinks the kinnôr is a lyre or small harp, and the 'ûgâr the syrinx or Pandæan pipes.

[7] Θοβελ, LXX. See note on chap. x. 2.   [8] 'Pleasant.'

24 If Qaîn shall be avenged sevenfold.
Truly Lamech seventy and sevenfold.[1]

25 And Âdâm knew his wife again; and she bare a son, and calleth his name Shêth: For, said she, Elôhîm hath appointed (*shâth*) me another seed instead of Hâbel; for Qaîn slew him.

26 And to Shêth, to him also there was born a son; and he called his name Enôsh: then began men to call upon the name of Yahveh.[2]

CHAPTER V.

1 This is the book of the genealogy of Âdâm.

In the day that Elôhîm created man, in the likeness of Elôhîm made he him;

2 Male and female created he them; and blessed them, and called their name Âdâm, in the day when they were created.

3 And Âdâm lived an hundred and thirty years, and begat a son in his own likeness, after his image: and called his name Shêth[3]:

[1] The Talmud explains this obscure passage to mean that when Lamech or Lemech grew old and blind, Tubal-Cain led him by the hand into the fields to hunt, and said to his father, 'Lo, yonder is a beast of prey, shoot thy arrow in that direction,' and Lamech having done so the arrow killed Cain, who was walking afar off. Lamech, when he discovered what he had done, clapped his hands together, and not seeing his son, struck the lad's head between his hands, killing him instantly.

[2] The latest editor has not preserved the rest of the statement of the posterity of Shêth as the Jehovist gave it. He gives the Elohistic genealogy in its place, introducing only one incidental verse taken from the other document.—L.

[3] According to the Elohist, Shêth, not Qaîn, is Adam's first-born. The genealogies are as follows:

4 And the days of Âdâm after he begat Shêth were eight hundred years: and he begat sons and daughters:

5 And all the days that Âdâm lived were nine hundred and thirty years: and he died.

6 And Shêth lived an hundred and five years, and begat Enôsh:

7 And Shêth lived after he begat Enôsh eight hundred and seven years, and begat sons and daughters:

8 And all the days of Shêth were nine hundred and twelve years: and he died.

9 And Enôsh lived ninety years, and begat Qênân:

10 And Enôsh lived after he begat Qênân eight hundred and fifteen years, and begat sons and daughters:

11 And all the days of Enôsh were nine hundred and five years: and he died.

12 And Qênân lived seventy years, and begat Mahalalêl:

13 And Qênân lived after he begat Mahalalêl eight hundred and forty years, and begat sons and daughters:

Genesis IV.	Genesis V.
Âdâm	Âdâm
Qain and Hâbel, his sons	Shêth
'Hanôch, Qain's son	Enôsh
Yirâd, 'Hanôch's son	Qênân
Me'hûyâêl, son of Yirâd	Mahalalêl
Methûshâêl, son of Me'hûyâêl	Yâred
Lâmech, son of Methûshâêl	'Hanôch
	Methûshala'h
	Lâmech.

The Rabbis (Nork, *Hebr. Rabbin. Wörterbuch*, art. Shêth) say that Shêth was the first who gave names to the celestial signs and marked the divisions of the year. Josephus says that the science of astrology was due to the children of Seth, and that as Adam had told them the world was to perish by water or by fire they constructed two columns, one of brick, the other of stone, on which they engraved the knowledge they had acquired, so that if a deluge destroyed the column of brick, the stone one might remain.

14 And all the days of Qênân were nine hundred and ten years: and he died.

15 And Mahalalêl lived sixty and five years, and begat Yâred:

16 And Mahalalêl lived after he begat Yâred eight hundred and thirty years, and begat sons and daughters:

17 And all the days of Mahalalêl were eight hundred ninety and five years: and he died.

18 And Yâred lived an hundred sixty and two years, and begat 'Hanôch:

19 And Yâred lived after he begat 'Hanôch eight hundred years, and begat sons and daughters:

20 And all the days of Yâred were nine hundred sixty and two years: and he died.

21 And 'Hanôch lived sixty and five years, and begat Methûshâla'h:

22 And 'Hanôch walked with God[1] after he begat Methûshâla'h three hundred years, and begat sons and daughters:

23 And all the days of 'Hanôch were three hundred sixty and five years:

24 And 'Hanôch walked with God: and he was not; for Elôhim took him.[2]

---

[1] Elôhim is translated 'God' when the Divine name is preceded by the article, which makes it a substantive of importance; *ha 'elôhim*, '*the* God,' 'the only God.'—L.

[2] Death and imperfectness was the result of Âdâm's sin according to the Rabbis, but Abrâhâm would partly counteract this imperfection, and the Messiah would wholly remove it. 'Hanôch did not sin, and therefore he did not die. Original sin was entirely unknown to the Rabbis. They held (*Ber.* 61 *a*) that God originally created man with two propensities, one to good, Yetser tobh, and one to evil, Yetser hara (*Sanh.* 91 *b*). The evil impulse began immediately after birth, but it could be overcome, and man could attain perfect righteousness.

25 And Methûshâla'h lived an hundred eighty and seven years, and begat Lâmech :

26 And Methûshâla'h lived after he begat Lâmech seven hundred eighty and two years, and begat sons and daughters :

27 And all the days of Methûshâla'h were nine hundred sixty and nine years : and he died.

28 And Lâmech lived an hundred eighty and two years, and he begat *a son*.[1]

29 And he called his name Nôa'h, saying, This same shall comfort us (*yenà'hamênù*) for our work and for the toil of our hands, which cometh from the ground which Yahveh hath cursed.[2]

30 And Lâmech lived after he begat Nô'ah five hundred ninety and five years, and begat sons and daughters :

31 And all the days of Lâmech were seven hundred seventy and seven years : and he died.

32 And Nôa'h was five hundred years old : and Nôa'h begat Shêm, 'Hâm, and Yâpheth.

[1] The original word must have been 'Nôa'h.' The latest editor has inserted the words 'a son' to connect this verse better with the next, which has been taken from another source.—L.

[2] This verse has been taken from the genealogy of Shêth in the Jehovistic document, the first two verses of which have been preserved in chap. iv. 25, 26. The remainder has been omitted, as being identical with the genealogy of the Elohistic document, which the editor has adopted.—L. M. Lenormant elsewhere observes that when the LXX in this verse explain the name of Nôa'h by ουτος αναπαυσει ημας απο των εργων ημων, 'This one will cause us to cease from our works,' they show that the Hebrew text they had before them differed from the one we have, and made it nearer to the radical navabh. This conveys an idea of 'rest' which agrees very well with the meaning of the Accadian Éa, the third god of the principal triad of the Chaldæo-Assyrian religion. This was the deity who warned 'Hasisadra (Xisuthros) that the deluge was about to take place, and who in consequence is frequently called Salman, 'the saviour.'

CHAPTER VI.

1 And it came to pass, when men began to multiply on the face of the ground, and daughters were born unto them,

2 That the sons of God saw the daughters of men that they were fair; and they took them wives of all that they chose.

3 And Yahveh said, My spirit shall not rule in man for ever, for that he also is flesh: yet shall his days be an hundred and twenty years.[1]

4 The Nephilim were in the earth in those days, and also after that, when the sons of God came in unto the daughters of men, and they bare children to them: the same were the mighty men which were of old, the men of renown.[2]

5 And Yahveh saw that the wickedness of man was great in the earth, and that every imagination of the thoughts of his heart was only evil continually.

6 And it repented Yahveh that he had made man on the earth, and it grieved him at his heart.

7 And Yahveh said, I will destroy man whom I have created from the face of the ground; both man, and beast, and creeping thing, and fowl of the air; for it repenteth me that I have made them.

8 But Nóa'h found grace in the eyes of Yahveh.

9 These are the genealogies of Nóa'h.

---

[1] This probably refers, not to the duration of man's life, for Abraham, for instance, died at a hundred and seventy-five years of age, but to the corruption of mankind, which reached its maximum a hundred and twenty years before the Deluge, or to the intercourse with the Benê-ha 'Elóhim, or sons of God. Is. vii. 8, xvi. 14, and especially Jonah iii. 4, are instances of the short periods allowed for repentance. The Benê-ha 'Elóhim are mentioned again in Job i. 6, but we never hear of sons of Yahveh.

[2] See Numb. xiii. 33, 'And there we saw the Nephilim (the Giants), the Benê-'Anâq, which come of the Nephilim.' Giant nations are mentioned in Deut. ii. 10, iii. 11. Goliath (1 Sam. xvii. 4) was six cubits and a span in height. Eusebius (*Præp. Ev.* lib. vii. cap. 8) says the Nephilim endeavoured to establish $\theta\epsilon o\mu\alpha\chi\iota\alpha\iota$ like the Greeks, besides being the authors of sorcery and witchcraft.

Nôa'h was a righteous man and upright in his generations: Nôa'h walked with God.

10 And Nôa'h begat three sons, Shêm, 'Ham, and Yâpheth.

11 And the earth was corrupt before God, and the earth was filled with violence.

12 And Elôhim saw the earth, and, behold, it was corrupt: for all flesh had corrupted his way upon the earth.

13 And Elôhim said unto Nôa'h, The end of all flesh is come before me; for the earth is filled with violence through them; and, behold, I will destroy them with the earth.

14 Make thee an ark[1] of cypress wood[2]; cells shalt thou make in the ark, and shalt pitch it within and without with pitch.

15 And this is how thou shalt make it: the length of the ark three hundred cubits, the breadth of it fifty cubits, and the height of it thirty cubits.

16 A light shalt thou make to the ark,[3] and to a cubit shalt thou finish it upwards; and the door of the ark shalt thou set in the side thereof; with lower, second, and third stories shalt thou make it.

17 And I, behold, I do bring the deluge[4] of waters

---

[1] Heb. têbâh, a chest or coffer. The word is only used of Nôa'h's vessel and the ark in which Moses was exposed, Exod. ii. 5. LXX, κιβωτος, and also θιβη, θηβη in LXX interp.

[2] 'Of square timber,' εκ ξυλων τετραγωνων, LXX. Buxtorf says gopher was a species of cypress wood. The word means pitch; hence resinous trees, such as were used in ship-building.

[3] LXX, Επισυναγων ποιησεις την κιβωτον, 'thou shalt narrow the ark in making it.' The light or window is omitted.

[4] Mabbûl, LXX, κατακλυσμον, υδωρ επι την γην. The word only occurs once again, in Ps. xxix. 10, 'Yahveh sat as king at the Deluge.' It is evidently a very old word, as it has to be explained as a deluge 'of waters.'

upon the earth, to destroy all flesh, wherein is the breath of life, from under heaven; every thing that is in the earth shall die.

18 But I will establish my covenant with thee; and thou shalt come into the ark, thou, and thy sons, and thy wife, and thy sons' wives with thee.

19 And of every living thing of all flesh, two of every sort shalt thou bring into the ark, to keep them alive with thee; they shall be male and female.

20 Of the fowl after their kind, and of the cattle after their kind, of every creeping thing of the ground after its kind, two of every sort shall come unto thee, to keep them alive.

21 And take thou unto thee of all food that is eaten, and gather it to thee; and it shall be for food for thee, and for them.

22 Thus did Nôa'h; according to all that Elôhîm commanded him, so did he.

CHAPTER VII.

1 And Yahveh said unto Nôa'h, Come thou and all thy house into the ark [1]; for thee have I seen righteous before me in this generation.

2 Of every clean beast thou shalt take to thee seven and seven, the male and his female; and of the beasts that are not clean two, the male and his female;

---

[1] The Jehovistic document evidently placed the directions given to Nôa'h by Yahveh respecting the construction of the ark before this verse, but the latest editor has no doubt omitted them because they repeated those of the Elohist almost word for word.—L.

3 Of the fowl also of the air [which are clean], seven and seven, male and female; [and of birds which are not clean, two, male and female [1]]: to keep seed alive upon the face of all the earth.

4 For yet seven days, and I will cause it to rain upon the earth forty days and forty nights; and every living thing that I have made will I destroy from off the face of the ground.

5 And Nôa'h did according unto all that Yahveh commanded him.

6 And Nôa'h was six hundred years old when the deluge of waters was upon the earth.[2]

7 And Nôa'h went in, and his sons, and his wife, and his sons' wives with him, into the ark, because of the waters of the deluge.

8 Of clean beasts, and of beasts that are not clean, and of [clean] fowls [and of fowls that are not clean], and of every thing that creepeth upon the ground,[3]

9 There went in two and two unto Nôa'h into the ark, male and female, as *Elôhîm*[4] commanded Nôa'h.

10 And it came to pass, after the seven days, that the waters of the deluge were upon the earth.

11 In the six hundredth year of Nôa'h's life, in the second month, on the seventeenth day of the month,[5]

---

[1] This verse, which is mutilated in the Hebrew text, is restored from the LXX.—L.

[2] This number corresponds to the Babylonian *ner*, νηρος, Assyr. ní-í-ru. It is the original astronomical cosmic year, at the end of which the equation of the solar and lunar years took place. Sixty solar years equal 742 lunations, that is sixty years of twelve months, and twenty-two intercalated months; 618 years and four months are therefore required for a cosmic year of 600 years. Shêm's cycle is also 600 years (Gen. xi. 10, 11).

[3] This verse is also incomplete in the Hebrew, and has been restored from the LXX.—L.

[4] The use of this name here instead of Yahveh is exceptional and peculiar, for the verse evidently belongs to the Elobistic document. Its presence here is doubtless owing to the latest editor.—L.

[5] On the twenty-seventh day of the month.—LXX. Conf. chap. viii. 14. According to the Hebrew text the deluge began on the seventeenth day of the second month. The tops of the mountains were seen on the first day of

on the same day were all the fountains of the great deep broken up, and the floodgates[1] of heaven were opened.

12 And the rain[2] was upon the earth forty days and forty nights.

13 In the selfsame day entered Nôa'h, and Shêm, and 'Hâm, and Yâpheth, the sons of Nôa'h, and Nôa'h's wife, and the three wives of his sons with them, into the ark[3];

---

the tenth month (viii. 5), and they were nearly dried up on the first day of the first month, and Nôa'h left the ark on the twenty-seventh day of the second month (viii. 14). Thus the flood lasts according to the Elohist exactly a solar year instead of forty days as in the Jehovist. The LXX and Josephus by making the deluge begin on the twenty-seventh of the month have altered this into a lunar year. The solar year in Egypt was preceded by a lunar year of 354¼ days.

[1] Οἱ καταρράκται.—LXX. These flood-gates are mentioned again in chap. viii. 2, 2 Kings vii. 19, Is. xxiv. 18 (where the LXX translate the word θυρίδες), and Mal. iii. 10. They were supposed to be opened when it rained. The primary meaning of the word is network or lattices. The word râqui'ah, which we translate firmament, was a material vault variously described as being 'of paved work like a sapphire stone,' Ex. xxiv. 10; 'like the terrible crystal,' Ezek. i. 22, or 'like a molten mirror,' Job xxxvii. 18. Above this was the heavenly ocean; 'Praise him . . . ye waters that be above the heavens,' Ps. cxlviii. 4. R. Yuda (Tr. Berakoth, chap. 1) says it would take a man fifty years, travelling at the rate of forty miles a day, to traverse the firmament. Above it was supposed to be the abode of God and the angels, Ps. ii. 4, Deut. xxxiii. 26. This conception of a solid firmament was not peculiar to the Jews. In Egypt the sky was supposed to be of iron, portions of which became detached occasionally and fell on the earth. Hence the Egyptian name for iron, ba en pe, 'matter from heaven.' The Greek name for iron also, σίδηρος, which appears again in the Latin sidus, a star, signifies the metal which was first known as having a sidereal origin.

[2] According to the Jehovist the rain is the sole agent in bringing about the deluge.

[3] The Rabbis say that Nôa'h's taking his sons into the ark before his wife and daughters-in-law shows that the sexes were to be separated in the ark, so that no increase was to be apprehended. It thus came to pass that though Shêm was a married man of the ripe age of a hundred years, neither he nor his brothers had any offspring till after the deluge. Three creatures, however, disobeyed the command, and are still being punished for it—Ham, from whom the negro race descended, the dog, and the raven.

14 They, and every beast after its kind, and all the cattle after their kind, and every creeping thing that creepeth upon the earth after its kind, and every fowl after its kind, every bird of every sort.

15 And they went in unto Nóa'h into the ark, two and two of all flesh wherein is the breath of life.

16 And they that went in, went in male and female of all flesh, as Elôhîm commanded him.

And Yahveh shut him in.[1]

17 And the deluge was forty days upon the earth; and the waters increased, and bare up the ark, and it was lift up above the earth.

18 And the waters prevailed, and increased greatly upon the earth; and the ark went upon the face of the waters.

19 And the waters prevailed exceedingly upon the earth; and all the high mountains that were under the whole heaven were covered.

20 Fifteen cubits upwards did the waters prevail: and the mountains were covered.

21 And all flesh died that moved upon the earth, both fowl, and cattle, and beast, and every creeping thing that creepeth upon the earth, and every man:

22 All in whose nostrils was the breath of the spirit of life, of all that was in the dry land, died.

23 And every living thing was destroyed which was upon the face of the ground, both man, and cattle, and creeping

---

[1] R. Ahia b. Zeira (*Tr. Pes.* i.) says that when Nóa'h went into the ark he took with him pearls and precious stones; when they gave but little light he knew it was day, but when they shone brilliantly he knew it was night: he was thus able to feed the animals which required food in the daytime and those which required food at night, else, as the planets had ceased to give light, he would not have known the difference between day and night.

thing, and fowl of the heaven, and they were destroyed from the earth: and Nôa'h only was left, and they that were with him in the ark.

24 And the waters prevailed upon the earth an hundred and fifty days.

CHAPTER VIII.

1 And Elôhim remembered Nôa'h, and every living thing, and all the cattle that were with him in the ark; and Elôhim made a wind to pass over the earth, and the waters assuaged;

2 The fountains also of the deep and the floodgates of heaven were stopped, and the rain from heaven was restrained.

3 And the waters returned from off the earth continually: and after the end of an hundred and fifty days the waters decreased.

4 And the ark rested in the seventh month, on the seventeenth day of the month,[1] upon the mountains of Arârât.[2]

5 And the waters decreased continually until the tenth month: in the tenth month, on the first day of the month, were the tops of the mountains seen.

6 And it came to pass at the end of forty days, that Nôa'h opened the window of the ark which he had made:

7 And he sent forth a raven,[3] and it went forth to and fro, until the waters were dried up from off the earth.

---

[1] Twenty-seventh.—LXX.
[2] The Jehovist does not mention any landing-place.
[3] The raven.—LXX.

8 [And Nôa'h stayed seven days], and he sent forth a dove from him to see if the waters were abated from off the face of the ground;

9 But the dove found no rest for the sole of her foot, and she returned unto him to the ark, for the waters were on the face of the whole earth; and he put forth his hand, and took her, and brought her in unto him into the ark.

10 And he stayed yet other seven days; and again he sent forth the dove out of the ark;

11 And the dove came in to him at eventide; and, lo, in her mouth a fresh olive leaf pluckt off: so Nôa'h knew that the waters were abated from off the earth.

12 And he stayed yet other seven days; and sent forth the dove; and she returned not again unto him any more.[1]

13 And it came to pass, in the six hundred and first year, in the first month, the first day of the month, the waters were dried up from off the earth: and Nôa'h removed the covering of the ark, and looked, and, behold, the face of the ground was dried.

14 And in the second month, on the seven and twentieth day of the month, was the earth dry.

15 And Elôhîm spake unto Nôa'h, saying,

16 Go forth of the ark, thou, and thy wife, and thy sons, and thy sons' wives with thee.

17 Bring forth with thee every living thing that is

---

[1] Schrader has shown the superior originality of the cuneiform story of the Flood with reference to the despatch of the birds. In the cuneiform account there are three birds, the dove (?), the swallow, and the raven, the two first of which return. The third does not return, and this is the proof for which Xisuthros is looking. In the Jehovistic account four birds are sent out, the *first* of which does not return, but flies to and fro. In the Babylonian account the birds are sent one after the other; in the Jehovistic seven days elapse between the sendings forth, a wholly unnecessary period. In the Babylonian account the raven sees the corpses floating on the water and eats them; but the Babylonian deluge only lasts six days, and corpses might still be visible, which they would scarcely be after the lapse of forty days.

with thee of all flesh, both fowl, and cattle, and every creeping thing that creepeth upon the earth ; that they may breed abundantly in the earth, and be fruitful, and multiply in the earth.

18 And Nôa'h went forth, and his sons, and his wife, and his sons' wives with him :

19 Every beast, every creeping thing, and every fowl, whatsoever moveth upon the earth, after their families, went forth out of the ark.

20 And Noah builded an altar unto Yahveh ; and took of every clean beast, and of every clean fowl, and offered burnt offerings upon the altar.

21 And Yahveh smelled the sweet savour; and Yahveh said in his heart, I will not again curse the ground any more for the sake of the man, for that the imagination of man's heart is evil from his youth ; neither will I again smite any more every thing living, as I have done.

22 While the earth remaineth, seedtime and harvest, and cold and heat, and summer and winter, and day and night, shall not cease.[1]

[1] The Jews say the Deluge was brought about by the Most Holy taking two stars from Kimâh (the Pleiades, Job ix. 9), which brought about the terrestrial cataclysm by means of torrential rains, and when he wished to put an end to it he took two stars from the Aïsh (the Great Bear, whose sons appear in her tail in Job xxxviii. 32) to refill the cavity.—*Tr. Berakoth*, F. 59 a.

CHAPTER IX.

1 And Elôhim blessed Nôa'h and his sons, and said unto them, Be fruitful, and multiply, and replenish the earth.

2 And the fear of you and the dread of you shall be upon every beast of the earth, and upon every fowl of the air; with all wherewith the ground creepeth, and all the fishes of the sea, into your hand are they delivered.

3 Every moving thing that liveth shall be food for you; as the green herb have I given you all.

4 But flesh with the life thereof, which is the blood thereof, shall ye not eat.

5 And surely your blood, the blood of your lives, will I require; at the hand of every beast will I require it: and at the hand of every man, even at the hand of every man's brother, will I require the life of man.

6 Whoso sheddeth man's blood, by man shall his blood be shed: for in the image of Elôhim made he man.

7 And you, be ye fruitful, and multiply; bring forth abundantly in the earth, and multiply therein.

8 And Elôhim spake unto Nôa'h, and to his sons with him, saying,

9 And I, behold, I establish my covenant with you, and with your seed after you;

10 And with every living creature that is with you, the fowl, the cattle, and every beast of the earth with

you: of all that go out of the ark, even every beast of the earth.

11 And I will establish my covenant with you; neither shall all flesh be cut off any more by the waters of the deluge; neither shall there any more be a deluge to destroy the earth.

12 And Elóhîm said, This is the token of the covenant which I make between me and you and every living creature that is with you, for perpetual generations.

13 I have set my bow in the cloud, and it shall be for a token of a covenant between me and the earth.

14 And it shall come to pass, when I bring a cloud over the earth, that the bow shall be seen in the cloud,

15 And I will remember my covenant, which is between me and you and every living creature of all flesh; and the waters shall no more become a deluge to destroy all flesh.

16 And the bow shall be in the cloud; and I will look upon it, that I may remember the everlasting covenant between Elóhîm and every living creature of all flesh that is upon the earth.

17 And Elóhîm said unto Nóa'h, This is the token of the covenant which I have established between me and all flesh that is upon the earth.

18 And the sons of Nóa'h, that went forth from the ark, were Shêm, and 'Hám, and Yâpheth; and 'Hám is the father of Kenâ'an.[1]

19 These three were the sons of Nóa'h; and of these was the whole earth overspread.

[1] 'Merchant.'

20 And Nôa'h began to be an husbandman, and planted a vineyard:

21 And he drank of the wine, and was drunken; and he was uncovered within his tent.

22 And 'Hâm, the father of Kenâ'an, saw the nakedness of his father, and told his two brethren without.

23 And Shêm and Yâpheth took a garment, and laid it upon both their shoulders, and went backward, and covered the nakedness of their father; and their faces were backward, and they saw not their father's nakedness.

24 And Nôa'h awoke from his wine, and knew what his youngest son had done unto him.

25 And he said,
 Cursed be Kenâ'an;
 A servant of servants shall he be unto his brethren!

26 And he said,
 Blessed be Yahveh, the God of Shêm;
 And let Kenâ'an be their servant!

27 Elôhîm enlarge Yâpheth,
 And let him dwell in the tents of Shêm;
 And let Kenâ'an be their servant.

28 And Nôa'h lived after the deluge three hundred and fifty years.

29 And all the days of Nôa'h were nine hundred and fifty years: and he died.

CHAPTER X.

1 Now these are the genealogies of the sons of Nôa'h, Shêm, 'Hâm, and Yâpheth : and unto them were sons born after the deluge.

2 The sons of Yâpheth: Gômer,[1] and Mâgôg,[2] and Mâday,[3] and Yâvân,[4] and Tubâl,[5] and Meshech,[6] and Tirâs.[7]

3 And the sons of Gômer : Ashkenaz,[8] and Riphath,[9] and Togarmâh.[10]

[1] Gômer, the Cimmerii, Assyr. Gimir.   [2] Probably the Scythians.
[3] Media, Assyr. Madai.   [4] Ionia.
[5] Generally supposed to be a Caucasian tribe, the Tibareni, neighbours of the Chalybes, the aborigines of the mountains on the coast of the Euxine, forgers of iron and workers in brass, who were celebrated in the time of the Argonauts. The Tibareni are described as having numerous flocks, and the Mosynœci, their neighbours, as living in their houses constructed of wood, in the midst of their forests, and at the foot of their mountains. In Ezek. xxvii. 13 they 'trade the persons of men and vessels of brass' to Tyre. In chap. xxxii. 26 Tubal is again mentioned in connection with Meshech, and also in chap. xxxviii. 2, 3, and xxxix. 1, and 1 Chron. i. 5. In Isa. lxvi. 19, however, it is mentioned in connection with Yâvân, or Ionia. In the inscriptions Salmanassar II. says, 'In my twenty-second campaign' (835 B.C.) 'I crossed the Purat' (Euphrates) 'for the twenty-second time, and advanced towards the land of Tabal' (Tubal). 'At that time I imposed tributes on twenty-four kings of the land of Tabal, and I went on towards those countries where mines of silver, salt (?), and alabaster are found.' From inscriptions of Sar-kin (the Sargôn of Isa. xx. 1) it seems clear that Tubal or Tabal was identical with the Cappadocia of later times. In his list of conquests from the commencement of his reign (701 B.C.) to his fifteenth campaign he says, 'Amris, of the land of Tubal, had been placed on the throne of his father Khulli; I gave him the land of Khilakku (Cilicia), which had not been conquered by my ancestors.'
[6] The Μοσχοι, Muski (Mu-us-ki) or Muški (Mu-uš-ki), LXX Μοσοχ. They inhabited the Moschian mountains, N.E. of Cappadocia.
[7] Jonath. and Targ. Jer. identify Tirâs with Thracia.
[8] Mentioned in Jer. li. 27 in conjunction with the kingdoms of Ararat and Minni, which is on the E. of Elam.
[9] Perhaps inhabitants of the Riphæan mountains.
[10] Probably Armenia. The Armenians say they are descended from Haik, a son of Togarmâh.

4 And the sons of Yâvân: Elisháh,[1] and Tarshish,[2] and the Kittim,[3] and the Dodánim.[4]

5 Of these were the coast-lands of the nations divided in their lands, every one after his tongue; after their families, in their nations.

6 And the sons of Hâm: Kûsh, and Miçraim,[5] and Phût,[6] and Kená'an.[7]

---

[1] Elis. See Ezek. xxvii. 7, 'Blue and purple from the isles of Elishah was thine awning.' This was a name for the whole Peloponnesus. Purple was found in Laconia, in the Gulf of Corinth, and in the islands of the Ægean.

[2] Tarshish, Tartessus, Ταρτησσος, was situated on an island at the mouth of the Tartessus, now the Guadalquivir in Spain. It was of great antiquity, and had ceased to exist in the time of Strabo. The 'kings of Tarshish' are mentioned in Ps. lxxii. 10. It was a great Phœnician emporium. In 1 Kings x. 22 and 2 Chron. ix. 21 Solomon has ships that go to Tarshish with the servants of Hiram; 'once every three years came the ships of Tarshish bringing gold, and silver, ivory, and apes, and peacocks.' The peacocks are omitted in the LXX. The Rev. R. Caldwell (*Comparative Grammar of the Dravidian Languages*) points out that Thukkiyyim, the word used in these passages for 'peacock' is evidently borrowed from the Tamil-Malayalam. With them Tokei or Tókei denotes the bird with the (resplendent) tail. It is called togeï in Malabar. There are no peacocks in Arabia or Africa.

[3] The Kittim are another Phœnician colony. Cyprus, whose capital was Kition, now Larnaka, is meant.

[4] The Rhodians,' LXX, Sam., and 1 Chron. i. 7, where they are called Ródánim.

[5] Egypt, Assyrian Musri, a plural noun to signify Upper and Lower Egypt. In Isa. xix. 6, &c., it is used in the singular, Mázór, to denote Lower Egypt as distinct from Pathrós or Upper Egypt.

[6] Phût is called Libya by the LXX, Ezek. xxvii. 10, &c. Josephus says they inhabited Mauritania. Pliny (*Hist. Nat.* v. 1) mentions a river Phut in Mauritania.

[7] Kená'an means the lowlands. In Isa. xxiii. 11, the name is applied to Phœnicia; in Zeph. ii. 5 to Philistia, &c., but in Gen. xv. 18 it is said to extend from the torrent of Miçráim to the river Phráth (Euphrates). The Babylonians and Assyrians only knew it as Kur Martu (Akkadian) and Mât Aḥarri, or the 'West Country.' The Assyrians included in this designation Omri (Samaria), Edom and Palastar (Philistia and other small states). The Mediterranean is described as 'the great sea of the setting

7 And the sons of Kûsh: Sebâ, and Havilâh, and Sabtâh, and Ra'emâh, and Sabtekâ: and the sons of Ra'emâh, Shebâ, and Dedân.

8 And Kûsh begat Nimród: he began to be a mighty one in the earth.

9 He was a mighty hunter before Yahveh; wherefore it is said, Like Nimród a mighty hunter before Yahveh.

10 And the beginning of his kingdom was Bâbel, and Erech, and Akkad, and Kalneh, in the land of Shine'âr.

11 Out of that land went forth Asshûr, and he built Nineveh, and Rehoboth-Ir, and Kâla'h.

12 And Resen between Nineveh and Kâla'h (the same is the great city).

13 And Miçraim begat the Lûdim, and the 'Anâmim, and the Lehâbim, and the Naphtu'him,

14 And the Patrusim, and the Kaslu'him (whence went forth the Pelishtîm), and the Kaphtôrîm.

15 And Kenâ'an begat Çidón his firstborn, and 'Héth;

16 And the Yebûsy, and the Amóry, and the Girgâshy;

17 And the 'Hivy, and the 'Arqy, and the Siny;

18 And the 'Arvâdy, and the Çemâry, and the 'Hamâthy; and afterward were the families of the Kena'any spread abroad.

19 And the border of the Kena'any was from Çidón, as thou goest towards Gerâr, unto 'Azâh; as thou goest towards Sedôm and 'Amôrâh, and Admâh and Çebóyim unto Lâsha'h.

20 These are the sons of 'Hâm, after their families, after their tongues, in their lands, in their nations.

sum.' For the other tribes mentioned in this chapter see note on chap. xxv. 16.

21 And unto Shêm, the father of all the children of 'Ēber, the elder brother of Yāpheth, to him also were children born.¹
22 The sons of Shêm: 'Elâm, and Asshûr, and Arpakshâd, and Lûd, and Arâm.
23 And the sons of Arâm: 'Ûç, and 'Hûl, and Gether, and Mash.
24 And Arpakshâd begat Shela'h; and Shela'h begat 'Ēber.
25 And unto 'Eber were born
two sons²: the name of the one was Peleg; for in his days was the earth divided (niphlegâh): and his brother's name was Yoqtân.¹
26 And Yoqtân begat Almôdad and Shâleph, and 'Haçarmâveth, and Yârah,
27 And Hadôrâm, and Ûzâl, and Diqlâh;
28 And 'Obal, and Abimâ'el, and Shebâ,
29 And Ophir, and 'Havîlâh, and Yobâb: all these were the sons of Yoqtân.
30 And their dwelling was from Mêshâ, as thou goest towards Sephâr, the mountain of the east.
31 These are the sons of Shêm, after their families, after their tongues, in their lands, after their nations.
32 These are the families of the sons of Nôa'h after their generations, in their nations: and of these were the nations divided in the earth after the deluge.

¹ This verse does not belong to the genealogy: it is evidently an addition to the original document which can only be attributed to the latest editor.—L.

² All the concluding portion of this verse bears the unmistakable impress of the Jehovistic editing; it is the only remaining fragment of the list which the latter document doubtless contained of the generations between Shêm and Abrâhâm. The original text of the Elohist in this place must have been ' And unto 'Hêber were born Peleg and Yoqtân.'—L.

CHAPTER XI.

1 And the whole earth had the same language and the same words.

2 And it came to pass, as they journeyed east, that they found a plain in the land of Shine'âr [1]; and they dwelt there.

3 And they said one to another,[2] Go to, let us make brick, and burn them thoroughly. And they had brick for stone, and bitumen had they for mortar.

4 And they said, Go to, let us build us a city, and a tower,[3] whose top may reach unto heaven, and let us make us a name; lest we be scattered abroad upon the face of the whole earth.

5 And Yahveh came down to see the city and the tower, which the children of men builded.

6 And Yahveh said, Behold, they are all one people, and they have all one language; and this is what they begin to do: and now nothing will be withholden from them, which they purpose to do.

7 Go to, let us go down, and there confound their language, that they may not understand one another's speech.

8 So Yahveh scattered them abroad from thence upon the face of all the earth: and they left off to build the city.[4]

9 Therefore was the name of it called Bâbel,[5] because Yahveh did there confound (balal) the language of all the earth: and from thence did Yahveh scatter them abroad upon the face of all the earth.

10 These are the genealogies of Shêm. Shêm was an hundred years old, and begat Arpakshâd two years after the deluge:

11 And Shêm lived after he begat Arpakshâd five hundred years, and begat sons and daughters.

---

[1] Sumâr, or South Babylonia.
[2] 'And a man said to his neighbour.' —LXX.
[3] Probably the tower of Borsippa (Bâr-sip, Bâr-sap, or Bar-sip), which was built in seven terraces, and was the temple of the seven lights or spheres of Heaven and Earth. It was dedicated to Bel-Nebo, was destroyed by rain and storm, and restored by Nebuchadnezzar. It is now called Birs-Nimrûd.
[4] 'And the tower.'—LXX.   [5] Bâbil or Bâbilu, 'God's gate-way.'

12 And Arpakshâd lived five and thirty years, and begat Shêla'h.¹

13 And Arpakshâd lived after he begat Shêla'h four hundred and three years, and begat sons and daughters.

14 And Shêla'h lived thirty years, and begat 'Êber:

15 And Shêla'h lived after he begat 'Êber four hundred and three years, and begat sons and daughters.

16 And 'Êber lived four and thirty years, and begat Peleg:

17 And 'Êber lived after he begat Peleg four hundred and thirty years, and begat sons and daughters.

18 And Peleg lived thirty years, and begat Re'û;²

19 And Peleg lived after he begat Re'û two hundred and nine years, and begat sons and daughters.

20 And Re'û lived two and thirty years, and begat Serûg:

21 And Re'û lived after he begat Serûg two hundred and seven years, and begat sons and daughters.

22 And Serûg lived thirty years, and begat Nâ'hôr:

23 And Serûg lived after he begat Nâ'hôr two hundred years, and begat sons and daughters.

24 And Nâ'hôr lived nine and twenty years, and begat Tera'h:

25 And Nâ'hôr lived after he begat Tera'h an hundred and nineteen years, and begat sons and daughters.

26 And Tera'h lived seventy years, and begat Abrâm,³ Nâ'hôr, and Hârân.

---
¹ 'And begat Cainan . . . and Cainan begat Salah.'—LXX.
² ' Friend of God.'
³ ' Father of elevation.' Philo (*De Gigantibus*) says this name was given to him to denote a mind entirely given up to the contemplation of

27 Now these are the genealogies of Tera'h.
Tera'h begat Abrâm, Nâ'hôr, and Hârân; and Hârân begat Lot.
28 And Hârân died in the presence of his father Tera'h in the land of his nativity, in Ûr of the Kasdim.[1]
29 And Abrâm and Nâ'hôr took them wives: the name of Abrâm's wife was Sâray[2]; and the name of Nâ'hôr's wife Milkâh, the daughter of Hârân, *the father of Milkâh, and the father of Yiskâh*.[3]

meteors and the celestial bodies. Tera'h here begets Abrâm after he had lived seventy years, and dies at Hârân when he is two hundred and five years old (verse 32). In chap. xii. 1, Abrâm leaves Chaldæa when he was one hundred and thirty-five years old, but in verse 4 it is said he was seventy-five years old when he left Hârân. Jerome and Augustine are agreed that this difficulty is insuperable.

[1] Renan thinks Ûr Casdim is Arpakshâd, for in Gen. x. 24, xi. 10, Arpakshâd is the head of the lineage of 'Êber and Tera'h, for in the style of the Tóledóth to say that 'Êber and Tera'h are descendants of Arpakshâd means that they have come from that country. The LXX do not mention Ûr, but merely speak of 'the country of the Chaldees.' Schrader thinks that by Arpakshâd we should understand the land of the Chaldæans or Babylonians, not that of the Armenian Chaldæans, who, he thinks, should be identified with the Chalybes. Eupolemos (Euseb. *Præp. Evang.* lib. ix. chap. 17) says Abraham was born εν τη πολει της Βαβυλωνιας Καμαρινη (ην τινας λεγειν πολιν Ουριην, ειναι δε μεθερμηνευομενην Χαλδαιων πολιν). Scaliger thinks this town should be spelt Ουρην, not Ουριην, and that it is identical with the town called Ura by Pliny, lib. v. chap. 21; that the expression 'town of the Chaldæans' results from the name Καμαρινη, and that 'Chaldæans' does not signify the inhabitants of Chaldæa, but the magicians or astrologers who are sometimes called by this name. Schrader remarks that Καμαρινη, when explained from the Arabic, signifies 'moon-town,' and Ura or Ουριη was the seat of the worship of the moon-deity, as Harrân (Hârân) was of the moon-god Sin. Kasdim may be formed from the Assyrian Casadu, 'to possess.' The Kasdim would thus be the lords of the land.

[2] Sâray is identified by Josephus and other Jewish writers with Yiskâh, a daughter of Hârân and sister of Lôt and Milkâh. This would make Hârân's mother to be a former wife of Tera'h, and not the mother of Abrâm. The Talmud says the name of the latter was Amthela or Amtelai, the daughter of Karnebo. Kar-Nebo (Kar-Nabu, fortress of Nebo) was also the name of a town in Assyria.

[3] This is evidently a marginal gloss which has passed into the text, and with two different readings, so that it is quite certain that these genealogies

30 And Sâray was barren ; she had no child.

31 And Tera'h took Abrâm his son, and Lôt the son of Hârân, his son's son, and Sâray his daughter-in-law, his son Abrâm's wife ; and they went forth with them from Ur of the Kasdim to go into the land of Kenâ'an : and they came unto Hârân,[1] and dwelt there.

32 And the days of Tera'h were two hundred and five years, and Tera'h died in Hârân.

CHAPTER XII.

1 Now Yahveh said unto Abrâm, Get thee out of thy country, and from thy kindred, and from thy father's house, unto the land that I will show thee :

2 And I will make of thee a great nation, and I will bless thee, and make thy name great ; and be thou a blessing :

3 And I will bless them that bless thee, and him that curseth thee will I curse : and in thee shall all the families of the earth be blessed.

4 So Abrâm went as Yahveh had spoken unto him ; and Lôt went with him : and Abrâm was seventy and five years old when he departed out of Hârân.

were revised during the Captivity in combination with parallel genealogies in existence among the Babylonians written in cuneiform characters. In fact, the name Yiskâh, which has been a *crux interpretum* up to the present time, is merely a second reading, which the most simple and natural mode of spelling Milkâh would be susceptible of in the cuneiform system of writing, in consequence of the polyphony of the initial portion of the name.—L.

[1] An ancient town situated on the Belias, a tributary of the Euphrates. Like Ůr, it was a chief seat of the worship of the moon-god Sin. In chap. xii. 4, 5, and xv. 7, however, it is Abrâm who is said to have migrated to Hârân. In Deut. xxvi. 5 Abrâm is called 'a wandering Aramæan.' Conf. Isa. xxvii. 13, 'they that wander (were exiled) in the land of Asshur.'

5 And Abrâm took Sâray his wife, and Lôt his brother's son, and all their substance that they had gathered, and the souls that they had gotten in Hârân; and they went forth to go into the land of Kenâ'an; and into the land of Kenâ'an they came.

6 And Abrâm passed through the land unto the place of Shechem, unto the terebinth of Môreh.¹ And the Kena'any was then in the land.

7 And Yahveh appeared unto Abrâm, and said, Unto thy seed will I give this land: and there builded he an altar unto Yahveh, who appeared unto him.

8 And he removed from thence unto the mountain on the east of Bêth-Êl, and pitched his tent, having Bêth-Êl on the west, and 'Ay on the east: and there he builded an altar unto Yahveh, and called upon the name of Yahveh.

9 And Abrâm journeyed, going on still toward the south.

10 And there was a famine in the land: and Abrâm went down into Miçraîm to sojourn there; for the famine was sore in the land.

11 And it came to pass, when he was come near to enter into Miçraîm, that he said unto Sâray his wife, Behold, now, I know that thou art a fair woman to look upon:

12 And it shall come to pass, when the inhabitants of Miçraîm shall see thee, that they shall say, This is his wife: and they will kill me, but they will save thee alive.

13 Say, I pray thee, thou art my sister: that it may be well with me for thy sake, and that my soul may live because of thee.

14 And it came to pass, that, when Abrâm was come into Miçraîm, the inhabitants of Miçraîm beheld the woman that she was very fair.

15 And the princes of Para'oh saw her, and praised her to Para'oh: and the woman was taken into Para'oh's house.

16 And he entreated Abrâm well for her sake: and he had sheep, and oxen, and he-asses, and male and female slaves, and she-asses, and camels.

¹ LXX, εἰς τὴν δρῦν τὴν ὑψηλήν, 'to the high oak.'

17 And Yahveh plagued Para'oh and his house with great plagues, because of Sâray Abrâm's wife.

18 And Para'oh called Abrâm, and said, What is this that thou hast done unto me? Why didst thou not tell me that she was thy wife?

19 Why saidst thou, She is my sister? so that I took her to be my wife: now therefore behold thy wife, take her, and go thy way.

20 And Para'oh gave men charge concerning him: and they brought him on the way, and his wife, and all that he had.

CHAPTER XIII.

1 And Abrâm went up out of Miçraîm, he, and his wife, and all that he had, and Lôt with him, into the Negeb.[1]

2 And Abrâm was very rich in cattle, in silver, and in gold.

3 And he went on his journeys from the Negeb even to Bêth-Êl, unto the place where his tent had been at the beginning, between Bêth-Êl and 'Ay;

4 Unto the place of the altar, which he had made there at the first: and there Abrâm called on the name of Yahveh.

5 And Lôt also, which went with Abrâm, had flocks, and herds, and tents.

6 And the land was not able to bear them, that they might dwell together: for their substance was great, so that they could not dwell together.

7 And there was a strife between the herdmen of Abrâm's cattle and the herdmen of Lôt's cattle: and the Kena'any and the Perizzy dwelled then in the land.

---

[1] The desert of Southern Palestine.—L. Negeb means the South, the south country (Exod. xxvi. 18, Numb. xiii. 29, &c.), and in Dan. xi. 5 *sqq.* it refers to Egypt.

8 And Abrâm said unto Lôt, Let there be no strife, I pray thee, between me and thee, and between my herdmen and thy herdmen, for we are brethren.

9 Is not the whole land before thee? separate thyself, I pray thee, from me: if thou wilt take the left hand, then I will go to the right; or if thou take the right hand, then I will go to the left.

10 And Lôt lifted up his eyes, and beheld all the circuit of the Yardên,[1] that it was well watered everywhere, before Yahveh destroyed Sedôm[2] and 'Amôrâh, like the garden of Yahveh, like the land of Miçraîm, as thou goest unto Ço'ar.[3]

11 So Lôt chose him all the circuit of the Yardên; and Lôt journeyed east: and they separated themselves the one from the other.

12 Abrâm dwelled in the land of Kenâ'an, and Lôt dwelled in the cities of the circuit (of the Yardên), and moved his tent as far as Sedôm.

13 *Now the men of Sedôm were wicked and sinners against Yahveh exceedingly.*[4]

14 And Yahveh said unto Abrâm, after that Lôt was separated from him, Lift up now thine eyes, and look from the place where thou art, northward and southward and eastward and westward:

15 For all the land which thou seest, to thee will I give it, and to thy seed for ever.

16 And I will make thy seed as the dust of the earth: so that if a man can number the dust of the earth, then shall thy seed also be numbered.

---

[1] The Jordan, so called from flowing down.

[2] 'Burning, conflagration.'

[3] The Massoretic pointing for this word must be inaccurate. The genuine ancient reading was very probably Çâr. It is not Ço'ar in the Pentapolis, but the Egyptian town Tsar (the first town met with in going from Palestine to the commencement of the irrigated lands of the Delta) that is meant.—L.

[4] This verse seems to have been added by the latest editor in order to prepare the narrative of the destruction of Sedôm and 'Amôrâh in chaps. xviii. and xix.—L.

17 Arise, walk through the land in the length of it and in the breadth of it; for unto thee will I give it.

18 And Abrâm moved his tent, and came and dwelt by the terebinths of Mamrê, which are in Hebrôn, and built there an altar unto Yahveh.

CHAPTER XIV.

1 And it came to pass in the days of Amràphel,[1] king of Shine'âr, Ariôch[2] king of Ellâsâr, Kedorlâ'ômer[3] king of Ê'lâm, and Tide'âl king of the Gôyîm,[4]

2 That they made war with Bera'h, king of Sedôm, and with Birsha' king of 'Amôrâh, Shinâb king of Admah, and Shemêber king of Çeboyîm, and the king of Bela' (*the same is Ço'ar*).

3 All these joined together in the vale of Siddîm (*the same is the salt sea*).

4 Twelve years they served Kedorlâ'ômer, and in the thirteenth year they rebelled.

5 And in the fourteenth year came Kedorlâ'ômer, and the kings that were with him, and smote the Rephaîm in 'Ashterôth-Qarnâyîm,[5] and the Zûzîm in Hâm, and the Êmîm in Shâvêh-Qiryathâyîm,[6]

6 And the 'Horîm in their mountain of Sê'îr unto the oak of Pârân, which is by the wilderness.

7 And they returned, and came to 'Ên-Mishpât[7] (*the same is*

---

[1] Amar-pal, an Accadian name.'—L.

[2] Iri-Aku, a king respecting whom several cuneiform inscriptions are in existence.—L. The name signifies 'servant of the moon-god,' and he was king of Larsa or Larsar, now Senkereh, where Samas or the sun-god was worshipped.

[3] Χοδολλογομορ, LXX. Koudour-Lagamar.—L. There was an Elamite deity Lagamar (La-ga-ma-ru), whose image was carried off by Assurbanipal. Koudour-Lagamar's Syrian campaign probably took place about 2,100 B.C.

[4] A people who dwell on the mountains on the east bank of the Tigris, called Guti and Kuti in the cuneiform inscriptions.—L.

[5] The two-horned Astarte. [6] The plain near the city of Qiryathâyîm.

[7] Fountain of judgment.

Qâdêsh), and smote all the plain of 'Amâlêqy, and also the Amóry, that dwelt in 'Haçaçôn-Tâmâr.¹

8 And there went out the king of Sedôm, and the king of 'Amôrâh, and the king of Admâh, and the king of Çeboyîm,² and the king of Bela' (*the same is Çó'ar*); and they set the battle in array against them in the vale of Siddîm³;

9 Against Kedorlâ'ômer, king of 'Êlam, Tide'âl king of the Góyîm, Amrâphêl king of Shine'âr, and Ariôch king of Ellâsâr; four kings against the five.

10 Now the vale of Siddîm was full of bitumen pits; and the kings of Sedôm and 'Amôrâh fled, and they fell there, and they that remained returned to the mountain.

11 And they took all the goods of Sedôm and 'Amôrâh, and all their victuals, and went away.

12 And they took Lôt, Abrâm's brother, who dwelt in Sedôm, and his goods, and departed.

13 And there came one that had escaped, and told Abrâm the 'Ebry⁴: now he dwelt by the terebinths of Mamrê the 'Amóry, brother of Eshkol, and brother of 'Anêr; and these were confederate with Abrâm.

14 And when Abrâm heard that his brother was taken captive, he led forth his trained men, born in his house, three hundred and eighteen, and pursued as far as Dân;

15 And he divided himself against them by night, he and his servants, and smote them, and pursued them unto 'Hôbâh, which is on the left hand of Dammâseq.⁵

16 And he brought back all the goods, and also brought again his brother Lôt, and his goods, and the women also, and the people.

17 And the king of Sedôm went out to meet him, after his return from the slaughter of Kedorlâ'ômer and the kings that were with him, at the vale of Shâvêh (*the same is the King's vale*).

¹ Pruning of the palm. 'Haçaçon was celebrated for its palms.
² Gazelles.   ³ Valley of the plains.
⁴ Περάτης, LXX. A stranger from the land beyond the Euphrates.
⁵ Assyrian Dimaški or Dimaška. The kingdom of Damascus is called (mât) Mûri-su or (mât) Gar-Mûri-su, probably 'fortress Mûrisu' (Schrader).

18 And Malkî-ṣedeq, king of Shâlôm, brought forth bread and wine: and he was priest of Êl-'Eliôn.[1]

19 And he blessed him and said, Blessed be Abrâm of Êl-'Eliôn, possessor of heaven and earth:

20 And blessed be Êl-'Eliôn, which hath delivered thine enemies into thy hand. And he gave him a tenth of all.

21 And the king of Sedôm said unto Abrâm, Give me the persons, and take the goods[2] to thyself.

22 And Abrâm said to the king of Sedôm, I have lift up mine eyes unto Yahveh, God Most High ('Êl-'Eliôn), possessor of heaven and earth,

23 That I will not take a thread nor a shoelatchet nor aught that is thine, lest thou shouldest say, I have made Abrâm rich:

24 Save only that which the young men have eaten, and the portion of the men which went with me; 'Ânêr, Eshkôl, and Mamrê, let them take their portion.

CHAPTER XV.

1 After these things the word of Yahveh came unto Abrâm in a vision, saying, Fear not, Abrâm: I am thy shield, and thy exceeding great reward.

2 And Abrâm said, O my lord, Yahveh, what wilt thou give me, seeing I go childless, and he that shall be possessor of my house is from Dammeseq, Eli'ezer?[3]

[1] A sacred name, which the fragments of Sanchoniathon show us was also in use among the Phœnicians, and which signifies 'The Most High God'; hence the mode in which Abrâm applies it to Yahveh in verse 22.—L.

[2] 'The cavalry.'—LXX.

[3] LXX. 'And Abram said, Master and Lord, what wilt thou give me? whereas I am departing without a child, but the son of Masek my homeborn female slave, this Eliezer of Damascus, is mine heir.' Nicolaus of Damascus, secretary to Herod the Great, says, 'Abram ruled at Damascus, a foreigner, who had come with an army out of the land beyond Babylon (ὑπερ Βαβυλωνος), called the land of the Chaldæans' (Jos. Ant. i. cap. 7), and adds that he migrated to Canaanea.

3 And Abrâm said, Behold, to me thou hast given no seed; and lo, one born in mine house is mine heir.

4 And behold, the word of Yahveh came unto him saying, This man shall not be thine heir; but he that shall come forth out of thine own bowels shall be thine heir.

5 And he brought him forth abroad, and said, Look now toward heaven, and tell the stars,[1] if thou be able to tell them: and he said unto him, So shall thy seed be.

6 And he believed in Yahveh, and He counted it to him for righteousness.

7 And he said unto him, I am Yahveh that brought thee out of Ûr of the Kasdîm, to give thee this land to inherit it.

8 And he said, My lord, Yahveh, whereby shall I know that I inherit it?

9 And he said unto him, Take me an heifer of three years old, and a she-goat of three years old, and a ram of three years old, and a turtledove, and a young pigeon.

10 And he took him all these, and divided them in the midst, and laid each half over against the other: but the birds divided he not.

11 And the birds of prey came down upon the carcases, and Abrâm drove them away.

12 And when the sun was going down, a deep sleep fell upon Abrâm; and lo, an horror of great darkness fell upon him.

13 And he said unto Abrâm, Know of a surety that thy seed shall be a stranger in a land that is not theirs, and shall serve them; and they shall afflict them four hundred years;

14 And also that nation, whom they shall serve, will I judge; and afterward they shall come out with great substance.

---

[1] Schrader points out that this comparison, which frequently recurs (Gen. xx. 17, xxvi. 4, Exod. xxxii. 13, Deut. i. 10, &c), is met with in Assyrian, expressed in precisely the same words in an inscription of Ašurnâṣirhabal. The Assyrian Kakkab, 'star,' strongly resembles the Hebrew Kôkab. Bereshith Rabba on this verse says, 'The Eternal called forth Abraham and his posterity out of the dominion of the stars; by nature, the Israelite was a servant of the stars, and born under their influence, as are the heathen; but by virtue of the law given on Mount Sinai he became liberated from this degrading servitude.'

15 But thou shalt go to thy fathers in peace ; thou shalt be buried in a good old age.

16 And in the fourth generation they shall come hither again : for the iniquity of the 'Amóry is not yet full.

17 And it came to pass, that, when the sun went down, and it was dark, behold, a smoking furnace, and a flaming torch that passed between these pieces.

18 In that day Yahveh made a covenant with Abrâm, saying, Unto thy seed have I given this land, from the torrent of Miçraîm [1] unto the great river, the river Phrâth :

19 The Qêny, and the Qenizzy, and the Qadmôny,

20 And the 'Hitty, and the Perizzy, and the Rephaîm,

21 And the 'Amóry, and the Kena'any,[2] and the Girgâshy, and the Yebûsy.

CHAPTER XVI.

1 Now Sâray Abrâm's wife bare him no children : and she had a female slave, a native of Miçraîm, whose name was Hâgâr.

2 And Sâray said unto Abrâm, Behold, now, Yahveh hath restrained me from bearing ; go in, I pray thee, unto my slave ; it may be that I shall obtain children by her. And Abrâm hearkened unto the voice of Sâray.

3 And Sâray Abrâm's wife took Hâgâr the Egyptian, her slave, after Abrâm had dwelt ten years in the land of Kenâ'an, and gave her to Abrâm her husband to be his wife.

4 And he went in unto Hâgâr, and she conceived : and when she saw that she had conceived, her mistress was despised in her eyes.

[1] The torrent which formed the extreme north-east frontier of Egypt, now Wady el-'Areesh, upon which Rhinocolura, now El 'Areesh, was situated.

[2] 'And the Evites.'— LXX.

5 And Sâray said unto Abrâm, My wrong be upon thee: I gave my handmaid into thy bosom; and when she saw that she had conceived, I was despised in her eyes: Yahveh judge between me and thee.

6 But Abrâm said unto Sâray, Behold, thy maid is in thy hand; do to her that which is good in thine eyes. And Sâray dealt hardly with her, and she fled from her face.

7 And the angel [1] of Yahveh found her by a spring of water in the wilderness, by the spring in the way to Shûr.[2]

8 And he said, Hâgâr, Sâray's handmaid, whence comest thou? and whither goest thou? And she said, I flee from the face of my mistress Sâray.

9 And the angel of Yahveh said unto her, Return to thy mistress, and submit thyself under her hands.

10 And the angel of Yahveh said unto her, I will greatly multiply thy seed, that it shall not be numbered for multitude.

11 And the angel of Yahveh said unto her, Behold, thou art with child, and shalt bear a son; and thou shalt call his name Yishmâ'êl, because Yahveh hath heard thy affliction.

12 And he shall be as a wild-ass among men; his hand shall be against every man, and every man's hand against him; and he shall dwell in the presence of all his brethren.

13 And she called the name of Yahveh that spake unto her,

---

[1] Mal'ak, a messenger of God. R. Simon b. Lakisch says, 'The names of the angels were imported, like the names of the months, by the Israelites on their return from Babylon. Originally it was said (Isa. vi. 6) *Then flew one of the Seráphim unto me*; or (ib. 2): *Above him stood the Seráphim*. But since that time the Bible says (Dan. ix. 21) the man Gabriël, &c., or (ib. x. 21), merely *Michaël your prince*' (*Tr. Rosh Hasshanah*, chap. i.). Maimoindes (*Mor. Neb.* part i. c. 48) says that the corporeal figures of the angels only existed in the minds of those who saw them, and had no real existence. They are sometimes called angels, sometimes men (Gen. xvii. 2), sometimes winds or spirits (Ps. civ. 4 and 1 Kings xxii. 21), and sometimes women (Zech. v. 9), 'and, behold, there came forth two women, and the wind was in their wings,' &c.

[2] Suez, or perhaps the Shûr (wall) of Egypt, which was built to keep the Sakti or foreigners out of Egypt by Amenemhat I., the first king of the twelfth dynasty, about 2380 B.C.—(Lepsius.)

Thou art a God that seeth (*attâh êl roy*) : for she said, Have I even here looked after him that seeth me?[1]

14 Wherefore the well was called Beêr-la'hay-roy (the well of the Living One who seeth me) : behold, it is between Qâdêsh and Bârâd.

15 And Hâgâr bare Abrâm a son : and Abrâm called the name of his son, which Hâgar bare, Yishmâ'êl.

16 And Abrâm was fourscore and six years old, when Hâgâr bare Yishmâ'êl to Abrâm.

CHAPTER XVII.[2]

1 And when Abrâm was ninety years old and nine Yahveh[3] appeared to Abrâm, and said unto him, I am El-Shadday (God Almighty) ; walk before me, and be thou perfect.

2 And I will make my covenant between me and thee, and will multiply thee exceedingly.

3 And Abrâm fell on his face : and Elôhîm talked with him, saying,

4 As for me, behold, my covenant is with thee, and thou shalt be the father of a multitude of nations.

5 Neither shall thy name any more be called Abrâm,

---

[1] 'For I have openly seen him that appeared to me.'—LXX.

[2] We have evidently here the Elohistic version of the narrative of which chap. xv. gave us the version taken from the Jehovistic document.—L.

[3] This name of God must have been inserted by the latest editor: the word in the original text was no doubt Elôhîm, as in the rest of the chapter.—L.

but thy name shall be Abrâhâm (the father of a multitude)[1]: for the father of a multitude of nations have I made thee.

6 And I will make thee exceeding fruitful, and I will make nations of thee, and kings shall come out of thee.

7 And I will establish my covenant between me and thee and thy seed after thee throughout their generations for an everlasting covenant, to be a God unto thee and to thy seed after thee.

8 And I will give unto thee, and to thy seed after thee, the land of thy sojourning, all the land of Kenâ'an, for an everlasting possession : and I will be their God.

9 And Elôhim said unto Abrâhâm, And as for thee, thou shalt keep my covenant, thou, and thy seed after thee throughout their generations.

10 This is my covenant, which ye shall keep, between me and you and thy seed after thee; every male among you shall be circumcised.

11 And ye shall be circumcised in the flesh of your foreskin ; and it shall be a token of a covenant betwixt me and you.

12 And he that is eight days old shall be circumcised among you, every male throughout your generations, he that is born in the house, or bought with money of any stranger, which is not of thy seed.

13 He that is born in thy house, and he that is bought with thy money, must needs be circumcised:

---

[1] This change of names is unhistorical, there being no word râhâm in Hebrew, and no root with the three letters רהם. The old reading of Sârâh's name was also Sâray, and Abrâm and Sâray are the original names.

and my covenant shall be in your flesh for an everlasting covenant.

14 And the uncircumcised male who is not circumcised in the flesh of his foreskin, that soul shall be cut off from his people : he hath broken my covenant.

15 And Elóhîm said unto Abrâhâm, As for Sâray thy wife, thou shalt not call her name Sâray, but Sârâh shall her name be.

16 And I will bless her, and moreover I will give thee a son of her: yea, I will bless her, and she shall be a mother of nations : kings of peoples shall be of her.

17 Then Abrâhâm fell upon his face, and laughed (yiçe'hâq), and said in his heart, Shall a child be born unto him that is an hundred years old ? and shall Sârâh, that is ninety years old, bear ?

18 And Abrâhâm said unto Elóhim, Oh that Yishmâ'êl might live before thee !

19 And Elóhim said, Nay, but Sârâh thy wife shall bear thee a son ; and thou shalt call his name Yiçe'hâq : and I will establish my covenant with him for an everlasting covenant for his seed after him.

20 And as for Yishmâ'êl, I have heard thee : behold, I have blessed him, and will make him fruitful, and will multiply him exceedingly ; twelve princes shall he beget, and I will make him a great nation.

21 But my covenant will I establish with Yiçe'hâq, which Sârâh shall bear unto thee at this set time in the next year.

22 And he left off talking with him, and Elóhim went up from Abrâhâm.

23 And Abrâhâm took Yishmâ'êl his son, and all that were born in his house, and all that were bought with his money, every male among the men of Abrâhâm's house, and circumcised the flesh of their foreskin in the selfsame day, as Elôhîm had said unto him.

24 And Abrâhâm was ninety years old and nine, when he was circumcised in the flesh of his foreskin.

25 And Yishmâ'êl his son was thirteen years old when he was circumcised in the flesh of his foreskin.

26 In the selfsame day was Abrâhâm circumcised, and Yishmâ'êl his son.

27 And all the men of his house, those born in the house, and those bought with money of the stranger, were circumcised with him.

CHAPTER XVIII.

1 And Yahveh appeared unto him[1] by the terebinths of Mamrê, as he sat in the tent door in the heat of the day;

2 And he lift up his eyes and looked, and, lo, three men stood over against him: and when he saw them, he ran to meet them from the tent door, and bowed himself to the earth,

3 And said, my Lord, if now I have found favour in thy sight, pass not away, I pray thee, from thy servant:

4 Let now a little water be fetched, and wash your feet, and rest yourselves under the tree:

5 And I will fetch a morsel of bread, and comfort ye your

---

[1] 'Unto him' has evidently been inserted by the latest editor instead of 'unto Abraham,' so as to connect this narrative with the preceding chapter. L.

heart; after that ye shall pass on: for therefore are ye come to your servant. And they said, So do, as thou hast said.

6 And Abrâhâm hastened into the tent unto Sârâh, and said, Make ready quickly three measures of fine meal, knead it, and make cakes.

7 And Abrâhâm ran unto the herd, and fetched a calf tender and good, and gave it unto the servant; and he hasted to dress it.

8 And he took butter, and milk, and the calf which he had dressed, and set it before them; and he stood by them under the tree, and they did eat.

9 And they said unto him, Where is Sârâh thy wife? And he said, Behold, in the tent.

10 And (one of them) said, I will certainly return unto thee when the season cometh round; and, lo, Sârâh thy wife shall have a son. And Sârâh heard in the tent door, which was behind him.

11 Now Abrâhâm and Sârâh were old, and well stricken in age; it had ceased to be with Sârâh after the manner of women.

12 And Sârâh laughed within herself, saying, After I am waxed old shall I have pleasure, my lord being old also?

13 And Yahveh said unto Abrâhâm, Wherefore did Sârâh laugh, saying, Shall I of a surety bear a child, which am old?

14 Is anything too hard for Yahveh? At the set time I will return unto thee, when the season cometh round, and Sârâh shall have a son.

15 Then Sârâh denied, saying, I laughed not; for she was afraid. And he said, Nay, but thou didst laugh.

16 And the men rose up from thence, and looked towards Sedôm; and Abrâhâm went with them to bring them on the way.

17 And Yahveh said, Shall I hide from Abrâhâm that which I do;

18 Seeing that Abrâhâm shall surely become a great and mighty nation, and all the nations of the earth shall be blessed in him?

19 For I have known him, to the end that he may command his children and his household after him, that they may keep the way of Yahveh, to do justice and judgment; to the end that Yahveh may bring upon Abrâhâm that which he hath spoken of him.

20 And Yahveh said, Because the cry of Sedôm and 'Amôrâh is great, and because their sin is very grievous;

21 I will go down now, and see whether they have done altogether according to the cry of it, which has come unto me; and if not, I will know.

22 And the men turned from thence, and went toward Sedôm; but Abrâhâm stood yet before Yahveh.[1]

23 And Abrâhâm drew near, and said, Wilt thou consume the righteous with the wicked?

24 Peradventure there be fifty righteous within the city; wilt thou consume and not spare the place for the fifty righteous that are therein?

25 That be far from thee to do after this manner, to slay the righteous with the wicked, that so the righteous should be as the wicked; that be far from thee: shall not the Judge of all the earth do right?

26 And Yahveh said, if I find in Sedôm fifty righteous within the city, then I will spare all the place for their sake.

27 And Abrâhâm answered and said, Behold now, I have taken unto me to speak unto my Lord which am but dust and ashes:

28 Peradventure there shall lack five of the fifty righteous: wilt thou destroy all the city for the lack of five? And he said, I will not destroy it, if I find there forty and five.

29 And he spake unto him yet again, and said, Peradventure there shall be forty found there? And he said, I will not do it for the forty's sake.

30 And he said, Oh let not my Lord be angry, and I will

---

[1] The Jewish tradition, preserved in the Midrashim, says the original text was, 'And Yahveh stood yet before Abrâhâm.' The present reading is reckoned among 'the amendments of the Scribes.'—L. In *Tr. Rosh Hasshanah*, i. 3, it is said that God declares in Gen. xviii. 22 that he himself instituted the custom of rising in the presence of old men.

speak: peradventure there shall thirty be found there. And he said, I will not do it if I find thirty there.

31 And he said, Behold now, I have taken upon me to speak unto my Lord: peradventure there shall be twenty found there. And he said, I will not destroy it for the twenty's sake.

32 And he said, Oh let not my Lord be angry, and I will speak yet but this once: peradventure ten shall be found there. And he said, I will not destroy it for the ten's sake.

33 And Yahveh went his way, as soon as he had left communing with Abrâhâm: and Abrâhâm returned unto his place.

CHAPTER XIX.

1 And the two angels came to Sedôm at even; and Lôt sat in the gate of Sedôm; and Lôt saw them, and rose up to meet them; and he bowed himself with his face to the earth;

2 And he said, Behold now, my lords, turn aside, I pray you, into your servant's house, and tarry all night, and wash your feet, and ye shall rise up early, and go on your way. And they said, Nay, but we will abide in the street all night.

3 And he urged them greatly; and they turned in unto him, and entered into his house; and he made them a feast, and did take unleavened bread, and they did eat.

4 But before they lay down, the men of the city, even the men of Sedôm, compassed the house round, both young and old, all the people from every quarter:

5 And they called unto Lôt, and said unto him, Where are the men which came in to thee this night? bring them out unto us that we may know them.

6 And Lôt went out unto them to the door, and shut the door after him.

7 And he said, I pray you, my brethren, do not so wickedly.

8 Behold, now, I have two daughters which have not known

man; let me, I pray you, bring them out unto you, and do ye to them as is good in your eyes: only unto these men do nothing; forasmuch as they are come under the shadow of my roof.

9 And they said, Stand back. And they said, This one fellow came in to sojourn, and he will needs be a judge: now we will deal worse with thee, than with them. And they pressed sore upon the man, even Lôt, and drew near to break the door.

10 But the men put forth their hand, and brought Lôt into the house to them, and shut the door.

11 And they smote the men that were at the door of the house with blindness, both small and great: so that they wearied themselves to find the door.

12 And the men said unto Lôt, Hast thou any here besides? son in law, and thy sons, and thy daughters, and whomsoever thou hast in the city; bring them out of the place:

13 For we will destroy this place, because the cry of them is waxen great before Yahveh; and Yahveh hath sent us to destroy it.

14 And Lôt went out, and spake unto his sons in law, which married his daughters, and said, Up, get you out of this place; for Yahveh will destroy the city. But he seemed unto his sons in law as one that mocked.

15 And when the morning arose, then the angels hastened Lôt, saying, Arise, take thy wife, and thy two daughters which are here; lest thou be consumed in the iniquity of the city.

16 But he lingered; and the men laid hold upon his hand, and upon the hand of his wife, and upon the hand of his two daughters; Yahveh being merciful unto him: and they brought him forth, and set him without the city.

17 And it came to pass, when they had brought them forth abroad, that he said, Escape for thy life; look not behind thee, neither stay thou in all the circuit; escape to the mountain, lest thou be consumed.

18 And Lôt said unto them, Oh, not so, my lord:

19 Behold now, thy servant hath found grace in thy sight,

and thou hast magnified thy mercy, which thou hast showed unto me in saving my life ; and I cannot escape to the mountain, lest the evil overtake me, and I die :

20 Behold now, this city is near to flee unto, and it is a little one : Oh let me escape thither, (is it not a little one ?) and my soul shall live.

21 And he said unto him, See, I have accepted thee concerning this thing also, that I will not overthrow the city of which thou hast spoken.

22 Haste thee, escape thither ; for I cannot do anything till thou be come thither. Therefore the name of the city was called Çô'ar (little).

23 The sun was risen upon the earth when Lôt came to Çô'ar,

24 Then Yahveh rained upon Sedôm and 'Amôrâh brimstone [1] and fire from Yahveh out of heaven ;

25 And he overthrew those cities, and all the circuit, and all the inhabitants of the cities, and that which grew upon the ground.

26 But his wife looked back from behind him, and she became a pillar of salt.

27 And Abrâhâm gat up early in the morning to the place where he had stood before Yahveh :

28 And he looked toward Sedôm and 'Amôrâh, and toward all the land of the circuit, and beheld, and, lo, the smoke of the land went up as the smoke of a furnace.[2]

---

[1] Gophrith, pitch ; hence sulphur and other inflammable substances. See Gôpher, vi. 14.

[2] M. Lartet (*Ecole des Hautes Etudes, Sect. des Sciences Naturelles*, t. 2, p. 263) thinks that the Dead Sea terminated at one time at the peninsula known by the name of Lisan, and that the space of land which is now a lagune, and extends to the opening of the Wady Zeib, and which is still covered by the waters when they rise higher than usual, was the vale of Siddim which is the salt sea (xiv. 3). Traces of land-slips have been observed on the sides of Djebel. Usdom, the Mountain of Salt, and Sedôm may have been overwhelmed by one of these catastrophes, the result of earthquakes, and afterwards have been covered by the waters of the Dead Sea and the alluvial deposits of the southern streams which flow into the lagune.

29 And it came to pass, when Elôhim destroyed the cities of the circuit, that Elôhim remembered Abrâhâm, and sent Lôt out of the midst of the overthrow, when he overthrew the cities in which Lôt dwelt.

30 And Lôt went up out of Çô'ar, and dwelt in the mountain, and his two daughters with him; for he feared to dwell in Çô'ar: and he dwelt in a cave, he and his two daughters.

31 And the firstborn said unto the younger, Our father is old, and there is not a man in the earth to come in unto us after the manner of all the earth:

32 Come, let us make our father drink wine, and we will lie with him, that we may preserve seed of our father.

33 And they made their father drink wine that night: and the firstborn went in, and lay with her father; and he knew not when she lay down, nor when she arose.

34 And it came to pass on the morrow, that the firstborn said unto the younger, Behold, I lay yesternight with my father: let us make him drink wine this night also; and go thou in, and lie with him, that we may preserve seed of our father.

35 And they made their father drink wine that night also: and the younger arose, and lay with him: and he knew not when she lay down, nor when she arose.

36 Thus were both the daughters of Lôt with child by their father.

37 And the firstborn bare a son, and called his name Môâb (progeny of a father): the same is the father of the people of Môâb to this day.

38 And the younger, she also bare a son, and called his name Ben-'Ammy (son of my people): the same is the father of the Benê-'Ammôn to this day.

CHAPTER XX.[1]

1 *And Abráhám journeyed from thence toward the land of Negeb, and dwelt between Qádésh and Shûr; and he sojourned in Gerâr.*
2 *And Abráhám said of Sáráh his wife, She is my sister: and Abímelech king of Gerâr sent, and took Sáráh.*
3 *And Elóhîm came to Abímelech in a dream of the night, and said to him, Behold, thou art but a dead man, because of the woman which thou hast taken; for she is a man's wife.*
4 *Now Abímelech had not come near her: and he said, Lord, wilt thou slay even a righteous nation?*

[1] This chapter is one of the most embarrassing in Genesis as regards the settlement of its authorship. It certainly does not come from the Jehovist, and it is evidently a second version of the Jehovistic narrative which we have in the existing text in chap. xii. 10–20. As God is called Elóhîm throughout except in verse 18 critics formerly considered it as taken from the Elohistic document. Recent criticism, however, has clearly shown the difficulty of maintaining this opinion. Neither the language, nor the grammatical construction, nor the method and spirit of its narrative resemble the usual style of the Elohist. The fragment differs from his mode of writing as much and perhaps even more than it does from that of the Jehovist. The latest editor must have taken it from some other source to place it here between the two leading documents which he was publishing. It is one of the passages which certain critics consider to have been taken from a book which the latest editor borrowed but little from, the author of which they call 'the second Elohist,' or 'the theocratical narrator.'

Whatever the truth may be, whether the editor has introduced the text as we have it, or whether it has been introduced by later copyists, this narrative is certainly not in its natural and logical place. It is inserted contrary to all probability and to the natural sequence of events, between the promise of a son to Abráhám and Sáráh and the birth of that son—that is to say, during Sáráh's miraculous pregnancy. The amorous feelings which the beauty of Abráhám's wife aroused in the king of Gerâr presuppose a young woman, not the aged woman of ninety-nine, who is spoken of in chap. xviii. 11–14. Voltaire and others have sneered with more wit than piety at the improbability of the facts which results from the present position of this narrative in the later portion of Abráhám's biography.

If this fragment must, notwithstanding the serious difficulties of so doing, be referred to the Elohist, it would have to take the place of that which now occupies xii. 5–xiii. 3 to put it in its natural and proper place in the Book of Genealogies.—L.

5 *Said he not himself unto me, She is my sister? and she, even she herself said, He is my brother: in the integrity of my heart and the innocency of my hands have I done this.*

6 *And God said unto him in the dream, Yea, I know that in the integrity of thy heart thou hast done this, and I also withheld thee from sinning against me: therefore suffered I thee not to touch her.*

7 *Now therefore restore the man's wife; for he is a prophet, and he shall pray for thee, and thou shalt live: and if thou restore her not, know thou that thou shalt surely die, thou, and all that are thine.*

8 *And Abimelech rose early in the morning, and called all his servants, and told all these things in their ears: and the men were sore afraid.*

9 *Then Abimelech called Abrahám, and said unto him, What hast thou done unto us? and wherein have I sinned against thee, that thou hast brought on me and on my kingdom a great sin? thou hast done deeds unto me that ought not to be done.*

10 *And Abimelech said unto Abrahám, What sawest thou, that thou hast done this thing?*

11 *And Abrahám said, Because I thought, Surely the fear of Elóhim is not in this place; and they will slay me for my wife's sake.*

12 *And moreover she is indeed my sister, the daughter of my father, but not the daughter of my mother; and she became my wife:*

13 *And it came to pass, when Elóhim* [1] *caused me to wander from my father's house, that I said unto her, This is thy kindness which thou shalt show unto me: at every place whither we shall come, say of me, He is my brother.*

14 *And Abimelech took sheep and oxen, and menservants and womenservants, and gave them unto Abrahám, and restored him Sárah his wife.*

15 *And Abimelech said, Behold, my land is before thee: dwell where it pleaseth thee.*

---

[1] The sacred name Elóhim, though plural in form, always governs the verb in the singular. In this place the verb is in the plural, which is quite irregular.—L.

16 And unto Sârâh he said, Behold, I have given thy brother a thousand pieces of silver : behold, it is for thee a covering of the eyes to all that are with thee¹ ; and before all men thou art righted.

17 And Abrâhâm prayed unto God : and Elôhîm healed Abîmelech, and his wife, and his maidservants ; and they bare children.

18 For Yahveh had fast closed up all the wombs of the house of Abîmelech, because of Sârâh Abrâhâm's wife.

CHAPTER XXI.

1 And Yahveh visited Sârâh as he had said, and Yahveh did unto Sârâh as he had spoken.

2 And Sârâh conceived, and bare Abrâhâm a son in his old age, at the set time of which Elôhîm had spoken to him.

3 And Abrâhâm called the name of his son that was born unto him, whom Sârâh bare to him, Yiçe'hâq.

4 And Abrâhâm circumcised his son Yiçe'hâq when he was eight days old, as Elôhîm had commanded him.

5 And Abrâhâm was an hundred years old when his son Yiçe'hâq was born unto him.

6 And Sârâh said, Elôhîm hath prepared laughter for me ; every one that heareth will laugh (yiçe'hâq) at me.

7 And she said, Who would have said unto Abrâhâm, that Sârâh should give children suck ? for I have borne him a son in his old age.

8 And the child grew, and was weaned: and

¹ An honourable satisfaction.—L.

Abrâhâm made a great feast on the day that Yiçe'hâq was weaned.

9 And Sârâh saw the son of Hâgâr, the Egyptian, which she had borne unto Abrâhâm, mocking.

10 Wherefore she said unto Abrâhâm, Cast out this bondwoman and her son: for the son of this bondwoman shall not be heir with my son, even with Yiçe'haq.

11 And the thing was very grievous in Abrâhâm's sight on account of his son.

12 And Elóhim said unto Abrâhâm, Let it not be grievous in thy sight because of the lad, and because of thy bondwoman; in all that Sârâh saith unto thee, hearken unto her voice; for in Yiçe'haq shall thy seed be called.

13 And also of the son of the bondwoman will I make a nation, because he is thy seed.

14 And Abrâhâm rose up early in the morning, and took bread and a skin of water, and gave it unto Hâgâr, putting it on her shoulder, and the child, and sent her away: and she departed, and wandered in the wilderness of Bêr-Shâb'a.

15 And the water in the bottle was spent, and she cast the child under one of the shrubs.

16 And she went, and sat her down against him a long way off, as it were a bowshot: for she said, Let me not look upon the death of the child. And she sat over against him, and lift up her voice, and wept.

17 And Elóhim heard the voice of the lad; and the angel of Elóhim called to Hâgâr out of heaven, and said unto her, What aileth thee, Hâgâr? fear not; for Elóhim hath heard the voice of the lad where he is.

18 Arise, lift up the lad, and hold him in thine hand; for I will make him a great nation.

19 And Elôhim opened her eyes, and she saw a well of water; and she went and filled the bottle with water, and gave the lad drink.[1]

20 And Elôhim was with the lad, and he grew; and he dwelt in the wilderness, and became an archer.

21 And he dwelt in the wilderness of Pârân: and his mother took him a wife out of the land of Miçraim.

22 *And it came to pass*[2] *at that time, that Abimelech*[3] *and Phichol the captain of his host spake unto Abrâhâm, saying, Elôhim is with thee in all that thou doest:*

23 *Now therefore swear unto me here by Elôhim that thou wilt not deal falsely with me, nor with my son, nor with my son's son: but according to the kindness that I have done unto thee, thou shalt do unto me, and to the land wherein thou hast sojourned.*

24 *And Abrâhâm said, I will swear.*

25 *And Abrâhâm reproved Abimelech because of the well of water, which Abimelech's servants had violently taken away.*

26 *And Abimelech said, I know not who hath done this thing: neither didst thou tell me, neither yet heard I of it, but to-day.*

27 *And Abrâhâm took sheep and oxen, and gave them unto Abimelech; and they two made a covenant.*

28 *And Abrâhâm set seven ewe lambs of the flock by themselves.*

29 *And Abimelech said unto Abrâhâm, What mean those seven ewe lambs which thou hast set by themselves?*

30 *And he said, These seven ewe lambs shalt thou take of my hand, that it may be a witness unto me, that I have digged this well.*

---

[1] It is clear that this was originally the Elohistic narrative, parallel to the Jehovistic narrative in chap. xvi. 5-15.—L.

[2] This is the continuation of the narrative in chap. xx. taken from the same document.—L.

[3] Και Οχοζαθ ο νυμφαγωγος αυτου, 'and Ochozath his friend' (his attendant at marriage, or friend of the bridegroom).—LXX.

31 Wherefore he called that place Bêr-Shâb'a; because there they sware both of them.

32 So they made a covenant at Bêr-Shâb'a: and Abimelech rose up, and Phichôl the captain of his host, and they returned into the land of the Pelishtim.

33 And Abrâhâm planted a tamarisk tree in Bêr-Shâb'a, and called there on the name of Yahveh, the Everlasting God.

34 And Abrâhâm sojourned in the land of the Pelishtim many days.

CHAPTER XXII.[1]

1 And it came to pass after these things that God did prove Abrâhâm, and said unto him, Abrâhâm: and he said, Here am I.

2 And he said, Take now thy son, thine only son, whom thou lovest, even Yiçe'hâq, and get thee into the land of Môriyâh[2]; and offer him there for a burnt offering upon one of the mountain which I will tell thee of.

3 And Abrâhâm rose early in the morning, and saddled his ass, and took two of his young men with him, and Yiçe'hâq his son; and he clave the wood for the burnt offering, and rose up, and went unto the place of which God had told him.

4 On the third day Abrâhâm lift up his eyes, and saw the place afar off.

---

[1] For the origin of verses 1-18 of this chapter, see the note on them in the attempted restoration of the Jehovistic document.—I.

[2] 'Into the high land.'—LXX. In 2 Chron. iii. 1 the LXX has εν ορει του Αμωρια, 'in the mount of Amoria,' and the Syriac has 'in the land of the Amorites.' It would evidently be absurd that a district should be called, as it is usually supposed to be called, after an appearance which had not yet taken place. Accordingly Aquila has, somewhat similarly to the LXX, εις την γην την καταφανη, 'to the conspicuous land,' Symmachus, εις την γην της οπτασιας, 'to the land of the vision,' and the Vulgate has also *in terram visionis*, 'to the land of vision.'

5 And Abrâhâm said to his young men, Abide ye here with the ass, and I and the lad will go yonder; and we will worship, and come again to you.

6 And Abrâhâm took the wood of the burnt offering, and laid it upon Yiçe'hâq his son; and he took in his hand the fire and the knife; and they went both of them together.

7 And Yiçe'hâq spake unto Abrâhâm his father, and said, My father: and he said, Here am I, my son. And he said, Behold the fire and the wood: but where is the lamb for a burnt offering?

8 And Abrâhâm said, Elôhîm will provide himself the lamb for a burnt offering, my son: so they went both of them together.

9 And they came to the place which God had told him of; and Abrâhâm built the altar there, and laid the wood in order, and bound Yiçe'hâq his son, and laid him on the altar, upon the wood.

10 And Abrâhâm stretched forth his hand, and took the knife to slay his son.

11 And the angel of Yahveh called unto him out of heaven, and said, Abrâhâm, Abrâhâm: and he said, Here am I.

12 And he said, Lay not thy hand upon the lad, neither do thou any thing to him: for now I know thou fearest Elôhîm, seeing thou hast not withheld thy son, thine only son, from me.

13 And Abrâhâm lifted up his eyes, and looked, and behold, behind him a ram caught in the thicket[1] by his horns: and Abrâhâm went and took the ram, and offered him up for a burnt offering in the stead of his son

14 And Abrâhâm called the name of that place Yahveh-yireh (Yahveh will provide): as it is said to this day, In the mount of Yahveh it shall be provided.[2]

15 And the angel of Yahveh called unto Abrâhâm a second time out of heaven,

16 And said, By myself have I sworn, saith Yahveh, because

---

[1] 'In a plant of Sabec.'—LXX.

[2] The proverb alluded to here is now unintelligible. It was a play upon the name of Mount Moriyâh.— L. The LXX have it 'The Lord hath seen; that they might say to-day, In the mount the Lord was seen.'

thou hast done this thing, and hast not withheld thy son, thine only son :

17 That in blessing I will bless thee, and in multiplying I will multiply thy seed as the stars of the heaven, and as the sand which is upon the sea shore; and thy seed shall possess the gate of his enemies.

18 And in thy seed shall all the nations of the earth be blessed, because thou hast obeyed my voice.

19 So Abrâhâm returned unto his young men, and they rose up and went together *to Bêr-Shâbʿa ; and Abrâhâm dwelt at Bêr-Shâbʿa.*[1]

20 And it came to pass after these things, that it was told Abrâhâm, saying, Behold, Milkâh, she also hath borne children unto thy brother Nâʿhôr [2];

21 ʿÛç his firstborn,[3] and Bûz his brother,[4] and Qemûêl the father of Arâm ;

22 And Kesed, and ʾHazô, and Pildâsh, and Yidlâph, and Bethûêl.

23 And Bethûêl begat Ribqâh : these eight did Milkâh bear to Nâʿhôr, Abrâhâm's brother.

24 And his concubine, whose name was Reûmâh, she also bare Tebaʿh, and Gaʿham, and Taʿhash, and Maʿachâh.

[1] These words have evidently been added to the text of the Jehovist by the latest editor, so as to make this narrative connect with the one which he had caused to precede it. L.

[2] Although verses 20–24 are purely genealogical they do not in the least resemble the Book of Genealogies drawn up by the Elohist, neither do they fit naturally into his plan. They must, therefore, be attributed to the Jehovist, who inserted them as a preparation for and introduction to the account of the marriage between Yiçeʿhâq and Ribqâh. —L.

[3] Ἐν χωρᾳ τῃ Αυσιτιδι, 'in the land of Ausis,' Job i. 1, LXX ; a tribe of North Arabia. In Gen. x. 23, ʿÛç is called the son of Arâm, and in chap. xxxvi. 28, the son of Dishân.

[4] A people and region of Arabia Deserta. See Job xxxii. 2.

CHAPTER XXIII.

1 And the life of Sârâh was an hundred and seven and twenty years: these were the years of the life of Sârâh.

2 And Sârâh died in Qiryath-Arb'a (*the same is Hebrôn*), in the land of Kenâ'an: and Abrâhâm came to mourn for Sârâh, and to weep for her.

3 And Abrâhâm rose up from before his dead, and spake unto the Benê-'Hêth, saying,

4 I am a stranger and a sojourner with you: give me a possession of a buryingplace with you, that I may bury my dead out of my sight.

5 And the Benê-'Hêth answered Abrâhâm, saying unto him,

6 Hear us, my lord: Thou art a prince of Elóhim among us: in the choice of our sepulchres bury thy dead; none of us shall withhold from thee his sepulchre, but that thou mayest bury thy dead.

7 And Abrâhâm rose up, and bowed himself to the people of the land, even to the Benê-'Hêth.

8 And he communed with them, saying, If it be your mind that I should bury my dead out of my sight, hear me, and intreat for me to 'Ephrôn the son of Ço'har,

9 That he may give me the cave[1] of Machpêlâh, which he hath, which is in the end of his field; for the full price let him give it to me in the midst of you for a possession of a buryingplace.

---

[1] 'The double cave,' τὸ σπήλαιον τὸ διπλοῦν.—LXX.

10 Now 'Ephrôn was sitting in the midst of the Bênê-'Hêth: and 'Ephrôn[1] the 'Hitty[2] answered Abrâhâm in the audience of the Benê-'Heth, even of all that went in at the gate of his city, saying,

11 Nay, my lord, hear me: the field give I thee, and the cave that is therein; in the presence of the sons of my people give I it thee: bury thy dead.

12 And Abrâhâm bowed himself down before the people of the land,

13 And he spake unto 'Ephrôn in the audience of the people of the land, saying, But if thou wilt, I pray thee, hear me: I will give the price of the field; take it of me, and I will bury my dead there.

14 And 'Ephrôn answered Abrâhâm, saying unto him,

15 My lord, hearken unto me: a piece of land worth four hundred shekels of silver, what is that betwixt me and thee? bury therefore thy dead.

16 And Abrâhâm hearkened unto 'Ephrôn; and Abrâhâm weighed to 'Ephrôn the silver, which he had named in the audience of the Benê-'Hêth, four

---

[1] 'Ephrôn means 'of or belonging to a calf.' It is a Hebrew name.

[2] The 'Hitty were the great and warlike nation called Kheta by the Egyptians, and Khatti by the Assyrians. Their country lay between the Orontes and the Euphrates, and there is no evidence that they ever existed in Palestine, but rather there is evidence to the contrary. See 1 Kings x. 29, 2 Kings vii. 6. They are mentioned in the tablets drawn up for Sargon king of Argane about 1900 B.C. 'On the twentieth day an eclipse happens. The king of the Hittites [or the king of the Khatti] lives and on the throne seizes.' Tuklat-pal-Asar (Tiglath Pilesar) I., about 1130 B.C., mentions in his inscription the subjugation of four thousand men of the Kaskaya and Hurumaya rebellious tribes of the Khatti, who had brought the cities of Subarta under their power. They refused to fight, and the king took their valuables and two soss (120) of their chariots fitted to the yoke, and gave them to his own people.

hundred shekels of silver,[1] current money with the merchant.

17 So the field of 'Ephrôn, which was in Machpêlâh, which was before Mamrê, the field, and the cave which was therein, and all the trees that were in the field, that were in all the border thereof round about, were made sure

18 Unto Abrâhâm for a possession in the presence of the children of 'Hêth, before all that went in at the gate of his city.

19 And after this, Abrâhâm buried Sârâh his wife in the cave of the field of Machpêlâh before Mamrê (*the same is Hebrôn in the land of Kenâ'an*).

20 And the field, and the cave that is therein, were made sure unto Abrâhâm for a possession of a burying-place by the Benê-'Hêth.

CHAPTER XXIV.

1 And Abrâhâm was old, and well stricken in age: and Yahveh had blessed Abrâhâm in all things.

2 And Abrâhâm said unto his servant, the elder of his house, that ruled over all that he had, Put, I pray thee, thy hand under my thigh:

3 And I will make thee swear by Yahveh, the God of heaven and the God of earth, that thou shalt not take a wife for

---

[1] LXX, Διδραχμοι. The gêrâh, or bean (probably the seeds of the carob-tree), twenty of which went to the shekel, was the basis of the early Hebrew money, which, whatever its form, was valued according to its weight. The value of the silver shekel was about three shillings.

my son of the daughters of the Kena'any, among whom I dwell;

4 But thou shalt go unto my country, and to my kindred, and take a wife for my son Yice'hâq.

5 And the servant said unto him, Peradventure the woman will not be willing to follow me unto this land: must I needs bring thy son again unto the land from whence thou camest?

6 And Abrâhâm said unto him, Beware that thou bring not my son thither again.

7 Yahveh, the God of heaven, that took me from my father's house, and from the land of my nativity, and that spake unto me, and that sware unto me, saying, Unto thy seed will I give this land; he shall send his angel before thee, and thou shalt take a wife for my son from thence.

8 And if the woman be not willing to follow thee, then thou shalt be clear from this my oath; only thou shalt not bring my son thither again.

9 And the servant put his hand under the thigh of Abrâhâm his master, and sware to him concerning this matter.

10 And the servant took ten camels, of the camels of his master, and departed; having all goodly things of his master's in his hand; and he arose and went to Aram Naharaîm,[1] unto the city of Nâ'hôr.

11 And he made the camels to kneel down without the city by the well of water at the time of evening, the time that women go out to draw water.

12 And he said, O Yahveh, God of my master Abrâhâm, send me, I pray thee, good speed this day, and show kindness unto my master Abrâhâm.

13 Behold, I stand by the fountain of water; and the daughters of the men of the city come out to draw water;

14 And let it come to pass, that the damsel to whom I shall say, Let down thy pitcher, I pray thee, that I may drink; and she shall say, Drink, and I will give thy camels drink also: let

---

[1] Syria of the two rivers, Mesopotamia. The Jehovist always uses the word Paddan-Arâm, the plain of Syria, xxv. 20, &c. This word only occurs in Genesis.

the same be she that thou hast appointed for thy servant Yiçe'hâq; and thereby shall I know that thou hast shown kindness unto my master.

15 And it came to pass, before he had done speaking, that, behold, Ribqâh came out, who was born to Bethûêl the son of Milkâh, the wife of Nâ'hôr, Abrâhâm's brother, with her pitcher upon her shoulder.

16 And the damsel was very fair to look upon, a virgin, neither had any man known her: and she went down to the fountain, and filled her pitcher, and came up.

17 And the servant ran to meet her, and said, Give me to drink, I pray thee, a little water of thy pitcher.

18 And she said, Drink, my lord: and she hasted, and let down her pitcher upon her hand, and gave him drink.

19 And when she had done giving him drink, she said, I will draw for thy camels also, until they have done drinking.

20 And she hasted, and emptied her pitcher into the trough, and ran again unto the well to draw, and drew for all his camels.

21 And the man looked stedfastly on her; holding his peace, to know whether Yahveh had made his journey prosperous or not.

22 And it came to pass, as the camels had done drinking, that the man took a golden ring of half a beq'a weight,[1] and two bracelets for her hands of ten shekels weight of gold;

23 And said, Whose daughter art thou? tell me, I pray thee. Is there room in thy father's house for us to lodge in?

24 And she said unto him, I am the daughter of Bethûêl the son of Milkâh, which she bare unto Nâ'hôr.

25 She said moreover to him, We have both straw and provender enough, and room to lodge in.

26 And the man bowed his head, and worshipped Yahveh.

27 And he said, Blessed be Yahveh, the God of my master Abrâhâm, who hath not forsaken his mercy and truth toward my master: as for me, Yahveh hath led me in the way to the house of my master's brethren.

[1] 'Took golden earrings, each of a drachm weight.'—LXX.

28 And the damsel ran, and told her mother's house according to these words.

29 And Ribqâh had a brother, and his name was Lâbân: and Lâbân ran out unto the man, unto the fountain.

30 And it came to pass, when he saw the ring, and the bracelets upon his sister's hands, and when he heard the words of Ribqâh his sister, saying, Thus spake the man to me; that he came unto the man; and, behold, he stood by the camels at the fountain.

31 And he said, Come in, thou blessed of Yahveh; wherefore standest thou without? for I have prepared the house, and room for the camels.

32 And the man came into the house, and he ungirded the camels; and he gave straw and provender for the camels, and water to wash his feet and the men's feet that were with him.

33 And there was set meat before him to eat; but he said, I will not eat, until I have told mine errand. And he said, Speak on.

34 And he said, I am Abrâhâm's servant.

35 And Yahveh hath blessed my master greatly; and he is become great: and he hath given him flocks, and herds, and silver and gold, and male and female slaves, and camels and asses.

36 And Sârâh my master's wife bare a son to my master when she was old; and unto him hath he given all that he hath.

37 And my master made me swear, saying, Thou shalt not take a wife for my son of the daughters of the Kena'any, in whose land I dwell:

38 But thou shalt go unto my father's house, and to my kindred, and take a wife for my son.

39 And I said unto my master, Peradventure the woman will not follow me.

40 And he said unto me, Yahveh, before whom I walk, will send his angel with thee, and prosper thy way; and thou shalt take a wife for my son of my kindred, and of my father's house.

41 Then shalt thou be clear from my oath, when thou comest to my kindred; and if they give her not to thee, thou shalt be clear from my oath.

42 And I came this day unto the fountain, and said, O Yahveh, God of my master Abrâhâm, if now thou do prosper my way which I go :

43 Behold, I stand by the fountain of water; and let it come to pass, that the maiden which cometh forth to draw, to whom I shall say, Give me, I pray thee, a little water of thy pitcher to drink;

44 And she shall say to me, Both drink thou, and I will also draw for thy camels: let the same be the woman whom Yahveh hath appointed for my master's son.

45 And before I had done speaking in my heart, behold, Ribqâh came forth with her pitcher on her shoulder; and she went down unto the fountain, and drew : and I said to her, Let me drink, I pray thee.

46 And she made haste, and let down her pitcher from her shoulder, and said, Drink, and I will give thy camels drink also; so I drank, and she made the camels drink also.

47 And I asked her, and said, Whose daughter art thou? And she said, The daughter of Bethûêl, Nâ'hôr's son, whom Milkâh bare unto him : and I put the ring upon her nose, and the bracelets upon her hands.

48 And I bowed my head, and worshipped Yahveh, and blessed Yahveh, the God of my master Abrâhâm, which had led me in the right way to take my master's brother's daughter for his son.

49 And now if ye will deal kindly and truly with my master, tell me : and if not, tell me ; that I may turn to the right hand or to the left.

50 Then Lâbân and Bethûêl answered and said, The thing proceedeth from Yahveh : we cannot speak unto thee good or bad.

51 Behold, Ribqâh is before thee, take her, and go, and let her be thy master's son's wife, as Yahveh hath spoken.

52 And it came to pass, that, when Abrâhâm's servant heard their words, he bowed himself down to the earth before Yahveh.

53 And the servant brought forth jewels of silver, and jewels of gold, and raiment, and gave them to Ribqâh : he gave also to her brother and to her mother precious things.

54 And they did eat and drink, he and the men that were with him, and tarried all night; and they rose up in the morning, and he said, Send me away unto my master.

55 And her brother and her mother said, Let the damsel abide with us a few days, at the least ten; after that she shall go.

56 And he said unto them, Hinder me not, seeing that Yahveh hath prospered my way; send me away that I may go to my master.

57 And they said, We will call the damsel, and inquire at her mouth.

58 And they called Ribqâh, and said unto her, Wilt thou go with this man? And she said, I will go.

59 And they sent away Ribqâh their sister, and her nurse and Abrâhâm's servant, and his men.

60 And they blessed Ribqâh, and said unto her, Our sister, be thou the mother of thousands of ten thousands, and let thy seed possess the gates of those that hate them.

61 And Ribqâh arose, and her damsels, and they rode upon the camels, and followed the man: and the servant took Ribqâh and went his way.

62 And Yiçe'hâq came from the way[1] of Beêr-la'hay-rôy[2] (the well of the Living One that seeth me); for he dwelt in the land of Negeb.

63 And Yiçe'hâq went out to meditate in the field at the eventide: and he lifted up his eyes, and saw, and behold, there were camels coming.

64 And Ribqâh lifted up her eyes, and when she saw Yiçe'hâq, she lighted off the camel.

65 And she, said unto the servant, What man is this that walketh in the field to meet us? And the servant said, It is my master: and she took her veil, and covered herself.

66 And the servant told Yiçe'hâq all the things that he had done.

---

[1] The LXX and the author of the Samaritan version have had before them here a text which had bimadbar, 'in the desert,' instead of mibbô.—L.

[2] See chap. xvi. 14. L.

67 And Yiçe'hâq brought her into his mother Sârâh's tent, and took Ribqâh, and she became his wife; and he loved her: and Yiçe'haq was comforted after his mother's death.

CHAPTER XXV.

1 And Abrâhâm took another wife and her name was Qetûrâh.[1]

2 And she bare him Zimrân, and Yoqshân, and Medân, and Midyân, and Yishbâq, and Shûâ'h.

3 *And Yoqshân begat Shebâ and Dedân*,[2] and the sons of *Dedân* were the Aphûrîm, and the Letûshîm and the Leummîm.

4 And the sons of Midyân; 'Êphâh, and 'Êpher, and 'Hanôch, and Abîd'a, and Eldâ'â. All these were the children of Qetûrâh.

5 And Abrâhâm gave all that he had to Yiçe'hâq.

6 But unto the sons of the concubines, which Abrâhâm had, Abrâhâm gave gifts; and he sent them away from Yiçe'hâq his son, while he yet lived, eastward, into the east country.

7 And these are the days of Abrâhâm's life which he lived, an hundred three score and fifteen years.

---

[1] She is called Abrâhâm's concubine in 1 Chron. i. 32. Qetûrâh means 'incense,' and her descendants are, therefore, the tribes who brought incense from the south of Arabia to Palestine and the Mediterranean.

[2] The verb used here for 'begat' does not belong to the ordinary phraseology of the Elohist; besides which, the Elohist places Shebâ and Dedân among the descendants of 'Hâm in chap. x. 7. The commencement of this verse, therefore, cannot have been written by him, but must have been added by the latest editor, who perhaps also added verse 5 in accordance with chap. xxiv. 36. This, however, is not so certain.—L.

8 And Abrâhâm gave up the ghost, and died in a good old age, an old man, and full of years; and was gathered to his people.

9 And Yiçe'hâq and Yishmâ'êl his sons buried him in the cave of Machpêlâh, in the field of 'Ephrôn the son of Ço'ar the 'Hitty, which is before Mamrê.

10 The field which Abrâhâm purchased of the Benê-'Hêth; there was Abrâhâm buried, and Sârâh his wife.

11 And it came to pass after the death of Abrâhâm, Elôhîm blessed Yiçe'hâq his son; *and Yiçe'hâq dwelt by Beêr-la'hay-rôy.*

12 Now these are the generations of Yishmâ'êl Abrâhâm's son, whom Hâgar the Egyptian, Sârâh's handmaid, bare unto Abrâhâm.

13 And these are the names of the sons of Yishmâ'êl by their names, according to their generations: the first born of Yishmâ'êl, Nebâyôth, and Qêdâr, and Adbeêl, and Mibsâm,

14 And Mishmâ', and Dûmâh, and Massâ,

15 And 'Hadâd, and Têmâ, Yetûr, Nâphish, and Qêdmâh.

16 These are the sons of Yishmâ'êl, and these are their names, by their villages, and by their encampments[1]: twelve princes according to their nations.[2]

---

[1] This expression signifies that the tribes indicated by the author were partly settled and partly nomad.--L.

[2] The name of Kûsh which was formerly supposed to apply exclusively to the African Ethiopia has been shown to apply to Arabia, not Africa. When Moses is said in Numb. xii. 1 to have married a woman of Kûsh it is evident from Ex. ii. 15 21 that she was a native of Midiân or Madiân in Arabia, on the northern coast of the Red Sea. See also 2 Kings xix. 9 and 2 Chron. xiv. 9, 12 15, in all which passages Kûsh is mis-translated Ethiopia in the Revised Version. Wilford (*As. Res.* vol. viii. p. 206) says that in the old Sanscrit geography Cuśa was the second dwipa, the first

17 And these are the years of the life of Yishmâ'êl,

being Jambu, or India. It is so called either from a sage called Cuśa, or from the grass Cuśa or Poa which is supposed to grow there plentifully. It includes all the countries from the Indus to the Persian Gulf and the Caspian Sea. Cuśa is Kûsh. In the Puranas Cusha-dwipa, the land of Cush, includes Arabia and the other countries from the borders of India to the Mediterranean, while at a later period a second Cusha-dwipa, situated beyond the straits of Bab-el-Mandeb in Africa, was called Cusha-dwipa *without*, as having been colonised from Cusha-dwipa *within*.

In Genesis Arabia is originally peopled by the Kûshites, a leading nation of the Hamitic race. Niebuhr says the Kûshites can be traced all along the coast of Yemen from Hali (the Alikoi) to Zebid ('Sesippi portus'). Beni Khusi is the name of a small district in the province or department of Rema, as Beit el Khûsi is the name of a village in Haschid ir Bekil, while the name of the town of Kúsma, in the department of Kúsma or Kus'úmma resembles closely the name of Khûs. The Yoqtânids, descendants of Yoqtân (Arab. Kahtân), are said to have established themselves near the Kûshites, while numerous tribes descended from Hâgâr and Qetûrâh joined them subsequently. The list is as follows:—

1. Descendants of Kûsh: Sebâ, 'Havilâh, Sabtâh, Ra'emâh or Regma, Sabtekâ, and the sons of Ra'emâh, Shebâ and Dedân.
2. Descendants of Yoqtân: Almodâd, Shâleph, 'Haçarmâveth, Yâra'h, Hadôrâm, Ûzâl, Diqlâh, Obâl, Abimâêl, Shebâ, Ophir, 'Havilâh, and Yôbâb.
3. Descendants of Qetûrâh: Zimrân, Yoqshân, Medân, Midyân, Yishbâq, and Shûû'h. Yoqshân begat Shebâ and Dedân, and the sons of Dedân were the Asshûrim, the Letûshim, and the Lemmmîn. The sons of Midyân were 'Ephâh, 'Ępher, 'Hanôch, Abid'â, and Eldâ'â.
4. Descendants of Yishmâ'êl: Nebâyôth, Qêdâr, Adbeêl, Mibsâm, Mishmâ', Dûmâh, Massâ, 'Hadad, Têmâ, Yetûr, Nâphish, Qêdemâh.

In each of the first three divisions there is a tribe called Shebâ; there are two tribes called Dedân—one Kûshite, the other descended from Qetûrâh; and two tribes called 'Havilâh—one Kûshite, the other descended from Yoqtân.

Caussin de Perceval says that most Arab authors divide their nation into extinct races, Baïda, and existing races, Moutéakkhara, and the latter into Ariba, Moutéarriba and Moustariba. Of these the Ariba are Arabians of pure blood, and the Moustariba are descendants of Yishmâ'êl, who married a Kûshite princess. The Kûshite race is said to have consisted of twelve tribes, Ad, Thamoud, Tasm, Djachi, Amlik, Oumayim, Abil, Djourhoum, Wabar, Jasm, Antem, and Hashem. Of these the tribe of Ad may be recognised in the Oaditæ of Ptolemy; the tribe of Thamoud, in the Thamiditæ of the Arabian Gulf, whence as late as Justinian 'Saracen horsemen of the tribe of Thamud' are enrolled as auxiliaries in his armies; the tribe of Amlik (Amalek), the tribes of 'Esâr stretching 'from Havilah to Shûr' in Ptolemy's Saracena, called Amalekites by Theophanes.

an hundred and thirty and seven years; and he gave

Shebâ (Saba), now Mâreb, was once the metropolis of Yemen. Pliny calls it Mariaba, 'lords of all.' Abulfeda says it is still inhabited by the Kahtan (Yoqtan?) Arabs. A tribe called Beni-Sabya still exists in the neighbourhood. 'Havilâh is the territory between San'â and Mareb, called Khaonlân. Osiander has identified Sabta (Sabota) with an ancient town situated about four days' journey S.E. of Mâreb, and celebrated for the sixty temples which it contained. Ra'emâh or Regma (LXX) is mentioned in Ezek. xxvii. 20-22 with Shebâ and Dedân as trading with Tyre: 'the merchants of Shebâ and Ra'emâh, they were thy traffickers; they traded for thy wares, with chief of all spices, and with all precious stones, and gold' (verse 22). Niebuhr thinks it is the departments of Dsjêbi and Kúsma in the Yemen, which are collectively called Rêma by the Arabs. A more probable opinion, however, places it on the opposite side to Dedân on the promontory at the mouth of the Persian Gulf.

The dwelling of the children of Yoqtân is said in Gen. x. 30 to be 'from Meshâ, as thou goest towards Sephâr, the mountain of the east.' Meshâ appears to be the frontier towards the west, and there is still in existence a village named Musa in the neighbourhood of Mocha the name of which the Arabs consider to be of great antiquity. Sephâr is the Sephar of Ptolemy, and is situated to the east of Meshâ. Haçarmâveth is no doubt the great province of Hadramaut, on the east of Yemen. Hadramaut and Yemen together formed Arabia Felix. Hadoram (LXX, Οδορρα) is Darrhâ, in Omân. Ûzzâl is Sabe Regia, now called Sanaa, and was once the Yoqtanite capital of Yemen.

Ezek. xxvii. 19 should read 'Vedân also and Yavân traded from Ûzzâl with yarn for thy wares: bright iron, cassia, and calamus, were among thy merchandise.' Yavân is a city of Yemen, perhaps situated in the Deibân of Niebuhr. Diqlâh would appear to be represented by the Dulkhelaitæ, or tribe of Dhu l'Khalnah, between Ûzzâl and Mâreb. Bochart, however, who derives the name from an unused root signifying palm-tree, places it in the district of the Minæi, on the south coast of Arabia, which Pliny says was rich in palm-trees. Obal (Eval, LXX, and Ebal, 1 Chron. i. 22) which means 'stripped,' ' bare of leaves,' is identical with the Avalitæ (Ptolemy) or Abaliti (Pliny) on the African coast of the Straits of Bab-el-Mandeb. Abimael means 'father of Mael, identical with the Mali, who lived in the neighbourhood of Medina, and are mentioned by Theophrastus as producing frankincense, myrrh, cassia, and cinnamon. Shebâ, called Mâreb and Saba by the Arabs, has been already noticed.

Great differences of opinion have existed as to the site of Ophir. In the LXX, in 1 Kings ix. 28, it is spelt Σωφιρα, and in chap. x. 11 Σουφιρ. In 2 Chron. viii. 18 and ix. 10 there is the same difference of spelling. In Job ii. 24 and xxviii. 16 it is called Σωφιρ. In Ps. xlv. 9 it is omitted altogether, and in Is. xiii. 12 it is spelt Συφιρ. From these various spellings it has been thought that Σουπαρα (now Goa) in India was meant. It has also been identified with Pliny's ' littus Hammæum, ubi auri metalla,' or the Gold Coast,

up the ghost and died; and was gathered unto his people.

on the east coast of Arabia, where there is still a village called El Ophir. Ophir, however, is placed between Shebâ and 'Havilâh. The name seems to be formed on a Sabæan adjective derived from a word signifying dust, or small sand, and M. Halévy considers it to be the province formerly known as Maphartis or Mapharitis, which extended as far as Ocelis or Okela, the principal port of Bab-el-Mandeb. There is a popular adage in the Wady Saba, 'Turab-el-Djaouf dhahab'—the dust of the Sabæan district (the Djaouf) is gold. The Hebrew word Kethem, which is used in Job xxviii. 16, Is. xiii. 12 and Dan. x. 5 to denote the gold of Ophir, exists in the Sabæan language only. The wealth of Arabia is alluded to in Judges viii. 24, 26. Diodorus Siculus (lib. iii. c. 3) says of them: 'Having never been conquered, by reason of the largeness of their country, they flow in streams of gold and silver; and likewise their beds, chairs, and stools have their feet of silver, and all their household stuff is so sumptuous and magnificent that it is incredible. The porticoes of their houses and temples, in some cases, are overlaid with gold. The like wonderful cost they are at throughout their whole buildings, adorning them, in some parts, with silver and gold, and in others with ivory, precious stones, and other things of great value, for they have enjoyed a constant and uninterrupted peace for many ages and generations.'

Agatharcides says: 'The Sabæans surpass in wealth and magnificence not only the neighbouring barbarians, but all other nations whatsoever. As their distant situation protects them from all foreign plunders, immense stores of precious metals have been accumulated among them, especially in the capital. Curiously wrought gold and silver drinking vessels in great variety; couches and tripods with silver feet; an incredible profusion of costly furniture in general; porticoes, with large columns partly gilt, and capitals ornamented with wrought silver figures; roofs and doors ornamented with gold fretwork set with precious stones, besides an extraordinary magnificence reigning in the decorations of their houses, where they use silver, gold, ivory, and the most precious stones, and all other things that men deem most valuable. These people have enjoyed their good fortune from the earliest times undisturbed.'

Eupolemus, quoted by Eusebius (*Præp. Ev.* lib. ix. c. 30), says that David, having been advised by an angel to leave the building of the temple to his son, had vessels built at Elan in Arabia in order to send them to the island of Ophir in the Erythræan Sea to collect precious metals there. This island, he says, contained gold mines, and the gold was afterwards taken to Judæa. Pliny speaks of the once famous cities of the people of Oman, which in his time were wildernesses. He says of the Arabians, 'Take them all in all, they are the richest nation in the world.'

Yobâb is identical with Ptolemy's Jobaritæ, whose name survives in the Benê Yubar in the country of the Beni Yoqtân, towards Mâreb, and the

18 And they dwelt from 'Havîlâh unto Shûr, that is

Beni Yobub or Yobâb are near Mount Sephar, between Senaa and Zebid. Niebuhr thinks that Beni Dsjobûb, a small district in the southern portion of the department of Kúsma may have been named after Yobâb.
Zimrân (LXX, Ζεμβραμ, Ζομβραμ), the eldest son of Qetûrâh, is to be traced in the Banizomaneis (that is the Beni Zoman) of Diodorus Siculus and Agatharcides. Burckhardt recognised the Beni Zoman in the Beni Omran or 'Amrân (Robinson). They are a very independent and strong tribe, much given to plunder. Yoqshân signifies ' fowler' (LXX, Ιεζαν and Ιεξαν). No trace of this tribe can be discovered. Perhaps from their occupation they were a wandering tribe. Medân (LXX, Μαδαλ, Μαδιαμ) is identified with the Maadeni or the inhabitants of Maadan al Nokra, the site of Hedjer, the ancient capital of the Thamiditæ or tribe of Thamoud, and the Madiana of Ptolemy. Hedjer is also called Medayen by the Arabs. Midiân (LXX, Μαδιαμ, Μαδαμ) is referred to in Isa. lx. 6, 'The multitude of camels shall cover thee, the young camels of Midiân and 'Ephâh; they all shall come from Sheba; they shall bring gold and frankincense, and shall proclaim the praises of Yahveh.'
Yishbâq (LXX, Ιεσβωκ, Σοβακ) is identical with Shobak, the Sebomita or Esbuta of Ptolemy, on the southern border of the Amalekites. Shûa'h (LXX, Σωιε, Σωε) is mentioned again in Job ii. 11, where the LXX speak of Baldad king of the Sanchæans. It is probably the Σακκαια of Ptolemy (v. 15), to the east of Batanæa. Dedân bordered upon Edôm. The travelling companies of the Dedânim are mentioned in Isa. xxi. 13. The Asshûrim appear to be the Asyr or El-Asyr Arabs, who inhabit the district called Hasoros by Strabo, the people of which are called Elesoai by Ptolemy. Ibn-el-Shayr, of the Asyr tribe, is mentioned by Burckhardt. The Letûshim may be the Tedium of Ptolemy, bordering on Chaldæa. The Leummim are the sons of Luma. Luma is a city mentioned by Ptolemy on the eastern side of Arabia Deserta, not far from the supposed seat of the Letûshim. Niebuhr mentions another Luma in Yemen, in the department of Kúsma, between Sûk es Sept and Abid. These three sons of Dedân are omitted in 1 Chron. i.
'Ephâh (LXX, Γεφαρ) appears to be to the south of Midiân, where there is a watering station on the coast called Makar Efa, or the wells of 'Ephâh, 'Epher (LXX, Αφειρ, Οφερ) is probably Shor Afar, a town on the coast of Midiân, some twenty miles north of the town of Modiana. Pliny mentions the Pharanitæ at the head of the Elanitic Gulf. This people extended to the southern extremity of the peninsula of Sinai, where ' Pharan civitas ' and ' Pharan promontorium ' denote their presence, and probably took their name from the wilderness of Parân.
'Hanôch (LXX, Ενωχ), Hanak, or Hank-krue, a town at the northern foot of Djebel Sheick, the Hippos Mons of Ptolemy. To the east of this town is another large town called Henekeh or Hanake, on the caravan route from Medina to Bosra. Abid'â, ' father of knowledge,' survives in Ptolemy's Abida, under the range of the Anti-Libanus. Burckhardt discovered a

tribe of Abyda Arabs in the country south of the Asyr mountains in Yemen. Eldâ'à, 'whom God called,' supposed to be the Audia or Ludia of Ptolemy, now Eldii or Eldji, forming a connecting link of the northern settlements of Midian between Adida and Modiana.

Nebâyóth, 'high places,' was the eldest son of Yishmá'êl. Josephus asserts the identity of Nebâyóth and the well-known nation of the Nabatæans. This, however, has been doubted on account of the difference in spelling, the name Nabatæan being spelled with ṭ, not t (נבטו) on the inscriptions, Arabic Nabaṭ, Nabíṭ, &c). Nebâyóth appears as a pastoral people in Isa. lx. 7. The Nabatæans are described by Diodorus as being in 312 B.C., when Antigonus unsuccessfully attacked them in Petra, a powerful tribe of some 10,000 warriors, nomads, eschewing agriculture, fixed houses, and the use of wine (all which were forbidden on pain of death), and living on flesh and milk. They were, however, enormously wealthy, for Diodorus mentions 500 talents of silver and enormous stores of aromatics as being among the spoils of Petra when it was surprised by the Syrians during the absence of its garrison. Strabo also speaks of their wealth in gold and silver, purple robes, pictures, statues, &c. Qêdâr, 'black skin,' 'a black-skinned man' (a name applied by the Rabbis to all the Arabians), is identical with the Arab tribe called Cedrei, Cedareni, or Gedranitæ by Pliny, and which, he says, border, as well as the Arab tribes of the Cauchlei, on the territory of the Nabatæi (*N. H.* lib. v. c. 2). They thus belong to the northern portion of the Hedjaz.

Adbeél (LXX, Ναβδεηλ), written Abdeel in Josephus, may, it is thought, be recognised in Niebuhr's Beni Abdillah, a somewhat extensive tract of country in the district of Bellád el Kobail in Yemen. Mibsâm (LXX, Μασσαμ), 'sweet odour,' is thought by Calmet to be Mepsa, a town placed by Ptolemy on the boundary line between Arabia Petræa and Palestine. Mishmá' (LXX, Μασμα), called Masmaos by Josephus, is probably the Masæmanes of Ptolemy, who dwelt near Mount Zames (Mount Mesha). Dûmáh (LXX, Δουμα, Ιδουμα) is no doubt the Δουμαιθα of Ptolemy. It is called in Arabic 'stony Dumah.' 'Dumætha (Daumat al Gendal) is noticed by Ptolemy and Abulfeda [and by Pliny under the name of Domatha]; and may be found in D'Anville's maps, in the mid-desert between Chaibar and Tadmor' (Gibbon, *Decline and Fall*, vol. ix. p. 248). Massà, the Masani of Ptolemy, a people bordering on Chaldæa, frequently mentioned in the inscriptions of Tiglath-Pileser II. and Asurbanipal in the form Maṣ' as the name of a North-Arabian tribe. 'Hadad (LXX, Χοδδαν, Χουδαν), 'sharpness,' may be traced in the tribe of Hadad, the chief town of which is Hadéddo, in the department of Dsjébi in Yemen. Têmâ (LXX, Θαιμαν) is the modern Beni Temin, on the western border of Nejed. Pliny says the Thimanæi were adjacent to the Nabathæans. It is mentioned in Jer. xxv. 23, 'Dedân, and Têmâ, and Búz' (LXX, Ρως), and also in Job vi. 19,

'The caravans of Têmâ looked,
The companies of Shebâ waited for them,'

before Miçraim, as thou goest towards Asshûr: he abode in the presence of all his brethren.[1]

19 And these are the generations of Yiçe'hâq, Abrâhâm's son: Abrâhâm begat Yiçe'hâq:

20 And Yiçe'hâq was forty years old when he took Ribqâh the daughter of Bethûêl the Aramy of Paddan-Arâm, the sister of Lâbân the Aramy, to be his wife.

21 And Yiçe'hâq intreated Yahveh for his wife because she was barren: and Yahveh was intreated of him, and Ribqâh conceived.

22 And the children struggled together within her; and she said, If it be so, wherefore do I live? And she went to inquire of Yahveh.

23 And Yahveh said unto her,

Two nations are in thy womb,

or, as the LXX has it, 'Behold the ways of the Thaemanites, ye that mark the paths of the Sabœans.' Têmâ is the Túnai of Tiglath-Pileser II.

Yetûr is mentioned again in 1 Chron. v. 19. The name of Yetûr reappears in the Iturœans, who dwelt to the south of Damascus, between that city and the half tribe of Mênassheh. This was afterwards the province of Iturœa, and is now the district of Jeidûr. Náphish (LXX, Ναφες): this tribe is supposed to have existed on the borders of Gilead. Qêdemâh (LXX, Κεδμα), 'eastward,' is El Kadema, a celebrated commercial town in the upper part of the Persian Gulf, the 'Itauros portus' of Ptolemy, and the Ammea of Pliny.

There were numerous tribes in Northern Arabia from the frontiers of Egypt to the banks of the Euphrates and the marshes of Babylonia (Gen. xxv. 18, Plin. vi. 118). The Assyrian inscriptions speak of Eastern Arabians on the Susian coast of the Persian Gulf (*Inscriptions of Khorsabad*, 69). Egyptian documents speak of the brigand populations of the desert long before the time of Abrâhâm. They are called Shasou or Herouschu. M. Halévy says that a fixed period is known, about 115 B.C. (it cannot be earlier), at which the Sabœan nation was still in all its power. Augustus, however, heard of their wealth, and about 24 B.C. Ælius Gallus set out in command of a Roman army of 10,000 men, assisted by Obodas king of Petra, with a thousand Nabathæans and five hundred Jews, and eventually took Mariaba and Mar Saba.

[1] This verse bears on the face of it the impress of the historical Assyrian period, and has evidently been added by the latest editor. It is not even in its proper place, for it refers to the sons of Yishmâ'êl.—L.

And two peoples shall be separated even from thy bowels :
And the one people shall be stronger than the other people ;
And the elder shall serve the younger.

24 And when her days to be delivered were fulfilled, behold, there were twins in her womb.

25 And the first came forth ruddy, all over like an hairy garment, and they called his name 'Ēsâv.

26 And after that came forth his brother, and his hand had hold on 'Ēsâv's heel ('âqeb) ; and his name was called Ya'aqôb : and Yiçe'hâq was threescore years old when she bare them.

27 And the boys grew : and 'Ēsâv was a cunning hunter, a man of the field ; and Ya'aqôb was a peaceable man, living in tents.

28 Now Yiçe'hâq loved 'Ēsâv, because he did eat of his venison ; and Ribqâh loved Ya'aqôb.

29 And Ya'aqôb sod pottage : and 'Ēsâv came in from the field, and he was faint :

30 And 'Ēsâv said to Ya'aqôb, Feed me, I pray thee, with that same red (âdôm) *pottage* ; for I am faint : therefore was his name called Edôm.

31 And Ya'aqôb said, Sell me this day thy birthright.

32 And 'Ēsâv; said, Behold, I am at the point to die, and what good shall my birthright do to me ?

33 And Ya'aqôb said, Swear to me this day ; and he sware unto him : and he sold his birthright unto Ya'aqôb.

34 And Ya'aqôb gave 'Ēsâv bread and pottage of lentils ; and he did eat, and drink, and rose up, and went his way : so 'Ēsâv despised his birthright.

CHAPTER XXVI.

1 And there was a famine in the land, beside the first famine that was in the days of Abrâhâm. And Yiçe'hâq went unto Abîmelech king of the Pelishtîm unto Gerâr.

2 And Yahveh appeared unto him, and said, Go not down into Miçraîm; dwell in the land which I shall tell thee of:

3 Sojourn in this land, and I will be with thee, and will bless thee, for unto thee, and unto thy seed, I will give all these lands, and I will establish the oath which I sware unto Abrâhâm thy father;

4 And I will multiply thy seed as the stars of heaven, and will give unto thy seed all these lands; and in thy seed shall all the nations of the earth be blessed;

5 Because that Abrâhâm obeyed my voice, and kept my charge, my commandments, my statutes, and my laws.

6 And Yiçe'hâq dwelt in Gerâr:

7 And the men of the place asked him of his wife; and he said, She is my sister; for he feared to say, My wife; lest, said he, the men of the place should kill me for Ribqâh; because she was fair to look upon.[1]

8 And it came to pass, when he had been there a long time, that Abîmelech king of the Pelishtîm looked out at a window, and saw, and behold Yiçe'hâq was sporting with Ribqâh his wife.

9 And Abîmelech called Yiçe'hâq, and said, Behold, of a surety she is thy wife: and how saidst thou, She is my sister? And Yiçe'hâq said unto him, Because I said, Lest I die for her.

10 And Abîmelech said, What is this that thou hast done unto us? one of the people might lightly have lien with thy wife, and thou shouldest have brought guiltiness upon us.

11 And Abîmelech charged all the people, saying, He that toucheth this man or his wife shall surely be put to death.

12 And Yiçe'hâq sowed in that land, and found in the same year an hundredfold, and Yahveh blessed him.

13 And the man waxed great, and grew more and more until he became very great:

14 And he had possessions of flocks, and possessions of herds, and a great household; and the Pelishtîm envied him.

---

[1] The whole of this passage, verses 7–11, is the Jehovistic version of the story respecting Abrâhâm in chap. xx, taking place at the same spot, but taken from a different document.—L.

15 Now all the wells which his father's servants had digged in the days of Abrâhâm his father, the Pelishtîm had stopped them, and filled them with earth.

16 And Abîmelech said unto Yiçe'hâq, Go from us, for thou art much mightier than we.

17 And Yiçe'hâq departed thence, and encamped in the valley of Gerâr, and dwelt there.

18 *And Yiçe'hâq digged again the wells of water, which they had digged in the days of Abrâhâm his father; for the Pelishtîm had stopped them after the death of Abrâhâm: and he called their names after the names by which his father had called them.*[1]

19 And Yiçe'hâq digged in the valley, and found there a well of springing water.

20 And the herdmen of Gerâr strove with Yiçe'hâq's herdmen, saying, The water is ours: and he called the name of the well 'Eseq (Contention); because they contended with him.

21 And they digged another well, and they strove for that also: and he called the name of it Sitnâh (Enmity).

22 And he removed from thence, and digged another well; and for that they strove not: and he called the name of it Re'hobôth (Broad places); and he said, For now Yahveh hath made room for us, and we shall be fruitful in the land.

23 And he went up from thence to Beêr-Shâb'a.

24 And *Yahveh* appeared unto him *the same* night, and said, I am the God of Abrâhâm thy father: fear not, for I am with thee, and will bless thee, and multiply thy seed for my servant Abrâhâm's sake.[2]

25 And he builded an altar there, and called upon the name

[1] There is no mention of these wells or of their names in the preceding chapter, so the latest editor must have taken this verse from a different document.—L.

[2] Chap. xxxv. 12 and Exod. vi. 3 distinctly show that the work of the Elohist contained an appearance of God to Yiçe'hâq. It seems to us that this must be the same, for it is unconnected with verses 23-25, the latter of which continues the Jehovistic narrative in a natural manner, while verse 24 is in no way connected with it, and seems to have been inserted at the last moment in the latest revision.—L.

of Yahveh, and pitched his tent there, and there Yiçe'hâq's slaves digged a well.

26 Then Abîmelech went to him from Gerâr, and A'huzzath his friend, and Phichôl the captain of his host.[1]

27 And Yiçe'hâq said unto them, Wherefore are ye come unto me, seeing ye hate me, and have sent me away from you?

28 And they said, We saw plainly that Yahveh was with thee; and we said, Let there now be an oath betwixt us, even betwixt us and thee, and let us make a covenant with thee;

29 That thou wilt do us no hurt, as we have not touched thee, and as we have done unto thee nothing but good, and have sent thee away in peace: thou art now the blessed of Yahveh.

30 And he made them a feast, and they did eat and drink.

31 And they rose up betimes in the morning, and sware one to another: and Yiçe'hâq sent them away, and they departed from him in peace.

32 And it came to pass the same day, that Yiçe'hâq's slaves came, and told him concerning the well which they had digged, and said unto him, We have found water.

33 And he called it Shib'âh (oath); therefore the name of the city is Beêr-Shâb'a unto this day.

34 And when 'Êsâv was forty years old he took to wife Yehûdith the daughter of Beêry, the 'Hitty, and Bâsemath the daughter of Elôn the 'Hitty[2]:

35 And they were a grief of mind unto Yiçe'hâq and to Ribqâh.

---

[1] Verses 26-33 give the parallel narrative to the one in chap. xxi. 22-34, but taken from another source, and made to belong to the period of Abrâhâm.—L.

[2] In chap. xxxvi. 3, 4, 13, Bâsemath is called the daughter of Yishmâ'êl, sister of Nebâyôth.

CHAPTER XXVII.

1 And it came to pass, that when Yiçe'hâq was old, and his eyes were dim, so that he could not see, he called 'Êsâv his elder son, and said unto him, My son : and he said unto him, Here am I.

2 And he said, Behold now, I am old, I know not the day of my death :

3 Now therefore take, I pray thee, thy weapons, thy quiver and thy bow, and go out to the field, and take me venison ;

4 And make me savoury meat such as I love, and bring it to me, that I may eat ; that my soul may bless thee before I die.

5 And Ribqâh heard when Yiçe'hâq spake to 'Êsâv his son. And 'Êsâv went to the field to hunt for venison and to bring it.

6 And Ribqâh spake unto Ya'aqôb her son, saying, Behold, I heard thy father speak unto 'Êsâv thy brother, saying,

7 Bring me venison, and make me savoury meat, that I may eat, and bless thee before Yahveh before my death.

8 Now therefore, my son, obey my voice according to that which I command thee.

9 Go now to the flock, and fetch me from thence two good kids of the goats ; and I will make them savoury meat for thy father, such as he loveth :

10 And thou shalt bring it to thy father, that he may eat, so that he may bless thee before his death.

11 And Ya'aqôb said to Ribqâh his mother, Behold, 'Êsâv my brother is a hairy man, and I am a smooth man.

12 My father peradventure will feel me, and I shall seem to him as a deceiver ; and I shall bring a curse upon me, and not a blessing.

13 And his mother said unto him, Upon me be thy curse, my son : only obey my voice, and go fetch me them.

14 And he went, and fetched, and brought them to his mother : and his mother made savoury meat, such as his father loved.

15 And Ribqâh took the goodly raiment of 'Êsâv her elder

son, which were with her in the house, and put them upon Ya'aqôb her younger son :

16 And she put the skins of the kids of the goats upon his hands, and upon the smooth of his neck :

17 And she gave the savoury meat and the bread, which she had prepared, into the hand of her son Ya'aqôb.

18 And he came unto his father, and said, My father; and he said, Here am I; who art thou, my son ?

19 And Ya'aqôb said unto his father, I am 'Ēsâv thy first-born; I have done according as thou badest me : arise, I pray thee, sit and eat of my venison, that thy soul may bless me.

20 And Yiçe'hâq said unto his son, How is it that thou hast found it so quickly, my son ? And he said, Because Yahveh thy God sent me good speed.

21 And Yiçe'hâq said unto Ya'aqôb, Come near, I pray thee, that I may feel thee, my son, whether thou be my very son 'Ēsâv, or not.

22 And Ya'aqôb went near unto Yiçe'hâq his father ; and he felt him, and said, The voice is Ya'aqôb's voice, but the hands are the hands of 'Ēsâv.

23 And he discovered him not, because his hands were hairy, as his brother 'Ēsâv's hands : so he blessed him.

24 And he said, Art thou my very son, 'Ēsâv ? And he said, I am.

25 And he said, Bring it near to me, and I will eat of my son's venison, that my soul may bless thee. And he brought it near to him, and he did eat : and he brought him wine, and he drank.

26 And his father Yiçe'hâq said unto him, Come near now, and kiss me, my son.

27 And he came near, and kissed him : and he smelled the smell of his raiment, and blessed him, and said,

    See, the smell of my son
    Is as the smell of a field which Yahveh hath blessed :

28 And God give thee of the dew of heaven
    And of the fatness of the earth,
    And plenty of corn and wine :

29 Let peoples serve thee,
And nations bow down to thee;
Be lord over thy brethren,
And let thy mother's sons bow down to thee;
Cursed be every one that curseth thee,
And blessed be every one that blesseth thee.

30 And it came to pass, as soon as Yiçe'hâq had made an end of blessing Ya'aqôb, and Ya'aqôb was yet scarce gone out from the presence of Yiçe'hâq his father, that 'Êsâv his brother came in from his hunting.

31 And he also made savoury meat, and brought it unto his father; and he said unto his father, Let my father arise, and eat of his son's venison, that thy soul may bless me.

32 And Yiçe'hâq his father said unto him, Who art thou? And he said, I am thy son, thy firstborn, 'Êsâv.

33 And Yiçe'hâq trembled very exceedingly, and said, Who then is he that hath taken venison, and brought it me, and I have eaten of all before thou camest, and have blessed him? yea, and he shall be blessed.

34 When 'Êsâv heard the words of his father, he cried with an exceeding great and bitter cry, and said unto his father, Bless me, even me also, O my father.

35 And he said, Thy brother came with guile, and hath taken away thy blessing.

36 And he said, Is he not rightly named Ya'aqôb, for he hath supplanted me (Ya'eqbêny) these two times: he took away my birthright; and, behold, now he hath taken away my blessing. And he said, Hast thou not reserved a blessing for me?

37 And Yiçe'hâq answered and said unto 'Êsâv, Behold, I have made him thy lord, and all his brethren have I given to him for servants; and with corn and wine have I sustained him: and what then shall I do for thee, my son?

38 And 'Êsâv said unto his father, Hast thou but one blessing, my father? bless me, even me also, O my father. And 'Êsâv lift up his voice, and wept.

39 And Yiçe'hâq his father answered and said unto him,

Behold, away from the fatness of the earth shall be thy
blessing,
And away from the dew of heaven from above;
40 And by thy sword shalt thou live,
And thou shalt serve thy brother;
And it shall come to pass, when thou shalt break loose,
That thou shalt shake his yoke from off thy neck.
41 And 'Êsâv hated Ya'aqôb because of the blessing wherewith his father blessed him : and 'Êsâv said in his heart, The days of mourning for my father are at hand ; then will I slay my brother Ya'aqôb.
42 And the words of 'Êsâv her elder son were told to Ribqâh : and she sent and called Ya'aqôb her younger son, and said unto him, Behold, thy brother 'Êsâv, as touching thee, doth comfort himself, purposing to kill thee.
43 Now therefore, my son, obey my voice ; and arise, flee thou to Lâbân my brother to Hârân ;
44 And tarry with him a few days, until thy brother's fury turn away ;
45 Until thy brother's anger turn away from thee, and he forget that which thou has done to him : then I will send, and fetch thee from thence : why should I be bereaved of you both in one day ?
46 And Ribqâh said to Yiçe'hâq, I am weary of my life because of the daughters of 'Hêth : if Ya'aqôb take a wife of the daughters of 'Hêth, such as these, of the daughters of the land, what good shall my life do me ?

CHAPTER XXVIII.

1 And Yiçe'hâq called Ya'aqôb, and blessed him, and charged him, and said unto him, Thou shalt not take a wife of the daughters of Kenâ'an.

2 Arise, go to Paddan-Arâm, to the house of Bethûêl thy mother's father: and take thee a wife from thence of the daughters of Lâbân thy mother's brother.

3 And El-Shadday (God Almighty) bless thee, and make thee fruitful, and multiply thee, that thou mayest be a company of peoples ;

4 And give thee the blessing of Abrâhâm, to thee, and to thy seed with thee; that thou mayest inherit the land of thy sojournings, which Elôhîm gave unto Abrâhâm.

5 And Yiçe'hâq sent away Ya'aqôb: and he went to Paddan-Arâm unto Lâbân, son of Bethûêl the Aramy, the brother of Ribqâh, Ya'aqôb's and 'Êsâv's mother.

6 Now 'Êsâv saw that Yiçe'hâq had blessed Ya'aqôb and sent him away to Paddan-Arâm, to take him a wife from thence ; and that, as he blessed him, he gave him a charge, saying, Thou shalt not take a wife of the daughters of Kenâ'an ;

7 And that Ya'aqôb obeyed his father and his mother, and was gone to Paddan-Arâm :

8 And 'Êsâv saw that the daughters of Kenâ'an pleased not Yiçe'hâq his father ;

9 And 'Êsâv went unto Yishmâ'êl, and took unto the wives which he had Ma'halath the daughter of

Yishmá'él, Abrâhâm's son, the sister of Nebâyôth, to be his wife.

10 And Ya'aqôb went out from Beêr-Shâb'a, and went toward Hârân.

11 And he lighted upon a certain place, and tarried there all night, because the sun was set; and he took one of the stones of the place, and put it under his head, and lay down in that place to sleep.

12 And he dreamed, and behold a ladder set up on the earth, and the top of it reached to heaven : and behold the angels of God ascending and descending upon it.

13 And, behold, Yahveh stood above it, and said, I am Yahveh, the God of Abrâhâm thy father, and the God of Yiçe'-hâq : the land whereon thou liest, to thee will I give it, and to thy seed ;

14 And thy seed shall be as the dust of the earth, and thou shall spread abroad to the west, and to the east, and to the north, and to the south ; and in thee and in thy seed shall all the families of the earth be blessed.

15 And, behold, I am with thee, and will keep thee whithersoever thou goest, and will bring thee again into this land; for I will not leave thee, until I have done unto thee that which I have spoken to thee of.

16 And Ya'aqôb wakened out of his sleep, and he said, Surely Yahveh is in this place ; and I knew it not.

17 And he was afraid, and said, How dreadful is this place! this is none other but the house of God, and this is the gate of heaven.

18 And Ya'aqôb rose up early in the morning, and took the stone that he had put under his head, and set it up for a pillar, and poured oil upon the top of it.[1]

19 And he called the name of that place Bêth-Êl (the house of God) : but the name of the city was Lûz at the first.

[1] Mazzêvâh, a pillar or menhir. It was one of those anointed or living stones which Philo calls βαιτυλια, and which according to him were made by Uranus. In chap. xxxv. 15, the place was not named Bêth-Êl till long after, when Jacob was old. A numen dwelt in these anointed stones, which Philo speaks of as λιθοι εμψυχοι.

20 And Ya'aqôb vowed a vow, saying, If Yahveh Elôhîm will be with me, and will keep me in this way that I go, and will give me bread to eat, and raiment to put on,

21 So that I come again to my father's house in peace, then shall Yahveh be my God.

22 And this stone, which I have set up for a column, shall be God's house : and of all that thou shalt give me, I will surely give the tenth unto thee.

CHAPTER XXIX.

1 Then Ya'aqôb went on his journey,[1] and came to the land of the Benê-Qedem.[2]

2 And he looked, and behold a well in the field, and lo, three flocks of sheep lying there by it: for out of that well they watered the flocks : and the stone upon the well's mouth was great.

3 And thither were all the flocks gathered: and they rolled the stone from the well's mouth, and watered the sheep, and put the stone again from the well's mouth in its place.

4 And Ya'aqôb said unto them, My brethren, whence be ye ? And they said, Of Hârân are we.

5 And he said unto them, Know ye Lâbân the son of Na'hôr ? and they said, We know him.

6 And he said unto them, Is it well with him ? And they said, It is well: and, behold, Râ'hêl his daughter cometh with the sheep.

7 And he said, Lo, it is yet high day, neither is it time that the cattle should be gathered together: water ye the sheep, and go and feed them.

8 And they said, We cannot, until all the flocks be gathered together, and they roll the stone from the well's mouth ; then we water the sheep.

---

[1] Literally, 'lifted up his feet.'—L.   [2] The children of the East.—L.

9 While he yet spake with them, Râ'hêl came with her father's sheep: for she kept them.

10 And it came to pass, when Ya'aqôb saw Râ'hêl the daughter of Lâbân his mother's brother, and the sheep of Lâbân his mother's brother, that Ya'aqôb went near, and rolled the stone from the well's mouth, and watered the flock of Lâbân his mother's brother.

11 And Ya'aqôb kissed Râ'hêl, and lifted up his voice, and wept.

12 And Ya'aqôb told Râ'hêl that he was her father's brother, and that he was Ribqâh's son: and she ran and told her father.

13 And it came to pass, when Lâbân heard the tidings of Ya'aqôb his sister's son, that he ran to meet him, and embraced him, and kissed him, and brought him to his house. And he told Lâbân all these things.

14 And Lâbân said unto him, Surely thou art my bone and my flesh. And he abode with him the space of a month.

15 And Lâbân said unto Ya'aqôb, Because thou art my brother, shouldest thou therefore serve me for nought? tell me, what shall thy wages be?

16 And Lâbân had two daughters: the name of the elder was Lêâh, and the name of the younger was Râ'hêl.

17 And Lêâh's eyes were tender; but Râ'hêl was beautiful and well favoured.

18 And Ya'aqôb loved Râ'hêl; and he said, I will serve thee seven years for Râ'hêl thy younger daughter.

19 And Lâbân said, It is better that I give her to thee, than that I should give her to another man: abide with me.

20 And Ya'aqôb served seven years for Râ'hêl; and they seemed unto him but a few days for the love he had to her.

21 And Ya'aqôb said unto Lâbân, Give me my wife, for my days are fulfilled, that I may go in unto her.

22 And Lâbân gathered together all the men of the place, and made a feast.[1]

[1] Certain peculiarities of expression make one suspect that this verse is taken from the book of the Elohist.—L.

23 And it came to pass in the evening, that he took Lêâh his daughter, and brought her to him; and he went in unto her.

24 And Lâbân gave Zilpâh his handmaid unto his daughter Lêâh for an handmaid.

25 And it came to pass in the morning that, behold, it was Lêâh; and he said to Lâbân, What is this that thou hast done unto me? did not I serve with thee for Râ'hêl? Wherefore then has thou beguiled me?

26 And Lâbân said, It is not so done in our place, to give the younger before the firstborn.

27 Fulfil the week of this one, and we will give thee the other also for the service which thou shalt serve with me yet seven other years.

28 And Ya'aqôb did so, and fulfilled her week: and he gave him Râ'hêl his daughter to wife.

29 And Lâbân gave to Râ'hêl his daughter Bil'hâh his handmaid to be her handmaid.

30 And he went in also unto Râ'hêl, and he loved also Râ'hêl more than Lêâh, and served with him yet seven other years.

31 And Yahveh saw that Lêâh was hated, and he opened her womb: but Râ'hêl was barren.

32 And Lêâh conceived, and bare a son, and she called his name Reûbên: for she said, Because Yahveh hath looked upon my affliction (*rââh be'onyí*); for now my husband will love me.

33 And she conceived again, and bare a son; and said, Because Yahveh hath heard (*shâma'a*) that I am hated, he hath therefore given me this son also: and she called his name Shime'òn.

34 And she conceived again, and bare a son; and said, Now this time will my husband be joined (*yillâveh*) unto me, because I have borne him three sons: therefore was his name called Lêvy.

35 And she conceived again, and bare a son; and she said, This time will I praise Yahveh (*ôdeh eth-Yahveh*): therefore she called his name Yehûdâh; and she left bearing.

CHAPTER XXX.

1 And when Râ'hêl saw that she bare Ya'aqôb no children, Râ'hêl envied her sister; and she said unto Ya'aqôb, Give me children, or else I die.

2 *And Ya'aqôb's anger was kindled against Râ'hêl; and he said, Am I in Elôhîm's stead, who hath withheld from thee the fruit of the womb?*

3 And she said, Behold my maid Bil'hâh, go in unto her; that she may bear upon my knees, and I also may obtain children by her.

4 And she gave him Bil'hâh her handmaid to wife: and Ya'aqôb went in unto her.

5 And Bil'hâh conceived, and bare Ya'aqôb a son.

6 And Râ'hêl said, Elôhîm hath judged me (*dinanny*), and hath also heard my voice, and hath given me a son: therefore called she his name Dân.

7 And Bil'hâh Râ'hêl's handmaid conceived again, and bare Ya'aqôb a second son.

8 And Râ'hêl said, With mighty wrestlings of Elôhîm have I wrestled (*naphtâly*) with my sister, and have prevailed: and and she called his name Naphtâly.

9 When Lêâh saw that she had left bearing, she took Zilpâh, her handmaid, and gave her to Ya'aqôb to wife.

10 And Zilpâh Lêâh's handmaid bare Ya'aqôb a son.

11 And Lêâh said, Fortunate (*bâgâd*)! and she called his name Gâd.

12 And Zilpâh Lêâh's handmaid bare Ya'aqôb a second son.

13 And Lêâh said, Happy am I (*beâshry*)! for the daughters will call me happy: and she called his name Âshêr.

14 And Reûbên went in the days of wheat harvest, and found mandrakes in the field, and brought them unto his mother Lêâh. Then Râ'hêl said to Lêâh, Give me, I pray thee, of thy son's mandrakes.

15 And she said unto her, Is it a small matter that thou hast

taken away my husband? and wouldest thou take away my son's mandrakes also? And Râ'hêl said, Therefore he shall lie with thee to-night for thy son's mandrakes.

16 And Ya'aqôb came from the field in the evening, and Lêâh went out to meet him, and said, Thou must come in unto me; for I have surely hired thee with my son's mandrakes. And he lay with her that night.

17 And Elôhîm hearkened unto Lêâh, and she conceived, and bare Ya'aqôb a fifth son.

18 And Lêâh said, Elôhîm hath endowed me with a good dowry (*shechâry*), because I gave my handmaid to my husband: and she called his name Yissâchâr.

19 And Lêâh conceived again, and bare a sixth son to Ya'aqôb.

20 And Lêâh said, Elôhîm hath endowed me with a good dowry; now will my husband live with me (*yizbelêny*), because I have borne him six sons: and she called his name Zebulûn.

21 *And afterwards she bare a daughter, and called her name Dînâh.*

22 And Elôhîm remembered Râ'hêl, and Elôhîm hearkened to her, and opened her womb.

23 And she conceived, and bare a son: and said, Elôhîm hath taken away my reproach:

24 And she called his name Yôsêph, saying, Yahveh add to me (*yôsêph*) another son.

25 And it came to pass, when Râ'hêl had borne Yôsêph, that Ya'aqôb said unto Lâbân, Send me away, that I may go unto mine own place, and to my country.

26 Give me my wives and my children for whom I have served thee, and let me go: for thou knowest my service wherewith I have served thee.

27 And Lâbân said unto him, If now I have found favour in thine eyes, tarry: for I have divined that Yahveh hath blessed me for thy sake.

28 And he said, Appoint me thy wages, and I will give it.

29 And he said unto him, Thou knowest how I have served thee, and how thy cattle hath fared with me.

30 For it was little which thou hadst before I came, and it hath increased unto a multitude; and Yahveh hath blessed thee whithersoever I turned: and now when shall I provide for mine own house also?

31 And he said, What shall I give thee? And Ya'aqôb said, Thou shalt not give me aught: if thou wilt do this thing for me, I will again feed thy flock and keep it.

32 I will pass through all thy flock to-day, removing from thence every speckled and spotted one, and every black one among the sheep, and the spotted and speckled among the goats: and of such shall be my hire.

33 So shall my righteousness answer for me hereafter, when thou shalt come concerning my hire that is before thee: every one that is not speckled and spotted among the goats, and black among the sheep, that, if found with me, shall be counted stolen.

34 And Lâbân said, Behold, I would it might be according thy word.

35 And he removed that day the he-goats that were ringstraked and spotted, and all the she-goats that were speckled and spotted, every one that had white in it, and all the black ones among the sheep, and gave them into the hand of his sons;

36 And he set three days' journey betwixt himself and Ya'aqôb; and Ya'aqôb fed the rest of Lâbân's flocks.

37[1] *And Ya'aqôb took him rods of fresh styrax, and of the almond and of the plane-tree; and peeled white strakes in them, and made the white appear which was in the rods.*

38 *And he set the rods which he had peeled over against the flocks in the gutters in the watering troughs where the flocks came to drink; and they conceived when they came to drink.*

39 *And the flocks conceived before the rods, and the flocks brought forth ringstraked, and speckled, and spotted.*

---

[1] Most modern critics consider verses 31-42 to be an addition by the latest editor, taken from some document not generally used by him, probably from the same which furnished the whole of chap. xx. and chap. xxi. 32-34. It seems to me, however, that the addition of the latest editor to the text of the Jehovist consists merely in the description of Ya'aqôb's strange conduct.—L.

40 And Ya'aqôb separated the lambs, and set the faces of the flocks toward the ringstraked, and all the black in the flock of Lâbân [1]; and he put his own droves apart, and put them not unto Lâbân's flock.

41 *And it came to pass, whensoever the stronger of the flock did conceive, that Ya'aqôb laid the rods before the eyes of the flock in the gutters, that they might conceive among the rods;*

42 *But when the flock were feeble, he put them not in: so the feebler were Lâbân's, and the stronger Ya'aqôb's.*

43 And the man increased exceedingly, and had large flocks, and maidservants and slaves, and camels and asses.

CHAPTER XXXI.

1 And he heard the words of Lâbân's sons, saying, Ya'aqôb hath taken away all that was our father's; and of all that which was our father's hath he gotten all this wealth.

2 And Ya'aqôb beheld the countenance of Lâbân, and, behold, it was not toward him as beforetime.

3 And Yahveh said unto Ya'aqôb, Return unto the land of thy fathers, and to thy kindred; and I will be with thee.

4 And Ya'aqôb sent and called Râ'hêl and Lêâh to the field unto his flock.

5 And said unto them, I see your father's countenance that it is not toward me as beforetime; but the God of my father hath been with me.

6 And ye know that with all my power I have served your father.

7 And your father hath deceived me, and changed my wages ten times [2]; but Elôhîm suffered him not to hurt me.

---

[1] That is, he made the rest of the flock go away from the speckled and spotted animals, which he set apart for himself.—L.

[2] For the ten lambs.—LXX.

8 If he said thus, The speckled shall be thy wages; then all the flock bare speckled: and if he said thus, The ringstraked shall be thy wages; then bare all the flock ringstraked.

9 Thus Elôhîm hath taken away the cattle of your father, and given them to me.

10 And it came to pass at the time that the flock conceived, that I lifted up mine eyes, and saw in a dream, and, behold, the he-goats which leaped upon the flock were ringstraked, speckled, and grisled.

11 And the angel of Elôhîm said unto me in the dream, Ya'aqôb; and I said, Here am I.

12 And he said, Lift up now thine eyes, and see, all the he-goats which leap upon the flock are ringstraked, speckled, and grisled; for I have seen all that Lâbân doeth unto thee.

13 I am the God of Bêth-Êl, where thou anointedst a column, where thou vowedst a vow unto me: now arise, get thee out from this land, and return unto the land of thy nativity.

14 And Râ'hêl and Lêâh answered and said unto him, Is there yet any portion or inheritance for us in our father's house?

15 Are we not counted of him strangers? for he hath sold us, and hath also quite devoured our money.

16 For all the riches which Elôhîm hath taken away from our father, that is ours and our children's: now then, whatsoever Elôhîm hath said unto thee, do.

17 Then Ya'aqôb rose up, and set his sons and his wives upon camels:

18 And he carried away all his cattle, and all his substance which he had gathered, the cattle of his getting, which he had gathered in Paddan-Arâm, for to go to Yiçe'hâq his father unto the land of Kenâ'an.

19 Now Lâbân was gone to shear his sheep: and Râ'hêl stole the Terâphîm [1] that were her father's.

20 And Ya'aqôb stole away unawares to Lâbân the Aramy; in that he told him not that he fled.

[1] Domestic idols.—L.

21 So he fled with all that he had; and he rose up, and passed over the River, and set his face toward the mountain of Gile'âd.

22 And it was told Lâbân on the third day that Ya'aqôb was fled.

23 And he took his brethren with him, and pursued after him seven days' journey; and he overtook him in the mountain of Gile'âd.

24 And Elôhîm came to Lâbân the Aramy, in a dream of the night, and said unto him, Take heed to thyself that thou speak not to Ya'aqôb either good or bad.

25 And Lâbân came up with Ya'aqôb. Now Ya'aqôb had pitched his tent in the mountain : and Lâbân with his brethren pitched in the mountain of Gile'âd.

26 And Lâbân said to Ya'aqôb, What hast thou done ? that thou hast stolen away unawares to me, and carried away my daughters as captives of the sword ?

27 Wherefore didst thou flee secretly, and steal away from me ; and didst not tell me, that I might have sent thee away with mirth and with songs, to the sound of the tambourine [1] and the kinnôr ;

28 And hast not suffered me to kiss my sons and my daughters ? now hast thou done foolishly.

29 It is in the power of my hand to do you hurt : but the God of your father spake unto me yesternight, saying, Take heed to thyself that thou speak not unto Ya'aqôb either good or bad.

30 And now, though thou wouldest needs be gone, because thou sore longedst after thy father's house, yet wherefore hast thou stolen my gods ?

31 And Ya'aqôb answered and said to Lâbân, Because I was afraid : for I said, Lest thou shouldest take thy daughters from me by force, [and all my possessions].[2]

32 With whomsoever thou findest thy gods, he shall not live :

---

[1] The tôph is a tambourine or small hand-drum.—Engel.

[2] The LXX have these words, which are no longer in the Hebrew text.—L.

before our brethren discern thou what is thine with me, and take it to thee. For Ya'aqôb knew not that Râ'hêl had stolen them.

33 And Lâbân went into Ya'aqôb's tent, and into Lêâh's tent, and into the tent of the two maidservants; but he found them not. And he went out of Lêâh's tent, and entered into Râ'hêl's tent.

34 Now Râ'hêl had taken the Terâphîm, and put them in the camel's furniture, and sat upon them. And Lâbân felt about all the tent, but found them not.

35 And she said to her father, Let not my lord be angry that I cannot rise up before thee; for the manner of women is upon me. And he searched, but found not the Terâphîm.

36 And Ya'aqôb was wroth, and chode with Lâbân: and Ya'aqôb answered and said to Lâbân, What is my trespass? what is my sin? that thou hast so hotly pursued after me?

37 Whereas thou hast felt about all my stuff, what hast thou found of all thy household stuff? Set it here before my brethren and thy brethren, that they may judge betwixt us two.

38 This twenty years have I been with thee; thy ewes and thy she-goats have not cast their young, and the rams of thy flocks have I not eaten.

39 That which was torn of beasts I brought not unto thee; I bare the loss of it; of my hands didst thou require it, whether stolen by day or stolen by night.

40 Thus I was; in the day the drought consumed me, and the frost by night; and my sleep fled from mine eyes.

41 These twenty years have I been in thy house; I served thee fourteen years for thy two daughters, and six for thy flock: and thou hast changed my wages ten times.

42 Except the God of my father, the God of Abrâhâm, and the fear of Yiçe'hâq, had been with me, surely now hadst thou sent me away empty. Elôhîm hath seen mine affliction and the labour of my hands, and rebuked thee yesternight.

43 And Lâbân answered and said unto Ya'aqôb, The daughters are my daughters, and the children are my children, and the

flocks are my flocks, and all that thou seest is mine: and what can I do this day unto these my daughters, or unto their children which they have borne?

44 And now come, let us make a covenant, I and thou; and let it be for a witness between me and thee.

45 And Ya'aqôb took a stone, and set it up for a column.

46 And Ya'aqôb said unto his brethren, Gather stones; and they took stones, and made an heap: and they did eat there by the heap.

47 And Lâbân called it *Yegar-shâhadûthâ* (*the heap of witness*); but Ya'aqôb called it *Gale'êd*.

48 And Lâbân said [to Ya'aqôb, Behold this heap, and the column which I have set between me and thee [1]]. This heap is witness [and this pillar is witness between me and thee]. Therefore was the name of it called Gale'êd,

49 And Miçpâh, for he said, Yahveh watch (*Yiçeph*) between me and thee when we are hidden one from another.

50 If thou shalt afflict my daughters, and if thou shalt take wives beside my daughters, no man is with us; see, Elôhîm is witness betwixt me and thee.

51 And Lâbân said to Ya'aqôb, Behold this heap, and behold the column which I have set betwixt me and thee.

52 This heap be witness and the column be witness, that I will not pass over this heap to thee, and that thou shalt not pass over this heap and this column unto me, for harm.

53 The God of Abrâhâm and the God of Nâ'hôr, the God of their father, judge between us. And Ya'aqôb sware by the Fear of his father Yiçc'hâq.

54 And Ya'aqôb offered a sacrifice in the mountain, and called his brethren to eat bread: and they did eat bread, and tarried all night in the mountain.

55 And early in the morning Lâbân rose up, and kissed his sons and his daughters, and blessed them: and Lâbân departed, and returned unto his place.

---

[1] These supplementary portions of a verse which is evidently incomplete without them are taken from the LXX.—L.

CHAPTER XXXII.

1 And Ya'aqôb went on his way, [and having looked up, he saw the host of Elôhîm encamped [1]], and the angels of Elôhîm met him.

2 And Ya'aqôb said when he saw them, This is Elôhîm's host, and he called the name of that place Mâ'hanâîm (*encampments*).

3 And Ya'aqôb sent messengers before him to 'Êsâv his brother, unto the land of Sê'îr, the field of Edôm.

4 And he commanded them, saying, Thus shall ye say unto my lord 'Êsâv; Thus saith thy servant Ya'aqôb, I have sojourned with Lâbân and stayed until now:

5 And I have oxen, and asses, and flocks, and male and female slaves: and I have sent to tell my lord, that I may find grace in thy sight.

6 And the messengers returned to Ya'aqôb, saying, We came to thy brother 'Êsâv, and moreover he cometh to meet thee, and four hundred men with him.

7 Then Ya'aqôb was greatly afraid and was distressed: and he divided the people that was with him, and the flocks, and the herds, and the camels, into two companies;

8 And he said, If 'Êsâv come to the one company, and smite it, then the company which is left shall escape.

9 And Ya'aqôb said, O God of my father Abrâhâm, and God of my father Yiçc'hâq, O Yahveh, which saidst unto me, Return unto thy country, and to thy kindred, and I will do thee good:

10 I am not worthy of the least of all thy mercies, and of all the truth which thou hast showed unto thy servant; for with my staff I passed over this Yardên; and now I am become two companies.

11 Deliver me, I pray thee, from the hand of my brother,

[1] This portion of the verse is only in the LXX, and is missing from the Hebrew text.—L.

from the hand of 'Êsâv ; for I fear him, lest he come and smite me, the mother with the children.

12 And thou saidst, I will surely do thee good, and make thy seed as the sand of the sea, which cannot be numbered for multitude.

13 And he lodged there that night; and took of that which he had with him a present for 'Êsâv his brother ;

14 Two hundred she-goats, and twenty he-goats, two hundred ewes and twenty rams.

15 Thirty milch camels and their colts, forty kine and ten bulls, twenty she-asses and ten foals.

16 And he delivered them into the hand of his servants, every drove by itself; and said unto his servants, Pass over before me, and put a space betwixt drove and drove.

17 And he commanded the foremost, saying, When 'Êsâv my brother meeteth thee, and asketh thee, saying, Whose art thou, and whither goest thou ? and whose are these before thee ?

18 Then thou shalt say, They be thy servant Ya'aqôb's ; it is a present sent unto my lord 'Êsâv ; and, behold, he also is behind us.

19 And he commanded also the second, and the third, and all that followed the droves, saying, On this manner shall ye speak unto 'Êsâv, when ye find him ;

20 And ye shall say, Moreover, behold, thy servant Ya'aqôb is behind us. For he said, I will appease him with the present that goeth before me, and afterward I will see his face ; peradventure he will accept me.

21 So the present passed over before him : and he himself lodged that night in the company.

22 And he rose up that night, and took his two wives, and his two handmaids, and his eleven children, and passed over the ford of the Yabbok.

23 And he took them, and sent them over the stream, and sent over that he had.

24 And Ya'aqôb was left alone ; and there wrestled a man with him until the breaking of the day.

25 And when he saw that he prevailed not against him, he

touched the hollow of his thigh; and the hollow of Ya'aqôb's thigh was strained as he wrestled with him.

26 And he said, Let me go, for the day breaketh. And he said, I will not let thee go, except thou bless me.

27 And he said unto him, What is thy name? And he said, Ya'aqôb.

28 And he said, Thy name shall be called no more Ya'aqôb, but Yisrâêl, for thou hast striven with Elôhîm (*ki-sâritha 'im-Elôhîm*), and with men, and hast prevailed.

29 And Ya'aqôb asked him, and said, Tell me, I pray thee, thy name. And he said, Wherefore is it that thou dost ask after my name? And he blessed him there.

30 And Ya'aqôb called the name of the place Peny-Êl [1]; for, said he, I have seen Elôhîm face to face, and my life is preserved.

31 And the sun rose upon him as he passed over Peny-Êl, and he halted upon his thigh.

32 *Therefore the Bené-Yisráêl eat not the sinew of the hip which is upon the hollow of the thigh, unto this day: because he touched the hollow of Ya'aqôb's thigh in the sinew of the hip.*

CHAPTER XXXIII.

1 And Ya'aqôb lifted up his eyes, and looked, and behold, 'Êsâv came, and with him four hundred men. And he divided the children unto Lêâh, and unto Râ'hêl, and unto the two handmaids.

2 And he put the handmaids and their children foremost, and Lêâh and her children after, and Râ'hêl and Yôsêph hindmost.

3 And he himself passed over before them, and bowed himself to the ground seven times until he came near to his brother.

[1] The face of God.

4 And 'Êsâv ran to meet him, and embraced him, and fell on his neck, and kissed him: and they wept.

5 And he lifted up his eyes, and saw the women and the children; and said, Who are these with thee? And he said, The children which Elôhîm hath graciously given thy servant.

6 Then the handmaids came near, they and their children, and they bowed themselves.

7 And Lêâh also and her children came near, and bowed themselves; and after came Yôsêph near and Râ'hêl, and they bowed themselves.

8 And he said, What meanest thou by all this company which I met? And he said, To find grace in the sight of my lord.

9 And 'Êsâv said, I have enough; my brother, let that thou hast be thine.

10 And Ya'aqôb said, Nay, I pray thee, if now I have found grace in thy sight, then receive my present at my hand: forasmuch as I have seen thy face, as one seeth the face of Elôhîm, and thou wast pleased with me.

11 Take, I pray thee, my gift that is brought to thee; because Elôhîm hath dealt graciously with me, and because I have enough. And he urged him, and he took it.

12 And he said, Let us take our journey, and let us go, and I will go before thee.

13 And he said unto him, My lord knoweth that the children are tender, and that the flocks and herds with me give suck: and if they overdrive them one day, all the flocks will die.

14 Let my lord, I pray thee, pass over before his servant: and I will lead on softly, according to the pace of the cattle that is before me, and according to the pace of the children, until I come unto my lord unto Sê'îr.

15 And 'Êsâv said, Let me now leave with thee some of the folk that are with me. And he said, What needeth it? let me find grace in the sight of my lord.

16 So 'Êsâv returned that day on his way unto Sê'îr.

17 And Ya'aqôb journeyed unto Sukkôth, and built him an house, and made booths for his cattle: therefore the name of the place is called Sukkôth (Booths).

18 And Ya'aqôb came in peace to the city of Shechem, which is in the land of Kenâ'an, when he came from Paddan-Arâm; and encamped before the city.

19 And he bought the parcel of ground, where he had spread his tent, at the hand of the children of 'Hamôr, Shechem's father, for an hundred qesîtâh.[1]

20 And he erected there an altar, and called it Êl-Elôhê-Yisrâêl (Êl is the God of Yisrâêl).

CHAPTER XXXIV.

1 And Dinâh, the daughter of Lêâh, which she bare unto Ya'aqôb, went out to see the daughters of the land.

2 And Shechem, the son of 'Hamôr the 'Hivvy, the prince of the land, saw her; and he took her,

and lay with her, and humbled her.

3 And his soul clave unto Dinâh the daughter of Ya'aqôb, and he loved the damsel, and spake to the heart of the damsel.

4 And Shechem spake unto his father 'Hamôr, saying, Get me this damsel to wife.

5 Now Ya'aqôb heard that he had defiled Dinâh his daughter; and his sons were with his cattle in the field, and Ya'aqôb held his peace until they came.

6 And 'Hamôr the father of Shechem, went out unto Ya'aqôb to commune with him.

7 And the sons of Ya'aqôb came in from the field when they

---

[1] Something weighed out, containing about four shekels (conf. chap. xxiii. 16). The LXX translate it 'lambs,' but money was in use at this time. The word occurs again in Josh. xxiv. 32 and Job xlii. 11.

heard it: and the men were grieved, and they were very wroth, because he had wrought folly in Yisrâêl in lying with Ya'aqôb's daughter; which thing ought not to be done.

8 And 'Hamôr communed with them, saying, The soul of my son Shechem longeth for your daughter: I pray you give her unto him to wife.

9 And make ye marriage with us; give your daughters unto us, and take our daughters unto you.

10 And ye shall dwell with us: and the land shall be before you; dwell and trade ye therein, and get you possessions therein.

11 And Shechem said unto her father and unto her brethren, Let me find grace in your eyes, and what ye shall say unto me I will give.

12 Ask me never so much dowry and gift, and I will give according as ye shall say unto me: but give me the damsel to wife.

13 And the sons of Ya'aqôb answered Shechem and 'Hamôr his father with guile, and spake, because he had defiled Dinâh, their sister,

14 And said unto them, We cannot do this thing, to give our sister to one that is uncircumcised; for that were a reproach unto us.

15 Only on this condition will we consent with you; if ye will be as we be, that every male of you be circumcised;

16 Then will we give our daughters unto you, and we will take your daughters to us, and we will dwell with you, and we will become one people.

17 But if ye will not hearken to us, to be circumcised; then will we take our daughter, and we will be gone.

18 And their words pleased 'Hamôr, and Shechem 'Hamôr's son.

19 And the young man deferred not to do the thing, because he had delight in Ya'aqôb's daughter: and he was honoured above all the house of his father.

20 And 'Hamôr and Shechem his son came unto the gate of their city, and communed with the men of their city, saying,

21 These men are peaceable with us; therefore let them dwell in the land, and trade therein; for, behold, the land is large enough for them; let us take their daughters to us for wives, and let us give them our daughters.

22 Only on this condition will the men consent unto us to dwell with us, to become one people, if every male among us be circumcised, as they are circumcised.

23 Shall not their cattle and their substance and all their beasts be ours? only let us consent unto them, and they will dwell with us.

24 And unto 'Hamôr and unto Shechem his son hearkened all that went out of the gate of his city; and every male was circumcised, all that went out of the gate of his city.

25 And it came to pass on the third day, when they were sore, that two of the sons of Ya'aqôb, Shime'ôn and Lêvy, Dinâh's brethren, took each man his sword, and came upon the city unawares, and slew all the males.

26 And they slew 'Hamôr and Shechem his son with the edge of the sword, and took Dinâh out of Shechem's house, and went forth.

27 The sons of Ya'aqôb came upon the slain, and spoiled the city, because they had defiled their sister.

28 They took their flocks and their herds and their asses, and that which was in the city, and that which was in the fields.

29 And all their wealth, and all their little ones and their wives, took they captive and spoiled, even all that was in the house.

30 And Ya'aqôb said to Shime'ôn and Lêvy, Ye have troubled me, to make me to stink among the inhabitants of the land, among the Kena'any and the Perizzy : and I being few in number, they will gather themselves together against me and smite me ; and I shall be destroyed, I and my house.

31 And they said, Should he deal with our sister as with an harlot ?

CHAPTER XXXV.

1 And Elôhîm said unto Ya'aqôb, Arise, go up to Bêth-Êl, and dwell there : and make there an altar unto God, who appeared unto thee when thou fleddest from the face of 'Êsâv thy brother.

2 Then Ya'aqôb said unto his household, and to all that were with him, Put away the strange gods that are among you, and purify yourselves and change your garments :

3 And let us arise, and go up to Bêth-Êl ; and I will make there an altar unto God, who answered me in the day of my distress, and was with me in the way which I went.

4 And they gave unto Ya'aqôb all the strange gods which were in their hand, and the rings which were in their ears ; and Ya'aqôb hid them under the oak which was by Shechem.

5 And they journeyed : and the terror of Elôhîm was upon the cities that were round about them, and they did not pursue after the sons of Ya'aqôb.

6 So Ya'aqôb came to Lûz, which is in the land of Kenâ'an (the same is Bêth-Êl), he and all the people that were with him.

7 And he built there an altar, and called the place Êl-Bêth-Êl: because there God was revealed unto him, when he fled from the face of his brother.

8 And Debôrâh Ribqâh's nurse died, and she was buried below Bêth-Êl under the terebinth: and the name of it was called Allôn-Bâcûth (the Terebinth of weeping).

9 And Elôhîm appeared unto Ya'aqôb again, when he came from Paddan-Arâm, and blessed him.

10 And Elôhîm said unto him, Thy name is Ya'aqôb: thy name shall not be called any more Ya'aqôb, but Yisrâêl shall be thy name: and he called his name Yisrâêl.

11 And Elôhîm said unto him, I am El Shadday (God Almighty): be fruitful and multiply: a nation and a company of nations shall be of thee, and kings shall come out of thy loins.

12 And the land which I gave unto Abrâhâm and Yiçe'hâq, to thee will I give it, and to thy seed after thee will I give the land.

13 And Elôhîm went up from him in the place where he spake with him.

14 And Ya'aqôb set up a pillar in the place where he spake with him, a pillar of stone: and he poured out a drink offering thereon, and poured oil thereon.

15 And Ya'aqôb called the name of the place where Elôhîm spake with him, Bêth-Êl.

16 And they journeyed from Bêth-Êl, and there was still some way to come to Ephrâthâh: and Râ'hêl travailed, and she had hard labour.

17 And it came to pass, when she was in hard labour, that

the midwife said unto her, Fear not; for now thou shalt have another son.

18 And it came to pass, as she gave up the ghost (for she died), that she called his name Ben-Ôny (son of my sorrow): but his father called him Bin-Yâmîn (son of the right hand).

19 And Râ'hêl died, and was buried in the way to Ephrâthâh (the same is Bêth Le'hem).

20 And Ya'aqôb set up a column on her grave; the same is Maçebeth Qeturath-Râ'hêl (the column of Râ'hêl's grave) unto this day.

21 And Yisrâêl journeyed, and spread his tent beyond Mig-dal-'Êder.¹

22 And it came to pass, while Yisrâêl dwelt in that land, that Reûbên went and lay with Bil'hâh his father's concubine: and Yisrâêl heard of it.

Now the sons of Ya'aqôb were twelve:

23 The sons of Lêâh; Reûbên, Ya'aqôb's first born, and Shime'ôn, and Lêvy, and Yehûdâh, and Yissâchâr, and Zebulûn:

24 The sons of Râ'hêl; Yôsêph, and Binyâmîn;

25 And the sons of Bil'hâh, Râ'hêl's handmaid; Dân, and Naphtâly:

26 And the sons of Zilpâh, Lêâh's handmaid; Gâd, and Ashêr: these are the sons of Ya'aqôb, which were born to him in Paddan-Arâm.

27 And Ya'aqôb came unto Yiçe'hâq his father to Mamrê, to Qiryath-Arba' (*the same is Hebrôn*), where Abrâhâm and Yiçe'hâq sojourned.

28 And the days of Yiçe'hâq were an hundred and fourscore years.

29 And Yiçe'hâq gave up the ghost, and died, and was gathered unto his people old and full of days; and 'Êsâv and Ya'aqôb his sons buried him.

¹ 'Tower of the flock.'

CHAPTER XXXVI.

1 Now these are the generations of 'Ésâv (the same is Edôm).

2 'Ésâv took his wives of the daughters of Kenâ'an; 'Adâh the daughter of Elôn the 'Hitty, and Aholibâmâh the daughter of 'Anâh, the daughter of Çibe'ôn the 'Hivvy;

3 And Bàsemath Yishmâ'êl's daughter, sister of Nebâyôth.[1]

4 And 'Adâh bare to 'Ésâv Eliphàz; and Bàsemath bare Re'ûêl;

5 And Aholibâmâh bare Ye'ûsh, and Ya'elâm, and Qôra'h: these are the sons of 'Ésâv which were born unto him in the land of Kenâ'an.

6 And 'Ésâv took his wives, and his sons, and his daughters, and all the souls of his house, and his cattle, and all his beasts, and all his possessions, which he had gathered in the land of Kenâ'an; and went into a land away from his brother Ya'aqôb.

7 For their substance was too great for them to dwell together; and the land of their sojournings could not bear them because of their cattle.

8 And 'Ésâv dwelt in Mount Sê'ir: 'Ésâv is Edôm.

[1] There is a remarkable divergence between the names of 'Ésâv's wives as we have them here and as we have them in chap. xxvi. 34 and xxvii. 9. Yet in each case the writer follows the same book—that of the Elohist. We must therefore conclude either that this writer made use of different documents in these passages, or that in one or other of them his text has been altered. If the latter hypothesis is adopted the names given in this chapter are more worthy of credit than those given in chapters xxvi. and xxvii.—L.

9 And these are the generations of 'Êsâv, the father of Edôm, in Mount Sê'îr.

10 These are the names of 'Êsâv's sons; Eliphâz, the son of 'Adâh the wife of 'Êsâv, Re'ûel the son of Bâsemath the wife of 'Êsâv.

11 And the sons of Eliphâz were Têmân, Omâr, Çephô, and Ga'etâm, and Qenaz.

12 And Timnâ' was concubine to Eliphâz 'Êsâv's son; and she bare to Eliphâz 'Amâlêq: these are the sons of 'Adâh 'Êsâv's wife.

13 And these are the sons of Re'ûel; Na'hath, and Zera'h, Shammâh, and Mizzâh: these were the sons of Bâsemath 'Êsâv's wife.

14 And these were the sons of Aholibâmâh the daughter of 'Anâh, the daughter of Çibe'ôn, 'Êsâv's wife; and she bare to 'Êsâv Ye'ûsh, and Ya'elâm, and Qôra'h.

15 These are the phylarchs (allûphim)[1] of the Benê-'Êsâv; the sons of Eliphâz the firstborn of 'Êsâv; allûph Têmân, allûph Omâr, allûph Çephô, allûph Qenaz.

16 Allûph Qôra'h, allûph Ga'etâm, allûph 'Amâlêq: these are the phylarchs that came of Eliphâz in the land of Edôm; these are the sons of 'Adâh.

17 And these are the sons of Re'ûel 'Êsâv's son: allûph Na'hath, allûph Zera'h, allûph Shammâh, allûph Mizzâh: these are the phylarchs that came of Re'ûel in

---

[1] φύλαρχοι, LXX, ηγεμόνες. Allûph is used especially of the chiefs of the Edomites here and in Ex. xv. 15 and 1 Chron. i. 51-54; of the chiefs of the Jews in Zech. ix. 7, and xii. 5, 6; and of leaders generally in Ps. lv. 13, Prov. ii. 17, Jer. iii. 4, xiii. 21, &c.

the land of Edôm; these are the sons of Bâsemath 'Êsâv's wife.

18 And these are the sons of Aholibâmâh 'Êsâv's wife; allûph Ye'ûsh, allûph Ya'elâm, allûph Qôra'h: these are the phylarchs that came of Aholibâmah the daughter of 'Anâh, 'Êsâv's wife.

19 These are the sons of 'Êsâv, and these are their phylarchs: the same is Edôm.

20 These are the sons of Sê'ir the 'Hory, the inhabitants of the land; Lôtân, and Shôbâl, and Çibe'ôn, and 'Anâh,

21 And Dishôn, and Êçer, and Dishân: these are the phylarchs that came of the 'Hory, the children of Sê'ir in the land of Edôm.

22 And the children of Lôtân were 'Hory and Hêmâm; and Lôtân's sister was Timnâ'.

23 And these are the children of Shôbâl: 'Alvân, and Mana'hath, and 'Êbâl, Shephô, and Onâm.

24 And these are the children of Çibe'ôn; Ayâh and 'Anâh; this is 'Anâh who found the hot springs in the wilderness, as he fed the asses of Çibe'ôn his father.

25 And these are the children of 'Anâh: Dishôn, and Aholibâmâh the daughter of 'Anâh.

26 And these are the children of Dishôn; Hemdân, and Eshbân, and Yithrân, and Cherân.

27 These are the children of Êçer; Bilhân, and Zá'avân, and 'Aqân.

28 These are the children of Dishân; Uç, and Arân.

29 These are the phylarchs that came of the 'Hory: allûph Lôtân, allûph Shôbâl, allûph Çibe'ôn, allûph 'Anâh,

30 Allûph Dishôn, allûph Êçer, allûph Dishân : these are the phylarchs of the 'Hory, according to their phylarchs in the land of Sê'îr.

31 And these are the kings that reigned in the land of Edôm before there reigned any king over the Benê-Yisrâêl.

32 And Bela' the son of Be'ôr reigned in Edôm : and the name of his city was Dinhâbâh.

33 And Bela' died, and Yôbâb the son of Zera'h of Bocrâh reigned in his stead.

34 And Yôbâb died, and 'Hushâm of the land of Tê mân reigned in his stead.

35 And 'Hushâm died, and Hadad the son of Bedad, who smote Midyân in the field of Môâb, reigned in his stead : and the name of his city was 'Avîth.

36 And Hadad died, and Samlâh of Masrêqâh reigned in his stead.

37 And Samlâh died, and Shâûl of Rehôbôth-Hannâhâr reigned in his stead.

38 And Shâûl died, and Ba'al-'Hânân the son of 'Achbôr reigned in his stead.

39 And Ba'al-'Hânân the son of 'Achbôr died, and Hadar reigned in his stead : and the name of his city was Pâ'û ; and his wife's name was Mehêtabêl, the daughter of Matrêd, the daughter of Mê-zâhâb.

40 And these are the names of the phylarchs that came of 'Êsâv, according to their families, after their places, by their names; allûph Timnâ', allûph 'Alvâh, allûph Yethêth,

41 Allûph Aholîbâmâh, allûph Êlâh, allûph Pînôn,

42 Allûph Qenaz, allûph Têmân, allûph Mibçar,

43 Allûph Maqdyêl, allûph 'Irâm: these are the phylarchs of Edôm, according to their habitations in the land of their possession. This is 'Esâv the father of Edôm.

CHAPTER XXXVII.

1 And Ya'aqôb dwelt in the land of his father; sojourning in the land of Kenâ'an.

2 These are the generations of Ya'aqôb.

Yôsêph, being seventeen years old, was feeding the flock with his brethren;
and he was a lad with the sons of Bilhâh, and with the sons of Zilpâh, his father's wives:

And Yôsêph brought the evil report of them unto their father.

3 Now Yisrâêl loved Yôsêph more than all his children, *because he was the son of his old age*; and he made him a tunic of many colours.

4 And his brethren saw that their father loved him more than all his brethren, and they hated him; and could not speak peaceably unto him.

5 And Yôsêph dreamed a dream, and he told it to his brethren: and they hated him yet the more.

6 And he said unto them, Hear, I pray you, this dream which I have dreamed.

7 For, behold, we were binding sheaves in the field, and, lo, my sheaf arose, and also stood upright; and, and, behold, your sheaves came round about, and made obeisance to my sheaf.

8 And his brethren said to him, Shalt thou indeed

reign over us? or shalt thou indeed have dominion over us? And they hated him yet the more for his dreams, and for his words.

9 And he dreamed yet another dream, and told it to his brethren, and said, Behold, I have dreamed yet a dream ; and, behold, the sun and the moon and eleven stars made obeisance to me.[1]

10 And he told it to his father, and to his brethren : and his father rebuked him, and said unto him, What is this dream that thou hast dreamed? Shall I and thy mother and thy brethren indeed come to bow down ourselves to thee to the earth ?

11 And his brethren envied him ; but his father kept the saying in mind.

12 And his brethren went to feed their father's flock in Shechem.

13 And Yisrâêl said unto Yôsêph, Do not thy brethren feed

---

[1] The Jews believed the celestial bodies to be living and rational beings. Maimonides observes that when the Psalmist says (Ps. xix. 3),

'There is no speech nor language ;
Their voice cannot be heard,'

he means that the heavenly spheres have really a language among themselves, though it is not the language of the lips and of the tongue ; just as in Ps. iv. 4 it is said, 'Commune with your own heart upon your bed, and be still.' ' As to the learned men it is unnecessary to explain or to prove it. One need only consider their version of the " benediction of the moon"' [the prayer which should be offered up after the appearance of the new moon, in which it is said, speaking of the stars, 'they rejoice to fulfil the commands of their creator,'] &c., 'and what is frequently repeated in the prayers, as well as the texts of the Midrashim on Neh. ix. 6 and Job xxxviii. 7. In Bereshith Rabba they comment on Gen. i. 2, " And the earth was tohû and bohû," as follows : "The earth was tohû and bohû "' [that is, the earth lamented and grieved at its wretched condition]; '" I and it, it said, were created at the same time "' [that is, the earth and heaven]; '" but the things which are above live, while the things which are below are dead." They state clearly, therefore, that the heavenly bodies are alive, and are not dead bodies, like the elements.'

the flock in Shechem? Come, and I will send thee unto them. And he said to him, Here am I.

14 And he said to him, Go now, see whether it be well with thy brethren, and well with the flock; and bring me word again. So he sent him out to the vale of Hebrôn, and he came to Shechem.

15 And a certain man found him, and, behold, he was wandering in the field: and the man asked him, saying, What seekest thou?

16 And he said, I seek my brethren: tell me, I pray thee, where they are feeding the flock.

17 And the man said, They are departed hence; for I heard them say, Let us go to Dothân. And Yôsêph went after his brethren, and found them in Dothân.

18 And they saw him afar off, and before he came near unto them, they conspired against him to slay him.

19 And they said one to another, Behold this master of dreams cometh.

20 Come now therefore, let us slay him, and cast him into one of the cisterns, and we will say, An evil beast hath devoured him; and we shall see what will become of his dreams.

21 And Reûbên heard it, and delivered him out of their hand; and said, Let us not take his life.

22 And Reûbên said unto them, Shed no blood; cast him into this cistern that is in the wilderness, but lay no hand upon him: that he might deliver him out of their hand, to restore him to his father.

23 And it came to pass when Yôsêph was come unto his brethren, that they stript Yôsêph of his tunic, the tunic of many colours that was on him:

24 And they took him, and cast him into the cistern; and the cistern was empty, there was no water in it.

25 And they sat down to eat bread: and they lifted up their eyes and looked, and, behold, a travelling company of Yishma'êlîm came from Gile'âd, with their camels bearing spicery and balm and ladanum,[1] going to carry it down to Miçrâîm.[2]

26 And Yehûdâh said unto his brethren, What profit is it if we slay our brother, and conceal his blood?

27 Come, and let us sell him to the Yishma'êlîm, and let not our hand be upon him; for he is our brother, our flesh.[3]

28 And there passed by Midyânîm, merchantmen: and they drew and lifted up Yôsêph out of the cistern,

and they sold Yôsêph to the Yishma'êlîm for twenty (shekels) of silver. And they brought Yôsêph into Miçrâîm.

29 And Reûbên returned unto the cistern; and, behold, Yôsêph was not in the cistern; and he rent his clothes.

30 And he returned unto his brethren, and said, The child is not; and I, whither shall I go?

31 And they took Yôsêph's tunic, and killed a he-goat, and dipped the coat in the blood;

32 And they sent the tunic of many colours, and they brought it to their father; and said, This have we found: know now whether it be thy son's coat or not.

33 And he knew it, and said, It is my son's tunic; an evil beast hath devoured him; Yôsêph is without doubt torn in pieces.

34 And Ya'aqôb rent his garments, and put sackcloth upon his loins, and mourned for his son many days.

---

[1] The *Cistus ladanifera*.

[2] Yôsêph was sold only fifty years after the death of Yishma'êl. How could a nation of Yishma'êlîm carrying on commerce with Egypt have been formed in that time?

[3] In this verse Yehûdâh advises that Yôsêph shall be sold to the Yishma'êlîm. In the next verse the Midyânîm sell him to the Yishma'êlîm, and it is the latter who take Yôsêph to Egypt, while in verse 36 the Midyânîm sell him into Egypt.

35 And all his sons and all his daughters rose up to comfort him; but he refused to be comforted; and he said, For I will go down to Sheól [1] to my son mourning. And his father wept for him.

[1] The abode of the dead.—L. Gesenius says: 'I have no doubt that שְׁאוֹל is for שְׁעוֹל a hollow, a hollow and subterranean place, just as the German *Hölle* is of the same origin as *Höhle*, and the Latin *cœlum* is from the Greek κοῖλος, *hohl*, hollow. It is commonly derived from the idea of asking, from its asking for, demanding all, without distinction; hence *orcus rapax*, Catull. ii. 28, 29.' This place was situated below the earth (Numb. xvi. 30-33, where the earth opens and the rebels go down into Sheól). Job (xi. 8) says, speaking of the Almighty,

'It is as high as heaven; what can'st thou do?
Deeper than Sheól, what canst thou know?'

and Ezekiel (xxxi. 14) speaks of the Assyrians who 'are all delivered unto death, to the nether parts of the earth, in the midst of the children of men, with them that go down to the pit.' Deut. xxxii. 22 speaks of 'the lowest Sheól.' Eccles. ix. 10 says, 'There is no work, nor device, nor knowledge, nor wisdom, in Sheól, whither thou goest.' Job iii. 13,-17, speaks of it as a place of rest, 'where the wicked cease from raging.' In Ps. vi. 5, and xxx. 8, 9, we are told that God is forgotten there.

'In death there is no remembrance of thee!
In Sheól who shall give thee thanks?'

'I cried to thee, O Yahveh;
And unto Yahveh I made supplication:
What profit is there in my blood, when I go down to the pit?
Shall the dust praise thee? shall it declare thy truth?'

Sheól was inhabited by the manes, the Rephá'im, shades without blood or animal life. Isaiah (xxvi. 14) says, 'The dead live not, the deceased rise not; they are Rephá'im, they shall not rise.' In 1 Sam. xxviii. 13, 14, however, the woman says to Shâûl, 'I see Elóhim coming up out of the earth. And he said unto her, What form is he of? And she said, An old man cometh up, and he is covered with a robe.' Isaiah (xiv. 9) also says, 'Sheól from beneath is moved for thee to meet thee at thy coming: it stirreth up the Rephá'im for thee, even all the chief ones of the earth.' Ezek. xxxii. 27 speaks of 'the uncircumcised, which are gone down to Sheól with their weapons of war, and have laid their swords under their heads.'

In later times, when the doctrine of the resurrection of the dead had become generally accepted, the Jews adopted the Pagan view, and held that Gehenna and Paradise were close to each other. 'How far,' said they, 'are Gehenna and Paradise from each other?' One palm, was the answer; and R. Jochanan said, There is a wall between the two. But the other Rabbis said, No, they are on a level with each other: one can see from the one what

36 And the Midyânîm sold him into Miçràim unto Pôtiphar,[1] an eunuch of Para'ôh's, the chief of the executioners.

CHAPTER XXXVIII.

1 And it came to pass at that time, that Yehûdâh went down from his brethren, and turned in to a certain man of Adullâm, whose name was 'Hirâh.

2 And Yehûdâh saw there a daughter of a certain Kena'any whose name was Shû'a, and he took her, and went in unto her.

3 And she conceived, and bare a son: and he called his name 'Êr,

4 And she conceived again, and bare a son; and she called his name Ônan.

5 And she yet again bare a son, and called his name Shêlâh; and he was at Chezib when she bare him.

6 And Yehudâh took a wife for 'Êr his firstborn, and her name was Tâmâr.

7 And 'Êr, Yehûdâh's firstborn, was wicked in the eyes of Yahveh; and Yahveh slew him.

8 And Yehûdâh said unto Ônân, Go in unto thy brother's wife, and marry her as brother of her husband, and raise up seed to thy brother.

9 And Ônân knew that the seed should not be his; and it came to pass, when he went in unto his brother's wife, that he spilled it on the ground, lest he should give seed to his brother.

10 And the thing which he did was evil in the sight of Yahveh: and he slew him also.

11 Then said Yehûdâh to Tâmâr his daughter in law, Remain a widow in thy father's house till Shêlâh my son be grown up:

is passing in the other, and there is a great abyss between them.' —*Midrash Koeleth*, f. 103, 2.

[1] Petephres.—LXX.

for he said, Lest he also die, like his brethren. And Tâmâr went and dwelt in her father's house.

12 And in process of time Shû'a's daughter, the wife of Yehûdâh, died; and Yehûdâh was comforted, and went up unto his sheepshearers to Timnâth, he and his friend 'Hirâh the 'Adullâmy.

13 And it was told Tâmâr, saying, Behold thy father in law goeth up to Timnâth to shear his sheep.

14 And she put off from her the garments of her widowhood, and covered herself with her veil, and wrapped herself, and sat in the gate of 'Énaîm, which is by the way to Timnâth; for she saw that Shêlâh was grown up, and she was not given unto him to wife.

15 When Yehûdâh saw her, he thought her to be an harlot; for she had covered her face.

16 And he turned unto her by the way, and said, Go to, I pray thee, let me come in unto thee; for he knew not that she was his daughter in law. And she said, What wilt thou give me, that thou mayest come in unto me?

17 And he said, I will send thee a kid of the goats from the flock. And she said, Wilt thou give me a pledge, till thou send it?

18 And he said, What pledge shall I give thee? And she said, Thy signet and thy cord, and thy staff that is in thine hand. And he gave them to her, and came in unto her, and she conceived by him.

19 And she arose, and went away, and put off her veil from her, and put on the garments of her widowhood.

20 And Yehûdâh sent the kid of the goats by the hand of his friend the 'Adullâmy, to receive the pledge from the woman's hand: but he found her not.

21 Then he asked the men of her place, saying, Where is the harlot that was at 'Énaîm by the way side? And they said, There hath been no harlot here.

22 And he returned to Yehûdâh, and said, I have not found her; and also the men of the place said, There hath been no harlot here.

23 And Yehûdâh said, Let her take it to her, lest we be put to shame: behold, I sent this kid and thou hast not found her.

24 And it came to pass, about three months after, that it was told Yehûdâh, saying, Tâmâr thy daughter in law hath played the harlot; and moreover, behold, she is with child by whoredom. And Yehûdâh said, Bring her forth, and let her be burnt.

25 When she was brought forth, she sent to her father in law, saying, By the man, whose these are, am I with child: and she said, Discern, I pray thee, whose are these, the signet, and the cords, and the staff.

26 And Yehûdâh acknowledged them, and said, She is more righteous than I; forasmuch as I gave her not to Shêlâh my son. And he knew her again no more.

27 And it came to pass in the time of her travail, that, behold, twins were in her womb.

28 And it came to pass, when she travailed, that one put out a hand: and the midwife took and bound upon his hand a scarlet thread, saying, This came out first.

29 And it came to pass, as he drew back his hand, that, behold, his brother came out: and she said, How hast thou made a breach (*pâraçtâ*)? And she called his name Pârec̦.

30 And afterward came out his brother, that had the scarlet thread upon his hand: and his name was called Zâra'h.

CHAPTER XXXIX.

1 And Yôsêph was brought down to Miçrâim; and Pôtiphar, an enuuch of Para'ôh's, the chief of the executioners, a Miçry,[1] bought him of the hand of the Yishma'êlîm, which had brought him down thither.

2 And Yahveh was with Yôsêph, and he was a prosperous man; and he was in the house of his master the Miçry.

[1] An Egyptian.—L.

3 And his master saw that Yahveh was with him, and that Yahveh made all that he did to prosper in his hand.

4 And Yôsêph found grace in his sight, and he ministered unto him: and he made him overseer over his house, and all that he had he put into his hand.

5 And it came to pass from the time that he made him overseer in his house, and over all that he had, that Yahveh blessed the Miçry's house for Yôsêph's sake; and the blessing of Yahveh was upon all that he had, in the house and in the field.

6 And he left all that he had in Yôsêph's hand; and he knew not ought that was with him, save the bread which he did eat.[1] And Yôseph was comely, and well favoured.

7 And it came to pass after these things, that his master's wife cast her eyes upon Yôsêph; and she said, Lie with me.

8 But he refused, and said unto his master's wife, Behold, my master knoweth not what is with me in the house, and he hath put all that he hath into my hand;

9 There is none greater in this house than I; neither hath he kept back anything from me but thee, because thou art his wife: how then can I do this great wickedness, and sin against Elôhîm?

10 And it came to pass, as she spake to Yôsêph day by day, that he hearkened not unto her, to lie by her, or to be with her.

11 And it came to pass about this time, that he went into the house to do his work; and there was none of the men of the house there within.

12 And she caught him by the garment, saying, Lie with me: and he left his garment in her hand, and fled, and got him out.

13 And it came to pass, when she saw that he had left his garment in her hand, and was fled forth,

14 That she called unto the men of her house, and spake unto them, saying, See, he hath brought in an 'Ębry unto us to

---

[1] Bread is used here for food in general. The Egyptians would not eat any food prepared by strangers.

mock us; he came in unto me to lie with me, and I cried with a loud voice:

15 And it came to pass, when he heard that I lifted up my voice and cried, that he left his garment by me, and fled, and got him out.

16 And she laid up his garment by her, until his master came home.

17 And she spake unto him according to these words, The Ĕbry slave, which thou hast brought unto us, came in unto me to mock me:

18 And it came to pass, as I lifted up my voice and cried, that he left his garment by me, and fled out.

19 And it came to pass, when his master heard the words of his wife, which she spake unto him, saying, After this manner did thy servant to me; that his wrath was kindled.

20 And Yôsêph's master took him, and put him into the prison, the place where the king's prisoners were bound: and he was there in the prison.

21 But Yahveh was with Yôsêph, and showed kindness unto him, and gave him favour in the sight of the keeper of the prison.

22 And the keeper of the prison committed to Yôsêph's hand all the prisoners that were in the prison; and whatsoever they did there, he was the doer of it.

23 The keeper of the prison looked not to anything that was under his hand, because Yahveh was with him, and that which he did, Yahveh made it to prosper.

CHAPTER XL.

1 And it came to pass after these things that the cup-bearer of the king of Miçrâim and his baker offended their lord the king of Miçrâim.

2 And Para'òh was wroth against his two officers, against the chief of the cup-bearers, and against the chief of the bakers.

3 And he put them in ward in the house of the chief of the executioners, into the prison, *the place where Yôsêph was bound.*

4 And the chief of the executioners charged Yôsêph with them, and he ministered unto them, and they continued a season in ward.

5 And they dreamed a dream both of them, each man his dream, in one night, each man according to the interpretation of his dream, the cup-bearer and the baker of the king of Miçrâim, which were bound in the prison.

6 And Yôsêph came in unto them in the morning, and saw them, and, behold, they were sad.

7 And he asked Para'òh's eunuchs *that were with him in ward in his master's house,* saying, Wherefore look ye so sadly to-day?

8 And they said unto him, We have dreamed a dream, and there is none that can interpret it. And Yôsêph said unto them, Do not interpretations belong to Elôhîm? tell it me, I pray you.

9 And the chief cup-bearer told his dream to Yôsêph, and said to him, In my dream, behold, a vine was before me;

10 And in the vine were three branches; and it was as though it budded, and its blossoms shot forth; and the clusters thereof brought forth ripe grapes:

11 And Para'òh's cup was in my hand; and I took the grapes, and pressed them into Para'òh's cup, and I gave the cup into Para'òh's hand.

12 And Yôsêph said unto him, This is the interpretation of it: the three branches are three days:

13 Within yet three days shall Para'ôh lift up thine head, and restore thee unto thine office; and thou shalt give Para'ôh's cup into his hand, after the former manner when thou wast his cup-bearer.

14 But have me in remembrance when it shall be well with thee, and show kindness, I pray thee, unto me, and make mention of me unto Para'ôh, and bring me out of this house:

15 For indeed I was stolen away out of the land of the 'Ébrim: *and here also have I done nothing that they should put me in the dungeon.*

16 When the chief baker saw that the interpretation was good, he said unto Yôsêph, I also was in my dream, and, behold, three baskets of white bread were on my head:

17 And in the uppermost basket there was all manner of bakemeats for Para'ôh; and the birds did eat them out of the basket upon my head.

18 And Yôsêph answered and said, This is the interpretation thereof: the three baskets are three days:

19 Within yet three days shall Para'ôh lift up thy head from off thee, and shall hang thee on a tree; and the birds shall eat thy flesh from off thee.

20 And it came to pass the third day, which was Para'ôh's birthday, that he made a feast unto all his servants: and he lifted up the head of the chief cup-bearer and the head of the chief baker among his servants.

21 And he restored the chief cup-bearer unto his

K

office of cup-bearer again; and he gave the cup into Para'ôh's hand:

22 But he hanged the chief baker, as Yôsêph had interpreted to them.

23 Yet did not the chief cup-bearer remember Yôsêph, but forgot him.

CHAPTER XLI.

1 And it came to pass at the end of two full years that Para'ôh dreamed: and, behold, he stood by the river.

2 And, behold, there came up out of the river seven kine, well favoured and fatfleshed; and they fed in the reed-grass.[1]

3 And, behold, seven other kine came up after them out of the river, ill favoured and leanfleshed; and stood by the other kine upon the brink of the river.

4 And the ill favoured and leanfleshed kine did eat up the seven well favoured and fat kine. So Para'ôh awoke.

5 And he slept and dreamed a second time: and, behold, seven ears of corn came up upon one stalk, rank and good.

6 And, behold, seven ears, thin and blasted with the east wind, sprung up after them.

---

[1] A'hû, reed-grass, corresponds exactly to the Egyptian word pe'hu, which designates the portion of each nome which consisted of half-inundated meadows.—L.

7 And the thin ears swallowed up the seven rank and full ears. And Para'ôh awoke, and, behold, it was a dream.

8 And it came to pass in the morning that his spirit was troubled ; and he sent for all the interpreters [1] of Miçrâim, and all the wise men thereof: and Para'ôh told them his dream ; but there was none that could interpret them unto Para'ôh.

9 Then spake the chief cup-bearer unto Para'ôh, saying, I will make mention of my faults this day :

10 Para'ôh was wroth with his servants, and put me in ward in the house of the chief of the executioners, me and the chief baker :

11 And we dreamed a dream in one night, I and he ; we dreamed each man according to the interpretation of his dream.

12 And there was with us there a young man, an 'Êbry,[2] a slave of the chief of the executioners ; and we told him, and he interpreted to us our dreams ; to each man according to his dream he did interpret.

13 And it came to pass, as he interpreted to us, so it was ; I was restored unto mine office, and he was hanged.

14 Then Para'ôh sent and called Yôsêph, *and they brought him hastily out of the dungeon* : and he shaved himself, and changed his raiment, and came in unto Para'ôh.

15 And Para'ôh said unto Yôsêph, I have dreamed a

---

[1] Εξεγηταs.—LXX.
[2] This is either an anachronism, or the name is used to designate ' foreigner.'

dream, and there is none that can interpret it: and I have heard say of thee, that when thou hearest a dream thou canst interpret it.

16 And Yôsêph answered Para'ôh, saying, It is not in me: Elôhim shall give Para'ôh an answer of peace.

17 And Para'ôh spake unto Yôsêph, In my dream, behold, I stood upon the brink of the river [1]:

18 And, behold, there came up out of the river seven kine, fatfleshed and well favoured; and they fed in the reed-grass:

19 And, behold, seven other kine came up after them, poor and very ill favoured and leanfleshed, such as I never saw in all the land of Miçráim for badness:

20 And the lean and ill favoured kine did eat up the first seven fat kine:

21 And when they had eaten them up, it could not be known that they had eaten them; but they were still ill favoured, as at the beginning. So I awoke.

22 And I saw in my dream, and, behold, seven ears came up upon one stalk, full and good:

23 And, behold, seven ears, withered, thin, and blasted with the east wind, sprung up after them:

24 And the thin ears swallowed up the seven good ears: and I told it unto the interpreters; but there was none that could declare it to me.

25 And Yôsêph said unto Para'ôh, The dream of Para'ôh is one: what Elôhim is about to do he hath declared unto Para'ôh.

26 The seven good kine are seven years; and the seven good ears are seven years: the dream is one.

---

[1] The Nile. The Nile is called in Coptic, Phiara, *the* river.

27 And the seven lean and ill favoured kine that came up after them are seven years, and also the seven empty ears blasted with the east wind ; they shall be seven years of famine.

28 That is the thing which I spake unto Para'ôh ; what Elóhîm is about to do he hath showed unto Para'ôh.

29 Behold, there come seven years of great plenty throughout all the land of Miçrâîm :

30 And there shall arise after them seven years of famine; and all the plenty shall be forgotten in the land of Miçrâîm ; and the famine shall consume the land ;

31 And the plenty shall not be known in the land by reason of that famine which followeth ; for it shall be very grievous.

32 And for that the dream was doubled unto Para'ôh twice, it is because the thing is established by Elóhîm, and Elóhîm will shortly bring it to pass.

33 Now therefore let Para'ôh look out a man discreet and wise, and set him over the land of Miçrâîm.

34 Let Para'ôh do this, and let him appoint overseers over the land, and take up the fifth part of the land of Miçrâîm in the seven plenteous years.

35 And let them gather all the food of these good years that come, and lay up *corn* under the hand of Para'ôh for food in the cities, and let them keep it.

36 And the food shall be for a store to the land against the seven years of famine, which shall be in the land of Miçrâîm ; that the land perish not through the famine.

37 And the thing was good in the eyes of Para'ôh, and in the eyes of all his servants.

38 And Para'ôh said unto his servants, Can we find such a one as this, a man in whom the spirit of Elôhim is?

39 And Para'ôh said unto Yôsêph, Inasmuch as Elôhim hath showed thee all this, there is none so discreet and wise as thou:

40 Thou shall be over my house, and according unto thy word shall all my people do homage: only in the throne will I be greater than thou.

41 And Para'ôh said unto Yôsêph, See, I have set thee over all the land of Miçrâim.

42 And Para'ôh took off his signet ring from his hand, and put it upon Yôsêph's hand, and arrayed him in vestures of fine byssus, and put a gold chain about his neck;

43 And he made him to ride in the second chariot which he had; and they cried before him, Bow the knee [1]: and he set him over all the land of Miçrâim.

44 And Para'ôh said unto Yôsêph, I am Para'ôh, and without thee shall no man lift up his hand or his foot in all the land of Miçrâim.

45 And Para'ôh called Yôsêph's name Çâphenath-Pa'anêah,[2] and he gave him to wife Âsenath, the

---

[1] Abrêch, probably a word of Egyptian origin, in which is concealed Au'rek, 'Let everyone bow himself,' or Asserek, 'bow the head.'

[2] Brugsch finds in this name the Egyptian title Tsa-p-u-nt-p-a-Ânkh, 'Ruler of the District of the Abode of the Living One'—that is, of the Sethroitic nome in which Ha-onar (the capital of the Shepherd Kings under whose rule Yôsêph lived) was situated.—L. The LXX call him Psonthomphanech, and his wife Aseneth, probably 'She who is of Neith,' the Egyptian Minerva.

daughter of Pôtî-phêrâ priest of On.¹ And Yôsêph went out over the land of Miçrâim.²

46 And Yôsêph was thirty years old when he stood before Para'ôh king of Miçrâim, and Yôsêph went out from the presence of Para'ôh, and went throughout all the land of Miçrâim.

47 And in the seven plenteous years the earth brought forth by handfuls.

48 And he gathered up all the food of the seven years which were in the land of Miçrâim, and laid up the food in the cities: the food of the field, which was round about every city, laid he up in the same.

49 And Yôsêph laid up corn as the sand of the sea, very much, until he left numbering; for it was without number.³

50 And unto Yôsêph were born two sons before the year of famine came, which Asenath the daughter of Pôtî-phêrâ priest of On bare unto him.

51 And Yôsêph called the name of the first-born Menassheh: For, said he, Elôhîm hath made me forget (*nasshany*) all my toil, and all my father's house.

52 And the name of the second called he Ephrâim: For Elôhîm hath made me fruitful (*hiphrany*) in the land of my affliction.

53 And the seven years of plenty, that was in the land of Miçrâim, came to an end.

54 And the seven years of famine began to come, according as Yôsêph had said: and there was famine in

---

[1] Heliopolis, LXX; called Bêth-shemesh, or house of the sun, in Jer. xliii. 13, and Âven, vanity (city of idolatry), in Ezek. xxx. 17.

[2] This sentence is not in the LXX.

[3] This verse seems to be in the usual style of the Jehovistic narrative in a very marked manner. It would seem to be almost the only one which the latest editor took from the Jehovist's account of the advancement of Yôsêph in Egypt, having preferred the narrative of the Elohist.—L.

all lands; but in all the land of Miçraim there was bread.

55 And when all the land of Miçraim was famished, the people cried to Para'ôh for bread: and Para'ôh said to all Miçraim, Go unto Yôsêph; what he saith to you, do.

56 And the famine was over all the face of the earth: and Yôsêph opened all the storehouses,[1] and sold unto Miçraim; *and the famine was sore in the land of Miçraim.*

57 And all countries came into Miçraim to Yôsêph for to buy corn; because the famine was sore in all the earth.

CHAPTER XLII.

1 Now Ya'aqôb saw that there was corn in Miçraim, and Ya'aqôb said unto his sons, Why do ye look one upon another?

2 And he said, Behold, I have heard that there is corn in Miçraim: get you down thither, and buy for us from thence; that we may live, and not die.

3 And Yôsêph's ten brethren went down to buy corn from Miçraim.

4 But Binyâmin, Yôsêph's brother, Ya'aqôb sent not with his brethren; for he said, Lest peradventure mischief befall him.

5 And the sons of Yisrâêl came to buy among those that came: for the famine was in the land of Kenâ'an.

---

[1] The storehouses he had built.—L.

6 And Yôsêph was the governor over the land: he it was that sold to all the people of the land: and Yôsêph's brethren came, and bowed down themselves to him with their faces to the earth.

7 And Yôsêph saw his brethren, and he knew them, but made himself strange unto them, and spake roughly with them; and he said unto them, Whence come ye? And they said, From the land of Kenâ'an to buy food.

8 And Yôsêph knew his brethren, but they knew not him.

9 And Yôsêph remembered the dreams which he dreamed of them, and said unto them, Ye are spies; to see the nakedness of the land ye are come.

10 And they said unto him, Nay, my lord, but to buy food are thy servants come.

11 We are all one man's sons; we are true men, thy servants are no spies.

12 And he said unto them, Nay, but to see the nakedness of the land ye are come.

13 And they said, We thy servants are twelve brethren, the sons of one man in the land of Kenâ'an; and, behold, the youngest is this day with our father, and one is not.

14 And Yôsêph said unto them, That is it that I spake unto you, saying, Ye are spies:

15 Hereby shall ye be proved: by the life of Para'ôh ye shall not go forth hence, except your youngest brother come hither.

16 Send one of you, and let him fetch your brother, and ye shall be bound, that your words may be proved,

whether there be truth in you: or else by the life of Para'òh surely ye are spies.

17 And he put them all together into ward three days.

18 And Yôsêph said unto them the third day, This do, and live; for I fear God:

19 And if ye be true men, let one of your brethren be bound in your prison house; but go ye, carry corn for the famine of your houses:

20 And bring your youngest brother unto me; so shall your words be verified, and ye shall not die. And they did so.

21 And they said one to another, We are verily guilty concerning our brother, in that we saw the distress of his soul, when he besought us, and we would not hear; therefore is this distress come upon us.

22 And Reûbên answered them, saying, Spake I not unto you, saying, Do not sin against the child; and ye would not hear? therefore also, behold, his blood is required.

23 And they knew not that Yôsêph understood them, for there was an interpreter between them.

24 And he turned himself about from them, and wept; and he returned to them, and spake to them, and took Shime'ôn from among them, and bound him before their eyes.

25 Then Yôsêph commanded to fill their vessels with corn, and to restore every man's money into his sack, and to give them provision for the way: and thus was it done unto them.

26 And they loaded their asses with their corn, and departed thence.

27 And as one of them opened his sack to give his ass provender in the lodging place, he espied his money; and, behold, it was in the mouth of his sack.

28 And he said unto his brethren, My money is restored; and, lo, it is even in my sack: and their heart failed them, and they turned trembling one to another, saying, What is this that Elôhîm hath done unto us?

29 And they came unto Ya'aqôb their father unto the land of Kenâ'an, and told him all that had befallen them; saying,

30 The man, the lord of the land, spake roughly with us, and took us for spies of the country.

31 And we said unto him, We are true men, we are no spies:

32 We be twelve brethren, sons of our father; one is not, and the youngest is this day with our father in the land of Kenâ'an.

33 And the man, the lord of the land, said unto us, Hereby shall I know that ye are true men; leave one of your brethren with me, and take corn for the famine of your houses, and go your way:

34 And bring your youngest brother unto me; then shall I know that ye are no spies, but that ye are true men: so will I deliver you your brother, and ye shall traffick in the land.

35 And it came to pass as they emptied their sacks, that, behold, every man's purse of money was in his sack: and when they and their father saw their purses of money, they were afraid.

36 And Ya'aqôb their father said unto them, Me have ye bereaved of my children: Yôsêph is not, and Shime'ôn is not, and ye will take Binyâmîn away: all these things are upon me.

37 And Reûbên spake unto his father, saying, Slay my two sons, if I bring him not to thee; deliver him into my hand, and I will bring him to thee again.

38 And he said, My son shall not go down with you; for his brother is dead, and he only is left: if mischief befall him by the way in which ye go, then shall ye bring down my gray hairs with sorrow to Sheôl.

CHAPTER XLIII.[1]

1 And the famine was sore in the land.

2 And it came to pass, when they had eaten up the corn which they had brought out of Miçràîm, their father said unto them, Go again, buy us a little food.

3 And Yehûdâh spake unto him, saying, The man did solemnly protest unto us, saying, Ye shall not see my face, except your brother be with you.

4 If thou wilt send our brother with us, we will go down and buy thee food:

---

[1] Both the style and the choice of expressions show that this chapter had a different editor to the preceding one. It is certainly the work of a different author, and the peculiar characteristics of the Jehovist appear in a manner which it is impossible to mistake. There is also a serious difference in the narrative. Yehûdâh here takes the part which Reûbên played in the last chapter. Chapter xlii. is therefore no doubt taken from the same document as chap. xxxvii. 5-11, 18-24, and 29, 30, and the present chapter from the same document as chap. xxxvii. 12-17 and 25-28. The two chapters are, however, consecutive, and the facts narrated in chap. xliii. presuppose those narrated in chap. xlii. The Jehovist and Elohist must therefore each of them have related the two successive interviews between Yôsêph and his brethren. The latest editor has taken the account of the first interview from the Elohist, and the account of the second from the Jehovist, with the exception of three verses inserted by him in chap. xlii (verses 5, 27 and 28), which bear the unmistakable impress of a different editorship to that of the rest of the text.—L.

5 But if thou wilt not send him, we will not go down : for the man said unto us, Ye shall not see my face, except your brother be with you.

6 And Yisraêl said, Wherefore dealt ye so ill with me, as to tell the man whether ye had yet a brother?

7 And they said, The man asked straitly concerning ourselves, and concerning our kindred, saying, Is your father yet alive? have ye another brother? and we told him according to the tenor of these words: could we in any wise know that he would say, Bring your brother down?

8 And Yehûdâh said unto Yisrâêl his father, Send the lad with me, and we will arise and go ; that we may live and not die, both we and thou, and also our little ones.

9 I will be surety for him ; of my hand shalt thou require him: if I bring him not unto thee, and set him before thee, then I shall have sinned against thee for ever :

10 For except we had lingered, surely we had now returned a second time.

11 And their father Yisrâêl said unto them, If it be so now, do this : take of the choice fruits of the land in your vessels, and carry down the man a present, a little balm, and a little honey, spicery, and ladanum, pistachio nuts and almonds :

12 And take double money in your hand ; and the money that was returned in the mouth of your sacks carry again in your hand ; peradventure it was an oversight :

13 Take also your brother, and arise, go again unto the man :

14 And Êl-Shadday (God Almighty) give you mercy before the man, that he may release unto you your other brother and Binyâmîn. And if I am bereaved of my children, I am bereaved.

15 And the men took the present, and they took double money in their hand, and Binyâmîn ; and rose up, and went down to Miçrâîm, and stood before Yôsêph.

16 And when Yôsêph saw Binyâmîn with them, he said to the steward of his house, Bring the men into the house, and slay, and make ready ; for the men shall dine with me at noon.

17 And the man did as Yôsêph bade; and the man brought the men into Yôsêph's house.

18 And the men were afraid, because they were brought into Yôsêph's house; and they said, Because of the money that was returned in our sacks at the first time are we brought in; that he may roll himself upon us, and fall upon us, and take us for bondmen, and our asses.

19 And they came near to the steward of Yôsêph's house, and they spake unto him at the door of the house,

20 And said, Oh my lord, we came indeed down at the first time to buy food:

21 And it came to pass, when we came to the lodging place, that we opened our sacks, and, behold, every man's money was in the mouth of his sack, our money in full weight: and we have brought it again in our hand.

22 And other money have we brought down in our hand to buy food: we know not who put our money in our sacks.

23 And he said, Peace be to you, fear not: your God and the God of your father hath given you treasure in your sacks: I had your money. And he brought Shime'ôn out unto them.

24 And the man brought the men into Yôsêph's house, and gave them water, and they washed their feet: and he gave their asses provender.

25 And they made ready the present against Yôsêph came at noon: for they heard that they should eat bread there.

26 And when Yôsêph came home, they brought him the present which was in their hand into the house, and bowed down themselves to him to the earth.

27 And he asked them of their welfare, and said, Is your father well, the old man of whom ye spake? Is he yet alive?

28 And they said, Thy servant our father is well, he is yet alive. And they bowed the head, and made obeisance.

29 And he lifted up his eyes, and saw Binyâmîn his brother, his mother's son, and said, Is this your youngest brother, of whom ye spake unto me? And he said, Elôhîm be gracious unto thee, my son.

30 And Yôsêph made haste, for his bowels did yearn upon

his brother: and he sought where to weep; and he entered into his chamber, and wept there.

31 And he washed his face, and came out; and he refrained himself, and said, Set on bread.

32 And they set on for him by himself, and for them by themselves, and for the Miçry, which did eat with him, by themselves: because the Miçry might not eat bread with the 'Ĕbrîm; for that is an abomination unto the Miçry.

33 And they sat before him, the firstborn according to his birthright, and the youngest according to his youth: and the men marvelled one with another.

34 And messes were taken unto them from before him: but Binyâmîn's mess was five times so much as any of theirs. And they drank, and drank largely with him.

CHAPTER XLIV.

1 And he commanded the steward of his house, saying, Fill the men's sacks with food, as much as they can carry, and put every man's money in his sack's mouth.

2 And put my cup, the silver cup, in the sack's mouth of the youngest, and his corn money. And he did according to the word that Yôsêph had spoken.

3 As soon as the morning was light, the men were sent away, they and their asses.

4 And when they were gone out of the city, and were not yet far off, Yôsêph said unto his steward, Up, follow after the men; and when thou dost overtake them, say unto them, Wherefore have ye rewarded evil for good?

5 Is not this it in which my lord drinketh, and whereby he indeed divineth [1]? ye have done evil in so doing.

---

[1] Οιωνισμῷ οιωνιζεται, divines augury.—LXX.

6 And he overtook them, and he spake unto them these words.

7 And they said unto him, Wherefore speaketh my lord such words as these? far be it from thy servants to do such a thing.

8 Behold, the money which we found in our sacks' mouths, we brought again unto thee out of the land of Kenâ'an: how then should we steal out of thy lord's house silver or gold?

9 With whomsoever of thy servants it be found, let him die, and we also will be my lord's bondmen.

10 And he said, Now also let it be according unto your words: he with whom it is found shall be my bondman; and ye shall be blameless.

11 Then they hasted, and took down every man his sack to the ground, and opened every man his sack.

12 And he searched, and began at the eldest, and left at the youngest: and the cup was found in Binyâmîn's sack.

13 Then they rent their clothes, and laded every man his ass, and returned to the city.

14 And Yehûdâh and his brethren came to Yôsêph's house; and he was yet there: and they fell before him on the ground.

15 And Yôsêph said unto them, What deed is this that ye have done? Know ye not that such a man as I can indeed divine?

16 And Yehûdâh said, What shall we say unto my lord? what shall we speak? or how shall we clear ourselves? God hath found out the iniquity of thy servants: behold, we are my lord's bondmen, both we, and he also in whose hand the cup is found.

17 And he said, Far be it from me that I should do so: the man in whose hand the cup is found, he shall be my bondman; but as for you, get you up in peace unto your father.

18 Then Yehûdâh came near unto him, and said, Oh my lord, let thy servant, I pray thee, speak a word in my lord's ears, and let not thine anger burn against thy servant: for thou are even as Para'ôh.

19 My lord asked his servants, saying, Have ye a father, or a brother?

20 And we said unto my lord, We have a father, an old man, and a child of his old age, a little one [1]; and his brother is dead, and he alone is left of his mother, and his father loveth him.

21 And thou saidst unto thy servants, Bring him down unto me, that I may set mine eyes upon him.

22 And we said unto my lord, The lad cannot leave his father: for if he should leave his father, his father would die.

23 And thou saidst unto thy servants, Except your youngest brother come down with you, ye shall see my face no more.

24 And it came to pass when we came up unto thy servant my father, we told him the words of my lord.

25 And our father said, Go again, buy us a little food.

26 And we said, We cannot go down: if our youngest brother be with us, then will we go down; for we may not see the man's face, except our youngest brother be with us.

27 And thy servant my father said unto us, Ye know that my wife bare me two sons:

28 And the one went out from me, and I said, Surely he is torn in pieces; and I have not seen him since.

29 And if ye take this one also from me, and mischief befall him, ye shall bring down my gray hairs with sorrow to Sheôl.

30 Now therefore, when I come to thy servant my father, and the lad be not with us; seeing that his life is bound up in the lad's life;

31 It shall come to pass, when he seeth that the lad is not with us, that he will die: and thy servants shall bring down the gray hairs of thy servant with sorrow to Sheôl.

32 For thy servant became surety for the lad unto my father, saying, If I bring him not unto thee, then shall I bear the blame to my father for ever.

33 Now therefore, let thy servant, I pray thee, abide instead

---

[1] Binyâmin, however, was more than twenty-two years of age at this time, for he was born before Yôsêph, 'being seventeen years old' (chap. xxxvii. 2), was sold into Egypt, and had ten sons of his own (chap. xlvi. 21).

of the lad as bondman to my lord; and let the lad go up with his brethren.

34 For how shall I go up to my father, and the lad be not with me? lest I see the evil that shall come upon my father.

CHAPTER XLV.

1 Then Yôsêph could not refrain himself before all them that stood by him; and he cried, Cause every man to go out from me. And there stood no man with him, while Yôsêph made himself known unto his brethren.

2 And he wept aloud: and the Egyptians heard, and the house of Para'ôh heard.

3 And Yôsêph said unto his brethren, I am Yôsêph; doth my father yet live [1]? And his brethren could not answer him : for they were troubled at his presence.

4 And Yôsêph said unto his brethren, Come near to me, I pray you. And they came near. And he said, I am Yôsêph your brother, whom ye sold into Miçrâim.

5 And now be not grieved, nor angry with yourselves, that ye sold me hither: for Elôhîm did send me before you to preserve life.

6 For these two years hath the famine been in the land: and there are yet five years, in the which there shall be neither plowing nor harvest.

7 And Elôhîm sent me before you to preserve you a

---

[1] It is evident that the portion taken by the latest editor from some other document than that from which the preceding portion was taken begins here, for Yôsêph had previously ascertained (in the portion taken from the Jehovist, chap. xliii. 27) that his father was alive as soon as he saw his brethren, and before he had ceased to put them to the proof.—L.

remnant in the earth, and to save you alive by a great deliverance.

8 So now it was not you that sent me hither, but Elôhîm; and he hath made me a grand-master of Para'ôh's,[1] and lord over all his house, and ruler over all the land of Miçraîm

9 Haste ye, and go up to my father, and say unto him, Thus saith thy son Yôsêph, Elôhîm hath made me lord of all Miçraîm : come down unto me, tarry not :

10 And thou shalt dwell in the land of Gôshen,[2] and thou shalt be near unto me, thou and thy children, and thy children's children, and thy flocks, and thy herds, and all that thou hast :

11 And there will I nourish thee ; for there are yet five years of famine ; lest thou come to poverty, thou, and thy household, and all that thou hast.

12 And, behold, your eyes see, and the eyes of my brother Binyâmîn, that it is my mouth that speaketh unto you.

13 And ye shall tell my father of all my glory in Miçraîm, and of all that ye have seen ; and ye shall haste and bring down my father hither.

14 And he fell upon his brother Binyâmîn's neck, and wept ; and Binyâmîn wept upon his neck.

15 And he kissed all his brethren, and wept upon them : and after that his brethren talked with him.

16 And the fame thereof was heard in Para'ôh's house, saying. Yôsêph's brethren are come : and it pleased Para'ôh well, and his servants.

[1] The expression 'ab lepara'ôh' is identical with the Egyptian title 'ab en pir-âa,' 'grand-master of the king's house.'—L.
[2] Gesem of Arabia.—LXX. Ebers (*Durch Gosen*, s. 505 *sqq.*) thinks the name corresponds to Keshem, a province in Lower Egypt.

17 And Para'òh said unto Yôsêph, Say unto thy brethren, This do ye; lade your beasts, and go, get you unto the land of Kenâ'an;

18 And take your father and your households, and come unto me; and I will give you the good of the land of Miçráim, and ye shall eat the fat of the land.

19 Now thou art commanded, this do ye; take you chariots out of the land of Miçráim for your little ones, and for your wives, and bring your father, and come.

20 Also regard not your stuff; for the good of all the land of Miçráim is yours.

21 And the sons of Yisráêl did so: and Yôsêph gave them chariots, according to the commandment of Para'òh, and gave them provision for the way.

22 To all of them he gave each man changes of raiment; but to Binyámin he gave three hundred pieces of silver,[1] and five changes of raiment.

23 And to his father he sent after this manner; ten asses laden with the good things of Miçráim, and ten she-asses laden with corn and bread and victual for his father by the way.

24 So he sent his brethren away, and they departed; and he said unto them, See that ye fall not out by the way.

25 And they went up out of Miçráim, and came into the land of Kenâ'an unto Ya'aqôb their father.

26 And they told him, saying, Yôsêph is yet alive, and he is ruler over all the land of Miçráim. And his heart fainted, for he believed them not.

27 And they told him all the words of Yôsêph, which he had said unto them: and when he saw the chariots which Yôsêph had sent to carry him, the spirit of Ya'aqôb their father revived:

28 And Yisráêl said, It is enough; Yôsêph my son is yet alive: I will go and see him before I die.

---

[1] LXX, 'three hundred pieces of gold.'

CHAPTER XLVI.

1 And Yisrâêl took his journey with all that he had, and came to Beêr-Shâb'a, and sacrificed victims there to the God of his father Yiçe'hâq.

2 And Elôhîm spake unto Yisrâêl in the visions of the night, and said, Ya'aqôb, Ya'aqôb. And he said, Here am I.

3 And he said, I am God, the God of thy father: fear not to go down into Miçrâîm; for I will there make of thee a great nation:

4 I will go down with thee into Miçrâîm; and I will also surely bring thee up again: and Yôsêph shall put his hand upon thine eyes.

5 And Ya'aqôb rose up from Beêr-Shâb'a: and the sons of Yisrâêl carried Ya'aqôb their father, and their little ones, and their wives, in the chariots which Para'ôh had sent to carry him.

6 And they took their cattle, and their goods, which they had gotten in the land of Kenâ'an, and came into Miçrâîm, Ya'aqôb and all his seed with him:

7 His sons, and his sons' sons with him, his daughters, and his sons' daughters, and all his seed brought he with him into Miçrâîm.

8 And these are the names of the children of Yisrâêl, which came into Miçrâîm, Ya'aqôb and his sons: Reûbên, Ya'aqôb's firstborn.

9 And the sons of Reûbên; 'Hanôch, and Phallû, and 'Heçrôn, and Karmy.

10 And the sons of Shime'ôn; Yemûêl, and Yâmin, and Ohad, and Yâchîn, and Ço'har, and Shâ'ûl, the son of the Kena'anîth.

11 And the sons of Lêvy ; Gêrshôn, and Qehâth, and Merâry.

12 And the sons of Yehûdâh ; 'Êr, and Onân, and Shêlâh, and Pereç, and Zâra'h ; but 'Êr and Onân died in the land of Kenâ'an. And the sons of Pereç were 'Heçrôn and 'Hâmûl.

13 And the sons of Yissâchâr ; Tôla', and Puvâh, and Yôb, and Shimrôn.

14 And the sons of Zebulûn ; Sered, and Êlôn, and Ya'hleêl.

15 These are the sons of Lêâh, which she bare unto Ya'aqôb in Paddan-Arâm, with his daughter Dinâh : his sons and his daughters were thirty and three persons in all.[1]

16 And the sons of Gâd ; Çiphyôn, and 'Haggy, Shûny, and Eçbôn, 'Êry, and Arôdy, and Arêly.

17 And the sons of Âshêr ; Yimnâh, and Yishvâh, and Yishvy, and Bery'âh, and Sera'h their sister : and the sons of Bery'âh ; 'Heber, and Malkiêl.

18 These are the sons of Zilpâh, which Lâbân gave to Lêâh his daughter, and these she bare unto Ya'aqôb, even seventeen persons.

19 The sons of Râ'hêl Ya'aqôb's wife ; Yôsêph, and Binyâmîn.

20 And unto Yôsêph in the land of Miçrâim were born Menassheh and Ephrâim, which Asenath the daughter of Pôti-Phêrâ priest of On bare unto him.

21 And the sons of Binyâmîn ; Belâ', and Beker, and Ashbêl, Gêrâ, and Na'amân, Ê'hy, and Rôsh, Muppim, and 'Huppim, and Ârd.

[1] There are only thirty-two names in the text. To make up thirty-three Ya'aqôb himself would have to be counted.—L.

22 These are the sons of Râ'hêl, which were born to Ya'aqôb: in all fourteen persons.

23 And the sons of Dân; 'Hushîm.

24 And the sons of Naphtâly; Ya'hçeêl, and Gûny, and Yeçer, and Shillêm.

25 These are the sons of Bilhâh, which Lâbân gave unto Râ'hêl his daughter, and these she bare unto Ya'aqôb: in all seven persons.

26 All the persons that came with Ya'aqôb into Miçrâim, which came out of his loins, besides Ya'aqôb's sons' wives, were threescore and six in number.[1]

27 And the sons of Yôsêph, which were born to him in Miçrâim, were two: all the persons of the house of Ya'aqôb, which came into Miçrâim were threescore and ten.[2]

28 And he sent Yehûdâh before him unto Yôsêph to show the way before him unto Gôshen[3]; and they came into the land of Gôshen.

29 And Yôsêph made ready his chariot, and went up to meet Yisrâêl his father, to Gôshen; and he presented himself unto him, and fell on his neck, and wept on his neck a good while.

30 And Yisrâêl said unto Yôsêph, Now let me die, since I have seen thy face, that thou art yet alive.

31 And Yôsêph said unto his brethren, and unto his father's house, I will go up, and tell Para'òh, and will say unto him, My brethren and my father's house, which were in the land of Kenâ'an, are come unto me;

32 And the men are shepherds, for they have been keepers of cattle: and they have brought their flocks, and their herds, and all that they have.

---

[1] This number is obtained by omitting Yôsêph and his two sons born in Egypt from the descendants of Ya'aqôb.—L.

[2] Including Ya'aqôb himself, and also Yôsêph and his two sons.—L.

[3] 'To the City of Heroes, in the land of Ramesses.'—LXX.

33 And it shall come to pass, when Para'ôh shall call you, and shall say, What is your occupation ?
34 That ye shall say, Thy servants have been keepers of cattle from our youth even until now, both we, and our fathers: that ye may dwell in the land of Gôshen; for every shepherd is an abomination unto the Egyptians.

CHAPTER XLVII.

1 Then Yôsêph went in and told Para'ôh, and said, My father and my brethren, and their flocks, and their herds, and all that they have, are come out of the land of Kenâ'an; and, behold, they are in the land of Gôshen.
2 And from among his brethren he took five men, and presented them unto Para'ôh.
3 And Para'ôh said unto his brethren, What is your occupation ? And they said unto Para'ôh, Thy servants are shepherds, both we, and our fathers.
4 And they said unto Para'ôh, To sojourn in the land are we come; for there is no pasture for thy servants' flocks; for the famine is sore in the land of Kenâ'an; now, therefore, we pray thee, let thy servants dwell in the land of Gôshen.
5 And Para'ôh spake unto Yôsêph, saying, Thy father and thy brethren are come unto thee:
6 The land of Miçrâîm is before thee; in the best of the land make thy father and thy brethren to dwell; in the land of Gôshen let them dwell; and if thou knowest any able men among them, then make them rulers over my cattle.
7 And Yôsêph brought in Ya'aqôb his father, and set him before Para'ôh: and Ya'aqôb blessed Para'ôh.
8 And Para'ôh said unto Ya'aqôb, How many are the days of the years of thy life ?

9 And Ya'aqôb said unto Para'ôh, The days of the years of my pilgrimage are an hundred and thirty years: few and evil have been the days of the years of my life, and they have not attained unto the days of the years of the life of my fathers in the days of their pilgrimage.

10 And Ya'aqôb blessed Para'ôh, and went out from the presence of Para'ôh.

11 And Yôsêph placed his father and his brethren, and gave them a possession in the land of Miçràîm, *in the best of the land,* in the land of Ra'mesês, as Para'ôh had commanded.

12 And Yôsêph nourished his father, and his brethren, and all his father's household, with bread, according to the number of their little ones.

13.[1] *And there was no bread in all the land; for the famine was very sore, so that the land of Miçràîm and the land of Kenâ'an fainted by reason of the famine.*

14 *And Yôsêph gathered up all the money that was found in the land of Miçràîm, and in the land of Kenâ'an, for the corn which they bought: and Yôsêph brought the money into Para'ôh's house.*

15 *And when the money was all spent in the land of Miçràîm, and in the land of Kenâ'an, all the Egyptians came unto Yôsêph, and said, Give us bread: for why should we die in thy presence? for our money faileth.*

16 *And Yôsêph said, Give your cattle; and I will give you for your cattle, if money fail.*

17 *And they brought their cattle unto Yôsêph: and Yôsêph gave them bread in exchange for the horses, and for the cattle of*

---

[1] I can only think of verses 13–26 as an addition by the latest editor, taken from some document or compilation which gave a specially economic importance to the transactions of Yôsêph in corn during the famine, and which made this the starting-point of a social revolution in Egypt. It certainly does not proceed from the same source as the notices we had on the same subject in chap. xii. 33–36, 47–49, and 53–57.—L.

*the flocks, and for the cattle of the herds, and for the asses: and
he fed them with bread in exchange for all their cattle for that
year.*

*18 And when that year was ended, they came unto him the
second year, and said unto him, We will not hide from my lord,
how that our money is all spent; and the herds of cattle are my
lord's; there is nought left in the sight of my lord, but our bodies,
and our lands:*

*19 Wherefore should we die before thine eyes, both we and our
land? buy us and our land for bread, and we and our land will
be servants unto Para'ôh: and give us seed, that we may live and
not die, and that the land be not desolate.*

*20 So Yôsêph bought all the land of Miçrâim for Para'ôh; for
the Egyptians sold every man his field, because the famine was
sore upon them: and the land became Para'ôh's.*

*21 And as for the people, he removed them to the cities
from one end of the border of Miçrâim even unto the other end
thereof.*

*22 Only the land of the priests bought he not: for the priests
had a portion from Para'ôh, and did eat their portion which
Para'ôh gave them; wherefore they sold not their land.*

*23 Then Yôsêph said unto the people, Behold, I have bought
you this day and your land for Para'ôh: lo, here is seed for you,
and ye shall sow the land.*

*24 And it shall come to pass at the ingatherings, that ye shall
give a fifth unto Para'ôh, and four parts shall be your own, for
seed of the field, and for your food, and for them of your households, and for food for your little ones.*

*25 And they said, Thou hast saved our lives: let us find grace
in the sight of my lord, and we will be Para'ôh's servants.*

*26 And Yôsêph made it a statute concerning the land of
Miçrâim unto this day, that Para'ôh should have the fifth; only
the land of the priests alone became not Para'ôh's.*

27 And Yisrâêl dwelt in Miçrâim, in the land of Gôshen;
and they gat them possessions therein, and were fruitful, and
multiplied exceedingly.

28 And Ya'aqôb lived in the land of Miçrâim seven-

teen years: so the days of Ya'aqôb, the days of his life, were an hundred forty and seven years.

29 And the time drew near that Yisrâêl must die: and he called his son Yôsêph, and said unto him, If now I have found grace in thy sight, put, I pray thee, thy hand under my thigh, and deal kindly and truly with me; bury me not, I pray thee, in Miçrâîm:

30 But when I sleep with my fathers, thou shalt carry me out of Miçrâîm, and bury me in their buryingplace. And he said, I will do as thou hast said.

31 And he said, Swear unto me: and he sware unto him. And Yisrâêl bowed himself upon the bed's head.[1]

CHAPTER XLVIII.

1 And it came to pass after these things, that one said to Yôsêph, Behold, thy father is sick: and he took with him his two sons, Menassheh and Ephrâîm.

2 And one told Ya'aqôb, and said, Behold thy son Yôsêph cometh unto thee: *and Yisrâêl strengthened himself, and sat upon the bed.*

3 And Ya'aqôb said unto Yôsêph, Êl-Shadday (God Almighty) appeared unto me at Lûz, in the land of Kenâ'an, and blessed me,

4 And said unto me, Behold, I will make thee fruitful, and multiply thee, and I will make of thee a company of peoples; and will give this land to thy seed after thee for an everlasting possession.

5 And now thy two sons, which were born unto thee

---
[1] 'Leaning on the top of his staff.'—LXX.

in the land of Miçrâîm before I came unto thee in Miçrâîm, are mine; Ephrâîm and Menassheh, even as Reûbên and Shime'ôn shall be mine.

6 And thy issue, which thou hast begotten after them, shall be thine; they shall be called after the name of their brethren in their inheritance.

7 And as for me, when I came from Paddân, Râ'hêl died by me in the land of Kenâ'an in the way, when there was still some way to come unto Ephrâth[1]: and I buried her there in the way to Ephrâth (*the same is Bêth-Le'hem.*)

8 And Yisrâêl beheld Yôsêph's sons, and said, Who are these?

9 And Yôsêph said unto his father, They are my sons, whom Elôhîm hath given me here. And he said, Bring them, I pray thee, unto me, and I will bless them.

10 Now the eyes of Yisrâêl were dim for age, so that he could not see. And he brought them near unto him; and he kissed them, and embraced them.

11 And Yisrâêl said unto Yôsêph, I had not thought to see thy face; and, lo, Elôhîm hath let me see thy seed also.

12 And Yôsêph brought them out from between his knees; and he bowed himself with his face to the earth.

13 And Yôsêph took them both, Ephrâîm in his right hand, and Menassheh in his left hand toward Yisrâêl's right hand, and brought them near unto him.

14 And Yisrâêl stretched out his right hand, and laid it upon Ephrâîm's head, who was the younger, and his left hand upon Menassheh's head, crossing his hands wittingly; for Manassheh was the firstborn.

15 And he blessed Yôsêph, and said, The God before whom my fathers Abrâhâm and Yiçe'hâq did walk, the God which hath fed me all my life long unto this day,

---

[1] 'As I drew nigh to the horse-course of Chabratha in the land of Chanaan, so as to come to Ephratha.'—LXX.

16 The angel which hath redeemed me from all evil, bless the lads; and let my name be named on them, and the name of my fathers Abrâhâm and Yiçc'hâq; and let them grow into a multitude in the midst of the earth.

17 And when Yôsêph saw that his father laid his right hand upon the head of Ephrâîm, it displeased him; and he held up his father's hand, to remove it from Ephrâîm's head unto Menassheh's head.

18 And Yôsêph said unto his father, Not so, my father: for this is the firstborn; put thy right hand upon his head.

19 And his father refused, and said, I know it, my son, I know it: he also shall become a people, and he also shall be great: howbeit his younger brother shall be greater than he, and his seed shall become a multitude of nations.

20 And he blessed them that day, saying, By thee shall Yisrâêl bless, saying, Elôhîm make thee as Ephrâîm and as Menassheh: and he set Ephrâîm before Menassheh.

21 And Yisrâêl said unto Yôsêph, Behold, I die: but Elôhîm shall be with you, and bring you again unto the land of your fathers.

22 Moreover I have given to thee one portion[1] above thy brethren, which I took out of the hand of the 'Amôry with my sword and with my bow.

CHAPTER XLIX.

1 And Ya'aqôb called unto him his sons, and said, Gather yourselves together, that I may tell you that which shall befall you in the latter days.

2 Assemble yourselves together, and hear, ye sons of Ya'aqôb;

[1] *Shechem a'had,* an expression which seems to be a play upon the name of the town of Shechem, the capture and sack of which were narrated in chap. xxxiv.—L.

And hearken unto Yisrâêl your father.
3 Reûbên, thou art my firstborn,
My might, and the first-fruits of my strength ;
The excellency of dignity, and the excellency of power.[1]
4 Impetuous as water, thou shalt not have the excellency ;
Because thou wentest up to thy father's bed :
Then defiledst thou it : he went up to my couch.
5 Shime'ôn and Lêvy are brethren ;
Weapons of violence are their compacts.[2]
6 O my soul, come not thou into their secret councils ;
Unto their assembly, my honour, be not thou united ;
For in their anger they slew men,
And in their selfwill they houghed oxen.
7 Cursed be their anger, for it was fierce ;
And their wrath, for it was cruel :
I will divide them in Ya'aqôb,
And scatter them in Yisrâêl.
8 Yehûdâh, thee shall thy brethren praise :
Thy hand shall be on the neck of thine enemies ;
Thy father's sons shall bow down before thee.
9 Yehûdâh is a lion's whelp ;
From the prey, my son, thou art gone up :
He stooped down, he crouched as a lion,
And as a lioness ; who shall rouse him up ?
10 The sceptre shall not depart from Yehûdah,
Nor the ruler's staff from between his feet,
Until he come to Shilôh.[3]
And unto him shall the obedience of the peoples be.
11 Binding his foal unto the vine,
And his ass's colt unto the choice vine ;
He hath washed his garments in wine,
And his vesture in the blood of grapes.

[1] 'Hard to be endured, hard and self-willed.'—LXX.
[2] 'Symeon and Levi, brethren, accomplished the injustice of their cutting off.'—LXX.
[3] This is the meaning of the text according to the grammatical construction. The interpretation of this prophecy, however, is still the *crux* of commentators.—L.

12 His eyes shall be red with wine,
   And his teeth white with milk.
13 Zebulûn shall dwell at the haven of the sea:
   And he shall be for an haven of ships;
   And his border shall be by Çidôn.
14 Yissâchâr is a strong ass,
   Couching down between the sheepfolds:
15 And he saw a resting place that it was good,
   And the land that it was pleasant;
   And he bowed his shoulder to bear,
   And became a servant under taskwork.
16 Dân shall judge his people
   As one of the tribes of Yisrâêl.
17 Dân shall be a serpent in the way,
   An horned snake[1] in the path,
   That biteth the horse's heels,
   So that his rider falleth backward.
18 I have waited for thy salvation, O Yahveh.
19 Gâd, a troop shall press upon him,
   But he shall press upon their heel.
20 Âshêr, his bread shall be fat;
   And he shall yield royal dainties.[2]
21 Naphtâly is a hind let loose:
   He giveth goodly words.[3]
22 Yôsêph is a fruitful bough,
   A fruitful bough by a fountain;
   His branches run over the wall.[4]
23 The archers have sorely grieved him,
   And shot at him, and persecuted him:
24 But his bow abode in strength,
   And the arms of his hands were made strong,

---

[1] *Vipera Cerastes*, the horned sand-snake of Egypt. They bury themselves in the sand. Pliny (*Hist. Nat.* lib. viii. c. 23) says of them that by moving their horns they attract birds to them.

[2] 'Yield dainties to princes.'—LXX.

[3] 'Nepthalim is a spreading stem, bestowing beauty on its fruit.'—LXX.

[4] 'Joseph is a son increased; my dearly loved son is increased; my youngest son, turn to me.'—LXX.

By the hands of the Mighty One of Ya'aqôb,
(From thence is the shepherd, the stone of Yisrâêl,)
25 Even by the God of thy father, who shall help thee,
And by the Almighty, who shall bless thee.
With blessings of heaven above,
Blessings of the deep that coucheth beneath,
Blessings of the breasts, and of the womb.
26 The blessings of thy father have prevailed
Above the blessings of my progenitors
Unto the utmost bound of the everlasting hills :[1]
They shall be on the head of Yôsêph
And on the crown of the head of him that is prince among his brethren.
27 Binyâmîn is a wolf that ravineth :
In the morning he shall devour the prey,
And at even he shall divide the spoil.

28 And these are the twelve tribes of Yisrâêl :[2] and this it is that their father spake unto them and blessed them; every one according to his blessing he blessed them.

29 And he charged them, and said unto them, I am to be gathered to my people : bury me with my fathers in the cave that is in the field of 'Ephrôn the 'Hitty.

30 In the cave that is in the field of Machpêlâh, which is before Mamrê, in the land of Kenâ'an, which Abrâhâm bought with the field from 'Ephrôn the 'Hitty, for a possession of a buryingplace :

31 There they buried Abrâhâm and Sârâh his wife : there they buried Yiçe'haq and Ribqâh his wife; and there I buried Lêâh :

32 The field and the cave that is therein, which was purchased from the Benê-'Hêth.

---

[1] 'The blessings of thy father and thy mother—it has prevailed above the blessing of the lasting mountains, and beyond the blessings of the everlasting hills.'—LXX.
[2] Only eleven tribes are spoken of. Menassheh is omitted altogether.

33 And when Ya'aqôb made an end of charging his sons, he gathered up his feet into the bed, and yielded up the ghost, and was gathered unto his people.

CHAPTER L.

1 And Yôsêph fell upon his father's face, and wept upon him, and kissed him.

2 And Yôsêph commanded his slaves the physicians to embalm his father: and the physicians embalmed Yisrâêl.

3 And forty days were fulfilled for him; for so are fulfilled the days of embalming: and the Egyptians wept for him threescore and ten days.

4 And when the days of weeping for him were past, Yôsêph spake unto the house of Para'ôh, saying, If now I have found grace in your eyes, speak, I pray you, in the ears of Para'ôh, saying,

5 My father made me swear, saying, Lo, I die: in my grave which I have digged for me in the land of Kena'an, there shalt thou bury me. Now therefore let me go up, I pray thee, and bury my father, and I will come again.

6 And Para'ôh said, Go up, and bury thy father, according as he made thee swear.

7 And Yôsêph went up to bury his father: and with him went up all the servants of Para'ôh, the elders of his house, and all the elders of the land of Miçraîm,

8 And all the house of Yôsêph, and his brethren, and his father's house: only their little ones, and their flocks, and their herds, they left in the land of Gôshen.

9 And there went up with him both chariots and horsemen: and it was a very great company.

10 And they came to Gôren-haâtâd,[1] which is beyond the

[1] The threshing-floor of thistles; a place the exact site of which is very doubtful.—L.

Yardên,[1] and there they lamented with a very great and sore lamentation: and he made a mourning for his father seven days.

11 And when the inhabitants of the land, the Kena'any, saw the mourning at Gôren-hââtâd they said, This is a grievous mourning for Miçrâim: wherefore the name of it was called Âbêl-Miçrâim,[2] which is beyond the Yardên.

12 And his sons did unto him according as he commanded them:

13 For his sons carried him into the land of Kenâ'an, and buried him in the cave of Machpêlâh, which Abrâhâm brought with the field, for a possession of a buryingplace, of 'Ephrôn the 'Hitty, before Mamrê.

14 And Yôsêph returned into Miçrâim, he, and his brethren, and all that went up with him to bury his father, after he had buried his father.

15 And when Yôsêph's brethren saw that their father was dead, they said, It may be that Yôsêph will hate us, and will fully requite us all the evil which we did unto him.

16 And they sent a message unto Yôsêph, saying, Thy father did command before he died, saying,

17 So shall ye say unto Yôsêph, Forgive, I pray thee now, the transgression of thy brethren, and their sin, for that they did unto thee evil: and now, we pray thee, forgive the transgression of the servants of the God of thy father. And Yôsêph wept when they spake unto him.

18 And his brethren also went and fell down before his face; and they said, Behold, we be thy slaves.

19 And Yôsêph said unto them, Fear not, for am I in the place of Elôhîm?

20 And as for you, ye meant evil against me; but Elôhîm meant it for good, to bring to pass, as it is this day, to save much people alive.

[1] Hebrón being between Egypt and the Yardên, it is impossible to understand why they should have carried the body beyond the Yardên. The account of the Elohist is perfectly intelligible.

[2] The mourning of Egypt.

21 Now therefore fear ye not: I will nourish you, and your little ones. And he comforted them, and spake to their heart.

22 And Yôsêph dwelt in Miçrâim, he and his father's house: and Yôsêph lived an hundred and ten years.

23 And Yôsêph saw Ephrâîm's children of the third generation: the children also of Mâchîr the son of Menassheh were born upon Yôsêph's knees.

24 And Yôsêph said unto his brethren, I die: but Elôhîm will surely visit you, and bring you up out of this land unto the land which he sware to Abrâhâm, to Yiçe'hâq, and to Ya'aqôb.

25 And Yôsêph took an oath of the children of Yisrâêl, saying, Elôhîm will surely visit you, and ye shall carry up my bones from hence.

26 So Yôsêph died, being an hundred and ten years old: and they embalmed him, and he was put into a coffin in Miçrâim.

II.
THE BOOK OF ORIGINS
OR
JEHOVISTIC DOCUMENT

I.

THE CREATION OF MAN AND WOMAN.

II. 4 In the day that Yahveh Elôhîm made earth and heaven,

5 No bush of the field was yet in the earth, and no herb of the field had yet sprung up: for Yahveh Elôhîm had not caused it to rain upon the earth, and there was not a man to till the ground:

6 But there went up a mist from the earth, and watered the whole face of the ground.

7 And Yahveh Elôhîm formed man of the dust of the ground, and breathed into his nostrils the breath of life; and man became a living soul.

8 And Yahveh Elôhîm planted a garden eastward in Êden; and there he put the man whom he had formed.

9 And out of the ground made Yahveh Elôhîm to grow every tree that is pleasant to the sight, and good for food; the tree of life also in the midst of the garden, and the tree of the knowledge of good and evil.

10 And a river went out of Êden to water the garden; and from thence it was parted, and became four heads.

11 The name of the first is Pishôn: that is it which compasseth the whole land of 'Havilâh, where there is gold;

12 And the gold of that land is good: there is the bedóla'h and the shôham stone.

13 And the name of the second river is Gi'hôn: the same is it that compasseth the whole land of Kûsh.

14 And the name of the third river is 'Hiddeqel: that is it which goeth in front of Asshûr. And the fourth river is the P'hráth.

15 And Yahveh Elôhim took the man, and put him into the garden of Êden to dress it and to keep it.

16 And Yahveh Elôhim commanded the man, saying, Of every tree of the garden thou mayest freely eat:

17 But of the tree of the knowledge of good and evil, thou shalt not eat of it: for in the day that thou eatest thereof, thou shalt surely die.

18 And Yahveh Elôhim said, It is not good that the man should be alone; I will make him an help answering to him.

19 And out of the ground Yahveh Elôhim formed every beast of the field and every fowl of the air; and brought them unto the man to see what he would call them: and whatsoever the man called every living creature, that was the name thereof.

20 And the man gave names to all cattle, and to the fowl of the air, and to every beast of the field; but for man there was not found an help meet for him.

21 And Yahveh Elôhim caused a deep sleep to fall upon the man, and he slept; and he took one of his ribs, and closed up the flesh instead thereof.

22 And the rib which Yahveh Elôhim had taken from the man, made he a woman, and brought her unto the man.

23 And the man said, This is now bone of my bones, and flesh of my flesh: she shall be called woman (*isshâh*), because she was taken out of man (*ish*).

24 Therefore shall a man leave his father and his mother, and shall cleave unto his wife, and they shall be one flesh.

25 And they were both naked, the man and his wife, and were not ashamed.

II.

THE FIRST SIN.

III. 1 Now the serpent was more subtil than any beast of the field which Yahveh Elôhîm had made. And he said unto the woman, Yea, hath Elôhîm said, Ye shall not eat of any tree of the garden?

2 And the woman said unto the serpent, Of the fruit of the trees of the garden we may eat:

3 But of the fruit of the tree which is in the midst of the garden, Elôhîm hath said, Ye shall not eat of it, neither shall ye touch it, lest ye die.

4 And the serpent said unto the woman, Ye shall not surely die:

5 For Elôhîm doth know that in the day ye eat thereof, then your eyes shall be opened and ye shall be as Elôhîm, knowing good and evil.

6 And when the woman saw that the tree was good for food, and that it was a delight to the eyes, and

that the tree was to be desired to make one wise, she took of the fruit thereof, and did eat; and she gave also unto her husband with her, and he did eat :

7 And the eyes of both of them were opened, and they knew that they were naked; and they sewed fig leaves together, and made themselves girdles.

8 And they heard the voice of Yahveh Elôhîm walking in the garden in the breeze of the evening: and the man and his wife hid themselves from the presence of Yahveh Elôhîm amongst the trees of the garden.

9 And Yahveh Elôhîm called unto the man, and said unto him, Where art thou?

10 And he said, I heard thy voice in the garden, and I was afraid, because I was naked; and I hid myself.

11 And he said, Who told thee that thou wast naked? Hast thou eaten of the tree, whereof I commanded thee that thou shouldest not eat?

12 And the man said, The woman whom thou gavest to be with me, she gave me of the tree, and I did eat.

13 And Yahveh Elôhîm said unto the woman, What is this that thou hast done? And the woman said, The serpent beguiled me, and I did eat.

14 And Yahveh Elôhîm said unto the serpent, Because thou hast done this, cursed art thou from among all cattle, and from among every beast of the field: upon thy belly shalt thou go, and dust shalt thou eat all the days of thy life.

15 And I will put enmity between thee and the woman, and between thy seed and her seed; it shall bruise thy head, and thou shalt bruise his heel.

16 Unto the woman he said, I will greatly multiply thy sorrow and thy conception; in sorrow thou shalt bring forth children; and thy desire shall be to thy husband, and he shall rule over thee.

17 And unto the man he said, Because thou hast hearkened unto the voice of thy wife, and hast eaten of the tree, of which I commanded thee, saying, Thou shalt not eat of it: cursed is the ground for thy sake; in toil shalt thou eat of it all the days of thy life.

18 Thorns also and thistles shall it bring forth to thee; and thou shalt eat the herb of the field;

19 In the sweat of thy face shalt thou eat bread till thou return unto the ground; for out of it wast thou taken: for dust thou art, and unto dust shalt thou return.

20 And the man called his wife's name 'Havvâh; because she was the mother of all living (*hây*).

21 And Yahveh Elôhîm made for the man and for his wife tunics of skins, and clothed them.

22 And Yahveh Elôhîm said, Behold, the man is become as one of us, to know good and evil: and now, lest he put forth his hand, and take also of the tree of life, and eat, and live for ever:

23 Therefore Yahveh Elôhîm sent him forth from the garden of Êden to till the ground from whence he was taken.

24 So he drove out the man, and he placed at the east of the garden of Êden the Kerubîm, and the flame of a sword which turned every way, to keep the way of the tree of life.

III.

QAÎN AND HÂBEL.

IV. 1 And the man knew 'Havvâh his wife; and she conceived, and bare Qaîn, and said, I have gotten (*qânîthy*) a man with the help of Yahveh.

2 And again she bare his brother Hâbel. And Hâbel was a keeper of sheep, but Qaîn was a tiller of the ground.

3 And in process of time it came to pass, that Qaîn brought of the fruit of the ground an offering unto Yahveh.

4 And Hâbel, he also brought of the firstlings of his flock, and of the fat thereof. And Yahveh had respect unto Hâbel, and to his offering:

5 But unto Qaîn and to his offering he had not respect. And Qaîn was very wroth, and his countenance fell.

6 And Yahveh said unto Qaîn, Why art thou wroth? and why is thy countenance fallen?

7 If thou doest well, shall it not be lifted up? and if thou doest not well, sin coucheth at the door; and unto thee shall be his desire, and thou shalt rule over him.

8 And Qaîn said unto Hâbel his brother, Let us go out into the plain. And it came to pass, when they were in the plain, that Qaîn rose up against Hâbel his brother, and slew him.

9 And Yahveh said unto Qaîn, Where is Hâbel thy

brother? And he said, I know not: am I my brother's keeper?

10 And [Yahveh] said, What hast thou done? the voice of thy brother's blood crieth unto me from the ground.

11 And now, cursed art thou from the ground, which hath opened her mouth to receive thy brother's blood from thy hand;

12 When thou tillest the ground, it shall not henceforth yield unto thee her strength; a fugitive and a wanderer shalt thou be in the earth.

13 And Qaîn said unto Yahveh, Mine iniquity is greater than I can bear.

14 Behold, thou hast driven me out this day from the face of the ground; and from thy face shall I be hid; and I shall be a fugitive and a wanderer in the earth; and it shall come to pass, that whosoever findeth me shall slay me.

15 And Yahveh said unto him, Therefore, whosoever slayeth Qaîn, vengeance shall be taken on him sevenfold. And Yahveh appointed a sign for Qaîn, lest any finding him should smite him.

16 And Qaîn went out from the presence of Yahveh, and dwelt in the land of Nôd (exile) on the east of Êden.

IV.

THE TWO LINES OF ÂDÂM'S POSTERITY.

IV. 17 And Qaîn knew his wife; and she conceived, and bare 'Hanôch: and he builded a city, and called the name of the city, after the name of his son, 'Hanôch.

18 And unto 'Hanôch was born Yirâd: and Yirâd begat Me'hûyâêl: and Me'hûyâêl begat Methûshâêl: and Methûshâêl begat Lâmech.

19 And Lâmech took unto him two wives: the name of the one was 'Adâh, and the name of the other Çillâh.

20 And 'Adâh bare Yâbâl: he was the father of such as dwell in tents and have cattle.

21 And his brother's name was Yûbâl; he was the father of all such as handle the kinnôr and the 'ûgâr.

22 And Çillâh, she also bare Tûbal-qain, the forger of every cutting instrument of brass and iron: and the sister of Tûbal-qain was Na'amâh.

23 And Lâmech said unto his wives:
    'Adâh and Çillah, hear my voice;
    Ye wives of Lâmech, hearken unto my speech:
    For I have slain a man to my wounding,
    And a young man to my hurt.
24 If Qaîn shall be avenged sevenfold,
    Truly Lâmech seventy and sevenfold.

25 And Âdâm knew his wife again; and she bare a son, and called his name Shêth: For, said she, Elôhim

hath appointed me (*shâth-li*) another seed instead of Hâbel; for Qaîn slew him.

26 And to Shêth, to him also there was born a son; and he called his name Enôsh: then began men to call upon the name of Yahveh.

. . . .

V. 29 [And Lâmech begat a son], and he called his name Nôa'h, saying, This same shall comfort us (*yena'hamênû*) for our work and for the toil of our hands, which cometh from the ground which Yahveh hath cursed.

V.

THE SONS OF GOD AND THE DAUGHTERS OF MEN.

VI. 1 And it came to pass, when men began to multiply on the face of the ground, and daughters were born unto them,

2 That the sons of God saw the daughters of men that they were fair; and they took them wives of all that they chose.

3 And Yahveh said, My spirit shall not rule in man for ever, for that he also is flesh: therefore shall his days be an hundred and twenty years.

4 The giants were in the earth in those days, and also after that, when the sons of God came in unto the daughters of men, and they bare children to them: the same were the mighty men which were of old, the men of renown.

VI.

THE DELUGE.

VI. 5 And Yahveh saw that the wickedness of man was great in the earth, and that every imagination of the thoughts of his heart was only evil continually.

6 And it repented Yahveh that he had made man on the earth, and it grieved him at his heart.

7 And Yahveh said, I will destroy man whom I have created from the face of the ground; both man, and beast, and creeping thing, and fowl of the air; for it repenteth me that I have made them.

8 But Nôa'h found grace in the eyes of Yahveh.

. . . . .

VII. 1 And Yahveh said unto Nôa'h, Come thou and all thy house into the ark; for thee have I seen righteous before me in this generation.

2 Of every clean beast thou shalt take to thee seven and seven, the male and his female; and of the beasts that are not clean two, the male and his female;

3 Of the fowl also of the air which are clean, seven and seven, male and female: and of birds which are not clean, two, male and female: to keep seed alive upon the face of all the earth.

4 For yet seven days, and I will cause it to rain upon the earth forty days and forty nights; and every living thing that I have made will I destroy from off the face of the ground.

5 And Nôa'h did according unto all that Yahveh commanded him.

7 And Nôa'h went in, and his sons, and his wife, and his sons' wives with him, into the ark, because of the waters of the deluge.

8 Of clean beasts, and of beasts that are not clean, and of clean fowls and of fowls that are not clean, and of every thing that creepeth upon the ground,

9 There went in two and two unto Nôa'h into the ark, male and female, as [Yahveh] had commanded Nôa'h.

16 And Yahveh shut him in.[1]

10 And it came to pass, after the seven days, that the waters of the deluge were upon the earth.

12 And the rain was upon the earth forty days and forty nights.

17 And the deluge was forty days upon the earth; and the waters increased, and bare up the ark, and it was lift up above the earth.

23 And every living thing was destroyed which was upon the face of the ground, both man, and cattle, and creeping thing, and fowl of the heaven, and they were destroyed from the earth: and Nôa'h only was left, and they that were with him in the ark.

VIII. 2 And the rain from heaven was restrained;

3 And the waters returned from off the earth continually.

6 And it came to pass at the end of forty days, that Nôa'h opened the window of the ark which he had made:

7 And he sent forth a raven, and it went forth to

---

[1] This sentence, which is placed later in the narrative as the text is at present, is here restored to its place.

and fro, until the waters were dried up from off the earth.

8 [And Nôa'h stayed seven days¹] and he sent forth a dove from him to see if the waters were abated from off the face of the ground;

9 But the dove found no rest for the sole of her foot, and she returned unto him to the ark, for the waters were on the face of the whole earth; and he put forth his hand, and took her, and brought her in unto him into the ark.

10 And he stayed yet other seven days; and again he sent forth the dove out of the ark;

11 And the dove came in to him at eventide; and lo, in her mouth a fresh olive leaf pluckt off: so Nôa'h knew that the waters were abated from off the earth.

12 And he stayed yet other seven days; and sent forth the dove; and she returned not again unto him any more.

13 And Nôa'h removed the covering of the ark, and looked, and, behold, the face of the ground was dried.

20 And Nôa'h builded an altar unto Yahveh; and took of every clean beast, and of every clean fowl, and offered burnt offerings upon the altar.

21 And Yahveh smelled the sweet savour; and Yahveh said in his heart, I will not again curse the ground any more for the sake of the man, for that the imagination of man's heart is evil from his youth; neither will I again smite any more every thing living, as I have done.

¹ This verse shows a space which requires to be filled up in the present state of the text. I have endeavoured to fill it in accordance with the beginning of verses 10 and 12.

22 While the earth remaineth, seedtime and harvest, and cold and heat, and summer and winter, and day and night shall not cease.

VII.

THE CURSE UPON KENÂ'AN.

IX. 18 And the sons of Nôa'h, that went forth from the ark, were Shêm and 'Hâm, and Yâpheth; and 'Hâm is the father of Kenâ'an.

19 These three were the sons of Nôa'h: and of these was the whole earth overspread.

20 And Nôa'h began to be an husbandman, and planted a vineyard:

21 And he drank of the wine, and was drunken; and he was uncovered within his tent.

22 And 'Hâm, the father of Kenâ'an, saw the nakedness of his father, and told his two brethren without.

23 And Shêm and Yâpheth took a garment, and laid it upon both their shoulders, and went backward, and covered the nakedness of their father; and their faces were backward, and they saw not their father's nakedness.

24 And Nôa'h awoke from his wine, and knew what his youngest son had done unto him.

25 And he said,
    Cursed be Kenâ'an;
      A servant of servants shall he be unto his
        brethren!

26 And he said,
   Blessed be Yahveh, the God of Shêm;
   And let Kenâ'an be their servant!
27 Elôhim enlarge Yâpheth,
   And let him dwell in the tents of Shêm;
   And let Kenâ'an be their servant.

VIII.[1]

THE LINEAGE OF THE SONS OF NÔA'H.

. . . . . .

X. 8 And Kùsh begat Nimrôd: he began to be a mighty one in the earth.

9 He was a mighty hunter before Yahveh: wherefore it is said, Like Nimrôd a mighty hunter before Yahveh.

10 And the beginning of his kingdom was Bâbel, and Erech, and Akkad, and Kalneh in the land of Shine'âr.

11 Out of that land went forth Asshûr, and built Nineveh and Rehoboth-Ir, and Kâla'h,

12 And Resen between Nineveh and Kâla'h (the same is the great city).

. . . . . .

25 And unto 'Éber were born two sons: the name of the one was Peleg; for in his days was the earth divided (*niphlegâh*), and his brother's name was Yoqtân.

---

[1] Only two fragments of this section, which have been introduced into the genealogical table of the Elohist by the latest reviser, are left.

IX.

THE TOWER OF BÂBEL.

XI. 1 And the whole earth had the same language and the same words.

2 And it came to pass, as they journeyed east, that they found a plain in the land of Shineʾâr; and they dwelt there.

3 And they said one to another, Go to, let us make brick, and burn them thoroughly. And they had brick for stone, and bitumen had they for mortar.

4 And they said, Go to, let us build us a city, and a tower, whose top may reach unto heaven, and let us make us a name; lest we be scattered abroad upon the face of the whole earth.

5 And Yahveh came down to see the city and the tower, which the children of men builded.

6 And Yahveh said, Behold, they are one people, and they have all one language; and this is what they begin to do: and now nothing will be withholden from them, which they purpose to do.

7 Go to, let us go down, and there confound their language, that they may not understand one another's speech.

8 So Yahveh scattered them abroad from thence upon the face of all the earth: and they left off to build the city.

9 Therefore was the name of it called Bâbel; because Yahveh did there confound (*balâl*) the language of all the earth: and from thence did Yahveh scatter them abroad upon the face of all the earth.

X.

THE CALL OF ABRÂHÂM.

XII. 1 Now Yahveh said to Abrâm, Get thee out of thy country, and from thy kindred, and from thy father's house, unto the land that I will show thee:
2 And I will make of thee a great nation, and I will bless thee, and make thy name great; and be thou a blessing:
3 And I will bless them that bless thee, and him that curseth thee will I curse: and in thee shall all the families of the earth be blessed.
4 So Abrâm went, as Yahveh had spoken unto him; and Lôt went with him: and Abrâm was seventy and five years old when he departed out of Hârân.
5 And they came into the land of Kenà'an.
6 And Abrâm passed through the land unto the place of Shechem unto the terebinth of Môreh. And the Kena'any was then in the land.
7 And Yahveh appeared unto Abrâm, and said, Unto thy seed will I give this land: and there builded he an altar unto Yahveh, who appeared unto him.
8 And he removed from thence unto the mountain on the east of Bêth-Êl, and pitched his tent, having Bêth-Êl on the west, and 'Ay on the east: and there he builded an altar unto Yahveh, and called upon the name of Yahveh.
9 And Abrâm journeyed, going on still toward the south.

XI.

ABRÂHÂM IN EGYPT.

XII. 10 And there was a famine in the land: and Abrâm went down into Miçrâim to sojourn there; for the famine was sore in the land.

11 And it came to pass, when he was come near to enter into Miçrâim, that he said unto Sâray his wife, Behold, now, I know that thou art a fair woman to look upon:

12 And it shall come to pass, when the inhabitants of Miçrâim shall see thee, that they shall say, This is his wife: and they will kill me, but they will save thee alive.

13 Say, I pray thee, thou art my sister: that it may be well with me for thy sake, and that my soul may live because of thee.

14 And it came to pass, that, when Abrâm was come into Miçrâim, the inhabitants of Miçrâim beheld the woman that she was very fair.

15 And the princes of Para'ôh saw her, and praised her to Para'ôh: and the woman was taken to Para'ôh's house.

16 And he entreated Abrâm well for her sake: and he had sheep, and oxen, and he-asses, and male and female slaves, and she-asses, and camels.

17 And Yahveh plagued Para'ôh and his house with great plagues, because of Sâray Abrâm's wife.

18 And Para'ôh called Abrâm, and said, What is

this that thou hast done unto me? Why didst thou not tell me that she was thy wife?

19 Why saidst thou, She is my sister? so that I took her to be my wife: now therefore behold thy wife, take her, and go thy way.

20 And Para'ôh gave men charge concerning him: and they brought him on the way, and his wife, and all that he had.

XII.

ABRÂHÂM AND LÔT SEPARATE.

XIII. 1 And Abrâhâm went up out of Miçrâim, he, and his wife, and all that he had, and Lôt with him, into the Negeb.

3 And he went on his journeys from the Negeb even to Bêth-Êl, unto the place where his tent had been at the beginning, between Bêth-Êl and 'Ay;

4 Unto the place of the altar, which he had made there at the first: and there Abrâm called on the name of Yahveh.

7 And there was a strife between the herdmen of Abrâm's cattle and the herdmen of Lôt's cattle: and the Kena'any and the Perizzy dwelt then in the land.

8 And Abrâm said unto Lôt, Let there be no strife, I pray thee, between me and thee, and between my herdmen and thy herdmen, for we are brethren.

9 Is not the whole land before thee? separate thyself, I pray thee, from me: if thou wilt take the left

hand, then I will go to the right; or if thou take the right hand, then I will go to the left.

10 And Lôt lifted up his eyes, and beheld all the circuit of the Yardên, that it was well watered every where, before Yahveh destroyed Sedôm and 'Amôrâh, like the garden of Yahveh, like the land of Miçráim, as thou goest unto Çô'ar.

11 So Lôt chose him all the circuit of the Yardên; and Lôt journeyed east: and they separated themselves the one from the other.

14 And Yahveh said unto Abrâm, after that Lôt was separated from him, Lift up now thine eyes, and look from the place where thou art, northward and southward and eastward and westward:

15 For all the land which thou seest, to thee will I give it, and to thy seed for ever.

16 And I will make thy seed as the dust of the earth: so that if a man can number the dust of the earth, then shall thy seed also be numbered.

17 Arise, walk through the land in the length of it and in the breadth of it; for unto thee will I give it.

18 And Abrâm moved his tent, and came and dwelt by the terebinths of Mamrê, which are in Hebrôn, and built there an altar unto Yahveh.

XIII.

RESCUE OF LÔT BY ABRÂHÂM, AND BLESSING OF ABRÂHÂM BY MALKÎ'ÇEDEQ.[1]

XIV. 1 And it came to pass in the days of Amrâphel king of Shinc'âr, Ariôch king of Ellâsâr, Kedorlâ'ômer king of 'Elâm, and Tidc'âl king of the Gôyim,

2 That they made war with Bera'h king of Sedôm, and with Birsha' king of 'Amôrâh, Shinâb king of Admâh, and Shemêber king of Çeboyim, and the king of Bela'.

3 All these joined together in the vale of Siddim.

4 Twelve years they served Kedorlâ'ômer, and in the thirteenth year they rebelled.

5 And in the fourteenth year came Kedorlâ'ômer, and the kings that were with him, and smote the Rephaim in 'Ashteroth-Qarnâyim, and the Zûzim in Hâm, and the Êmim in Shâvêh-Qiryâthâyim,

6 And the 'Hôrim in their mountain of Sê'ir unto the oak of Pârân, which is by the wilderness.

7 And they returned, and came to Ên-Mishpât, and smote all the plain of the 'Amâlêqy, and also of the Amôry, that dwelt in 'Haçaçôn-Tâmâr.

8 And there went out the king of Sedôm, and the king of 'Amôrâh, and the king of Admâh, and the king

---

[1] The whole of this chapter is a remarkable compilation, both as to its language and its form. It differs so much from the usual compilation of the Jehovist that it seems certain he has taken a complete narrative of older date, and has inserted it textually into his work. Some critics see in it one of the fragments of the special composition which they call 'the second Elohist,' or 'the Theocratic Narrator.'

of Çeboyîm, and the king of Bela'; and they set the battle in array against them in the vale of Siddim;

9 Against Kedorlá'ômer king of 'Êlâm, and Tide'âl king of the Gôyîm, and Amrâphel king of Shine'âr, and Arioch king of Ellâsâr; four kings against the five.

10 Now the vale of Siddim was full of bitumen pits; and the kings of Sedôm and 'Amôrâh fled, and they fell there, and they that remained fled to the mountain.

11 And they took all the goods of Sedôm and 'Amôrâh, and all their victuals, and went away.

12 And they took Lôt, Abrâm's brother's son, who dwelt in Sedôm, and his goods, and departed.

13 And there came one that had escaped, and told Abrâm the 'Ebry: now he dwelt by the terebinths of Mamrê the 'Amôry, brother of Eshkôl, and brother of 'Anêr: and these were confederate with Abrâm.

14 And when Abrâm heard that his brother was taken captive, he led forth his trained men, born in his house, three hundred and eighteen, and pursued as far as Dân;

15 And he divided himself against them by night, he and his servants, and smote them, and pursued them unto 'Hôbâh, which is on the left hand of Dammâseq.

16 And he brought back all the goods, and also brought again his brother Lôt, and his goods, and the women also, and the people.

17 And the king of Sedôm went out to meet him, after his return from the slaughter of Kedorlá'ômer and the kings that were with him, at the vale of Shâvêh.

18 And Malki'çedeq, king of Shâlêm, brought forth bread and wine: and he was priest of Êl-'Eliôn.

19 And he blessed him and said, Blessed be Abrâm of Êl-'Eliôn, possessor of heaven and earth:

20 And blessed be Êl-'Eliôn, which hath delivered thine enemies into thy hand. And he gave him a tenth of all.

21 And the king of Sedôm said unto Abrâm, Give me the persons, and take the goods to thyself.

22 And Abrâm said to the king of Sedôm, I have lift up mine hand unto Yahveh, God Most High (Êl-'Eliôn), possessor of heaven and earth,

23 That I will not take a thread nor a shoelatchet nor aught that is thine, lest thou shouldest say, I have made Abrâm rich:

24 Save only that which the young men have eaten, and the portion of the men which went with me; 'Anêr, Eshkôl, and Mamrê, let them take their portion.

— ——— — —

XIV.

COVENANT BETWEEN YAHVEH AND ABRÂHÂM.

XV. 1 After these things the word of Yahveh came unto Abrâm in a vision, saying, Fear not, Abrâm: I am thy shield, and thy exceeding great reward.

2 And Abrâm said: O my lord, Yahveh, what wilt thou give me, seeing I go childless, and he that shall be possessor of my house is from Dammeseq, Eli'ezer?

3 And Abrâm said, Behold, to me thou hast given no seed: and, lo, one born in my house is mine heir.

4 And, behold, the word of Yahveh came unto him, saying, This man shall not be thine heir; but he that shall come forth out of thine own bowels shall be thine heir.

5 And he brought him forth abroad, and said, Look now toward heaven, and tell the stars, if thou be able to tell them: and he said unto him, So shall thy seed be.

6 And he believed in Yahveh; and he counted it to him for righteousness.

7 And he said unto him, I am Yahveh that brought thee out of Ûr of the Kasdim, to give thee this land to inherit it.

8 And he said, My lord, Yahveh, whereby shall I know that I inherit it?

9 And he said unto him, Take me an heifer of three years old, and a she-goat of three years old, and a ram of three years old, and a turtledove, and a young pigeon.

10 And he took him all these, and divided them in the midst, and laid each half over against the other: but the birds divided he not.

11 And the birds of prey came down upon the carcases, and Abrâm drove them away.

12 And when the sun was going down, a deep sleep fell upon Abrâm; and, lo, an horror of great darkness fell upon him.

13 And he said unto Abrâm, Know of a surety that thy seed shall be a stranger in a land that is not theirs, and shall serve them; and they shall afflict them four hundred years;

14 And also that nation, whom they serve, will I

judge: and afterward they shall come out with great substance.

15 But thou shalt go to thy fathers in peace; thou shalt be buried in a good old age.

16 And in the fourth generation they shall come hither again: for the iniquity of the 'Amóry is not yet full.

17 And it came to pass, that, when the sun went down, and it was dark, behold, a smoking furnace, and a flaming torch that passed between these pieces.

18 In that day Yahveh made a covenant with Abrâm, saying, Unto thy seed have I given this land, from the torrent of Miçrâim unto the great river, the river Phrâth:

19 The Qêny, and the Qenizzy, and the Qadmóny,

20 And the 'Hitty, and the Perizzy, and the Rephaim,

21 And the 'Amóry, and the Kena'any, and the Girgâshy, and the Yebûsy.[1]

[1] It is probable that the Jehovist related the change of Abrâm's name into Abrâhâm, and that of his wife's name Sâray into Sârâh, in this place. The verses in which Yahveh commanded this change must have been omitted by the latest reviser as being a reduplication of those in which the same events are narrated in the Elohistic document, and which he has placed a little further on in chap. xvii. of the present text. It would thus be this latest reviser who replaced the names Abrâm and Sâray instead of Abrâhâm and Sârâh in the narrative which follows the one just read, so as to evade mentioning the latter names until after the time when he mentions their adoption.

XV.

BIRTH OF YISHMÁ'ÉL.

XVI. 1 Now Sàray Abrám's wife bare him no children: and she had a female slave, a native of Miçráim, whose name was Hâgâr.

2 And Sàray said unto Abrám, Behold now, Yahveh hath restrained me from bearing; go in, I pray thee, unto my slave; it may be that I shall obtain children by her. And Abrám hearkened unto the voice of Sàray.

4 And he went in unto Hâgâr, and she conceived: and when she saw that she had conceived, her mistress was despised in her eyes.

5 And Sàray said unto Abrám, My wrong be upon thee: I gave my handmaid into thy bosom; and when she saw that she had conceived, I was despised in her eyes: Yahveh judge between me and thee.

6 But Abrám said unto Sàray, Behold, thy maid is in thy hand; do to her that which is good in thine eyes. And Sàray dealt hardly with her, and she fled from her face.

7 And the angel of Yahveh found her by a spring of water in the wilderness, by the spring in the way to Shûr.

8 And he said, Hâgâr, Sàray's handmaid, whence comest thou? and whither goest thou? And she said, I flee from the face of my mistress Sàray.

9 And the angel of Yahveh said unto her, Return to thy mistress, and submit thyself under her hands.

10 And the angel of Yahveh said unto her, I will greatly multiply thy seed, that it shall not be numbered for multitude.

11 And the angel of Yahveh said unto her, Behold, thou art with child, and shalt bear a son; and thou shalt call his name Yishmâ'él, because Yahveh hath heard thy affliction.

12 And he shall be as a wild-ass among men; his hand shall be against every man, and every man's hand against him; and he shall dwell in the presence of all his brethren.

13 And she called the name of Yahveh that spake unto her, Thou art a God that seeth (*attâh él roy*): for she said, Have I even here looked after him that seeth me?

14 Wherefore the well was called Beêr-la'hay-rôy (the well of the Living One who seeth me): behold, it is between Qâdêsh and Bârâd.[1]

XVI.

YIÇE'HÂQ'S BIRTH PROMISED.

XVIII. 1 And Yahveh appeared [to Abrâhâm] by the terebinths of Mamrê, as he sat in the tent door in the heat of the day;

---

[1] The 15th and 16th verses of chap. xvi. of the present text, which relate the birth of Yishmâ'él, belong to the Elohist. The narrative of the Jehovist must assuredly have ended by a similar verse, left out by the latest reviser, which stated the fact of the birth of the son promised in verse 11.

2 And he lift up his eyes and looked, and, lo, three men stood over against him: and when he saw them, he ran to meet them from the tent door, and bowed himself to the earth,

3 And said, My lord, if now I have found favour in thy sight, pass not away, I pray thee, from thy servant:

4 Let now a little water be fetched, and wash your feet, and rest yourselves under the tree:

5 And I will fetch a morsel of bread, and comfort ye your heart; after that ye shall pass on: for therefore are ye come to your servant. And they said, So do, as thou hast said.

6 And Abrâhâm hastened into the tent unto Sârâh, and said, Make ready quickly three measures of fine meal, knead it, and make cakes.

7 And Abrâhâm ran unto the herd, and fetched a calf tender and good, and gave it unto the servant; and he hasted to dress it.

8 And he took butter, and milk, and the calf which he had dressed, and set it before them; and he stood by them under the tree, and they did eat.

9 And they said unto him, Where is Sârâh thy wife? and he said, Behold, in the tent.

10 And (one of them) said, I will certainly return unto thee when the season cometh round; and, lo, Sârâh thy wife shall have a son. And Sârâh heard in the tent door, which was behind him.

11 Now Abrâhâm and Sârâh were old, and well stricken in age; it had ceased to be with Sârâh after the manner of women.

12 And Sârâh laughed within herself, saying, After I am waxed old shall I have pleasure, my lord being old also?

13 And Yahveh said unto Abrâhâm, Wherefore did Sârâh laugh, saying, Shall I of a surety bear a child, which am old?

14 Is any thing too hard for Yahveh? At the set time I will return unto thee, when the season cometh round, and Sârâh shall have a son.

15 Then Sârâh denied, saying, I laughed not; for she was afraid. And he said, Nay, but thou didst laugh.

XVII.

ABRÂHÂM INTERVENES ON BEHALF OF SEDÔM.

XVIII. 16 And the men rose up from thence, and looked toward Sedôm; and Abrâhâm went with them to bring them on the way.

17 And Yahveh said, Shall I hide from Abrâhâm that which I do;

18 Seeing that Abrâhâm shall surely become a great and mighty nation, and all the nations of the earth shall be blessed in him?

19 For I have known him, to the end that he may command his children and his household after him, that they may keep the way of Yahveh, to do justice and judgment; to the end that Yahveh may bring upon Abrâhâm that which he hath spoken of him.

20 And Yahveh said, Because the cry of Sedôm and 'Amôrâh is great, and because their sin is very grievous;

21 I will go down now, and see whether they have done altogether according to the cry of it, which has come unto me; and if not, I will know.

22 And the men turned from thence, and went towards Sedôm; [and Yahveh stood yet before Abrâhâm[1]].

23 And Abrâhâm drew near, and said, Wilt thou consume the righteous with the wicked?

24 Peradventure there be fifty righteous within the city; wilt thou consume and not spare the place for the fifty righteous that are therein?

25 That be far from thee to do after this manner, to slay the righteous with the wicked, that so the righteous should be as the wicked; that be far from thee: shall not the Judge of all the earth do right?

26 And Yahveh said, If I find in Sedôm fifty righteous within the city, then I will spare all the place for their sake.

27 And Abrâhâm answered and said, Behold now, I have taken upon me to speak unto my Lord, which am but dust and ashes:

28 Peradventure there shall lack five of the fifty righteous: wilt thou destroy all the city for the lack of five? And he said, I will not destroy it, if I find there forty and five.

29 And he spake unto him yet again, and said,

---

[1] Replaced according to the Jewish tradition. See note on this passage, *ante*, p. 54.

Peradventure there shall be forty found there. And he said, I will not do it for the forty's sake.

30 And he said, Oh let not my Lord be angry, and I will speak: peradventure there shall thirty be found there. And he said, I will not do it, if I find thirty there.

31 And he said, Behold now, I have taken upon me to speak unto my Lord: peradventure there shall be twenty found there. And he said, I will not destroy it for the twenty's sake.

32 And he said, Oh let not my Lord be angry, and I will speak yet but this once: peradventure ten shall be found there. And he said, I will not destroy it for the ten's sake.

33 And Yahveh went his way, as soon as he had left communing with Abráhám; and Abráhám returned unto his place.

XVIII.

DESTRUCTION OF SEDÔM AND 'AMÔRÁH.

XIX. 1 And the two angels came to Sedôm at even; and Lôt sat in the gate of Sedôm; and Lôt saw them, and rose up to meet them; and he bowed himself with his face to the earth;

2 And he said, Behold now, my lords, turn aside, I pray you, into your servant's house, and tarry all night, and wash your feet, and ye shall rise up early, and go

on your way. And they said, Nay; but we will abide in the street all night.

3 And he urged them greatly; and they turned in unto him, and entered into his house; and he made them a feast, and did bake unleavened bread, and they did eat.

4 But before they lay down, the men of the city, even the men of Sedôm, compassed the house round, both young and old, all the people from every quarter:

5 And they called unto Lôt, and said unto him, Where are the men which came in to thee this night? bring them out unto us, that we may know them.

6 And Lôt went out unto them to the door, and shut the door after him.

7 And he said, I pray you, my brethren, do not so wickedly.

8 Behold now, I have two daughters which have not known man; let me, I pray you, bring them out unto you, and do ye to them as is good in your eyes: only unto these men do nothing; forasmuch as they are come under the shadow of my roof.

9 And they said, Stand back. And they said, This one fellow came in to sojourn, and he will needs be a judge: now will we deal worse with thee, than with them. And they pressed sore upon the man, even Lôt, and drew near to break the door.

10 But the men put forth their hand, and brought Lôt into the house to them, and shut the door.

11 And they smote the men that were at the door of the house with blindness, both small and great: so that they wearied themselves to find the door.

12 And the men said unto Lôt, Hast thou any here besides? son in law, and thy sons, and thy daughters, and whomsoever thou hast in the city; bring them out of the place:

13 For we will destroy this place, because the cry of them is waxen great before Yahveh; and Yahveh hath sent us to destroy it.

14 And Lôt went out, and spake unto his sons in law, which married his daughters, and said, Up, get you out of this place; for Yahveh will destroy the city. But he seemed unto his sons in law as one that mocked.

15 And when the morning arose, then the angels hastened Lôt, saying, Arise, take thy wife, and thy two daughters which are here; lest thou be consumed in the punishment of the city.

16 But he lingered; and the men laid hold upon his hand, and upon the hand of his wife, and upon the hand of his two daughters; Yahveh being merciful unto him: and they brought him forth, and set him without the city.

17 And it came to pass, when they had brought them forth abroad, that he said, Escape for thy life; look not behind thee, neither stay thou in all the circuit; escape to the mountain, lest thou be consumed.

18 And Lôt said unto them, Oh, not so, my lord:

19 Behold now, thy servant hath found grace in thy sight, and thou hast magnified thy mercy, which thou hast showed unto me in saving my life; and I cannot escape to the mountain, lest the disaster overtake me, and I die:

20 Behold now, this city is near to flee unto, and it

is a little one: oh, let me escape thither (is it not a little one?) and my soul shall live.

21 And he said unto him, See, I have accepted thee concerning this thing also, that I will not overthrow the city of which thou hast spoken.

22 Haste thee, escape thither; for I cannot do anything till thou be come thither. Therefore the name of the city was called Çō'ăr (little).

23 The sun was risen upon the earth when Lôt came to Çō'ăr.

24 Then Yahveh rained upon Sedôm and upon 'Amôrâh brimstone and fire from Yahveh out of heaven;

25 And he overthrew those cities, and all the circuit, and all the inhabitants of the cities, and that which grew upon the ground.

26 But his wife looked back from behind him, and she became a pillar of salt.

27 And Abrâhâm gat up early in the morning to the place where he had stood before Yahveh:

28 And he looked towards Sedôm and 'Amôrâh, and toward all the land of the circuit, and beheld, and, lo, the smoke of the land went up as the smoke of a furnace.

XIX.

LÔT AND HIS DAUGHTERS.

XIX. 30 And Lôt went up out of Çô'âr, and dwelt in the mountain, and his two daughters with him; for he feared to dwell in Çô'âr: and he dwelt in a cave, he and his two daughters.

31 And the firstborn said unto the younger, Our father is old, and there is not a man in the earth to come in unto us after the manner of all the earth:

32 Come, let us make our father drink wine, and we will lie with him, that we may preserve seed of our father.

33 And they made their father drink wine that night: and the firstborn went in, and lay with her father: and he knew not when she lay down, nor when she arose.

34 And it came to pass on the morrow, that the firstborn said unto the younger, Behold, I lay yesternight with my father: let us make him drink wine this night also; and go thou in, and lie with him, that we may preserve seed of our father.

35 And they made their father drink wine that night also; and the younger arose, and lay with him: and he knew not when she lay down, nor when she arose.

36 Thus were both the daughters of Lôt with child by their father.

37 And the firstborn bare a son, and called his name Môâb (progeny of a father): the same is the father of the (people of) Môâb to this day.

38 And the younger, she also bare a son, and called his name Ben-'Ammy (son of my people): the same is the father of the Benê-'Ammôn to this day.

XX.

BIRTH OF YIÇE'HÂQ.

XXI. 1 And Yahveh visited Sârâh as he had said, [and Sârâh conceived, and bare Yiçe'hâq to Abrâhâm in his old age, at the set time of which Yahveh had spoken to him.[1]]

6 And Sârâh said, [Yahveh] hath prepared laughter for me; every one that heareth will laugh (*yiçe'hâq*) at me.

7 And she said, Who would have said unto Abrâhâm, that Sârâh should give children suck? for I have borne him a son in his old age.

[1] I restore conjecturally the verse which the latest editor has omitted in order to substitute for it the verse in which the Elohist related the same event, probably in almost exactly the same terms.

XXI.

THE SACRIFICE OF ABRÂHÂM.[1]

XXII. 1 And it came to pass after these things, that God did prove Abrâhâm, and said unto him, Abrâhâm ; and he said, Here am I.

2 And he said, Take now thy son, thine only son, whom thou lovest, even Yiçc'hâq, *and get thee into the land of Môriyâh* ; and offer him *there* for a burnt offering upon one of the mountains which I will tell thee of.

3 And Abrâhâm rose early in the morning, and saddled his ass, and took two of his young men with him, and Yiçc'hâq his son ; and he clave the wood for the burnt offering, and rose up, and went unto the place of which God had told him.

---

[1] There seems to be no question that the latest editor took this narrative from the Jehovistic document, and all critics are agreed upon this point. But in the editing of the Jehovistic narrative, which is evident in several places (e.g. in verses 11 and 14–18), a previous editing can be traced as distinctly which is due to a writer whose manner of writing is neither that of the Elohist nor that of the Jehovist, and who used the expressions ha'elôhim (which we have translated ' God ') or simply Elôhim to designate the Almighty. We have here, therefore, one of those passages in which the Jehovist has inserted in his book a narrative already complete, taken from some older writing, as we have already shown in chap. xiv. Many critics think that this fragment has been taken by him from the writer whom they call, with more or less precision, ' the second Elohist.' Whatever the truth of this conjecture, which is still very undecided, may be, the fact which seems beyond doubt here is that the Jehovist has adopted an older narrative, which he has gone over again, and to which he has made certain additions which bear the mark of his own hand. In order to show with more clearness this origin of the fragment, and the way in which two authors are traced in it, I have once more used two different kinds of type. All that is written by the first author, who uses the words ha'elôhim or Elôhim, is in ordinary type, while the additions which are themselves the witness that they are the personal work of the Jehovist are printed in italics.

4 On the third day Abrâhâm lifted up his eyes, and saw the place afar off.

5 And Abrâhâm said unto his young men, Abide ye here with the ass, and I and the lad will go yonder; and we will worship, and come again to you.

6 And Abrâhâm took the wood of the burnt offering, and laid it upon Yiçe'hâq his son; and he took in his hand the fire and the knife; and they went both of them together.

7 And Yiçe'hâq spake unto Abrâhâm his father, and said, My father: and he said, Here am I, my son. And he said, Behold the fire and the wood; but where is the lamb for a burnt offering?

8 And Abrâhâm said, Elôhim will provide himself the lamb for a burnt offering, my son: so they went both of them together.

9 And they came to the place which God had told him of; and Abrâhâm built the altar there, and laid the wood in order, and bound Yiçe'hâq his son, and laid him on the altar, upon the wood.

10 And Abrâhâm stretched forth his hand, and took the knife to slay his son.

11 *And the angel of Yahveh called unto him out of heaven, and said, Abrâhâm, Abrâhâm: and he said, Here am I.*

12 *And he (the angel) said*,[1] Lay not thine hand upon the lad, neither do thou any thing unto him: for now I know that thou fearest Elôhim, seeing thou hast not withheld thy son, thine only son, from me.

---

[1] The original narrative must have made Elôhim, who was speaking to Abrâhâm, interfere here without any intervention.

13 And Abrâhâm lifted up his eyes, and looked, and behold, behind him a ram caught in the thicket by his horns: and Abrâhâm went and took the ram, and offered him up for a burnt offering in the stead of his son.

14 *And Abrâhâm called the name of that place Yahveh-Yireh (Yahveh will provide): as it is said to this day, In the mount of Yahveh it shall be provided.*

15 *And the angel of Yahveh called unto Abrâhâm a second time out of heaven,*

16 *And said, By myself have I sworn, saith Yahveh, because thou hast done this thing, and hast not withheld thy son, thine only son:*

17 *That in blessing I will bless thee, and in multiplying I will multiply thy seed as the stars of the heaven, and as the sand which is upon the sea shore; and thy seed shall possess the gate of his enemies.*

18 *And in thy seed shall all the nations of the earth be blessed, because thou hast obeyed my voice.*

19 So Abrâhâm returned unto his young men, and they rose up and went together.

XXII.

THE CHILDREN OF NÂ'HÔR.

XXII. 20 And it came to pass after these things, that it was told Abrâhâm, saying, Behold, Milkâh, she also hath borne children unto thy brother Nâ'hôr;

21 'Uç his firstborn, and Bûz his brother, and Qemûêl the father of Arâm;

22 And Kesed, and 'Hazô, and Pildâsh, and Yidlâph, and Bethûêl.

23 And Bethûêl begat Ribqâh: these eight did Milkâh bear to Nâ'hôr, Abrâhâm's brother.

24 And his concubine, whose name was Reûmâh, she also bare Teba'h, and Ga'ham, and Ta'hash, and Ma'achâh.

XXIII.

THE MARRIAGE OF YIÇE'HÂQ AND RIBQÂH.

XXIV. 1 And Abrâhâm was old, and well stricken in age: and Yahveh had blessed Abrâhâm in all things.

2 And Abrâhâm said unto his servant, the elder of his house, that ruled over all that he had, Put, I pray thee, thy hand under my thigh:

3 And I will make thee swear by Yahveh, the God of heaven and the God of earth, that thou shalt not take a wife for my son of the daughters of the Kena'any, among whom I dwell;

4 But thou shalt go unto my country, and to my kindred, and take a wife for my son Yiçe'hâq.

5 And the servant said unto him, Peradventure the woman will not be willing to follow me unto this land: must I needs bring thy son again unto the land from whence thou camest?

6 And Abrâhâm said unto him, Beware that thou bring not my son thither again.

7 Yahveh, the God of heaven, that took me from my father's house, and from the land of my nativity, and that spake unto me, and that sware unto me, saying, Unto thy seed will I give this land; he shall send his angel before thee, and thou shalt take a wife for my son from thence.

8 And if the woman be not willing to follow thee, then thou shalt be clear from this my oath; only thou shalt not bring my son thither again.

9 And the servant put his hand under the thigh of Abrâhâm his master, and sware to him concerning this matter.

10 And the servant took ten camels, of the camels of his master, and departed; having all goodly things of his master's in his hand; and he arose, and went to Aram Naharaîm, unto the city of Nâ'hôr.

11 And he made the camels to kneel down without the city by the well of water at the time of evening, the time that women go out to draw water.

12 And he said, O Yahveh, God of my master Abrâhâm, send me, I pray. thee, good speed this day, and show kindness unto my master Abrâhâm.

13 Behold, I stand by the fountain of water; and the daughters of the men of the city come out to draw water;

14 And let it come to pass, that the damsel to whom I shall say, Let down thy pitcher, I pray thee, that I may drink; and she shall say, Drink, and I will give thy camels drink also: let the same be she that thou hast appointed for thy servant Yiçe'hâq; and thereby shall I know that thou hast showed kindness unto my master.

15 And it came to pass, before he had done speaking, that, behold, Ribqâh came out, who was born to Bethûêl the son of Milkâh, the wife of Nâ'hôr, Abrâhâm's brother, with her pitcher upon her shoulder.

16 And the damsel was very fair to look upon, a virgin, neither had any man known her: and she went down to the fountain, and filled her pitcher, and came up.

17 And the servant ran to meet her, and said, Give me to drink, I pray thee, a little water of thy pitcher.

18 And she said, Drink, my lord: and she hasted, and let down her pitcher upon her hand, and gave him drink.

19 And when she had done giving him drink, she said, I will draw for thy camels also, until they have done drinking.

20 And she hasted, and emptied her pitcher into the trough, and ran again unto the well to draw, and drew for all his camels.

21 And the man looked stedfastly on her; holding his peace, to know whether Yahveh had made his journey prosperous or not.

22 And it came to pass, as the camels had done drinking, that the man took a golden ring, of half a beq'a weight, and two bracelets for her hands of ten shekels weight of gold;

23 And said, Whose daughter art thou? tell me, I pray thee. Is there room in thy father's house for us to lodge in?

24 And she said, I am the daughter of Bethûêl the son of Milkâh, which she bare unto Nâ'hôr.

25 She said moreover unto him, We have both straw and provender enough, and room to lodge in.

26 And the man bowed his head, and worshipped Yahveh.

27 And he said, Blessed be Yahveh, the God of my master Abrâhâm, who hath not forsaken his mercy and truth toward my master: as for me, Yahveh hath led me in the way to the house of my master's brethren.

28 And the damsel ran, and told her mother's house according to these words.

29 And Ribqâh had a brother, and his name was Lâbân; and Lâbân ran out unto the man, unto the fountain.

30 And it came to pass, when he saw the ring, and the bracelets upon his sister's hands, and when he heard the words of Ribqâh his sister, saying, Thus spake the man unto me; that he came unto the man; and behold he stood by the camels at the fountain.

31 And he said, Come in, thou blessed of Yahveh; wherefore standest thou without? for I have prepared the house, and room for the camels.

32 And the man came into the house, and he ungirded the camels; and he gave straw and provender for the camels, and water to wash his feet and the men's feet that were with him.

33 And there was set meat before him to eat; but he said, I will not eat, until I have told mine errand. And he said, Speak on.

34 And he said, I am Abrâhâm's servant.

35 And Yahveh hath blessed my master greatly; and he is become great: and he hath given him flocks,

and herds, and silver and gold, and male and female slaves, and camels and asses.

36 And Sârâh my master's wife bare a son to my master when she was old ; and unto him hath he given all that he hath.

37 And my master made me swear, saying, Thou shalt not take a wife for my son of the daughters of the Kena'any, in whose land I dwell:

38 But thou shalt go unto my father's house, and to my kindred, and take a wife for my son.

39 And I said unto my master, Peradventure the woman will not follow me.

40 And he said unto me, Yahveh, before whom I walk, will send his angel with thee, and prosper thy way ; and thou shalt take a wife for my son of my kindred, and of my father's house.

41 Then shalt thou be clear from my oath, when thou comest to my kindred ; and if they give her not to thee, thou shalt be clear from my oath.

42 And I came this day unto the fountain, and said, O Yahveh, God of my master Abrâhâm, if now thou do prosper my way which I go:

43 Behold, I stand by the fountain of water ; and let it come to pass, that the maiden which cometh forth to draw, to whom I shall say, Give me, I pray thee, a little water of thy pitcher to drink ;

44 And she shall say to me, Both drink thou, and I will also draw for thy camels : let the same be the woman whom Yahveh hath appointed for my master's son.

45 And before I had done speaking in mine heart,

P

behold, Ribqâh came forth with her pitcher on her shoulder; and she went down unto the fountain, and drew: and I said unto her, Let me drink, I pray thee.

46 And she made haste, and let down her pitcher from her shoulder, and said, Drink. and I will give thy camels drink also: so I drank, and she made the camels drink also.

47 And I asked her, and said, Whose daughter art thou? And she said, The daughter of Bethûêl, Nâ'hôr's son, whom Milkâh bare unto him: and I put the ring upon her nose, and the bracelets upon her hands.

48 And I bowed my head, and worshipped Yahveh, and blessed Yahveh, the God of my master Abrâhâm, which had led me in the right way to take my master's brother's daughter for his son.

49 And now if ye will deal kindly and truly with my master, tell me: and if not, tell me; that I may turn to the right hand or to the left.

50 Then Lâbân and Bethûêl[1] answered and said, The thing proceedeth from Yahveh: we cannot speak unto thee bad or good.

51 Behold, Ribqâh is before thee, take her, and go, and let her be thy master's son's wife, as Yahveh hath spoken.

52 And it came to pass that, when Abrâhâm's servant heard their words, he bowed himself down to the earth before Yahveh.

[1] The mention of Bethûêl here is very likely a later addition to the original text. In fact the father of Ribqâh disappears from the rest of the narrative; everything seems to indicate that he is no longer among the living, and that his son Lâbân has become the head of the family in his place.

53 And the servant brought forth jewels of silver, and jewels of gold, and raiment, and gave them to Ribqâh: he gave also to her brother and to her mother precious things.

54 And they did eat and drink, he and the men that were with him, and tarried all night; and they rose up in the morning, and he said, Send me away unto my master.

55 And her brother and her mother said, Let the damsel abide with us a few days, at the least ten; after that she shall go.

56 And he said unto them, Hinder me not, seeing that Yahveh hath prospered my way; send me away that I may go to my master.

57 And they said, We will call the damsel, and inquire at her mouth.

58 And they called Ribqâh, and said unto her, Wilt thou go with this man? And she said, I will go.

59 And they sent away Ribqâh their sister, and her nurse, and Abrâhâm's servant, and his men.

60 And they blessed Ribqâh, and said unto her, Our sister, be thou the mother of thousands of ten thousands, and let thy seed possess the gate of those which hate them.

61 And Ribqâh arose, and her damsels, and they rode upon the camels, and followed the man: and the servant took Ribqâh, and went his way.

62 And Yiçe'hâq came from the way of Beêr-la'hay-rôy (the well of the Living One who seeth me); for he dwelt in the land of Negeb.

63 And Yiçe'hâq went out to meditate in the field at

the eventide: and he lifted up his eyes, and saw, and behold, there were camels coming.

64 And Ribqâh lifted up her eyes, and when she saw Yiçe'hâq, she lighted off the camel.

65 And she said unto the servant, What man is this that walketh in the field to meet us? And the servant said, It is my master: and she took her veil, and covered herself.

66 And the servant told Yiçe'hâq all the things that he had done.

67 And Yiçe'hâq brought her into his mother Sârâh's tent, and took Ribqâh, and she became his wife; and he loved her: and Yiçe'hâq was comforted after his mother's death.[1]

XXIV.

YA'AQÔB AND 'ÊSÂV.

XXV. 21 And Yiçe'hâq intreated Yahveh for his wife, because she was barren: and Yahveh was intreated of him, and Ribqâh his wife conceived.

22 And the children struggled together within her; and she said, If it be so, wherefore do I live? And she went to inquire of Yahveh.

23 And Yahveh said unto her,
  Two nations are in thy womb,

---

[1] The Jehovist ought to have mentioned the death of Abrâhâm here, but no doubt he did so very briefly, for the latest editor has omitted his narrative and inserted that of the Elohist, which is more exact and more detailed.

And two peoples shall be separated even from thy bowels;
And the one people shall be stronger than the other people;
And the elder shall serve the younger.

24 And when her days to be delivered were fulfilled, behold, there were twins in her womb.

25 And the first came forth ruddy, all over like an hairy garment, and they called his name 'Êsâv (hairy).

26 And after that came forth his brother, and his hand had hold on 'Êsâv's heel ('âqeb); and his name was called Ya'aqôb: and Yiçe'hâq was threescore years old when she bare them.

27 And the boys grew: and 'Êsâv was a cunning hunter, a man of the field; and Ya'aqôb was a peaceable man, dwelling in tents.

28 Now Yiçe'hâq loved 'Êsâv, because he did eat of his venison; and Ribqâh loved Ya'aqôb.

29 And Ya'aqôb sod pottage: and 'Êsâv came in from the field, and he was faint.

30 And 'Êsâv said to Ya'aqôb, Feed me, I pray thee, with that same red, with this red (âdôm) pottage; for I am faint: therefore was his name called Edôm.

31 And Ya'aqôb said, Sell me this day thy birthright.

32 And 'Êsâv said, Behold, I am at the point to die, and what profit shall the birthright do to me?

33 And Ya'aqôb said, Swear to me this day; and he sware unto him: and he sold his birthright unto Ya'aqôb.

34 And Ya'aqôb gave 'Êsâv bread and pottage of lentils; and he did eat, and drink, and rose up, and went his way: so 'Êsâv despised his birthright.

XXV.

YIÇE'HÂQ AND ABÎMELECH AT GERÂR.

XXVI. 1 And there was a famine in the land, beside the first famine that was in the days of Abrâhâm. And Yiçe'hâq went unto Abimelech king of the Pelishtîm unto Gerâr.

2 And Yahveh appeared unto him, and said, Go not down into Miçrâim; dwell in the land which I shall tell thee of:

3 Sojourn in this land, and I will be with thee, and will bless thee, for unto thee, and unto thy seed, I will give all these lands, and I will establish the oath which I sware unto Abrâhâm thy father;

4 And I will multiply thy seed as the stars of heaven, and will give unto thy seed all these lands; and in thy seed shall all the nations of the earth be blessed;

5 Because that Abrâhâm obeyed my voice, and kept my charge, my commandments, my statutes, and my laws.

6 And Yiçe'hâq dwelt in Gerâr:

7 And the men of the place asked him of his wife; and he said, She is my sister: for he feared to say, My wife; lest, said he, the men of the place should kill me for Ribqâh; because she was fair to look upon.

8 And it came to pass, when he had been there a long time, that Abimelech king of the Pelishtîm looked out at a window, and saw, and, behold, Yiçe'hâq was sporting with Ribqâh his wife.

9 And Abimelech called Yiçe'hâq, and said, Behold,

of a surety she is thy wife: and how saidst thou, She is my sister? And Yiçe'hâq said unto him, Because I said, Lest I die for her.

10 And Abîmelech said, What is this thou hast done unto us? one of the people might lightly have lien with thy wife, and thou shouldest have brought guiltiness upon us.

11 And Abîmelech charged all the people, saying, He that toucheth this man or his wife shall surely be put to death.

12 And Yiçe'hâq sowed in that land, and found in the same year an hundredfold, and Yahveh blessed him.

13 And the man waxed great, and grew more and more until he became very great:

14 And he had possessions of flocks, and possessions of herds, and a great household: and the Pelishtim envied him.

15 Now all the wells which his father's servants had digged in the days of Abrâhâm his father, the Pelishtim had stopped them, and filled them with earth.

16 And Abîmelech said unto Yiçe'hâq, Go from us, for thou art much mightier than we.

17 And Yiçe'hâq departed thence, and encamped in the valley of Gerâr, and dwelt there.

19 And Yiçe'hâq's slaves digged in the valley, and found there a well of springing water.

20 And the herdmen of Gerâr strove with Yiçe'hâq's herdmen, saying, The water is ours: and he called the name of the well 'Eseq (Contention); because they contended with him.

21 And they digged another well, and they strove for that also: and he called the name of it Sitnâh (Enmity).

22 And he removed from thence, and digged another well; and for that they strove not: and he called the name of it Re'hobôth (Broad places); and he said, For now Yahveh hath made room for us, and we shall be fruitful in the land.

23 And he went up thence to Beêr-Shâb'a.

25 And he builded an altar there, and called upon the name of Yahveh, and pitched his tent there, and there Yiçc'hâq's servants digged a well.

26 Then Abîmelech went to him from Gerâr, and A'huzzath his friend, and Phichôl the captain of his host.

27 And Yiçc'hâq said unto them, Wherefore are ye come unto me, seeing ye hate me, and have sent me away from you?

28 And they said, We saw plainly that Yahveh was with thee; and we said, Let there now be an oath betwixt us, even betwixt us and thee, and let us make a covenant with thee;

29 That thou wilt do us no hurt, as we have not touched thee, and as we have done unto thee nothing but good, and have sent thee away in peace: thou art now the blessed of Yahveh.

30 And he made them a feast, and they did eat and drink.

31 And they rose up betimes in the morning, and sware one to another: and Yiçc'hâq sent them away, and they departed from him in peace.

32 And it came to pass the same day, that Yiçc'hâq's

slaves came, and told him concerning the well which they had digged, and said unto him, We have found water.

33 And he called it Shib'âh (oath), therefore the name of the city is Beêr-Shâb'a unto this day.

XXVI.

YA'AQÔB OBTAINS HIS FATHER'S BLESSING BY STRATAGEM.

XXVII. 1 And it came to pass, that when Yiçe'hâq was old, and his eyes were dim, so that he could not see, he called 'Êsâv his elder son, and said unto him, My son : and he said unto him, Here am I.

2 And he said, Behold now, I am old, I know not the day of my death :

3 Now therefore take, I pray thee, thy weapons, thy quiver and thy bow, and go out to the field, and take me venison;

4 And make me savoury meat such as I love, and bring it to me, that I may eat; that my soul may bless thee before I die.

5 And Ribqâh heard when Yiçe'hâq spake to 'Êsâv his son. And 'Êsâv went to the field to hunt for venison, and to bring it.

6 And Ribqâh spake unto Ya'aqôb her son, saying, Behold, I heard thy father speak unto 'Êsâv thy brother, saying,

7 Bring me venison, and make me savoury meat,

that I may eat, and bless thee before Yahveh before my death.

8 Now therefore, my son, obey my voice according to that which I command thee.

9 Go now to the flock, and fetch me from thence two good kids of the goats; and I will make them savoury meat for thy father, such as he loveth:

10 And thou shalt bring it to thy father, that he may eat, so that he may bless thee before his death.

11 And Ya'aqôb said to Ribqâh his mother, Behold, 'Ésâv my brother is a hairy man, and I am a smooth man.

12 My father peradventure will feel me, and I shall seem to him as a deceiver; and I shall bring a curse upon me, and not a blessing.

13 And his mother said unto him, Upon me be thy curse, my son: only obey my voice, and go fetch me them.

14 And he went, and fetched, and brought them to his mother: and his mother made savoury meat, such as his father loved.

15 And Ribqâh took the goodly raiment of 'Ésâv her elder son, which were with her in the house, and put them upon Ya'aqôb her younger son:

16 And she put the skins of the kids of the goats upon his hands, and upon the smooth of his neck:

17 And she gave the savoury meat and the bread, which she had prepared, into the hand of her son Ya'aqôb.

18 And he came unto his father, and said, My father; and he said, Here am I; who art thou, my son?

19 And Ya'aqôb said unto his father, I am 'Êsav thy firstborn; I have done according as thou badest me: arise, I pray thee, sit and eat of my venison, that thy soul may bless me.

20 And Yiçe'hâq said unto his son, How is it that thou hast found it so quickly, my son? And he said, Because Yahveh thy God sent me good speed.

21 And Yiçe'hâq said unto Ya'aqôb, Come near, I pray thee, that I may feel thee, my son, whether thou be my very son 'Êsâv or not.

22 And Ya'aqôb went near unto Yiçe'hâq his father; and he felt him, and said, The voice is Ya'aqôb's voice, but the hands are the hands of 'Êsâv.

23 And he discerned him not, because his hands were hairy, as his brother 'Êsâv's hands: so he blessed him.

24 And he said, Art thou my very son 'Êsâv?

25 And he said, I am. And he said, Bring it near to me, and I will eat of my son's venison, that my soul may bless thee. And he brought it near to him, and he did eat: and he brought him wine, and he drank.

26 And his father Yiçe'hâq said unto him, Come near now, and kiss me, my son.

27 And he came near, and kissed him: and he smelled the smell of his raiment, and blessed him, and said,

> See, the smell of my son
> Is as the smell of a field which Yahveh hath blessed:

28 And God give thee of the dew of heaven
And of the fatness of the earth,
And plenty of corn and wine:

29 Let peoples serve thee,
>   And nations bow down to thee:
>   Be lord over thy brethren,
>   And let thy mother's sons bow down to thee;
>   Cursed be every one that curseth thee,
>   And blessed be every one that blesseth thee.

30 And it came to pass as soon as Yiçe'hâq had made an end of blessing Ya'aqôb, and Ya'aqôb was yet scarce gone out from the presence of Yiçe'hâq his father, that 'Êsâv his brother came in from his hunting.

31 And he also made savoury meat, and brought it unto his father; and he said unto his father, Let my father arise, and eat of his son's venison, that thy soul may bless me.

32 And Yiçe'hâq his father said unto him, Who art thou? And he said, I am thy son, thy firstborn, 'Êsâv.

33 And Yiçe'hâq trembled very exceedingly, and said, Who then is he that hath taken venison, and brought it me, and I have eaten of all before thou camest, and have blessed him? yea, and he shall be blessed.

34 When 'Êsâv heard the words of his father, he cried with an exceeding great and bitter cry, and said unto his father, Bless me, even me also, O my father.

35 And he said, Thy brother came with guile, and hath taken away thy blessing.

36 And he said, Is not he rightly named Ya'aqôb? for he hath supplanted me (Ya'eqbêny) these two times: he took away my birthright; and, behold, now he hath taken away my blessing. And he said, Hast thou not reserved a blessing for me?

37 And Yiçe'hâq answered and said unto 'Êsâv, Behold, I have made him thy lord, and all his brethren have I given to him for servants; and with corn and wine have I sustained him: and what then shall I do for thee, my son?

38 And 'Êsâv said unto his father, Hast thou but one blessing, my father? bless me, even me also, O my father. And 'Êsâv lifted up his voice, and wept.

39 And Yiçe'hâq his father answered and said unto him,

> Behold, away from the fatness of the earth shall be thy dwelling,
> And away from the dew of heaven from above;

40 And by thy sword shalt thou live,
> And thou shalt serve thy brother;
> And it shall come to pass, when thou shalt break loose,
> That thou shalt shake his yoke from off thy neck.

41 And 'Êsâv hated Ya'aqôb because of the blessing wherewith his father blessed him: and 'Êsâv said in his heart, The days of mourning for my father are at hand; then will I slay my brother Ya'aqôb.

42 And the words of 'Êsâv her elder son were told to Ribqâh: and she sent and called Ya'aqôb her younger son, and said unto him, Behold, thy brother 'Êsâv, as touching thee, doth comfort himself, purposing to kill thee.

43 Now therefore, my son, obey my voice; and arise, flee thou to Lâbân my brother to Hârân;

44 And tarry with him a few days, until thy brother's fury turn away;

45 Until thy brother's anger turn away from thee, and he forget that which thou hast done to him: then I will send, and fetch thee from thence: why should I be bereaved of you both in one day?

XXVII.

THE VISION OF YA'AQÔB.

XXVIII. 10 And Ya'aqób went out from Beér-Sháb'a, and went toward Hárán.

11 And he lighted upon a certain place, and tarried there all night, because the sun was set; and he took one of the stones of the place, and put it under his head, and lay down in that place to sleep.

12 And he dreamed, and behold a ladder set up on the earth, and the top of it reached to heaven: and behold the angels of God ascending and descending upon it.

13 And, behold, Yahveh stood above it, and said, I am Yahveh, the God of Abráhám thy father, and the God of Yiçe'háq: the land whereon thou liest, to thee will I give it, and to thy seed;

14 And thy seed shall be as the dust of the earth, and thou shalt spread abroad to the west, and to the east, and to the north, and to the south: and in thee and in thy seed shall all the families of the earth be blessed.

15 And, behold, I am with thee, and will keep thee whithersoever thou goest, and will bring thee again into this land; for I will not leave thee, until I have done that which I have spoken to thee of.

16 And Ya'aqôb awaked out of his sleep, and he said, Surely Yahveh is in this place: and I knew it not.

17 And he was afraid, and said, How dreadful is this place! this is none other but the house of God, and this is the gate of heaven.

18 And Ya'aqôb rose up early in the morning, and took the stone that he had put under his head, and set it up for a pillar, and poured oil upon the top of it.

19 And he called the name of that place Bêth-Êl (the house of God): but the name of the city was Lûz at the first.

20 And Ya'aqôb vowed a vow, saying, If Yahveh Elôhîm will be with me, and will keep me in this way that I go, and will give me bread to eat, and raiment to put on,

21 So that I come again to my father's house in peace, then shall Yahveh be my God.

22 And this stone, which I have set up for a pillar, shall be God's house[1]: and of all that thou shalt give me, I will surely give the tenth unto thee.

[1] The Bêth-Êl or betylus, by which name the sacred stones were known in the neighbouring nations to the Hebrews.

XXVIII.

LÂBÂN ENTERTAINS YA'AQÔB.

XXIX. 1 Then Ya'aqôb went on his journey, and came to the land of the Benê-Qedem.

2 And he looked, and behold a well in the field, and, lo, three flocks of sheep lying there by it: for out of that well they watered the flocks: and the stone upon the well's mouth was great.

3 And thither were all the flocks gathered: and they rolled the stone from the well's mouth, and watered the sheep, and put the stone again upon the well's mouth in its place.

4 And Ya'aqôb said unto them, My brethren, whence be ye? And they said, Of Hârân are we.

5 And he said unto them, Know ye Lâbân the son of Na'hôr? And they said, We know him.

6 And he said unto them, Is it well with him? And they said, It is well: and, behold, Râ'hêl his daughter cometh with the sheep.

7 And he said, Lo, it is yet high day, neither is it time that the cattle should be gathered together: water ye the sheep, and go and feed them.

8 And they said, We cannot, until all the flocks be gathered together, and they roll the stone from the well's mouth; then we water the sheep.

9 While he yet spake with them, Râ'hêl came with her father's sheep; for she kept them.

10 And it came to pass, when Ya'aqôb saw Râ'hêl

the daughter of Lâbân his mother's brother, and the sheep of Lâbân his mother's brother, that Ya'aqôb went near, and rolled the stone from the well's mouth, and watered the flock of Lâbân his mother's brother.

11 And Ya'aqôb kissed Râ'hêl, and lifted up his voice, and wept.

12 And Ya'aqôb told Râ'hêl that he was her father's brother, and that he was Ribqâh's son: and she ran and told her father.

13 And it came to pass, when Lâbân heard the tidings of Ya'aqôb his sister's son, that he ran to meet him, and embraced him, and kissed him, and brought him to his house. And he told Lâbân all these things.

14 And Lâbân said to him, Surely thou art my bone and my flesh. And he abode with him the space of a month.

15 And Lâbân said unto Ya'aqôb, Because thou art my brother, shouldest thou therefore serve me for nought? tell me, what shall thy wages be?

16 And Lâbân had two daughters: the name of the elder was Lêâh, and the name of the younger was Râ'hêl.

17 And Lêâh's eyes were tender; but Râ'hêl was beautiful and well favoured.

18 And Ya'aqôb loved Râ'hêl; and he said, I will serve thee seven years for Râ'hêl thy younger daughter.

19 And Lâbân said, It is better that I give her to thee, than that I should give her to another man: abide with me.

20 And Ya'aqôb served seven years for Râ'hêl: and

Q

they seemed unto him but a few days, for the love he had to her.

21 And Ya'aqôb said unto Lâbân, Give me my wife, for my days are fulfilled, that I may go in unto her.

22 And Lâbân gathered together all the men of the place, and made a feast.

23 And it came to pass in the evening, that he took Lêâh his daughter, and brought her to him; and he went in unto her.

24 And Lâbân gave Zilpâh his handmaid unto his daughter for an handmaid.

25 And it came to pass in the morning that, behold, it was Lêâh; and he said unto Lâbân, What is this thou hast done unto me? did not I serve with thee for Râ'hêl? Wherefore then hast thou beguiled me?

26 And Lâbân said, It is not so done in our place, to give the younger before the firstborn.

27 Fulfil the week of this one, and we will give thee the other also for the service which thou shalt serve with me yet seven other years.

28 And Ya'aqôb did so, and fulfilled her week: and he gave him Râ'hêl his daughter to wife.

29 And Lâbân gave to Râ'hêl his daughter Bil'hâh his handmaid to be her handmaid.

30 And he went in also unto Râ'hêl, and he loved also Râ'hêl more than Lêâh, and served with him yet seven other years.

31 And Yahveh saw that Lêâh was hated, and he opened her womb: but Râ'hêl was barren.

32 And Lêâh conceived, and bare a son, and she called his name Reûbên: for she said, Because Yahveh

hath looked upon my affliction (*râàh be'onyî*); for now my husband will love me.

33 And she conceived again, and bare a son; and said, Because Yahveh hath heard (*shâm'a*) that I am hated, he hath therefore given me this son also: and she called his name Shime'ôn.

34 And she conceived again, and bare a son; and said, Now this time will my husband be joined (*yillàveh*) unto me, because I have borne him three sons: therefore was his name called Lêvy.

35 And she conceived again, and bare a son; and she said, This time will I praise Yahveh (*ôdeh eth-Yahveh*): therefore she called his name Yehûdâh; and she left bearing.

XXX. 1[1] And when Râ'hêl saw that she bare Ya'aqôb no children, Râ'hêl envied her sister; and she said unto Ya'aqôb, Give me children, or else I die.

3 And she said, Behold my maid Bil'hâh, go in unto her; that she may bear upon my knees, and I also may obtain children by her.

4 And she gave him Bil'hâh her handmaid to wife: and Ya'aqôb went in unto her.

5 And Bil'hâh conceived, and bare Ya'aqôb a son.

6 *And Râ'hêl said, Elôhîm hath judged me* (dânanny), *and hath also heard my voice, and hath given me a son: therefore called she his name Dân.*

---

[1] In the existing text of chap. xxx. we see clearly what we have already stated with reference to the narrative of Abrâhâm's sacrifice. The Jehovist, while composing his book, had before him an older document which had been already published, in which God was called Elôhîm. He has followed it step by step, and has partly borrowed the narrative, for it can be recognised with certainty in certain passages which we have printed in italics.

7 And Bil'hâh Râ'hêl's handmaid conceived again, and bare Ya'aqôb a second son.

8 *And Râ'hêl said, With mighty wrestlings of Elôhîm have I wrestled* (naphtâly) *with my sister, and have prevailed: and she called his name Naphtâly.*

9 When Lêâh saw that she had left bearing, she took Zilpâh her handmaid, and gave her to Ya'aqôb to wife.

10 And Zilpâh Lêâh's handmaid bare Ya'aqôb a son.

11 And Lêâh said, Fortunate (*bâgâd*)! and she called his name Gâd.

12 And Zilpâh Lêâh's handmaid bare Ya'aqôb a second son.

13 And Lêâh said, Happy am I (*beâshry*)! for the daughters will call me happy: and she called his name Ashêr.

14 And Reûbên went in the days of wheat harvest, and found mandrakes in the field, and brought them unto his mother Lêâh. Then Râ'hêl said to Lêâh, Give me, I pray thee, of thy son's mandrakes.

15 And she said unto her, Is it a small matter that thou hast taken away my husband? and wouldest thou take away my son's mandrakes also? And Râ'hêl said, Therefore he shall lie with thee to-night for thy son's mandrakes.

16 And Ya'aqôb came from the field in the evening, and Lêâh went out to meet him, and said, Thou must come in unto me; for I have surely hired thee with my son's mandrakes. And he lay with her that night.

17 *And Elôhîm hearkened unto Lêâh,* and she conceived, and bare Ya'aqôb a fifth son.

18 *And Lêâh said, Elôhîm hath endowed me with a*

good dowry (shekâry), *because I gave my handmaid to my husband: and she called his name Yissâchâr.*

19 And Lêâh conceived again, and bare a sixth son to Ya'aqôb.

20 *And Lêâh said, Elôhîm hath endowed me with a good dowry; now will my husband live with me* (yizbelêny), *because I have borne him six sons: and she called his name Zebulûn.*

22 *And Elôhîm remembered Râ'hêl, and Elôhîm hearkened to her, and opened her womb.*

23 *And she conceived, and bare a son: and said, Elôhîm hath taken away my reproach:*

24 And she called his name Yôsêph, saying, Yahveh add (*yôsêph*) to me another son.

25 And it came to pass, when Râ'hêl had borne Yôsêph, that Ya'aqôb said unto Lâbân, Send me away, that I may go unto mine own place, and to my country.

26 Give me my wives and my children for whom I have served thee, and let me go: for thou knowest my service wherewith I have served thee.

27 And Lâbân said unto him, If now I have found favour in thine eyes, tarry: for I have divined that Yahveh hath blessed me for thy sake.

28 And he said, Appoint me thy wages, and I will give it.

29 And he said unto him, Thou knowest how I have served thee, and how thy cattle hath fared with me.

30 For it was little which thou hadst before I came, and it hath increased unto a multitude; and Yahveh hath blessed thee whithersoever I turned: and now when shall I provide for mine own house also?

31 And he said, What shall I give thee? And Ya'aqôb said, Thou shalt not give me aught: if thou wilt do this thing for me, I will again feed thy flock and keep it.

32 I will pass through all thy flock to-day, removing from thence every speckled and spotted one, and every black one among the sheep, and the spotted and speckled among the goats: and of such shall be my hire.

33 So shall my righteousness answer for me hereafter, when thou shalt come concerning my hire that is before thee: every one that is not speckled and spotted among the goats, and black among the sheep, that, if found with me, shall be counted stolen.

34 And Lâbân said, Behold, I would it might be according to thy word.

35 And he removed that day the he-goats that were ringstraked and spotted, and all the she-goats that were speckled and spotted, every one that had white in it, and all the black ones among the sheep, and gave them into the hand of his sons;

36 And he set three days' journey betwixt himself and Ya'aqôb: and Ya'aqôb fed the rest of Lâbân's flocks.

40 And Ya'aqôb separated the lambs, and set the faces of the flocks toward the ringstraked, and all the black in the flock of Lâbân; and he put his own droves apart, and put them not unto Lâbân's flock.

43 And the man increased exceedingly, and had large flocks, and maidservants and slaves, and camels and asses.

XXIX.

YA'AQÔB LEAVES LÂBÂN.[1]

XXXI. 1 And he heard the words of Lâbân's sons, saying, Ya'aqôb hath taken away all that was our father's; and of that which was our father's hath he gotten all this glory.

2 And Ya'aqôb beheld the countenance of Lâbân, and, behold, it was not toward him as beforetime.

3 [And Yahveh said to Ya'aqôb, Return unto the land of thy fathers, and to thy kindred; and I will be with thee.[2]]

4 And Ya'aqôb sent and called Râ'hêl and Lêâh to the field unto his flock.

5 And said unto them, I see your father's countenance, that it is not toward me as beforetime; but the God of my father hath been with me.

6 And ye know that with all my power I have served your father.

7 And your father hath deceived me, and changed my wages ten times; but Elôhîm suffered him not to hurt me.

8 If he said thus, The speckled shall be thy wages;

---

[1] In this portion the Jehovist has again followed the same older writer that he did in chap. xxx. of the present text, in whose document God was called Elôhîm. He has reproduced it so accurately that his peculiar mode of expression can only be detected in verse 3, in the first part of verse 13, the second part of verse 23, and vv. 48-50. These would seem to be the only additions this writer has made to the text which he borrowed and inserted bodily into his book.

[2] The verses which I have pointed out as being the only ones which are in the style of the Jehovist, and as having been added by him to the older text reproduced by him, are in brackets.

then all the flock bare speckled: and if he said thus, The ringstraked shall be thy wages; then bare all the flock ringstraked.

9 Thus Elôhîm hath taken away the cattle of your father, and given them to me.

10 And it came to pass at the time that the flock conceived, that I lifted up mine eyes, and saw in a dream, and, behold, the he-goats which leaped upon the flock were ringstraked, speckled, and grisled.

11 And the angel of Elôhîm said unto me in the dream, Ya'aqôb: and I said, Here am I.

12 And he said, Lift up now thine eyes, and see, all the he-goats which leap upon the flock are ringstraked, speckled, and grisled; for I have seen all that Lâbân doeth unto thee.

13 [I am the God of Bêth-Êl, where thou anointedst a column, where thou vowedst a vow unto me.] Now arise, get thee out from this land, and return unto the land of thy nativity.

14 And Râ'hêl and Lêâh answered and said unto him, Is there yet any portion or inheritance for us in our father's house?

15 Are we not counted of him strangers? for he hath sold us, and hath also quite devoured our money.

16 For all the riches which Elôhîm hath taken away from our father, that is ours and our children's: now then, whatsoever Elôhîm hath said unto thee, do.

19 Now Lâbân was gone to shear his sheep: and Râ'hêl stole the Terâphîm that were her father's.

20 And Ya'aqôb stole away unawares to Lâbân the Aramy, in that he told him not that he fled.

21 So he fled with all that he had; and he rose up, and passed over the River, and set his face toward the mountain of Gile'âd.

22 And it was told Lâbân on the third day that Ya'aqôb was fled.

23 And he took his brethren with him, and pursued after him seven days' journey; [and he overtook him in the mountain of Gile'âd.]

24 And Elôhîm came to Lâbân the Aramy, in a dream of the night, and said unto him, Take heed to thyself that thou speak not to Ya'aqôb either good or bad.

25 And Lâbân came up with Ya'aqôb. Now Ya'aqôb had pitched his tent in the mountain: and Lâbân with his brethren pitched in the mountain of Gile'âd.

26 And Lâbân said to Ya'aqôb, What hast thou done, that thou hast stolen away unawares to me, and carried away my daughters as captives of the sword?

27 Wherefore didst thou flee secretly, and steal away from me; and didst not tell me, that I might have sent thee away with mirth and with songs, to the sound of the tambourine and the kinnôr;

28 And hast not suffered me to kiss my sons and my daughters? now hast thou done foolishly.

29 It is in the power of my hand to do you hurt: but the God of your father spake unto me yesternight, saying, Take heed to thyself that thou speak not unto Ya'aqôb either good or bad.

30 And now, though thou wouldest needs be gone, because thou sore longedst after thy father's house, yet wherefore hast thou stolen my gods?

31 And Ya'aqôb answered and said to Lâbân, Because I was afraid: for I said, Lest thou shouldest take thy daughters from me by force [and all my possessions [1]].

32 With whomsoever thou findest thy gods, he shall not live: before our brethren discern thou what is thine with me, and take it to thee. For Ya'aqôb knew not that Râ'hêl had stolen them.

33 And Lâbân went into Ya'aqôb's tent, and into Lêâh's tent, and into the tent of the two maidservants; but he found them not. And he went out of Lêâh's tent, and entered into Râ'hêl's tent.

34 Now Râ'hêl had taken the Terâphim, and put them in the camel's furniture, and sat upon them. And Lâbân felt about all the tent, but found them not.

35 And she said to her father, Let not my lord be angry that I cannot rise up before thee; for the manner of women is upon me. And he searched, but found not the Terâphim.

36 And Ya'aqôb was wroth, and chode with Lâbân: and Ya'aqôb answered and said to Lâbân, What is my trespass? what is my sin, that thou hast so hotly pursued after me?

37 Whereas thou hast felt about all my stuff, what hast thou found of all thy household stuff? Set it here before my brethren and thy brethren, that they may judge betwixt us two.

38 This twenty years have I been with thee; thy ewes and thy she-goats have not cast their young, and the rams of thy flocks have I not eaten.

39 That which was torn of beasts I brought not

[1] See note *ante*, p. 101.

unto thee; I bare the loss of it; of my hand didst thou require it, whether stolen by day or stolen by night.

40 Thus I was; in the day the drought consumed me, and the frost by night; and my sleep fled from mine eyes.

41 These twenty years have I been in thy house; I served thee fourteen years for thy two daughters, and six for thy flock: and thou hast changed my wages ten times.

42 Except the God of my father, the God of Abrâhâm, and the fear of Yiçe'hâq, had been with me, surely now hadst thou sent me away empty. Elóhîm hath seen mine affliction and the labour of my hands, and rebuked thee yesternight.

43 And Lâbân answered and said unto Ya'aqôb, The daughters are my daughters, and the children are my children, and the flocks are my flocks, and all that thou seest is mine: and what can I do this day unto these my daughters, or unto their children which they have borne?

44 And now come, let us make a covenant, I and thou; and let it be for a witness between me and thee.

45 And Ya'aqôb took a stone, and set it up for a column.

46 And Ya'aqôb said unto his brethren, Gather stones; and they took stones, and made an heap: and they did eat there by the heap.

48 And Lâbân said [Behold this heap, and the column which I have set between me and thee[1]]; this heap is witness, [and this pillar also is witness] between me and

---

[1] See *ante*, p. 103.

thee this day. Therefore was the name of it called Galeʻêd,

49 And Miçpâh, for he said, Yahveh watch (*yiçeph*) between me and thee when we are absent one from another.

50 If thou shalt afflict my daughters, and if thou shalt take wives beside my daughters, no man is with us; see, Elôhîm is witness betwixt me and thee.

51 And Lâbân said to Yaʻaqôb, Behold this heap, and behold the column, which I have set betwixt me and thee.

52 This heap be witness, and the column be witness, that I will not pass over this heap to thee, and that thou shalt not pass over this heap and this column to me, for harm.

53 The God of Abrâhâm and the God of Nâʻhôr, the God of their father, judge betwixt us. And Yaʻaqôb sware by the Fear of his father Yiçeʻhâq.

54 And Yaʻaqôb offered a sacrifice in the mountain, and called his brethren to eat bread: and they did eat bread, and tarried all night in the mountain.

55 And early in the morning Lâbân rose up, and kissed his sons and his daughters, and blessed them: and Lâbân departed, and returned unto his place.

XXXII. 1 And Yaʻaqôb went on his way; [and, looking up, he saw the host of Elôhîm encamped;[1]] and the angels of Elôhîm met him.

2 And Yaʻaqôb said when he saw them, This is Elôhîm's host. And he called the name of that place Maʻhanâim (encampments).

[1] See note, p. 104.

XXX.

Ya'aqôb prepares to meet his brother.[1]

XXXII. 3 And Ya'aqôb sent messengers before him to 'Êsâv his brother, unto the land of Sê'ir, the field of Edôm.

4 And he commanded them, saying, Thus shall ye say unto my lord 'Êsâv; Thus saith thy servant Ya'aqôb, I have sojourned with Lâbân, and stayed until now :

5 And I have oxen, and asses, and flocks, and male and female slaves : and I have sent to tell my lord, that I may find grace in thy sight.

6 And the messengers returned to Ya'aqôb, saying, We came to thy brother 'Êsâv, and moreover he cometh to meet thee, and four hundred men with him.

7 Then Ya'aqôb was greatly afraid and was distressed : and he divided the people that was with him, and the flocks, and the herds, and the camels, into two companies ;

8 And he said, If 'Êsâv come to the one company, and smite it, then the company which is left shall escape.

9 And Ya'aqôb said, O God of my father Abrâhâm, and God of my father Yiçc'hâq, O Yahveh, which saidst unto me, Return unto thy country, and to thy kindred, and I will do thee good :

---

[1] The whole of this narrative is the Jehovist's own. He has not made any use of the older work he made use of in his account of Ya'aqôb. Verse xxxii. 7 in fact gives a different origin for the name of the locality of Mâ'hanâim to that set forth in chap. xxxii. 2.

10 I am not worthy of the least of all thy mercies, and of all the truth which thou hast showed unto thy servant; for with my staff I passed over this Yardén; and now I am become two companies.

11 Deliver me, I pray thee, from the hand of my brother, from the hand of 'Êsâv; for I fear him, lest he come and smite me, the mother with the children.

12 And thou saidst, I will surely do thee good, and make thy seed as the sand of the sea, which cannot be numbered for multitude.

13 And he lodged there that night; and took of that which he had with him a present for 'Êsâv his brother;

14 Two hundred she-goats and twenty he-goats, two hundred ewes and twenty rams,

15 Thirty milch camels and their colts, forty kine and ten bulls, twenty she-asses and ten foals.

16 And he delivered them into the hand of his servants, every drove by itself; and said unto his servants, Pass over before me, and put a space betwixt drove and drove.

17 And he commanded the foremost, saying, When 'Êsâv my brother meeteth thee, and asketh thee, saying, Whose art thou, and whither goest thou? and whose are these before thee?

18 Then thou shalt say, They be thy servant Ya'aqôb's; it is a present sent unto my lord 'Êsâv: and, behold, he also is behind us.

19 And he commanded also the second, and the third, and all that followed the droves, saying, On this manner shall ye speak unto 'Êsâv, when ye find him;

20 And ye shall say, Moreover, behold thy servant

Ya'aqôb is behind us. For he said, I will appease him with the present that goeth before me, and afterward I will see his face; peradventure he will accept me.

21 So the present passed over before him: and he himself lodged that night in the company.

22 And he rose up that night, and took his two wives, and his two handmaids, and his eleven children, and passed over the ford of the Yabbôk.

23 And he took them, and sent them over the stream, and sent over that he had.

XXXI.

YA'AQÔB WRESTLES WITH ELÔHÎM.[1]

XXXII. 24 And Ya'aqôb was left alone; and there wrestled a man with him until the breaking of the day.

25 And when he saw that he prevailed not against him, he touched the hollow of his thigh; and the hollow of Ya'aqôb's thigh was strained as he wrestled with him.

26 And he said, Let me go, for the day breaketh. And he said, I will not let thee go, except thou bless me.

27 And he said unto him, What is thy name? And he said, Ya'aqôb.

---

[1] It is not possible to doubt that this narrative was part of the Jehovist's document, but he has taken it bodily from that older document which is sometimes called the work of 'the second Elohist,' sometimes of 'the theocratical narrator.'

28 And he said, Thy name shall be called no more Ya'aqôb, but Yisrâêl, for thou hast striven with Elôhim (*ki-sârîtha 'im-Elôhim*) and with men, and hast prevailed.

29 And Ya'aqôb asked him, and said, Tell me, I pray thee, thy name. And he said, Wherefore is it that thou dost ask after my name? And he blessed him there.

30 And Ya'aqôb called the name of the place Peny-Êl; for, said he, I have seen Elôhim face to face, and my life is preserved.

31 And the sun rose upon him as he passed over Peny-Êl, and he halted upon his thigh.

XXXII.

MEETING OF YA'AQÔB AND 'ÊSÂV.[1]

XXXIII. 1 And Ya'aqôb lifted up his eyes, and looked, and behold, 'Êsâv came, and with him four hundred men. *And he divided the children unto Lêâh, and unto Râ'hêl, and unto the two handmaids.*

2 *And he put the handmaids and their children foremost, and Lêâh and her children after, and Râ'hêl and Yôsêph hindermost.*

3 And he himself passed over before them, and

---

[1] Here again the Jehovist has used the older document, in which God is called Elôhim, and has preserved the greater portion of the narrative. The passages in which peculiarities of language place the preservation of an older text (emanating from a different writer to the Jehovist) beyond doubt, are printed in italics.

bowed himself to the ground seven times, until he came near to his brother.

4 And 'Êsâv ran to meet him, and embraced him, and fell on his neck, and kissed him: and they wept.

5 *And he lifted up his eyes, and saw the women and the children; and said, Who are these with thee? And he said, The children which Elôhîm hath graciously given thy servant.*

6 Then the handmaids came near, they and their children, and they bowed themselves.

7 *And Lêâh also and her children came near, and bowed themselves; and after came Yôsêph near and Râ'hêl, and they bowed themselves.*

8 And he said, What meanest thou by all this company which I met? And he said, To find grace in the sight of my lord.

9 And 'Êsâv said, I have enough; my brother, let that thou hast be thine.

10 And Ya'aqôb said, Nay, I pray thee, if now I have found grace in thy sight, then receive my present at my hand; *forasmuch as I have seen thy face, as one seeth the face of Elôhîm, and thou wast pleased with me.*

11 *Take, I pray thee, my gift that is brought to thee: because Elôhîm hath dealt graciously with me, and because I have enough.* And he urged him, and he took it.

12 And he said, Let us take our journey, and let us go, and I will go before thee.

13 *And he said unto him, My lord knoweth that the children are tender, and that the flocks and herds with me*

give suck: and if they overdrive them one day, all the flocks will die.

14 *Let my lord, I pray thee, pass over before his servant: and I will lead on softly, according to the pace of the cattle that is before me, and according to the pace of the children, until I come unto my lord unto Sê'îr.*

15 And 'Ésâv said, Let me now leave with thee some of the folk that are with me. And he said, What needeth it? let me find grace in the sight of my lord.

16 So 'Ésâv returned that day on his way unto Sê'îr.

17 And Ya'aqôb journeyed to Sukkôth, and built him an house, and made booths for his cattle: therefore the name of the place is called Sukkôth (booths).

XXXIII.[1]

THE SONS OF YA'AQÔB AND THE INHABITANTS OF SHECHEM.

[2] [Ya'aqôb came to dwell near the town of Shechem.]

XXXIII. 19 And he bought the parcel of ground, where he had spread his tent, at the hand of the children of 'Hamôr, Shechem's father, for an hundred qesitâh.

[1] For this narrative the latest editor of Genesis has adopted the narrative of the Elohist as the fundamental basis. He has only taken a certain number of verses from the Jehovistic narrative, and these he introduces by way of complements. The result is that when the Jehovistic narrative is removed from the text there are several gaps, which we have endeavoured to fill up conjecturally, placing our restorations between brackets.

[2] To fill up these gaps we have preferred to restore the text of the Elohist when narrating the same facts, instead of inserting a narrative of our own which would not assimilate with the rest of the narrative.

20 And he erected there an altar, and called it Êl-Elôhê-Yisrâêl (Êl is the God of Yisrâêl).

¹ [And Shechem the son of 'Hamôr the 'Hivvy, the prince of the land, saw Dinâh, the daughter of Lêah, whom she bare unto Ya'aqôb.]

XXXIV. 3 And his soul clave unto Dinâh the daughter of Ya'aqôb, and he loved the damsel, and spake to the heart of the damsel.

2 And he took her, and lay with her, and humbled her.

5 Now Ya'aqôb heard that he had defiled Dinâh his daughter; and his sons were with his cattle in the field, and Ya'aqôb held his peace until they came.

7 And the sons of Ya'aqôb came in from the field when they heard it: and the men were grieved, and they were very wroth, because he had wrought folly in Yisrâêl in lying with Ya'aqôb's daughter; which thing should not be done.

11 And Shechem said unto her father and unto her brethren, Let me find grace in your eyes, and what ye shall say unto me I will give.

12 Ask me never so much dowry and gift, and I will give according as ye shall say unto me: but give me the damsel to wife.

13 And the sons of Ya'aqôb answered Shechem and 'Hamôr his father with guile, and spake, because he had defiled Dinâh, their sister.

14 And said unto them, We cannot do this thing, to give our sister to one that is uncircumcised; for that were a reproach unto us.

---

¹ See note ² on p 242.

[1] [Only on this condition will we consent unto you : if ye will be as we be, that every male of you be circumcised.]

19 And the young man deferred not to do the thing, because he had delight in Ya'aqôb's daughter : and he was honoured above all the house of his father.

[1] [And unto him hearkened all that went out of the gate of his city; and every male was circumcised like him.

And it came to pass on the third day, when they were sore, that two of the sons of Ya'aqôb, Shime'ôn and Lêvy, Dînâh's brethren, took each man his sword, and came upon the city unawares, and slew all the males.]

26 And they slew 'Hamôr and Shechem his son with the edge of the sword, and took Dînâh out of Shechem's house, and went forth.

27 The sons of Ya'aqôb came upon the slain, and spoiled the city, because they had defiled their sister.

29 All their wealth, and all their little ones and their wives, took they captive and spoiled, even all that was in the house.

[1] [And Ya'aqôb said to Shime'ôn and Lêvy, Ye have troubled me, to make me to stink among the inhabitants of the land. They will gather themselves together against me, and I shall be destroyed, I and my house.]

31 And they said, Should he deal with our sister as with an harlot?

[1] See note [2] on p. 242.

XXXIV.

BÊTH-ÊL RECONSECRATED.[1]

XXXV. 1 And Elóhim said unto Ya'aqôb, Arise, go up to Bêth-Êl, and dwell there: and make there an altar [unto God, who appeared unto thee when thou fleddest from the face of 'Ésáv thy brother.]

2 Then Ya'aqôb said unto his household, and to all that were him, Put away the strange gods that are among you, and purify yourselves, and change your garments.

3 And let us arise, and go up to Bêth-Êl; and I will make there an altar unto God, who answered me in the day of my distress, and was with me in the way which I went.

4 And they gave unto Ya'aqôb all the strange gods which were in their hand, and the rings which were in their ears: and Ya'aqôb hid them under the oak which was by Shechem.

5 And they journeyed, and the terror of Elóhim was upon the cities that were round about them, and they did not pursue after the sons of Ya'aqôb.

6 So Ya'aqôb came to Lûz, which is in the land of Kenâ'an (the same is Bêth-Êl), he and all the people that were with him.[2]

7 And he built there an altar, and called the place

---

[1] This is another fragment which the Jehovist has taken from the older document in which God is called Elóhim, and from which he has already borrowed so much. His own share in making additions to the text is only to be traced in the two portions of vv. 1 and 7, which we have put into brackets.

[2] There is some uncertainty respecting the origin of this verse. It may belong to the Elohist. M. Schrader thinks it does.

Êl-Beth-Êl: [because there Elóhîm was revealed unto him, when he fled from the face of his brother.]

8 And Debôrâh Ribqâh's nurse died, and she was buried below Bêth-Êl under the terebinth: and the name of it was called Allôn-Bâcûth (the terebinth of weeping).

XXXV.

DEATH OF RÂ'HÊL.

XXXV. 16 And they journeyed from Bêth-Êl; and there was still some way to come to Ephrâthâh: and Râ'hêl travailed, and she had hard labour.

17 And it came to pass, when she was in hard labour, that the midwife said unto her, Fear not; for now thou shalt have another son.

18 And it came to pass, as she gave up the ghost (for she died), that she called his name Ben-Ôny (son of my sorrow); but his father called him Bin-Yâmîn (son of the right hand).

19 And Râ'hêl died, and was buried in the way to Ephrâthâh (the same is Bêth-Le'hem).

20 And Ya'aqôb set up a column upon her grave: the same is Maçebeth Qeturâth-Râ'hêl (the column of Râ'hêl's grave) unto this day.

21 And Yisrâêl journeyed, and spread his tent beyond Migdal-'Êder.

22 And it came to pass, while Yisrâêl dwelt in that land, that Reûbên went and lay with Bil'hâh, his father's concubine, and Yisrâêl heard of it.[1]

[1] The Jehovist should relate here, as is done in our present copy of

XXXVI.

YÔSÊPH AND HIS BRETHREN.

XXXVII. 2 [Yôsêph] was a lad with the sons of Bil'hâh, and with the sons of Zilpâh, his father's wives. 3 Now Yisrâêl loved Yôsêph more than all his children; and he made him a tunic of many colours.

4 And his brethren saw that their father loved him more than all his brethren: and they hated him, and could not speak peaceably unto him.

12 And his brethren went to feed their father's flock in Shechem.

13 And Yisrâêl said unto Yôsêph, Do not thy brethren feed the flock in Shechem? Come, and I will send thee unto them. And he said to him, Here am I.

14 And he said to him, Go now, see whether it be well with thy brethren, and well with the flock; and bring me word again. So he sent him out of the vale of Hebrôn, and he came to Shechem.

15 And a certain man found him, and, behold, he was wandering in the field: and the man asked him, saying, What seekest thou?

16 And he said, I seek my brethren: tell me, I pray thee, where they are feeding the flock.

17 And the man said, They are departed hence; for I heard them say, Let us go to Dothân. And Yôsêph went after his brethren, and found them in Dothân.

Genesis, the death of Yiçe'hâq after the death of Râ'hêl. But this portion of his text is lost, the latest editor having preferred the narrative of the Elohist.

23 And it came to pass, when Yôsêph was come unto his brethren, that they stript Yôsêph of his tunic, the tunic of many colours that was on him.

25 And they sat down to eat bread: and they lifted up their eyes and looked, and, behold, a travelling company of Yishma'êlim came from Gile'âd, with their camels bearing spicery and balm and ladanum, going to carry it down to Miçraîm.

26 And Yehûdâh said unto his brethren, What profit is it if we slay our brother, and conceal his blood?

27 Come, and let us sell him to the Yishma'êlim, and let not our hand be upon him; for he is our brother, our flesh. And his brethren hearkened unto him,

28 And they sold Yôsêph to the Yishma'êlim for twenty (shekels) of silver. And they brought Yôsêph into Miçraîm.

31 And they took Yôsêph's tunic, and killed a he-goat, and dipped the coat in the blood;

32 And they sent the tunic of many colours, and they brought it to their father; and said, This have we found: know now whether it be thy son's coat or not;

33 And he knew it, and said, It is my son's tunic; an evil beast hath devoured him; Yôsêph is without doubt torn in pieces.

XXXVII.

YEHÛDÂH AND TÂMÂR.

XXXVIII. 1 And it came to pass at that time, that Yehûdâh went down from his brethren, and turned in to a certain man of 'Adullâm, whose name was 'Hirâh.

2 And Yehûdâh saw there a daughter of a certain Kena'any whose name was Shû'â; and he took her and went in unto her.

3 And she conceived, and bare a son; and he called his name 'Êr.

4 And she conceived again, and bare a son; and she called his name Ônân.

5 And she yet again bare a son, and called his name Shêlâh; and he was at Chezib when she bare him.

6 And Yehûdâh took a wife for 'Êr his firstborn, and her name was Tâmâr.

7 And 'Êr, Yehûdâh's firstborn, was wicked in the eyes of Yahveh; and Yahveh slew him.

8 And Yehûdâh said unto Ônân, Go in unto thy brother's wife, and marry her as brother of her husband, and raise up seed to thy brother.

9 And Ônân knew that the seed should not be his; and it came to pass, when he went in unto his brother's wife, that he spilled it on the ground, lest he should give seed to his brother.

10 And the thing which he did was evil in the sight of Yahveh: and he slew him also.

11 Then said Yehûdâh to Tâmâr his daughter in law, Remain a widow in thy father's house till Shêlâh

my son be grown up; for he said, Lest he also die, like his brethren. And Tâmâr went and dwelt in her father's house.

12 And in process of time Shû'a's daughter, the wife of Yehûdâh, died ; and Yehûdâh was comforted, and went up unto his sheepshearers to Timnâth, he and his friend 'Hirâh the 'Adullâmy.

13 And it was told Tâmâr, saying, Behold thy father in law goeth up to Timnâth to shear his sheep.

14 And she put off from her the garments of her widowhood, and covered herself with her veil, and wrapped herself, and sat in the gate of 'Ênaim, which is by the way to Timnâth ; for she saw that Shêlâh was grown up, and she was not given unto him to wife.

15 When Yehûdâh saw her, he thought her to be an harlot ; for she had covered her face.

16 And he turned unto her by the way, and said, Go to, I pray thee, let me come in unto thee: for he knew not that she was his daughter in law. And she said, What wilt thou give me, that thou mayest come in unto me?

17 And he said, I will send thee a kid of the goats from the flock. And she said, Wilt thou give me a pledge, till thou send it?

18 And he said, What pledge shall I give thee? And she said, Thy signet and thy cord, and the staff that is in thine hand. And he gave them to her, and came in unto her, and she conceived by him.

19 And she arose, and went away, and put off her veil from her, and put on the garments of her widowhood.

20 And Yehûdâh sent the kid of the goats by the hand of his friend the 'Adullâmy, to receive the pledge from the woman's hand: but he found her not.

21 Then he asked the men of her place, saying, Where is the harlot that was at 'Ênaim by the way side? And they said, There hath been no harlot here.

22 And he returned to Yehûdâh, and said, I have not found her; and also the men of the place said, There hath been no harlot here.

23 And Yehûdâh said, Let her take it to her, lest we be put to shame: behold, I sent this kid, and thou hast not found her.

24 And it came to pass, about three months after, that it was told Yehûdâh, saying, Tâmâr thy daughter in law hath played the harlot; and moreover, behold, she is with child by whoredom. And Yehûdâh said, Bring her forth, and let her be burnt.

25 When she was brought forth, she sent to her father in law, saying, By the man, whose these are, am I with child: and she said, Discern, I pray thee, whose are these, the signet, and the cords, and the staff.

26 And Yehûdâh acknowledged them, and said, She is more righteous than I; forasmuch as I gave her not to Shêlâh my son. And he knew her again no more.

27 And it came to pass, in the time of her travail, that, behold, twins were in her womb.

28 And it came to pass, when she travailed, that one put out a hand: and the midwife took and bound upon his hand a scarlet thread, saying, This came out first.

29 And it came to pass, as he drew back his hand, that, behold, his brother came out: and she said,

How hast thou made a breach (*pâraçtâ*)? And she called his name Pâreç.

30 And afterward came out his brother, that had the scarlet thread upon his hand: and his name was called Zára'h.

XXXVIII.

YÔSÊPH IN PÔTIPHAR'S HOUSE.

XXXIX. 1 And Yôsêph was brought down to Miçráîm, and Pôtiphar, an eunuch of Para'ôh's, the chief of the executioners, a Miçry (an Egyptian), bought him of the hand of the Yishma'êlim, which had brought him down thither.

2 And Yahveh was with Yôsêph, and he was a prosperous man ; and he was in the house of his master the Miçry.

3 And his master saw that Yahveh was with him, and that Yahveh made all that he did to prosper in his hand.

4 And Yôsêph found grace in his sight, and he ministered unto him ; and he made him overseer over his house, and all that he had he put into his hand.

5 And it came to pass from the time that he made him overseer in his house, and over all that he had, that Yahveh blessed the Miçry's house for Yôsêph's sake ; and the blessing of Yahveh was upon all that he had, in the house and in the field.

6 And he left all that he had in Yôsêph's hand ; and

he knew not ought that was with him, save the bread which he did eat. And Yôsêph was comely, and well favoured.

7 And it came to pass after these things, that his master's wife cast her eyes upon Yôsêph; and she said, Lie with me.

8 But he refused, and said unto his master's wife, Behold, my master knoweth not what is with me in the house, and he hath put all that he hath into my hand;

9 There is none greater in this house than I; neither hath he kept back any thing from me but thee, because thou art his wife: how then can I do this great wickedness, and sin against Elôhim?

10 And it came to pass, as she spake to Yôsêph day by day, that he hearkened not unto her, to lie by her, or to be with her.

11 And it came to pass about this time, that he went into the house to do his work; and there was none of the men of the house there within.

12 And she caught him by his garment, saying, Lie with me: and he left his garment in her hand, and fled, and got him out.

13 And it came to pass, when she saw that he had left his garment in her hand, and was fled forth,

14 That she called unto the men of her house, and spake unto them, saying, See, he hath brought in an 'Ebry unto us to mock us; he came in unto me to lie with me, and I cried with a loud voice:

15 And it came to pass, when he heard that I lifted up my voice and cried, that he left his garment by me, and got him out.

16 And she laid up his garment by her, until his master came home.

17 And she spake unto him according to these words, saying, The 'Ĕbry slave which thou hast brought unto us, came in unto me to mock me :

18 And it came to pass, as I lifted up my voice and cried, that he left his garment by me, and fled out.

19 And it came to pass, when his master heard the words of his wife, which she spake unto him, saying, After this manner did thy servant to me ; that his wrath was kindled.

20 And Yôsêph's master took him, and put him into the prison, the place where the king's prisoners were bound : and he was there in the prison.

21 But Yahveh was with Yôsêph, and showed kindness unto him, and gave him favour in the sight of the keeper of the prison.

22 And the keeper of the prison committed to Yôsêph's hand all the prisoners that were in the prison ; and whatsoever they did there, he was the doer of it.

23 The keeper of the prison looked not to any thing that was under his hand, because Yahveh was with him, and that which he did, Yahveh made it to prosper

XXXIX.

YÔSÊPH IS ADVANCED IN MIÇRÂÎM.[1]

. . . .

XLI. 49 And Yôsêph laid up corn as the sand of the sea, very much, until he left numbering; for it was without number.

*[And unto Yôsêph were born two sons before the year of famine came.]

51 And Yôsêph called the name of the firstborn Menassheh: For, said he, Elôhîm [2] hath made me forget (*nasshany*) all my toil, and all my father's house.

52 And the name of the second called he Ephrâîm: For Elôhîm hath made me fruitful (*hiphrany*) in the land of my affliction.

. . . . .

[1] The latest editor of Genesis has here adopted the text of the Elohist exclusively. The result is that the account of this portion of Yôsêph's life by the Jehovist is hopelessly lost. Only three verses, which have been introduced in the final revision by way of explanatory supplements into the narrative of the Elohist appear to have been preserved. But the way they have been inserted enables us to know them by their unquestionable characteristics.

[2] Here the Jehovist had borrowed from the editing of the older work to which the more or less correct name of the 'second Elohist' has been given, unless—which is not quite certain—these two verses, 51 and 52, have appeared in his own work, and the latest reviser did not take them directly from their original source.

XL.

FIRST MEETING OF YÔSÉPH AND HIS BRETHREN.[1]

. . . .

XLII. 5 And the sons of Yisrâél came to buy among those that came: for the famine was in the land of Kenâ'an.

. . . . . .

27 And as one of them opened his sack to give his ass provender in the lodging place, he espied his money; and, behold, it was in the mouth of his sack.

28 And he said unto his brethren, My money is restored; and, lo, it is even in my sack: and their heart failed them, and they turned trembling one to another, saying, What is this that Elóhim hath done unto us?

. . . . .

XLI.

SECOND MEETING OF YÔSÉPH AND HIS BRETHREN. YÔSÉPH MAKES HIMSELF KNOWN TO THEM.[2]

XLIII. 1 And the famine was sore in the land.

2 And it came to pass, when they had eaten up the

---

[1] Of this narrative, as of that which precedes it, only a few detached verses remain, which the latest editor of Genesis has inserted in the middle of the narrative of the Elohist, which he adopted. See note on chap. xliii.

The last two of these verses, while quite distinct from the rest of the chapter into which they have been inserted, do not show traces of the mode of narrating of the Jehovist himself, but of that of the older work from which he has borrowed so much.

[2] See note on chap. xliii.

corn which they had brought out of Miçráim, their father said unto them, Go again, buy us a little food.

3 And Yehûdâh spake unto him, saying, The man did solemnly protest unto us, saying, Ye shall not see my face, except your brother be with you.[1]

4 If thou wilt send our brother with us, we will go down and buy thee food:

5 But if thou wilt not send him, we will not go down: for the man said unto us, Ye shall not see my face, except your brother be with you.

6 And Yisrâêl said, Wherefore dealt ye so ill with me, as to tell the man whether ye had yet a brother?

7 And they said, The man asked straitly concerning ourselves, and concerning our kindred, saying, Is your father yet alive? have ye another brother? and we told him according to the tenor of these words; could we in any wise know that he would say, Bring your brother down?

8 And Yehûdâh said unto Yisrâêl his father, Send the lad with me, and we will arise and go; that we may live and not die, both we and thou, and also our little ones.

9 I will be surety for him; of my hand shalt thou require him: if I bring him not unto thee, and set him before thee, then I shall have sinned against thee for ever:

10 For except we had lingered, surely we had now returned a second time.

---

[1] From verses 3-7 it would be possible to partly restore the conversation of Yôsêph with his brethren at their first interview as the narrative of the Jehovist gave it. It was different to that given in chap. xlii. taken from the Elohist.

11 And their father Yisrâêl said unto them, If it be so now, do this: take of the choice fruits of the land in your vessels, and carry down the man a present, a little balm, and a little honey, spicery, and ladanum, pistachio nuts and almonds :

12 And take double money in your hand ; and the money that was returned in the mouth of your sacks carry again in your hand ; peradventure it was an oversight :

13 Take also your brother, and arise, go again unto the man :

14 And Êl-Shadday (God Almighty) give you mercy before the man, that he may release unto you your other brother and Binyâmin. And if I am bereaved of my children, I am bereaved.

15 And the men took the present, and they took double money in their hand, and Binyâmin : and rose up, and went down to Miçrâim, and stood before Yôsêph.

16 And when Yôsêph saw Binyâmin with them, he said to the steward of his house, Bring the men into the house, and slay, and make ready : for the men shall dine with me at noon.

17 And the man did as Yôsêph bade : and the man brought the men into Yôsêph's house.

18 And the men were afraid, because they were brought into Yôsêph's house ; and they said, Because of the money that was returned in our sacks at the first time are we brought in ; that he may roll himself upon us, and fall upon us, and take us for bondmen, and our asses.

19 And they came near to the steward of Yôsêph's house, and they spake unto him at the door of the house,

20 And said, Oh my lord, we came indeed down at the first time to buy food:

21 And it came to pass, when we came to the lodging place, that we opened our sacks, and, behold, every man's money was in the mouth of his sack, our money in full weight; and we have brought it again in our hand.

22 And other money have we brought down in our hand to buy food: we know not who put our money in our sacks.

23 And he said, Peace be to you, fear not: your God and the God of your father hath given you treasure in your sacks: I had your money. And he brought Shime'ôn out unto them.

24 And the man brought the men into Yôsêph's house, and gave them water, and they washed their feet: and he gave their asses provender.

25 And they made ready the present against Yôsêph came at noon: for they heard that they should eat bread there.

26 And when Yôsêph came home, they brought him the present which was in their hand into the house, and bowed down themselves to him to the earth

27 And he asked them of their welfare, and said, Is your father well, the old man of whom ye spake? Is he yet alive?

28 And they said, Thy servant our father is well, he

is yet alive. And they bowed the head, and made obeisance.

29 And he lifted up his eyes, and saw Binyâmîn his brother, his mother's son, and said, Is this your youngest brother, of whom ye spake unto me? And he said, Elôhîm be gracious unto thee, my son.[1]

30 And Yôsêph made haste, for his bowels did yearn upon his brother: and he sought where to weep; and he entered into his chamber, and wept there.

31 And he washed his face, and came out; and he refrained himself, and said, Set on bread.

32 And they set on for him by himself, and for them by themselves, and for the Miçry, which did eat with him, by themselves: because the Miçry might not eat bread with the 'Ébrim; for that is an abomination unto the Miçry.

33 And they sat before him, the firstborn according to his birthright, and the youngest according to his youth: and the men marvelled one with another.

34 And messes were taken unto them from before him: but Binyâmîn's mess was five times so much as any of theirs. And they drank, and drank largely with him.

XLIV. 1 And he commanded the steward of his house, saying, Fill the men's sacks with food, as much as they can carry, and put every man's money in his sack's mouth.

2 And put my cup, the silver cup, in the sack's mouth of the youngest, and his corn money. And he did according to the word that Yôsêph had spoken.

---

[1] This verse must have been taken by the Jehovistic writer from the older document which he had before him, in which God is called Elôhim.

3 As soon as the morning was light, the men were sent away, they and their asses.

4 And when they were gone out of the city, and were not yet far off, Yôsêph said unto his steward, Up, follow after the men; and when thou dost overtake them, say unto them, Wherefore have ye rewarded evil for good?

5 Is not this it in which my lord drinketh, and whereby he indeed divineth? ye have done evil in so doing.

6 And he overtook them, and he spake unto them these words.

7 And they said unto him, Wherefore speaketh my lord such words as these? Far be it from thy servants that they should do such a thing.

8 Behold, the money which we found in our sacks' mouths, we brought again unto thee out of the land of Kenâ'an: how then should we steal out of thy lord's house silver or gold?

9 With whomsoever of thy servants it be found, let him die, and we also will be my lord's bondmen.

10 And he said, Now also let it be according unto your words: he with whom it is found shall be my bondman; and ye shall be blameless.

11 Then they hasted, and took down every man his sack to the ground, and opened every man his sack.

12 And he searched, and began at the eldest, and left at the youngest: and the cup was found in Binyâmîn's sack.

13 Then they rent their clothes, and laded every man his ass, and returned to the city.

14 And Yehûdâh and his brethren came to Yôsêph's house; and he was yet there: and they fell before him on the ground.

15 And Yôsêph said unto them, What deed is this that ye have done? Know ye not that such a man as I can indeed divine?

16 And Yehûdâh said, What shall we say unto my lord? what shall we speak? or how shall we clear ourselves? God hath found out the iniquity of thy servants: behold, we are my lord's bondmen, both we, and he also in whose hand the cup is found.

17 And he said, Far be it from me that I should do so: the man in whose hand the cup is found, he shall be my bondman: but as for you, get you up in peace unto your father.

18 Then Yehûdâh came near unto him, and said, Oh my lord, let thy servant, I pray thee, speak a word in my lord's ears, and let not thine anger burn against thy servant: for thou art even as Para'ôh.

19 My lord asked his servants, saying, Have ye a father, or a brother?

20 And we said unto my lord, We have a father, an old man, and a child of his old age, a little one; and his brother is dead, and he alone is left of his mother, and his father loveth him.

21 And thou saidst unto thy servants, Bring him down unto me, that I may set mine eyes upon him.

22 And we said unto my lord, The lad cannot leave his father: for if he should leave his father, his father would die.

23 And thou saidst unto thy servants, Except your

youngest brother come down with you, ye shall see my face no more.

24 And it came to pass when we came up unto thy servant my father, we told him the words of my lord.

25 And our father said, Go again, buy us a little food.

26 And we said, We cannot go down: if our youngest brother be with us, then will we go down; for we may not see the man's face, except our youngest brother be with us.

27 And thy servant my father said unto us, Ye know that my wife bare me two sons:

28 And the one went out from me, and I said, Surely he is torn in pieces; and I have not seen him since.

29 And if ye take this one also from me, and mischief befall him, ye shall bring down my gray hairs with sorrow to Sheôl.

30 Now therefore, when I come to thy servant my father, and the lad be not with us; seeing that his life is bound up in the lad's life;

31 It shall come to pass, when he seeth that the lad is not with us, that he will die: and thy servants shall bring down the gray hairs of thy servant our father with sorrow to Sheôl.

32 For thy servant became surety for the lad unto my father, saying, If I bring him not unto thee, then shall I bear the blame to my father for ever.

33 Now therefore, let thy servant, I pray thee, abide instead of the lad a bondman to my lord; and let the lad go up with his brethren.

34 For how shall I go up to my father, and the lad

be not with me? lest I see the evil that shall come upon my father.

XLV. 1 Then Yôsêph could not refrain himself before all them that stood by him; and he cried, Cause every man to go out from me. And there stood no man with him, while Yôsêph made himself known unto his brethren.

2 And he wept aloud; and the Egyptians heard, and the house of Para'ôh heard.

14 And he fell upon his brother Binyâmîn's neck, and wept; and Binyâmin wept upon his neck.

15 And he kissed all his brethren, and wept upon them: and after that his brethren talked with him.

16 And the fame thereof was heard in Para'ôh's house, saying, Yôsêph's brethren are come: and it pleased Para'ôh well, and his servants.

17 And Para'ôh said unto Yôsêph, Say unto thy brethren, This do ye; lade your beasts, and go, get you unto the land of Kenâ'an;

18 And take your father and your households, and come unto me; and I will give you the good of the land of Miçrâim, and ye shall eat the fat of the land.

19 Now thou art commanded, this do ye; take you chariots out of the land of Miçrâim for your little ones, and for your wives, and bring your father, and come.

20 Also regard not your stuff; for the good of all the land of Miçrâim is yours.

21 And the sons of Yisrâêl did so: and Yôsêph gave them chariots, according to the commandment of Para'ôh, and gave them provision for the way.

*[And they came into the land of Kená'an unto Ya'aqôb their father.]

26 And they told him, saying, Yôsêph is yet alive, and he is ruler over all the land of Miçrâim. And his heart fainted, for he believed them not.

27 And they told him all the words of Yôsêph, which he had said unto them: and when he saw the chariots which Yôsêph had sent to carry him, the spirit of Ya'aqôb their father revived:

28 And Yisrâêl said, It is enough; Yôsêph my son is yet alive: I will go and see him before I die.

XLII.

THE FAMILY OF YA'AQÔB SETTLES IN MIÇRÂÎM.

XLVI.[1] 1 And Yisrâêl took his journey with all that he had, and came to Beêr-Shâb'a, and sacrificed victims there to the God of his father Yiçe'hâq.

2 And Elôhîm spake unto Yisrâêl in the visions of the night, and said, Ya'aqôb, Ya'aqôb. And he said, Here am I.

3 And he said, I am God, the God of thy father: fear not to go down into Miçrâim; for I will there make of thee a great nation:

4 I will go down with thee into Miçrâim; and I will also surely bring thee up again: and Yôsêph shall put his hand upon thine eyes.

[1] Verses 1-4 have been wholly taken by the Jehovist from the older document called the 'second Elohist.'

5 And Ya'aqôb rose up from Beêr-Shàb'a: and the sons of Yisraêl carried Ya'aqôb their father, and their little ones, and their wives, in the chariots which Para'ôh had sent to carry him.

28 And he sent Yehûdâh before him unto Yôsêph, to show the way before him unto Gôshen; and they came into the land of Gôshen.

29 And Yôsêph made ready his chariot, and went up to meet Yisraêl his father, to Gôshen; and he presented himself unto him, and fell on his neck, and wept on his neck a good while.

30 And Yisraêl said unto Yôsêph, Now let me die, since I have seen thy face, that thou art yet alive.

31 And Yôsêph said unto his brethren, and unto his father's house, I will go up, and tell Para'ôh, and will say unto him, My brethren and my father's house, which were in the land of Kenâ'an, are come unto me;

32 And the men are shepherds, for they have been keepers of cattle: and they have brought their flocks, and their herds, and all that they have.

33 And it shall come to pass, when Para'ôh shall call you, and shall say, What is your occupation?

34 That ye shall say, Thy servants have been keepers of cattle from our youth even until now, both we, and our fathers: that ye may dwell in the land of Gôshen; for every shepherd is an abomination unto the Egyptians.

XLVII. 1 Then Yôsêph went in and told Para'ôh, and said, My father and my brethren, and their flocks, and their herds, and all that they have, are come out of the land of Kenâ'an, and, behold, they are in the land of Gôshen.

2 And from among his brethren he took five men, and presented them unto Para'ôh.

3 And Para'ôh said unto his brethren, What is your occupation? And they said unto Para'ôh, Thy servants are shepherds, both we, and our fathers.

4 And they said unto Para'ôh, To sojourn in the land are we come; for there is no pasture for thy servants' flocks; for the famine is sore in the land of Kenâ'an; now, therefore, we pray thee, let thy servants dwell in the land of Gôshen.

5 And Para'ôh spake unto Yôsêph, saying, Thy father and thy brethren are come unto thee:

6 The land of Miçrâim is before thee; in the best of the land make thy father and thy brethren to dwell; in the land of Gôshen let them dwell; and if thou knowest any able men among them, then make them rulers over my cattle.

27 And Yisrâêl dwelt in the land of Miçrâim, in the land of Gôshen.

XLIII.

BLESSING OF THE SONS OF YÔSÊPH.

XLVII. 29 And the time drew near that Yisrâêl must die: and he called his son Yôsêph, and said unto him, If now I have found grace in thy sight, put, I pray thee, thy hand under my thigh, and deal kindly and truly with me; bury me not, I pray thee, in Miçrâim:

30 But when I sleep with my fathers, thou shalt carry me out of Miçráîm, and bury me in their burying-place. And he said, I will do as thou hast said. 31 And he said, Swear unto me: and he sware unto him. And Yisráél bowed himself upon the bed's head.

XLVIII. 8[1] And Yisráél beheld Yôsêph's sons, and said, Who are these? 9 And Yôsêph said unto his father, They are my sons, whom Elôhîm hath given me here. And he said, Bring them, I pray thee, unto me, and I will bless them. 10 Now the eyes of Yisráél were dim for age, so that he could not see. And he brought them near unto him; and he kissed them, and embraced them. 11 And Yisráél said unto Yôsêph, I had not thought to see thy face; and, lo, Elôhîm hath let me see thy seed also. 12 And Yôsêph brought them out from between his knees, and he bowed himself with his face to the earth. 13 And Yôsêph took them both, Ephráîm in his right hand toward Yisráél's left hand, and Menassheh in his left hand toward Yisráél's right hand, and brought them near unto him. 14 And Yisráél stretched out his right hand, and laid it upon Ephráîm's head, who was the younger, and his left hand upon Menassheh's head, guiding his hands wittingly; for Menassheh was the firstborn.

---

[1] The Jehovist has taken the groundwork of this narrative, and most of the expressions he makes use of, from the book where God is called Elôhîm; a different work from that of the Elohist properly so called, which has so often been the *substratum* to his narrative. The use, however, of the name of Yisráél to designate Ya'aqôb is one of the signs of his personal revision.

15 And he blessed Yôsêph, and said, The God before whom my fathers Abráhâm and Yiçe'hâq did walk, the God which hath fed me all my life long unto this day,

16 The angel which hath redeemed me from all evil, bless the lads; and let my name be named on them, and the name of my fathers Abráhâm and Yiçe'hâq; and let them grow into a multitude in the midst of the earth.

17 And when Yôsêph saw that his father laid his right hand upon the head of Ephrâim, it displeased him; and he held up his father's hand, to remove it from Ephrâim's head to Menassheh's head.

18 And Yôsêph said to his father, Not so, my father: for this is the firstborn; put thy right hand upon his head.

19 And his father refused, and said, I know it, my son, I know it: he also shall become a people, and he also shall be great; howbeit his younger brother shall be greater than he, and his seed shall become a multitude of nations.

20 And he blessed them that day, saying, By thee shall Yisrâêl bless, saying, Elôhim make thee as Ephrâim and as Menassheh: and he set Ephrâim before Menassheh.

21 And Yisrâêl said unto Yôsêph, Behold, I die: but Elôhim shall be with you, and bring you again unto the land of your fathers.

22 Moreover, I have given to thee one portion[1] above thy brethren, which I took out of the hand of the 'Amôry with my sword and with my bow.

---

[1] See note to chap. xlviii. 22.

XLIV.

BLESSING OF THE SONS OF YA'AQÔB.

XLIX. 1 And Ya'aqôb called unto his sons, and said: Gather yourselves together, that I may tell you that which shall befall you in the latter days.
 2 Assemble yourselves, and hear, ye sons of Ya'aqôb!
  And hearken unto Yisráêl your father.
 3 Reûbên, thou art my firstborn,
  My might, and the first-fruits of my strength;
  The excellency of dignity, and the excellency of power.
 4 Impetuous as water, thou shall not have the excellency;
  Because thou wentest up to thy father's bed:
  Then defiledst thou it: he went up to my couch.
 5 Shime'ôn and Lêvy are brethren;
  Weapons of violence are their compacts.
 6 O my soul, come not thou into their secret councils;
  Unto their assembly, my honour, be not thou united;
 For in their anger they slew men,
  And in their selfwill they houghed oxen.
 7 Cursed be their anger, for it was fierce;
  And their wrath, for it was cruel:
 I will divide them in Ya'aqôb,
  And scatter them in Yisráêl.
 8 Yehûdâh, thee shall thy brethren praise:
  Thy hand shall be on the neck of thine enemies;
  Thy father's sons shall bow down before thee.

9 Yehûdâh is a lion's whelp;
   From the prey, my son, thou art gone up:
   He stooped down, he couched as a lion,
   And as a lioness; who shall rouse him up?
10 The sceptre shall not depart from Yehûdâh,
   Nor the ruler's staff from between his feet,
   Until he come to Shilôh.
   And unto him shall the obedience of the peoples be.
11 Binding his foal unto the vine,
   And his ass's colt unto the choice vine;
   He hath washed his garments in wine,
   And his vesture in the blood of grapes.
12 His eyes shall be red with wine,
   And his teeth white with milk.
13 Zebulûn shall dwell at the haven of the sea:
   And he shall be for an haven of ships;
   And his border shall be by Çidôn.
14 Yissâchâr is a strong ass,
   Couching down between the sheepfolds:
15 And he saw a resting place that it was good,
   And the land that it was pleasant;
   And he bowed his shoulder to bear,
   And became a servant under taskwork.
16 Dân shall judge his people,
   As one of the tribes of Yisrâêl.
17 Dân shall be a serpent in the way,
   An horned snake in the path,
   That biteth the horse's heels,
   So that his rider falleth backward.
18 I have waited for thy salvation, O Yahveh.

19 Gâd, a troop shall press upon him,
   But he shall press upon their heel.
20 Ashêr his bread shall be fat ;
   And he shall yield royal dainties.
21 Naphtály is a hind let loose :
   He giveth goodly words.
22 Yôsêph is a fruitful bough,
   A fruitful bough by a fountain ;
   His branches run over the wall.
23 The archers have sorely grieved him,
   And shot at him, and persecuted him :
24 But his bow abode in strength,
   And the arms of his hands were made strong,
   By the hands of the Mighty One of Ya'aqôb,
   (From thence is the shepherd, the stone of Yisrâêl,)
25 Even by the God of thy father, who shall help thee,
   And by the Almighty, who shall bless thee,
   With blessings of heaven above,
   Blessings of the deep that coucheth beneath,
   Blessings of the breasts, and of the womb,
26 The blessings of thy father have prevailed
   Above the blessings of my progenitors
   Unto the utmost bound of the everlasting hills :
   They shall be on the head of Yôsêph,
   And on the crown of the head of him that is prince among his brethren.
27 Binyâmin is a wolf that ravineth :
   In the morning he shall devour the prey,
   And at even he shall divide the spoil.
28 All these are the twelve tribes of Yisrâêl ; and this it is that their father spake unto them and blessed them.

XLV.

DEATH AND FUNERALS OF YA'AQÔB AND YÔSÊPH.

. . . .[1]

L. 1 And Yôsêph fell upon his father's face, and wept upon him, and kissed him.

2 And Yôsêph commanded his slaves the physicians to embalm his father: and the physicians embalmed Yisrâêl.

3 And forty days were fulfilled for him; for so are fulfilled the days of embalming: and the Egyptians wept for him threescore and ten days.

4 And when the days of weeping for him were past, Yôsêph spake unto the house of Para'ôh, saying, If now I have found grace in your eyes, speak, I pray you, in the ears of Para'ôh, saying,

5 My father made me swear, saying, Lo, I die: in my grave which I have digged for me in the land of Kenâ'an, there shalt thou bury me. Now therefore let me go up, I pray thee, and bury my father, and I will come again.

6 And Para'ôh said, Go up, and bury thy father, according as he made thee swear.

7 And Yôsêph went up to bury his father: and with him went up all the servants of Para'ôh, the elders of his house, and all the elders of the land of Miçrâim,

8 And all the house of Yôsêph, and his brethren, and his father's house: only their little ones, and their flocks, and their herds, they left in the land of Gôshen.

---

[1] The verses in which the Jehovist related the death of Ya'aqôb are lost, the latest editor having adopted the text of the Elohist in place of them.

9 And there went up with him both chariots and horsemen : and it was a very great company.

10 And they came to Góren-háátád, which is beyond the Yardên, and there they lamented with a very great and sore lamentation: and he made a mourning for his father seven days.

11 And when the inhabitants of the land, the Kena'any, saw the mourning at Góren-háátád, they said, This is a grievous mourning for Miçráim : wherefore the name of it was called Abêl-Miçráim (Mourning of Miçráim), (the locality) which is beyond the Yardên.

14 And Yôsêph returned into Miçráim, he, and his brethren, and all that went up with him to bury his father, after he had buried his father.

15 And when Yôsêph's brethren saw that their father was dead, they said, It may be that Yôsêph will hate us, and will fully requite us all the evil which we did unto him.

16 And they sent a message unto Yôsêph, saying, Thy father did command before he died, saying,

17 So shall ye say unto Yôsêph, Forgive, I pray thee now, the transgression of thy brethren, and their sin, for that they did unto thee evil: and now, we pray thee, forgive the transgression of the servants of the God of thy father. And Yôsêph wept when they spake unto him.

18 And his brethren also went and fell down before his face ; and they said, Behold, we be thy slaves.

19 And Yôsêph said unto them, Fear not, for am I in the place of Elôhim ?[1]

---

[1] The Jehovist has taken these latter verses, almost without alteration, from the document improperly called that of the 'second Elohist.'

20 And as for you, ye meant evil against me; but Elôhim meant it for good, to bring to pass, as it is this day, to save much people alive.

21 Now therefore fear ye not: I will nourish you, and your little ones. And he comforted them, and spake to their heart.

23 And Yôsêph saw Ephrâim's children of the third generation: the children also of Mâchîr the son of Menassheh were born upon Yôsêph's knees.

24 And Yôsêph said unto his brethren, I die: but Elôhim will surely visit you, and bring you up out of this land unto the land which he sware to Abrâhâm, to Yiçe'hâq, and to Ya'aqôb.

25 And Yôsêph took an oath of the children of Yisrâêl, saying, Elôhim will surely visit you, and ye shall carry up my bones from hence.

26 So Yôsêph died, being an hundred and ten years old: and they embalmed him, and he was put into a coffin in Miçrâim.

III.
THE BOOK OF GENEALOGIES
OR
ELOHISTIC DOCUMENT

I.

THE GENEALOGIES OF THE HEAVEN AND OF THE EARTH.

II. 4 These are the genealogies of the heaven and of the earth when they were created.

I. 1 In the beginning Elôhim created the heaven and the earth.

2 And the earth was waste and void; and darkness was upon the face of the deep: and the spirit of Elôhim moved upon the face of the waters.

3 And Elôhim said, Let there be light: and there was light.

4 And Elôhim saw the light, that it was good: and Elôhim divided the light from the darkness.

5 And Elôhim called the light Day, and the darkness he called Night. And there was evening and there was morning, one day.

6 And Elôhim said, Let there be a firmament in the midst of the waters, and let it divide the waters from the waters. And it was so.

7 And Elôhim made the firmament, and divided the waters which were under the firmament from the waters which were above the firmament. And Elôhim saw the firmament, that it was good.

8 And Elôhim called the firmament Heaven. And there was evening and there was morning, a second day.

9 And Elôhîm said, Let the waters under the heaven be gathered together unto one place, and let the dry land appear: and it was so.

10 And Elôhîm called the dry land Earth; and the gathering together of the waters called he Seas: and Elôhîm saw that it was good.

11 And Elôhîm said, Let the earth put forth grass, herb yielding seed, and fruit-tree bearing fruit after its kind, wherein is the seed thereof, upon the earth: and it was so.

12 And the earth brought forth grass, herb yielding seed after its kind, and tree bearing fruit, wherein is the seed thereof, after its kind: and Elôhîm saw that it was good.

13 And there was evening and there was morning, a third day.

14 And Elôhîm said, Let there be lights in the firmament of the heaven to divide the day from the night; and let them be for signs and for seasons, and for days and years:

15 And let them be for lights in the firmament of the heaven to give light upon the earth: and it was so.

16 And Elôhîm made the two great lights; the greater light to rule the day, and the lesser light to rule the night: he made the stars also.

[1] [And Elôhîm placed them in the firmament of the heaven to give light upon the earth.]

17 And Elôhîm set them in the firmament of the heaven to give light upon the earth,

[1] The restoration of this verse, which is omitted from the text as we now have it, is absolutely necessary to make the history agree with the other verses.

18 And to rule over the day and over the night, and to divide the light from the darkness: and Elôhîm saw that it was good.

19 And there was evening and there was morning, a fourth day.

20 And Elôhîm said, Let the waters swarm with a living pullulation, and let fowl fly above the earth towards the face of the firmament of the heaven. And it was so.

21 And Elôhîm created the great sea-monsters, and all the living and creeping things with which the waters swarm, after their kinds, and every winged fowl after its kind: and Elôhîm saw that it was good.

22 And Elôhîm blessed them, saying, Be fruitful, and multiply, and fill the waters in the seas, and let fowl multiply in the earth.

23 And there was evening and there was morning, a fifth day.

24 And Elôhîm said, Let the earth bring forth the living creature after its kind, cattle, and creeping thing, and beast of the earth after its kind: and it was so.

25 And Elôhîm made the beast of the earth after its kind, and the cattle after their kind, and everything that creepeth upon the ground after its kind: and Elôhîm saw that it was good.

[1] [And Elôhîm blessed them, saying, Be fruitful, and multiply, and replenish the earth.]

26 And Elôhîm said, Let us make man in our image, after our likeness: and let them have dominion over the

[1] This is another verse which is wanting both in our present text and in the ancient versions, but which is also required to make the history of creation complete.

fish of the sea, and over the fowl of the air, and over the cattle, and over [every beast of] the earth, and over every creeping thing that creepeth upon the earth.

27 And Elôhim created man in his own image, in the image of Elôhim created he him; male and female created he them.

28 And Elôhim blessed them; and Elôhim said unto them, Be fruitful, and multiply, and replenish the earth, and subdue it; and have dominion over the fish of the sea, and over the fowl of the air, and over every living thing that moveth upon the earth.

29 And Elôhim said, Behold, I have given you every herb yielding seed, which is upon the face of all the earth, and every tree, in the which is the fruit of a tree yielding seed; to you it shall be for meat:

30 And to every beast of the earth, and to every fowl of the air, and to every thing that creepeth upon the earth, wherein there is the breath of life, I have given every green herb for meat: and it was so.

31 And Elôhim saw everything that he had made, and, behold, it was very good. And there was evening and there was morning, the sixth day.

II. 1 And the heaven and the earth were finished, and all the host of them.

2 And on the seventh day Elôhim finished his work which he had made; and he rested on the seventh day from all his work which he had made.

3 And Elôhim blessed the seventh day, and hallowed it; because that in it he rested from all his work which Elôhim had created and made.

II.

THE GENEALOGIES OF ÂDÂM.

V. 1 This is the book of the genealogies of Âdâm. In the day that Elôhîm created man, in the likeness of Elôhîm made he him;

2 Male and female created he them; and blessed them, and called their name Âdâm, in the day when they were created.

3 And Âdâm lived an hundred and thirty years, and begat a son in his own likeness, after his image: and called his name Shêth:

4 And the days of Âdâm after he begat Shêth were eight hundred years: and he begat sons and daughters:

5 And all the days that Âdâm lived were nine hundred and thirty years: and he died.

6 And Shêth lived an hundred and five years, and begat Enôsh:

7 And Shêth lived after he begat Enôsh eight hundred and seven years, and begat sons and daughters:

8 And all the days of Shêth were nine hundred and twelve years: and he died.

9 And Enôsh lived ninety years, and begat Qênân:

10 And Enôsh lived after he begat Qênân eight hundred and fifteen years, and begat sons and daughters:

11 And all the days of Enôsh were nine hundred and five years: and he died.

12 And Qênân lived seventy years, and begat Mahalalêl:

13 And Qênân lived after he begat Mahalalêl eight hundred and forty years, and begat sons and daughters :

14 And all the days of Qênân were nine hundred and ten years : and he died.

15 And Mahalalêl lived sixty and five years, and begat Yâred :

16 And Mahalalêl lived after he begat Yâred eight hundred and thirty years, and begat sons and daughters :

17 And all the days of Mahalalêl were eight hundred ninety and five years : and he died.

18 And Yâred lived an hundred sixty and two years, and begat 'Hanôch :

19 And Yâred lived after he begat 'Hanôch eight hundred years, and begat sons and daughters :

20 And all the days of Yâred were nine hundred sixty and two years : and he died.

21 And 'Hanôch lived sixty and five years, and begat Methûshâla'h :

22 And 'Hanôch walked with God after he begat Methûshâla'h three hundred years, and begat sons and daughters :

23 And all the days of 'Hanôch were three hundred sixty and five years :

24 And 'Hanôch walked with God : and he was not ; for Elôhîm took him.

25 And Methûshâla'h lived an hundred eighty and seven years, and begat Lâmech :

26 And Methûshâla'h lived after he begat Lâmech seven hundred eighty and two years, and begat sons and daughters :

27 And all the days of Methûshála'h were nine hundred sixty and nine years: and he died.

28 And Lâmech lived an hundred eighty and two years, and he begat [Nôa'h]:

30 And Lâmech lived after he begat Nôa'h five hundred ninety and five years, and begat sons and daughters:

31 And all the days of Lâmech were seven hundred seventy and seven years: and he died.

32 And Nôa'h was five hundred years old: and Nôa'h begat Shêm, 'Hâm, and Yâpheth.

III.

THE GENEALOGIES OF NÔA'H.

VI. 9 These are the genealogies of Nôa'h.

Nôa'h was a righteous man and upright in his generations: Nôa'h walked with God.

10 And Nôa'h begat three sons, Shêm, 'Hâm, and Yâpheth.

11 And the earth was corrupt before God, and the earth was filled with violence.

12 And Elôhîm saw the earth, and, behold, it was corrupt: for all flesh had corrupted his way upon the earth.

13 And Elôhîm said unto Nôa'h, The end of all flesh is come before me; for the earth is filled with violence through them; and, behold, I will destroy them with the earth.

14 Make thee an ark of cypress wood; cells shalt thou make in the ark, and shalt pitch it within and without with pitch.

15 And this is how thou shalt make it: the length of the ark three hundred cubits, the breadth of it fifty cubits, and the height of it thirty cubits.

16 A light shalt thou make to the ark, and to a cubit shalt thou finish it upward; and the door of the ark shalt thou set in the side thereof; with lower, second, and third stories shalt thou make it.

17 And I, behold, I do bring the deluge of waters upon the earth, to destroy all flesh, wherein is the breath of life, from under heaven; every thing that is in the earth shall die.

18 But I will establish my covenant with thee; and thou shalt come into the ark, thou, and thy sons, and thy wife, and thy sons' wives with thee.

19 And of every living thing of all flesh, two of every sort shalt thou bring into the ark, to keep them alive with thee; they shall be male and female.

20 Of the fowl after their kind, and of the cattle after their kind, of every creeping thing of the ground after its kind, two of every sort shall come unto thee, to keep them alive.

21 And take thou unto thee of all food that is eaten, and gather it to thee; and it shall be for food for thee, and for them.

22 Thus did Nôa'h; according to all that Elôhim commanded him, so did he.

VII. 6 And Nôa'h was six hundred years old when the deluge of waters was upon the earth.

11 In the six hundredth year of Nôa'h's life, in the second month, on the seventeenth day of the month, on the same day were all the fountains of the great deep broken up, and the floodgates of heaven were opened.

13 In the selfsame day entered Nôa'h, and Shêm, and 'Hâm, and Yâpheth, the sons of Nôa'h, and Nôa'h's wife, and the three wives of his sons with them, into the ark ;

14 They, and every beast after its kind, and all the cattle after their kind, and every creeping thing that creepeth upon the earth after its kind, and every fowl after its kind, every bird of every sort.

15 And they went in unto Nôa'h into the ark, two and two of all flesh wherein is the breath of life.

16 And they that went in, went in male and female of all flesh, as Elôhîm commanded him.

18 And the waters prevailed, and increased greatly upon the earth ; and the ark went upon the face of the waters.

19 And the waters prevailed exceedingly upon the earth ; and all the high mountains that were under the whole heaven were covered.

20 Fifteen cubits upwards did the waters prevail: and the mountains were covered.

21 And all flesh died that moved upon the earth, both fowl, and cattle, and beast, and every creeping thing that creepeth upon the earth, and every man :

22 All in whose nostrils was the breath of the spirit of life, of all that was in the dry land, died.

24 And the waters prevailed upon the earth an hundred and fifty days.

VIII. 1 And Elôhim remembered Nôa'h, and every living thing, and all the cattle that were with him in the ark: and Elôhim made a wind to pass over the earth, and the waters assuaged;

2 The fountains also of the deep and the floodgates of heaven were stopped;

3 And after the end of an hundred and fifty days the waters decreased.

4 And the ark rested in the seventh month, on the seventeenth day of the month, upon the mountains of Arârât.

5 And the waters decreased continually until the tenth month: in the tenth month, on the first day of the month, were the tops of the mountains seen.

13 And it came to pass, in the six hundred and first year, in the first month, the first day of the month, the waters were dried up from off the earth;

14 and in the second month, on the seven and twentieth day of the month, was the earth dry.

15 And Elôhim spake unto Nôa'h, saying,

16 Go forth of the ark, thou, and thy wife, and thy sons, and thy sons' wives with thee.

17 Bring forth with thee every living thing that is with thee of all flesh, both fowl, and cattle, and every creeping thing that creepeth upon the earth; that they may breed abundantly in the earth, and be fruitful, and multiply in the earth.

18 And Nôa'h went forth, and his sons, and his wife, and his sons' wives with him:

19 Every beast, every creeping thing, and every fowl, whatsoever moveth upon the earth, after their families, went forth out of the ark.

IX. 1 And Elôhim blessed Nôa'h and his sons, and said unto them, Be fruitful, and multiply, and replenish the earth.

2 And the fear of you and the dread of you shall be upon every beast of the earth, and upon every fowl of the air; with all wherewith the ground creepeth, and all the fishes of the sea; into your hand are they delivered.

3 Every moving thing that liveth shall be food for you; as the green herb have I given you all.

4 But flesh with the life thereof, which is the blood thereof, shall ye not eat.

5 And surely your blood, the blood of your lives, will I require; at the hand of every beast will I require it: and at the hand of man, even at the hand of every man's brother, will I require the life of man.

6 Whoso sheddeth man's blood, by man shall his blood be shed: for in the image of Elôhim made he man.

7 And you, be ye fruitful, and multiply; bring forth abundantly in the earth, and multiply therein.

8 And Elôhim spake unto Nôa'h, and to his sons with him, saying,

9 And I, behold, I establish my covenant with you, and with your seed after you;

10 And with every living creature that is with you, the fowl, the cattle, and every beast of the earth with

you: of all that go out of the ark, even every beast of the earth.

11 And I will establish my covenant with you; neither shall all flesh be cut off any more by the waters of the deluge; neither shall there any more be a deluge to destroy the earth.

12 And Elôhim said, This is the token of the covenant which I make between me and you and every living creature that is with you, for perpetual generations:

13 I have set my bow in the cloud, and it shall be for a token of a covenant between me and the earth.

14 And it shall come to pass, when I bring a cloud over the earth, that the bow shall be seen in the cloud,

15 And I will remember my covenant, which is between me and you and every living creature of all flesh; and the waters shall no more become a deluge to destroy all flesh.

16 And the bow shall be in the cloud; and I will look upon it, that I may remember the everlasting covenant between Elôhim and every living creature of all flesh that is upon the earth.

28 And Nôa'h lived after the deluge three hundred and fifty years.

29 And all the days of Nôa'h were nine hundred and fifty years: and he died.

IV.

THE GENEALOGIES OF THE SONS OF NÔA'H.

X. 1 Now these are the genealogies of the sons of Nôa'h, Shêm, 'Hâm, and Yâpheth : and unto them were sons born after the deluge.

2 The sons of Yâpheth : Gômer, and Mâgôg, and Mâday, and Yâvân, and Tubâl, and Meshech, and Tirâs.

3 And the sons of Gômer : Ashkenaz, and Riphath, and Togarmâh.

4 And the sons of Yâvân : Elishâh, and Tarshish, and the Kittim, and the Dôdânim.

5 Of these were the coast-lands of the nations divided in their lands, every one after his tongue ; after their families, in their nations.

6 And the sons of 'Hâm : Kûsh, and Miçraim, and Phût, and Kenâ'an.

7 And the sons of Kûsh : Sebâ, and Havîlâh, and Sabtâh, and Ra'emâh, and Sabtekâ : and the sons of Ra'emâh ; Shebâ, and Dedân.

13 And Miçraim begat the Lûdim, and the 'Anâmim, and the Lehâbim, and the Naphtu'him,

14 And the Patrusim, and the Kaslu'him (whence went forth the Pelishtim), and the Kaphtôrim.

15 And Kenâ'an begat Çidôn his firstborn, and 'Hêth ;

16 And the Yebûsy, and the Amôry, and the Girgâshy ;

17 And the 'Hivy, and the 'Arqy, and the Siny ;

18 And the 'Arvâdy, and the Çemáry, and the 'Hamâthy; and afterward were the families of the Kena'any spread abroad.

19 And the border of the Kena'any was from Çidôn, as thou goest towards Gerâr, unto 'Azâh; as thou goest towards Sedôm and 'Amôrâh, and Admâh and Çebôyim unto Lâsha'h.

20 These are the sons of 'Hâm, after their families, after their tongues, in their lands, in their nations.

22 The sons of Shêm: 'Êlâm, and Asshûr, and Arpakshâd, and Lûd, and Arâm.

23 And the sons of Arâm: 'Ûç, and 'Hûl, and Gether, and Mash.

24 And Arpakshâd begat Shela'h; and Shela'h begat 'Êber, [and 'Êber begat Peleg and Yoqtân.¹]

26 And Yoqtân begat Almôdad, and Shâleph, and 'Haçarmâveth, and Yârah,

27 And Hadôrâm, and Ûzâl, and Diqlâh,

28 And 'Obal, and Abimâ'el, and Shebâ,

29 And Ophir, and 'Havilâh, and Yobâb: all these were the sons of Yoqtân.

30 And their dwelling was from Môshâ, as thou goest towards Sephâr, the mountain of the east.

31 These are the sons of Shêm, after their families, after their tongues, in their lands, after their nations.

32 These are the families of the sons of Nôa'h after their genealogies, in their nations: and of these were the nations divided in the earth after the deluge.

¹ I replace here the verse for which the latest editor has substituted one from the Jehovistic document as it was probably written.

V.

THE GENEALOGIES OF SHÊM.

XI. 10 These are the genealogies of Shêm. Shêm was an hundred years old, and begat Arpakshâd two years after the deluge:

11 And Shêm lived after he begat Arpakshâd five hundred years, and begat sons and daughters.

12 And Arpakshâd lived five and thirty years, and begat Shêla'h.

13 And Arpakshâd lived after he begat Shêla'h four hundred and three years, and begat sons and daughters.

14 And Shêla'h lived thirty years, and begat 'Êber:

15 And Shêla'h lived after he begat 'Êber four hundred and three years, and begat sons and daughters.

16 And 'Êber lived four and thirty years, and begat Peleg:

17 And 'Êber lived after he begat Peleg four hundred and thirty years, and begat sons and daughters.

18 And Peleg lived thirty years, and begat Re'û;

19 And Peleg lived after he begat Re'û two hundred and nine years, and begat sons and daughters.

20 And Re'û lived two and thirty years, and begat Serûg:

21 And Re'û lived after he begat Serûg two hundred and seven years, and begat sons and daughters.

22 And Serûg lived thirty years, and begat Nâ'hôr:

23 And Serûg lived after he begat Nâ'hôr two hundred years, and begat sons and daughters.

24 And Nâ'hôr lived nine and twenty years, and begat Tera'h :

25 And Nâ'hôr lived after he begat Tera'h an hundred and nineteen years, and begat sons and daughters.

26 And Tera'h lived seventy years, and begat Abrâm, Nâ'hôr, and Hârân.

VI.

THE GENEALOGIES OF TERA'H.

XI. 27 Now these are the genealogies of Tera'h
Tera'h begat Abrâm, Nâ'hôr, and Hârân; and Hârân begat Lôt.

28 And Hârân died in the presence of his father Tera'h in the land of his nativity, in Ûr of the Kasdim.

29 And Abrâm and Nâ'hôr took them wives: the name of Abrâm's wife was Sâray; and the name of Nâ'hôr's wife Milkâh, the daughter of Hârân.

30 And Sâray was barren; she had no child.

31 And Tera'h took Abrâm his son, and Lôt the son of Hârân, his son's son, and Sâray his daughter-in-law, his son Abrâm's wife; and they went forth with them from Ûr of the Kasdim to go into the land of Kenâ'an: and they came unto Hârân, and dwelt there.

32 And the days of Tera'h were two hundred and five years, and Tera'h died in Hârân.

VII.

THE GENEALOGIES OF ABRÂHÂM.

*¹ [These are the genealogies of Abrâhâm.¹].

XII. 4 And Abrâm was seventy and five years old when he departed out of 'Hârân.

5 And Abrâm took Sâray his wife, and Lôt his brother's son, and all their substance that they had gathered, and the souls that they had gotten in Hârân; and they went forth to go into the land of Kenâ'an; and into the land of Kenâ'an they came.²

XIII. 2 And Abrâm was very rich in cattle, in silver, and in gold.

5 And Lôt also, which went with Abrâm, had flocks, and herds, and tents.

6 And the land was not able to bear them, that they might dwell together: for their substance was great, so that they could not dwell together.

12 Abrâm dwelled in the land of Kenâ'an, and Lôt dwelled in the cities of the circuit (of the Yardên), and moved his tent as far as Sedôm.

XVI. 3 And Sâray Abrâm's wife took Hâgâr the Egyptian, her slave, after Abrâm had dwelt ten years in the land of Kenâ'an, and gave her to Abrâm her husband to be his wife.

15 And Hâgâr bare Abrâm a son: and Abrâm

---

¹ I replace here the title which was certainly prefixed to this section of the Elohistic document similarly to those prefixed to the other sections of that work.

² The latter part of this sentence ought perhaps to be omitted, as inserted by the Jehovist.

called the name of his son, which Hâgar bare, Yishmâ'êl.

16 And Abrâm was fourscore and six years old, when Hâgar bare Yishmâ'êl to Abrâm.

XVII. 1 And when Abrâm was ninety years old and nine [Elôhim] appeared to Abrâm, and said unto him, I am Êl-Shadday (God Almighty); walk before me, and be thou perfect.

2 And I will make my covenant between me and thee, and will multiply thee exceedingly.

3 And Abrâm fell on his face: and Elôhim talked with him, saying,

4 As for me, behold, my covenant is with thee, and thou shalt be the father of a multitude of nations.

5 Neither shall thy name any more be called Abrâm, but thy name shall be Abrâhâm (the father of a multitude): for the father of a multitude of nations have I made thee.

6 And I will make thee exceeding fruitful, and I will make nations of thee, and kings shall come out of thee.

7 And I will establish my covenant between me and thee and thy seed after thee throughout their generations for an everlasting covenant, to be a God unto thee and to thy seed after thee.

8 And I will give unto thee, and to thy seed after thee, the land of thy sojourning, all the land of Kenâ'an, for an everlasting possession: and I will be their God.

9 And Elôhim said unto Abrâhâm, And as for thee, thou shalt keep my covenant, thou, and thy seed after thee throughout their generations.

10 This is my covenant, which ye shall keep, between me and you and thy seed after thee; every male among you shall be circumcised.

11 And ye shall be circumcised in the flesh of your foreskin; and it shall be a token of a covenant betwixt me and you.

12 And he that is eight days old shall be circumcised among you, every male throughout your generations, he that is born in the house, or bought with money of any stranger, which is not of thy seed.

13 He that is born in thy house, and he that is bought with thy money, must needs be circumcised: and my covenant shall be in your flesh for an everlasting covenant.

14 And the uncircumcised male who is not circumcised in the flesh of his foreskin, that soul shall be cut off from his people: he hath broken my covenant.

15 And Elôhîm said unto Abrâhâm, As for Sâray thy wife, thou shalt not call her name Sâray, but Sârâh shall her name be.

16 And I will bless her, and moreover I will give thee a son of her: yea, I will bless her, and she shall be a mother of nations: kings of peoples shall be of her.

17 Then Abrâhâm fell upon his face, and laughed (*yiçe'hâq*), and said in his heart, Shall a child be born unto him that is an hundred years old? and shall Sârâh, that is ninety years old, bear?

18 And Abrâhâm said unto Elôhîm, Oh that Yishmâ'êl might live before thee!

19 And Elôhîm said, Nay, but Sârâh thy wife shall bear thee a son; and thou shalt call his name Yiçe'bâq:

and I will establish my covenant with him for an everlasting covenant for his seed after him.

20 And as for Yishmâ'êl, I have heard thee: behold, I have blessed him, and will make him fruitful, and will multiply him exceedingly; twelve princes shall he beget, and I will make him a great nation.

21 But my covenant will I establish with Yiçe'hâq, which Sârâh shall bear unto thee at this set time in the next year.

22 And he left off talking with him, and Elôhîm went up from Abrâhâm.

23 And Abrâhâm took Yishmâ'êl his son, and all that were born in his house, and all that were bought with his money, every male among the men of Abrâhâm's house, and circumcised the flesh of their foreskin in the selfsame day, as Elôhîm had said unto him.

24 And Abrâhâm was ninety years old and nine, when he was circumcised in the flesh of his foreskin.

25 And Yishmâ'êl his son was thirteen years old, when he was circumcised in the flesh of his foreskin.

26 In the selfsame day was Abrâhâm circumcised, and Yishmâ'êl his son.

27 And all the men of his house, those born in the house, and those bought with money of the stranger, were circumcised with him.

XIX. 29 And it came to pass, when Elôhîm destroyed the cities (of the Yardên), that Elôhîm remembered Abrâhâm, and sent Lôt out of the midst of the overthrow, when he overthrew the cities in which Lôt dwelt.

XXI. 1 And [Elôhîm] visited Sârâh as he had said.

2 And Sârâh conceived, and bare Abrâhâm a son in his old age, at the set time of which Elôhîm had spoken to him.

3 And Abrâhâm called the name of his son that was born unto him, whom Sârâh bare to him, Yiçe'hâq.

4 And Abrâhâm circumcised his son Yiçe'hâq when he was eight days old, as Elôhîm had commanded him.

5 And Abrâhâm was an hundred years old when his son Yiçe'hâq was born unto him.

8[1] And the child grew, and was weaned: and Abrâhâm made a great feast on the day that Yiçe'hâq was weaned.

9 And Sârâh saw the son of Hâgâr, the Egyptian, which she had borne unto Abrâhâm, mocking.

10 Wherefore she said unto Abrâhâm, Cast out this bondwoman and her son: for the son of this bondwoman shall not be heir with my son, even with Yiçe'haq.

11 And the thing was very grievous in Abrâhâm's sight on account of his son.

12 And Elôhîm said unto Abrâhâm, Let it not be grievous in thy sight because of the lad, and because of thy bondwoman; in all that Sârâh saith unto thee, hearken unto her voice; for in Yiçe'haq shall thy seed be called.

13 And also of the son of the bondwoman will I make a nation, because he is thy seed.

14 And Abrâhâm rose up early in the morning, and took bread and a skin of water, and gave it unto Hâgâr,

---

[1] Many critics assign this passage, from verse 8 to verse 21, to the book of what they term 'the second Elohist.'

putting it on her shoulder, and the child, and sent her away: and she departed, and wandered in the wilderness of Beêr-Shâb'a.

15 And the water in the skin was spent, and she cast the child under one of the shrubs.

16 And she went, and sat her down over against him a long way off, as it were a bowshot : for she said, Let me not look upon the death of the child. And she sat over against him, and lift up her voice, and wept.

17 And Elôhîm heard the voice of the lad ; and the angel of Elôhîm called to Hâgâr out of heaven, and said unto her, What aileth thee, Hâgâr ? fear not ; for Elôhîm hath heard the voice of the lad where he is.

18 Arise, lift up the lad, and hold him in thy hand ; for I will make him a great nation.

19 And Elôhîm opened her eyes, and she saw a well of water ; and she went and filled the bottle with water, and gave the lad drink.

20 And Elôhîm was with the lad, and he grew ; and he dwelt in the wilderness, and became an archer.

21 And he dwelt in the wilderness of Pârân : and his mother took him a wife out of the land of Miçrâîm.

XXIII. 1 And the life of Sârâh was an hundred and seven and twenty years : these were the years of the life of Sârâh.

2 And Sârâh died in Qiryath-Arb'a, in the land of Kená'an : and Abrâhâm came to mourn for Sârâh, and to weep for her.

3 And Abrâhâm rose up from before his dead, and spake unto the Benê-'Hêth, saying,

4 I am a stranger and a sojourner with you : give

me a possession of a buryingplace with you, that I may bury my dead out of my sight.

5 And the Benê-'Hêth answered Abrâhâm, saying unto him,

6 Hear us, my lord: Thou art a prince of Elôhîm among us: in the choice of our sepulchres bury thy dead; none of us shall withhold from thee his sepulchre, but that thou mayest bury thy dead.

7 And Abrâhâm rose up, and bowed himself to the people of the land, even to the Benê-'Hêth.

8 And he communed with them, saying, If it be your mind that I should bury my dead out of my sight, hear me, and intreat for me to 'Ephrôn the son of Ço'har,

9 That he may give me the cave of Machpêlâh, which he hath, which is in the end of his field; for the full price let him give it to me in the midst of you for a possession of a buryingplace.

10 Now 'Ephrôn was sitting in the midst of the Benê-'Hêth: and 'Ephrôn the 'Hitty answered Abrâhâm in the audience of the Benê-'Hêth, even of all that went in at the gate of his city, saying,

11 Nay, my lord, hear me: the field give I thee, and the cave that is therein, I give it thee; in the presence of the sons of my people give I it thee: bury thy dead.

12 And Abrâhâm bowed himself down before the people of the land.

13 And he spake unto 'Ephrôn in the audience of the people of the land, saying, But if thou wilt, I pray thee, hear me: I will give the price of the field: take it of me, and I will bury my dead there.

14 And 'Ephrôn answered Abrâhâm, saying unto him,

15 My lord, hearken unto me : a piece of land worth four hundred shekels of silver, what is that betwixt me and thee? bury therefore thy dead.

16 And Abrâhâm hearkened unto 'Ephrôn ; and Abrâhâm weighed to 'Ephrôn the silver, which he had named in the audience of the Benê-'Hêth, four hundred shekels of silver, current money with the merchant.

17 So the field of 'Ephrôn, which was in Machpêlâh, which was before Mamrê, the field, and the cave which was therein, and all the trees that were in the field, that were in all the border thereof round about, were made sure

18 Unto Abrâhâm for a possession in the presence of the Benê-'Hêth, before all that went in at the gate of his city.

19 And after this, Abrâhâm buried Sârâh his wife in the cave of the field of Machpêlâh, before Mamrê.

20 And the field, and the cave that is therein, were made sure unto Abrâhâm for a possession of a burying-place by the Benê-'Hêth.

XXV. 1 And Abrâhâm took another wife and her name was Qetûrâh.

2 And she bare him Zimrân, and Yoqshân, and Medân, and Midyân, and Yishbâq, and Shûa'h.

3 And the sons of [Yoqshân] were the Asshûrim, and the Letûshim and the Leummim.

4 And the sons of Midyân ; 'Êphâh, and 'Êpher, and 'Hanôch, and Abid'a, and Eldâ'à. All these were the children of Qetûrâh.

5 And Abrâhâm gave all that he had to Yiçe'hâq.

6 But unto the sons of the concubines, which Abrâhâm had, Abrâhâm gave gifts; and he sent them away from Yiçe'hâq his son, while he yet lived, eastward, into the east country.

7 And these are the days of the years of Abrâhâm's life which he lived, an hundred three score and fifteen years.

8 And Abrâhâm gave up the ghost, and died in a good old age, an old man, and full of years; and was gathered to his people.

9 And Yiçe'hâq and Yishmâ'êl his sons buried him in the cave of Machpêlâh, in the field of 'Ephrôn the son of Ço'har the 'Hitty, which is before Mamrê,

10 The field which Abrâhâm purchased of the Benê-'Hêth; there was Abrâhâm buried, and Sârâh his wife.

11 And it came to pass after the death of Abrâhâm, that Elôhim blessed Yiçe'hâq his son.

VIII.

THE GENEALOGIES OF YISHMÂ'ÊL.

XXV. 12 Now these are the genealogies of Yishmâ'êl Abrâhâm's son, whom Hâgâr the Egyptian, Sârâh's handmaid, bare unto Abrâhâm.

13 And these are the names of the sons of Yishmâ'êl, by their names, according to their generations: the firstborn of Yishmâ'êl, Nebâyôth, and Qêdâr, and Adbeêl, and Mibsâm,

14 And Mishmâ', and Dûmâh, and Massâ,

15 And 'Hadâd, and Têmâ, Yetûr, Náphish, and Qêdmâh.

16 These are the sons of Yishmâ'êl, and these are their names, by their villages, and by their encampments: twelve princes according to their nations.

17 And these are the years of the life of Yishmâ'êl, an hundred and thirty and seven years; and he gave up the ghost and died; and was gathered unto his people.

IX.

THE GENEALOGIES OF YIÇE'HÂQ.

XXV. 19 These are the genealogies of Yiçe'hâq, Abrâhâm's son: Abrâhâm begat Yiçe'hâq:

20 And Yiçe'hâq was forty years old when he took Ribqâh, the daughter of Bethûêl the Aramy of Paddan-Arâm.

¹ [And Ribqâh bare him two sons, Êsâv and Ya'aqôb.]

26 And Yiçe'hâq was threescore years old when she bare them.

XXVI. 24 (Elôhim) appeared unto him in that night, and said, I am the God of Abrâhâm thy father: fear

---

¹ The verse of the Elohist stating the birth of the two sons of Yiçe'hâq has been omitted by the latest editor, who has substituted for it the more detailed account of the Jehovist. According to the usual mode of writing of the Elohist, he must have recorded the birth of the two brothers nearly in the mode which we have conjecturally restored.

not, for I am with thee, and will bless thee, and multiply thy seed for my servant Abrâhâm's sake.

34 And when 'Êsâv was forty years old, he took to wife Yehûdith the daughter of Beêry, the 'Hitty, and Bâsemath the daughter of Elôn the 'Hitty:
35 And they were a grief of mind unto Yiçe'hâq and to Ribqâh.

XXVII. 46 And Ribqâh said to Yiçe'hâq, I am weary of my life because of the daughters of 'Hêth: if Ya'aqôb take a wife of the daughters of 'Hêth, such as these, of the daughters of the land, what good shall my life do me?

XXVIII. 1 And Yiçe'hâq called Ya'aqôb, and blessed him, and charged him, and said unto him, Thou shalt not take a wife of the daughters of Kenâ'an.

2 Arise, go to Paddan-Arâm, to the house of Bethûêl thy mother's father: and take thee a wife from thence of the daughters of Lâbân thy mother's brother.

3 And El-Shadday (God Almighty) bless thee, and make thee fruitful, and multiply thee, that thou mayest be a company of peoples;

4 And give thee the blessing of Abrâhâm, to thee, and to thy seed with thee; that thou mayest inherit the land of thy sojournings, which Elôhim gave unto Abrâhâm.

5 And Yiçe'hâq sent away Ya'aqôb: and he went to Paddan-Arâm unto Lâbân, son of Bethûêl the Aramy, the brother of Ribqâh, Ya'aqôb and 'Êsâv's mother.

6 Now 'Êsâv saw that Yiçe'hâq had blessed Ya'aqôb and sent him away to Paddan-Arâm, to take him a wife from thence; and that, as he blessed him, he gave him

a charge, saying, Thou shalt not take a wife of the daughters of Kenâ'an;

7 And that Ya'aqôb obeyed his father and his mother, and was gone to Paddan-Arâm:

8 And 'Êsâv saw that the daughters of Kenâ'an pleased not Yiçe'hâq his father;

9 And 'Êsâv went unto Yishmâ'êl, and took unto the wives which he had Ma'halath the daughter of Yishmâ'êl, Abrâhâm's son, the sister of Nebâyôth, to be his wife.

. . . . . .¹

XXXI. 17 Then Ya'aqôb rose up, and set his sons and his wives upon camels:

18 And he carried away all his cattle, and all his substance which he had gathered, the cattle of his getting, which he had gathered in Paddan-Arâm, for to go to Yiçe'hâq his father unto the land of Kenâ'an.

XXXIII. 18 And Ya'aqôb came in peace to the city of Shechem, which is in the land of Kenâ'an, when he came from Paddan-Arâm; and encamped before the city.

XXXIV. 1 And Dinâh, the daughter of Lêâh, which she bare unto Ya'aqôb, went out to see the daughters of the land.

2 And Shechem, the son of 'Hamôr the 'Hivvy, the prince of the land, saw her, and he took her.

4 And Shechem spake unto his father 'Hamôr, saying, Get me this damsel to wife.

¹ The Elohist must have briefly narrated here Ya'aqôb's abiding with Lâbân and his marriage with Lâbân's two daughters. But his narrative, which was evidently a very concise one, has been set aside by the latest editor, who has put in its place the more developed narrative of the Jehovist, who has himself reproduced in its entirety an older document from the work sometimes called that of the 'second Elohist.'

THE GENEALOGIES OF YIÇEḤÂQ.

6 And 'Hamôr the father of Shechem went out unto Ya'aqôb to commune with him.

8 And 'Hamôr communed with [him], saying, The soul of my son Shechem longeth for your daughter: I pray you give her unto him to wife.

9 And make ye marriages with us; give your daughters unto us, and take our daughters unto you.

10 And ye shall dwell with us: and the land shall be before you; dwell and trade ye therein, and get you possessions therein.

*[Ya'aqôb and his sons answered 'Hamôr and Shechem, saying,]

15 Only on this condition will we consent with you: if ye will be as we be, that every male of you be circumcised;

16 Then will we give our daughters unto you, and we will take your daughters to us, and we will dwell with you, and we will become one people.

17 But if ye will not hearken to us, to be circumcised; then will we take our daughter, and we will be gone.

18 And their words pleased 'Hamôr, and Shechem 'Hamôr's son.

20 And 'Hamôr and Shechem his son came unto the gate of their city, and communed with the men of their city, saying,

21 These men are peaceable with us; therefore let them dwell in the land, and trade therein; for, behold, the land is large enough for them; let us take their daughters to us for wives, and let us give them our daughters.

22 Only on this condition will the men consent unto us to dwell with us, to become one people, if every male among us be circumcised, as they are circumcised.

23 Shall not their cattle and their substance and all their beasts be ours? only let us consent unto them, and they will dwell with us.

24 And unto 'Hamôr and unto Shechem his son hearkened all that went out of the gate of his city; and every male was circumcised, all that went out of the gate of his city.

25 And it came to pass on the third day, when they were sore, that two of the sons of Ya'aqôb, Shime'ôn and Lêvy, Dinâh's brethren, took each man his sword, and came upon the city unawares, and slew all the males.

28 They took their flocks and their herds and their asses, and that which was in the city, and that which was in the fields.

30 And Ya'aqôb said to Shime'ôn and Lêvy, Ye have troubled me, to make me to stink among the inhabitants of the land, among the Kena'any and the Perizzy: and I being few in number, they will gather themselves together against me and smite me; and I shall be destroyed, I and my house.

XXXV. 6 And Ya'aqôb came to Luz, which is in the land of Kenä'an, he and all the people that were with him.

9 And Elôhim appeared unto Ya'aqôb again, when he came from Paddan-Arâm, and blessed him.

10 And Elôhim said unto him, Thy name is Ya'aqôb:

thy name shall not be called any more Ya'aqôb, but Yisrâêl shall be thy name: and he called his name Yisrâêl.

11 And Elôhim said unto him, I am El Shadday (God Almighty): be fruitful and multiply: a nation and a company of nations shall be of thee, and kings shall come out of thy loins.

12 And the land which I gave unto Abrâhâm and Yiçe'hâq, to thee will I give it, and to thy seed after thee will I give the land.

13 And Elôhim went up from him in the place where he spake with him.

14 And Ya'aqôb set up a pillar in the place where he spake with him, a pillar of stone: and he poured out a drink offering thereon, and poured oil thereon.

15 And Ya'aqôb called the name of the place where Elôhim spake with him, Bêth-Êl.

22 Now the sons of Ya'aqôb were twelve:

23 The sons of Lêâh; Reûbên, Ya'aqôb's firstborn, and Shime'ôn, and Lêvy, and Yehûdâh, and Yissâchâr, and Zebulûn:

24 The sons of Râ'hêl; Yôsêph, and Binyâmîn;

25 And the sons of Bilhâh, Râ'hêl's handmaid; Dân, and Naphtâly:

26 And the sons of Zilpâh, Lêâh's handmaid; Gâd, and Ashêr: these are the sons of Ya'aqôb, which were born to him in Paddan-Arâm.

27 And Ya'aqôb came unto Yiçe'hâq his father to Mamrê, to Qiryath-Arba', where Abrâhâm and Yiçe'hâq sojourned.

28 And the days of Yiçc'hâq were an hundred and fourscore years.

29 And Yiçc'hâq gave up the ghost, and died, and was gathered unto his people old and full of days: and 'Êsâv and Ya'aqôb his sons buried him.

X.

THE GENEALOGIES OF 'ESÂV.

XXXVI 1 Now these are the genealogies of 'Ê'sâv (the same is Edôm).

2 'Êsâv took his wives of the daughters of Kenâ'an; 'Adâh the daughter of Elôn the 'Hitty, and Aholîbâmâh the daughter of 'Anâh, the daughter of Çibe'ôn the 'Hivvy;

3 And Bâsemath Yishmâ'êl's daughter, sister of Nebâyôth.[1]

4 And 'Adâh bare to 'Êsâv Eliphâz; and Bâsemath bare Re'ûêl;

5 And Aholîbâmâh bare Ye'ûsh, and Ya'elâm, and Qôra'h: these are the sons of 'Êsâv which were born unto him in the land of Kenâ'an.

6 And 'Êsâv took his wives, and his sons, and his daughters, and all the souls of his house, and his cattle, and all his beasts, and all his possessions, which he had gathered in the land of Kenâ'an; and went into a land away from his brother Ya'aqôb.

[1] See the note to chap. xxxvi. 3 in Part I.

7 For their substance was too great for them to dwell together; and the land of their sojournings could not bear them because of their cattle.

8 And 'Êsâv dwelt in Mount Sê'ir: 'Êsâv is Edôm.

9 And these are the generations of 'Êsâv, the father of Edôm, in Mount Sê'ir.

10 These are the names of 'Êsâv's sons; Eliphâz, the son of 'Adâh the wife of 'Êsâv, Re'ûêl the son of Bâsemath the wife of 'Êsâv.

11 And the sons of Eliphâz were Têmân, Omâr, Çephô, and Ga'etâm, and Qenaz.

12 And Timnâ' was concubine to Eliphâz 'Êsâv's son; and she bare to Eliphâz 'Amâlêq: these are the sons of 'Adâh 'Êsâv's wife.

13 And these are the sons of Re'ûêl; Na'hath, and Zera'h, Shammâh, and Mizzâh: these were the sons of Bâsemath 'Êsâv's wife.

14 And these were the sons of Aholibâmâh the daughter of 'Anâh, the daughter of Çibe'ôn, 'Êsâv's wife; and she bare to 'Êsâv Ye'ûsh, and Ya'elâm, and Qôra'h.

15 These are the phylarchs (allûphîm) of the Benê-'Êsâv; the sons of Eliphâz the firstborn of 'Êsâv; allûph Têmân, allûph Omâr, allûph Çephô, allûph Qenaz,

16 Allûph Qôra'h, allûph Ga'etâm, allûph 'Amâlêq: these are the phylarchs that came of Eliphâz in the land of Edôm; these are the sons of 'Adâh.

17 And these are the sons of Re'ûêl 'Êsâv's son; allûph Na'hath, allûph Zera'h, allûph Shammâh, allûph Mizzâh: these are the phylarchs that came of Re'ûêl in

the land of Edôm; these are the sons of Bâsemath 'Ēsâv's wife.

18 And these are the sons of Aholibâmâh 'Ēsâv's wife; allûph Ye'ûsh, allûph Ya'elâm, allûph Qôra'h: these are the phylarchs that came of Aholibâmah the daughter of 'Anâh, 'Ēsâv's wife.

19 These are the sons of 'Ēsâv, and these are their phylarchs: the same is Edôm.

20 These are the sons of Sê'îr the 'Hory, the inhabitants of the land; Lôtân, and Shôbâl, and Çibe'ôn, and 'Anâh,

21 And Dishôn, and Êçer, and Dìshân: these are the phylarchs that came of the 'Hory, the children of Sê'îr in the land of Edôm.

22 And the children of Lôtân were 'Hory and Hêmâm; and Lôtân's sister was Timnâ'.

23 And these are the children of Shôbâl: 'Alvân, and Mana'hath, and 'Ēbâl, Shephô, and Onâm.

24 And these are the children of Çibe'ôn; Ayâh and 'Anâh; this is 'Anâh who found the hot springs in the wilderness, as he fed the asses of Çibe'ôn his father.

25 And these are the children of 'Anâh; Dishôn, and Aholibâmâh the daughter of 'Anâh.

26 And these are the children of Dishôn; Hemdân, and Eshbân, and Yithrân, and Cherân.

27 These are the children of Êçer; Bilhân, and Za'avân, and 'Aqân.

28 These are the children of Dìshân; Uç, and Arân.

29 These are the phylarchs that came of the 'Hory: allûph Lôtân, allûph Shôbâl, allûph Çibe'ôn, allûph 'Anâh,

30 Allûph Dishôn, allûph Êçer, allûph Dishân: these are the phylarchs of the 'Hory, according to their phylarchs in the land of Sê'îr.

31 And these are the kings that reigned in the land of Edôm before there reigned any king over the Benê-Yisrâêl.

32 And Bela' the son of Be'ôr reigned in Edôm: and the name of his city was Dinhâbâh.

33 And Bela' died, and Yôbâb the son of Zera'h of Boçrâh reigned in his stead.

34 And Yôbâb died, and 'Hushâm of the land of Têmân reigned in his stead.

35 And 'Hushâm died, and Hadad the son of Bedad, who smote Midyân in the field of Môâb, reigned in his stead: and the name of his city was 'Avith.

36 And Hadad died, and Samlâh of Masrêqâh reigned in his stead.

37 And Samlâh died, and Shâûl of Rehôbôth-Hannâhâr reigned in his stead.

38 And Shâûl died, and Ba'al-'Hânân the son of 'Achbôr reigned in his stead.

39 And Ba'al-'Hânân the son of 'Achbôr died, and Hadar reigned in his stead: and the name of his city was Pâ'û; and his wife's name was Mehêtabêl, the daughter of Matrêd, the daughter of Mê-zâhâb.

40 And these are the names of the phylarchs that came of 'Êsâv, according to their families, after their places, by their names; allûph Timnâ', allûph 'Alvâh, allûph Yethêth,

41 Allûph Aholîbâmâh, allûph Êlâh, allûph Pînôn,

42 Allûph Qenaz, allûph Têmân, allûph Mibçar,

43 Allûph Maqdyêl, allûph 'Trâm: these are the phylarchs of Edôm, according to their habitations in the land of their possession. This is 'Esâv the father of Edôm.

XI.

THE GENEALOGIES OF YA'AQÔB.

XXXVII. 2 These are the genealogies of Ya'aqôb.

1 Ya'aqôb dwelt in the land of his father's sojournings, in the land of Kenâ'an.

2 Yôsêph, being seventeen years old, was feeding the flock with his brethren; and Yôsêph brought the evil report of them unto their father.

3 Now (Ya'aqôb) loved Yôsêph more than all his children, because he was the son of his old age.

5 And Yôsêph dreamed a dream, and he told it to his brethren: and they hated him yet the more.

6 And he said unto them, Hear, I pray you, this dream which I have dreamed.

7 For, behold, we were binding sheaves in the field, and, lo, my sheaf arose, and also stood upright; and, and, behold, your sheaves came round about, and made obeisance to my sheaf.

8 And his brethren said to him, Shalt thou indeed reign over us? or shalt thou indeed have dominion over us? And they hated him yet the more for his dreams, and for his words.

9 And he dreamed yet another dream, and told it to his brethren, and said, Behold, I have dreamed yet a

dream; and, behold, the sun and the moon and eleven stars made obeisance to me.

10 And he told it to his father, and to his brethren: and his father rebuked him, and said unto him, What is this dream that thou hast dreamed? Shall I and thy mother and thy brethren indeed come to bow down ourselves to thee to the earth?

11 And his brethren envied him; but his father kept the saying in mind.

*[Ya'aqôb sent Yôsêph to his brethren, who were feeding their father's flocks.]

18 And they saw him afar off, and before he came near unto them, they conspired against him to slay him.

19 And they said one to another, Behold, this master of dreams cometh.

20 Come now therefore, let us slay him, and cast him into one of the cisterns, and we will say, An evil beast hath devoured him; and we shall see what will become of his dreams.

21 And Reûbên heard it, and delivered him out of their hand; and said, Let us not take his life.

22 And Reûbên said unto them, Shed no blood; cast him into this cistern that is in the wilderness, but lay no hand upon him: that he might deliver him out of their hand, to restore him to his father.

24 And they took him, and cast him into the cistern; and the cistern was empty, there was no water in it.

28 And there passed by Midyânîm, merchantmen; and they drew and lifted up Yôsêph out of the cistern.

* (And they sold him to the Midyânîm).

29 And Reûbên returned unto the cistern; and, behold, Yôsêph was not in the cistern; and he rent his clothes.

30 And he returned unto his brethren, and said, The child is not; and I, whither shall I go?

*[And they sent and told their father, An evil beast hath devoured Yôsêph.]

34 And Ya'aqôb rent his garments, and put sackcloth upon his loins, and mourned for his son many days.

35 And all his sons and all his daughters rose up to comfort him; but he refused to be comforted; and he said, For I will go down to Sheól to my son mourning. And his father wept for him.

36 And the Midyânîm sold him into Miçrâim unto Pôtiphar, an eunuch of Para'ôh's, the chief of the executioners.

XL. 1 And it came to pass after these things that the cup-bearer of the king of Miçrâim and his baker offended their lord the king of Miçrâim.

2 And Para'ôh was wroth against his two officers, against the chief of the cup-bearers, and against the chief of the bakers.

3 And he put them in ward in the house of the chief of the executioners, into the prison.

4 And the chief of the executioners charged Yôsêph with them, and he ministered unto them, and they continued a season in ward.

5 And they dreamed a dream both of them, each man his dream, in one night, each man according to the interpretation of his dream, the cup-bearer and the

baker of the king of Miçràim, which were bound in the prison.

6 And Yôsêph came in unto them in the morning, and saw them, and, behold, they were sad.

7 And he asked Para'ôh's eunuchs, saying, Wherefore look ye so sadly to-day?

8 And they said unto him, We have dreamed a dream, and there is none that can interpret it. And Yôsêph said unto them, Do not interpretations belong to Elôhìm? tell it me, I pray you.

9 And the chief cup-bearer told his dream to Yôsêph, and said to him, In my dream, behold, a vine was before me;

10 And in the vine were three branches; and it was as though it budded, and its blossoms shot forth; and the clusters thereof brought forth ripe grapes:

11 And Para'ôh's cup was in my hand; and I took the grapes, and pressed them into Para'ôh's cup, and I gave the cup into Para'ôh's hand.

12 And Yôsêph said unto him, This is the interpretation of it: the three branches are three days:

13 Within yet three days shall Para'ôh lift up thine head, and restore thee unto thine office; and thou shalt give Para'ôh's cup into his hand, after the former manner when thou wast his cup-bearer.

14 But have me in remembrance when it shall be well with thee, and show kindness, I pray thee, unto me, and make mention of me unto Para'ôh, and bring me out of this house:

15 For indeed I was stolen away out of the land of the 'Ébrim.

16 When the chief baker saw that the interpretation was good, he said unto Yôsêph, I also was in my dream, and, behold, three baskets of white bread were on my head :

17 And in the uppermost basket there was all manner of bakemeats for Para'ôh; and the birds did eat them out of the basket upon my head.

18 And Yôsêph answered and said, This is the interpretation thereof: the three baskets are three days :

19 Within yet three days shall Para'ôh lift up thy head from off thee, and shall hang thee on a tree ; and the birds shall eat thy flesh from off thee.

20 And it came to pass the third day, which was Para'ôh's birthday, that he made a feast unto all his servants: and he lifted up the head of the chief cupbearer and the head of the chief baker among his servants.

21 And he restored the chief cup-bearer unto his office of cup-bearer again; and he gave the cup into Para'ôh's hand :

22 But he hanged the chief baker, as Yôsêph had interpreted to them.

23 Yet did not the chief cup-bearer remember Yôsêph, but forgot him.

XLI. 1 And it came to pass at the end of two full years, that Para'ôh dreamed: and, behold, he stood by the river.

2 And, behold, there came up out of the river seven kine, well favoured and fatfleshed; and they fed in the reed-grass.

3 And, behold, seven other kine came up after them

out of the river, ill favoured and leanfleshed; and stood by the other kine upon the brink of the river.

4 And the ill favoured and leanfleshed kine did eat up the seven well favoured and fat kine. So Para'ôh awoke.

5 And he slept and dreamed a second time: and, behold, seven ears of corn came up upon one stalk, rank and good.

6 And, behold, seven ears, thin and blasted with the east wind, sprung up after them.

7 And the thin ears swallowed up the seven rank and full ears. And Para'ôh awoke, and, behold, it was a dream.

8 And it came to pass in the morning that his spirit was troubled; and he sent for all the interpreters of Miçrâim, and all the wise men thereof: and Para'ôh told them his dream; but there was none that could interpret them unto Para'ôh.

9 Then spake the chief cup-bearer unto Para'ôh, saying, I will make mention of my faults this day:

10 Para'ôh was wroth with his servants, and put me in ward in the house of the chief of the executioners, me and the chief baker:

11 And we dreamed a dream in one night, I and he; we dreamed each man according to the interpretation of his dream.

12 And there was with us there a young man, an 'Ebry, a slave of the chief of the executioners; and we told him, and he interpreted to us our dreams; to each man according to his dream he did interpret.

13 And it came to pass, as he interpreted to us, so it

was; I was restored unto mine office, and he was hanged.

14 Then Para'ôh sent and called Yôsêph; and he shaved himself, and changed his raiment, and came in unto Para'ôh.

15 And Para'ôh said unto Yôsêph, I have dreamed a dream, and there is none that can interpret it: and I have heard say of thee, that when thou hearest a dream thou canst interpret it.

16 And Yôsêph answered Para'ôh, saying, It is not in me: Elôhim shall give Para'ôh an answer of peace.

17 And Para'ôh spake unto Yôsêph, In my dream, behold, I stood upon the brink of the river:

18 And, behold, there came up out of the river seven kine, fatfleshed and well favoured; and they fed in the reed-grass:

19 And, behold, seven other kine came up after them, poor and very ill favoured and leanfleshed, such as I never saw in all the land of Miçráim for badness:

20 And the lean and ill favoured kine did eat up the first seven fat kine:

21 And when they had eaten them up, it could not be known that they had eaten them; but they were still ill favoured, as at the beginning. So I awoke.

22 And I saw in my dream, and, behold, seven ears came up upon one stalk, full and good:

23 And, behold, seven ears, withered, thin, and blasted with the east wind, sprung up after them:

24 And the thin ears swallowed up the seven good ears: and I told it unto the interpreters; but there was none that could declare it to me.

25 And Yôsêph said unto Para'ôh, The dream of Para'ôh is one: what Elôhîm is about to do he hath declared unto Para'ôh.

26 The seven good kine are seven years; and the seven good ears are seven years: the dream is one.

27 And the seven lean and ill favoured kine that came up after them are seven years, and also the seven empty ears blasted with the east wind; they shall be seven years of famine.

28 That is the thing which I spake unto Para'ôh; what Elôhîm is about to do he hath showed unto Para'ôh.

29 Behold, there come seven years of great plenty throughout all the land of Miçrâim:

30 And there shall arise after them seven years of famine; and all the plenty shall be forgotten in the land of Miçrâim; and the famine shall consume the land;

31 And the plenty shall not be known in the land by reason of that famine which followeth; for it shall be very grievous.

32 And for that the dream was doubled unto Para'ôh twice, it is because the thing is established by Elôhîm, and Elôhîm will shortly bring it to pass.

33 Now therefore let Para'ôh look out a man discreet and wise, and set him over the land of Miçrâim.

34 Let Para'ôh do this, and let him appoint overseers over the land, and take up the fifth part of the land of Miçrâim in the seven plenteous years.

35 And let them gather all the food of these good years that come, and lay up corn under the hand

of Para'ōh for food in the cities, and let them keep it.

36 And the food shall be for a store to the land against the seven years of famine, which shall be in the land of Miçráim; that the land perish not through the famine.

37 And the thing was good in the eyes of Para'ōh, and in the eyes of all his servants.

38 And Para'ōh said unto his servants, Can we find such a one as this, a man in whom the spirit of Elōhīm is?

39 And Para'ōh said unto Yōsēph, Forasmuch as Elōhīm hath showed thee all this, there is none so discreet and wise as thou:

40 Thou shalt be over my house, and according unto thy word shall all my people do homage: only in the throne will I be greater than thou.

41 And Para'ōh said unto Yōsēph, See, I have set thee over all the land of Miçráim.

42 And Para'ōh took off his signet ring from his hand, and put it upon Yōsēph's hand, and arrayed him in vestures of fine byssus, and put a gold chain about his neck;

43 And he made him to ride in the second chariot which he had; and they cried before him, Bow the knee: and he set him over all the land of Miçráim.

44 And Para'ōh said unto Yōsēph, I am Para'ōh, and without thee shall no man lift up his hand or his foot in all the land of Miçráim.

45 And Para'ōh called Yōsēph's name Çāphenath-Pa'anēah, and he gave him to wife Āsenath, the

daughter of Pôti-phêrâ priest of On. And Yôsêph went out over the land of Miçrâim.

46 And Yôsêph was thirty years old when he stood before Para'ôh king of Miçrâim, and Yôsêph went out from the presence of Para'ôh, and went throughout all the land of Miçrâim.

47 And in the seven plenteous years the earth brought forth by handfuls.

48 And he gathered up all the food of the seven years which were in the land of Miçrâim, and laid up the food in the cities: the food of the field, which was round about every city, laid he up in the same.

50 And unto Yôsêph were born two sons before the year of famine came, which Asenath the daughter of Pôti-phêrâ priest of On bare unto him.

*[And the name of the eldest was Menassheh, and the name of the second Ephrâim.]

53 And the seven years of plenty, that was in the land of Miçrâim, came to an end.

54 And the seven years of famine began to come, according as Yôsêph had said: and there was famine in all lands; but in all the land of Miçrâim there was bread.

55 And when all the land of Miçrâim was famished, the people cried to Para'ôh for bread: and Para'ôh said to all Miçrâim, Go unto Yôsêph; what he saith to you, do.

56 And the famine was over all the face of the earth: and Yôsêph opened all the storehouses, and sold unto Miçrâim.

57 And all countries came into Miçrâim to Yôsêph

for to buy corn; because the famine was sore in all the earth.

XLII. 1 Now Ya'aqôb saw that there was corn in Miçráim, and Ya'aqôb said unto his sons, Why do ye look one upon another?

2 And he said, Behold, I have heard that there is corn in Miçráim: get you down thither, and buy for us from thence; that we may live, and not die.

3 And Yôsêph's ten brethren went down to buy corn from Miçráim.

4 But Binyâmîn, Yôsêph's brother, Ya'aqôb sent not with his brethren; for he said, Lest peradventure mischief befall him.

6 And Yôsêph was the governor over the land: he it was that sold to all the people of the land: and Yôsêph's brethren came, and bowed down themselves to him with their faces to the earth.

7 And Yôsêph saw his brethren, and he knew them, but made himself strange unto them, and spake roughly with them; and he said unto them, Whence come ye? And they said, From the land of Kená'an to buy food.

8 And Yôsêph knew his brethren, but they knew not him.

9 And Yôsêph remembered the dreams which he dreamed of them, and said unto them, Ye are spies; to see the nakedness of the land ye are come.

10 And they said unto him, Nay, my lord, but to buy food are thy servants come.

11 We are all one man's sons; we are true men, thy servants are no spies.

12 And he said unto them, Nay, but to see the nakedness of the land ye are come.

13 And they said, We thy servants are twelve brethren, the sons of one man in the land of Kenâ'an; and, behold, the youngest is this day with our father, and one is not.

14 And Yôsêph said unto them, That is it that I spake unto you, saying, Ye are spies:

15 Hereby shall ye be proved: by the life of Para'ôh ye shall not go forth hence, except your youngest brother come hither.

16 Send one of you, and let him fetch your brother, and ye shall be bound, that your words may be proved, whether there be truth in you: or else by the life of Para'ôh surely ye are spies.

17 And he put them all together into ward three days.

18 And Yôsêph said unto them the third day, This do, and live; for I fear God:

19 If ye be true men, let one of your brethren be bound in your prison house; but go ye, carry corn for the famine of your houses:

20 And bring your youngest brother unto me; so shall your words be verified, and ye shall not die. And they did so.

21 And they said one to another, We are verily guilty concerning our brother, in that we saw the distress of his soul, when he besought us, and we would not hear; therefore is this distress come upon us.

22 And Reûbên answered them, saying, Spake I not unto you, saying, Do not sin against the child; and ye would not hear? therefore also, behold, his blood is required.

23 And they knew not that Yôsêph understood them, for there was an interpreter between them.

24 And he turned himself about from them, and wept; and he returned to them, and spake to them, and took Shime'ôn from among them, and bound him before their eyes.

25 Then Yôsêph commanded to fill their vessels with corn, and to restore every man's money into his sack, and to give them provision for the way: and thus was it done unto them.

26 And they loaded their asses with their corn, and departed thence.

29 And they came unto Ya'aqôb their father, unto the land of Kenâ'an, and told him all that had befallen them; saying,

30 The man, the lord of the land, spake roughly with us, and took us for spies of the country.

31 And we said unto him, We are true men, we are no spies:

32 We be twelve brethren, sons of our father; one is not, and the youngest is this day with our father in the land of Kenâ'an.

33 And the man, the lord of the land, said unto us, Hereby shall I know that ye are true men; leave one of your brethren with me, and take corn for the famine of your houses, and go your way:

34 And bring your youngest brother unto me; then shall I know that ye are no spies, but that ye are true men: so will I deliver you your brother, and ye shall traffick in the land.

35 And it came to pass as they emptied their sacks,

that, behold, every man's purse of money was in his sack: and when they and their father saw their purses of money, they were afraid.

36 And Ya'aqôb their father said unto them, Me have ye bereaved of my children: Yôsêph is not, and Shime'ôn is not, and ye will take Binyâmîn away: all these things are upon me.

37 And Reûbên spake unto his father, saying, Slay my two sons, if I bring him not to thee; deliver him into my hand, and I will bring him to thee again.

38 And he said, My son shall not go down with you; for his brother is dead, and he only is left: if mischief befall him by the way in which ye go, then shall ye bring down my gray hairs with sorrow to Sheôl.

XLV. 3 And Yôsêph said unto his brethren, I am Yôsêph: doth my father yet live? And his brethren could not answer him: for they were troubled at his presence.

4 And Yôsêph said unto his brethren, Come near to me, I pray you. And they came near. And he said, I am Yôsêph your brother, whom ye sold into Miçrâim.

5 And now be not grieved, nor angry with yourselves, that ye sold me hither: for Elôhîm did send me before you to preserve life.

6 For these two years hath the famine been in the land: and there are yet five years, in the which there shall be neither plowing nor harvest.

[1] The latest editor having adopted the narrative of the Elohist for the second interview of Yôsêph with his brethren, and the mode in which he made himself known to them, the narrative of the Elohist is entirely lost, as far as this part of his work is concerned. His portion of the narrative recommences at the moment when Yôsêph makes himself known.

7 And Elôhim sent me before you to preserve you a remnant in the earth, and to save you alive by a great deliverance.

8 So now it was not you that sent me hither, but Elôhim; and he hath made me a grand-master of Para'ôh's, and lord over all his house, and ruler over all the land of Miçráim.

9 Haste ye, and go up to my father, and say unto him, Thus saith thy son Yôsêph, Elôhim hath made me lord of all Miçráim: come down unto me, tarry not:

10 And thou shalt dwell in the land of Gôshen, and thou shalt be near unto me, thou and thy children, and thy children's children, and thy flocks, and thy herds, and all that thou hast:

11 And there will I nourish thee; for there are yet five years of famine; lest thou come to poverty, thou, and thy household, and all that thou hast.

12 And, behold, your eyes see, and the eyes of my brother Binyâmîn, that it is my mouth that speaketh unto you.

13 And ye shall tell my father of all my glory in Miçráim, and of all that ye have seen; and ye shall haste and bring down my father hither.

21 [Yôsêph] gave them provision for the way.

22 To all of them he gave each man changes of raiment; but to Binyâmîn he gave three hundred (shekels) of silver, and five changes of raiment.

23 And to his father he sent after this manner; ten asses laden with the good things of Miçráim, and ten she-asses laden with corn and bread and victual for his father by the way.

24 So he sent his brethren away, and they departed; and he said unto them, See that ye fall not out by the way.

25 And they went up out of Miçrâim, and came into the land of Kenâ'an unto Ya'aqôb their father.

XLVI. 6 And they took their cattle, and their goods, which they had gotten in the land of Kenâ'an, and came into Miçrâim, Ya'aqôb and all his seed with him:

7 His sons, and his sons' sons with him, his daughters, and his sons' daughters, and all his seed brought he with him into Miçrâim.

8 And these are the names of the Benê-Yisrâêl, which came into Miçrâim, Ya'aqôb and his sons: Reûbên, Ya'aqôb's firstborn.

9 And the sons of Reûbên; 'Hanôch, and Phallû, and 'Heçrôn, and Karmy.

10 And the sons of Shime'ôn; Yemûêl, and Yâmîn, and Ohad, and Yâchîn, and Ço'har, and Shâ'ûl, the son of the Kena'anîth.

11 And the sons of Lêvy; Gêrshôn, and Qehâth, and Merâry.

12 And the sons of Yehûdâh; 'Êr, and Ônân, and Shêlâh, and Pereç, and Zâra'h; but 'Êr and Ônân died in the land of Kenâ'an. And the sons of Pereç were 'Heçrôn and 'Hâmûl.

13 And the sons of Yissâchâr; Tôlâ', and Puvâh, and Yôb, and Shimrôn.

14 And the sons of Zebulûn; Sered, and Êlôn, and Ya'hleêl.

15 These are the sons of Lêâh, which she bare unto

Ya'aqôb in Paddan-Arâm, with his daughter Dinâh: his sons and his daughters were thirty and three persons in all.[1]

16 And the sons of Gâd; Çiphyôn, and 'Haggy, Shûny, and Eçbôn, 'Êry, and Arôdy, and Arêly.

17 And the sons of Âshêr; Yimnâh, and Yishvâh, and Yishvy, and Bery'âh, and Sera'h their sister: and the sons of Bery'âh; 'Heber, and Malkiêl.

18 These are the sons of Zilpâh, which Lâbân gave to Lêah his daughter, and these she bare unto Ya'aqôb, even sixteen souls.

19 The sons of Râ'hêl Ya'aqôb's wife; Yôsêph, and Binyâmîn.

20 And unto Yôsêph in the land of Miçrâim were born Menassheh and Ephrâim, which Âsenath the daughter of Pôti-phêrâ priest of On bare unto him.

21 And the sons of Binyâmîn; Belâ', and Becher, and Ashbêl, Gêrâ, and Na'amân, Ê'hy, and Rôsh, Muppim, and 'Huppim, and Ârd.

22 These are the sons of Râ'hêl, which were born to Ya'aqôb: in all fourteen persons.

23 And the sons of Dân; 'Hushim.

24 And the sons of Naphtâly; Ya'hçeêl, and Gûny, and Yeçer, and Shillêm.

25 These are the sons of Bilhâh, which Lâbân gave unto Râ'hêl his daughter, and these she bare unto Ya'aqôb: in all seven persons.

26 All the persons that came with Ya'aqôb into Miçrâim, which came out of his loins, besides Ya'aqôb's sons' wives, were threescore and six in number.

[1] See note ante, on chap. xlvi. 15.

27 And the sons of Yôsêph, which were born to him in Miçrâim, were two: all the persons of the house of Ya'aqôb, which came into Miçrâim were threescore and ten.[1]

XLVII. 7 And Yôsêph brought in Ya'aqôb his father, and set him before Para'ôh: and Ya'aqôb blessed Para'ôh.

8 And Para'ôh said unto Ya'aqôb, How many are the days of the years of thy life?

9 And Ya'aqôb said unto Para'ôh, The days of the years of my pilgrimage are an hundred and thirty years: few and evil have been the days of the years of my life, and they have not attained unto the days of the years of the life of my fathers in the days of their pilgrimage.

10 And Ya'aqôb blessed Para'ôh, and went out from the presence of Para'ôh.

11 And Yôsêph placed his father and his brethren, and gave them a possession in the land of Miçrâim, in the land of Ra'mesês, as Para'ôh had commanded.

12 And Yôsêph nourished his father, and his brethren, and all his father's household, with bread, according to their families.

27 And they gat them possessions therein, and were fruitful, and multiplied exceedingly.

28 And Ya'aqôb lived in the land of Miçrâim seventeen years: so the days of Ya'aqôb, the years of his life, were an hundred forty and seven years.

XLVIII. 1 And it came to pass after these things, that one said to Yôsêph, Behold, thy father is sick: and he took with him his two sons, Menassheh and Ephrâim.

---

[1] As to these numbers see the note on chap. xlvi. 27.

2 And one told Ya'aqôb, and said, Behold thy son Yôsêph cometh unto thee.

3 And Ya'aqôb said unto Yôsêph, El-Shadday (God Almighty) appeared unto me at Lûz, in the land of Kenâ'an, and blessed me,

4 And said unto me, Behold, I will make thee fruitful, and multiply thee, and I will make of thee a company of peoples; and will give this land to thy seed after thee for an everlasting possession.

5 And now thy two sons, which were born unto thee in the land of Miçrâim before I came unto thee in Miçrâim, are mine; Ephrâim and Menassheh, even as Reûbên and Shime'ôn shall be mine.

6 And thy issue, which thou hast begotten after them, shall be thine; they shall be called after the name of their brethren in their inheritance.

7 And as for me, when I came from Paddân, Râ'hêl died by me in the land of Kenâ'an in the way, when there was still some way to come unto Ephrâth: and I buried her there.[1]

. . . . .

XLIX. 28 [Ya'aqôb called his sons together] and blessed them; every one according to his blessing he blessed them.

29 And he charged them, and said unto them, I am to be gathered to my people: bury me with my fathers in the cave that is in the field of 'Ephrôn the 'Hitty,

---

[1] Ya'aqôb's speech comes to this abrupt termination in the text as we have it, and there is no close to this verse. It must evidently have had one, however—some charge, probably, which was contained in a verse now lost.

30 In the cave that is in the field of Machpêlâh, which is before Mamrê, in the land of Kenâ'an, which Abrâhâm bought with the field from 'Ephrôn the 'Hitty, for a possession of a buryingplace :

31 There they buried Abrâhâm and Sârâh his wife : there they buried Yiçc'hâq and Ribqâh his wife; and there I buried Lêâh :

32 The field and the cave that is therein, which was purchased from the Benê-'Hêth.

33 And when Ya'aqôb had made an end of charging his sons, he gathered up his feet into the bed, and yielded up the ghost, and was gathered unto his people.

L. 12 And his sons did unto him according as he commanded them :

13 For his sons carried him into the land of Kenâ'an, and buried him in the cave of the field of Machpêlâh, which Abrâhâm bought with the field, for a possession of a buryingplace, of 'Ephrôn the 'Hitty, before Mamrê.

22 And Yôsêph dwelt in Miçrâim, he and his father's house : and Yôsêph lived an hundred and ten years.

January 1886.

Catalogue of Books

PUBLISHED BY

MESSRS. LONGMANS, GREEN, & CO.

39 PATERNOSTER ROW, LONDON, E.C.

Abbott.—*THE ELEMENTS OF LOGIC* By T. K. ABBOTT, B.D. 12mo. 2s. 6d. sewed, or 3s. cloth.

Acton. — *MODERN COOKERY FOR PRIVATE FAMILIES*, reduced to a System of Easy Practice in a Series of carefully tested Receipts. By ELIZA ACTON. With upwards of 150 Woodcuts. Fcp. 8vo. 4s. 6d.

Æschylus. — *THE EUMENIDES OF ÆSCHYLUS:* a Critical Edition, with Metrical English Translation. By JOHN F. DAVIES, M.A. Univ. Dub. Lit. D. Q.U.I. F.R.U.I. Professor of Latin in the Queen's College, Galway. 8vo. 7s.

A. K. H. B.—*THE ESSAYS AND CONTRIBUTIONS OF A. K. H. B.*—Uniform Cabinet Editions in crown 8vo.
Autumn Holidays of a Country Parson, 3s. 6d.
Changed Aspects of Unchanged Truths, 3s. 6d.
Commonplace Philosopher, 3s. 6d.
Counsel and Comfort from a City Pulpit, 3s. 6d.
Critical Essays of a Country Parson, 3s. 6d.
Graver Thoughts of a Country Parson. Three Series, 3s. 6d. each.
Landscapes, Churches, and Moralities, 3s. 6d.
Leisure Hours in Town, 3s. 6d.
Lessons of Middle Age, 3s. 6d.
Our Little Life. Two Series, 3s. 6d. each.
Present Day Thoughts, 3s. 6d.
Recreations of a Country Parson. Three Series, 3s. 6d. each.
Seaside Musings, 3s. 6d.
Sunday Afternoons in the Parish Church of a University City, 3s. 6d.

Aldridge. — *RANCH NOTES IN KANSAS, COLORADO, THE INDIAN TERRITORY AND NORTHERN TEXAS.* By REGINALD ALDRIDGE. Crown 8vo. with 4 Illustrations engraved on Wood by G. Pearson, 5s.

Allen.—*FLOWERS AND THEIR PEDIGREES.* By GRANT ALLEN. With 50 Illustrations engraved on Wood. Crown 8vo. 5s.

Alpine Club (The).—*GUIDES AND MAPS.*

THE ALPINE GUIDE. By JOHN BALL, M.R.I.A. Post 8vo. with Maps and other Illustrations:—

THE EASTERN ALPS, 10s. 6d.

CENTRAL ALPS, including all the Oberland District, 7s. 6d.

WESTERN ALPS, including Mont Blanc, Monte Rosa, Zermatt, &c. 6s. 6d.

THE ALPINE CLUB MAP OF SWITZERLAND, on the Scale of Four Miles to an Inch. Edited by R. C. NICHOLS, F.R.G.S. 4 Sheets in Portfolio, 42s. coloured, or 34s. uncoloured.

ENLARGED ALPINE CLUB MAP OF THE SWISS AND ITALIAN ALPS, on the Scale of Three English Statute Miles to One Inch, in 8 Sheets, price 1s. 6d. each.

ON ALPINE TRAVELLING AND THE GEOLOGY OF THE ALPS. Price 1s. Either of the Three Volumes or Parts of the 'Alpine Guide' may be had with this Introduction prefixed, 1s. extra.

Amos.—*WORKS BY SHELDON AMOS, M.A.*

A PRIMER OF THE ENGLISH CONSTITUTION AND GOVERNMENT. Crown 8vo. 6s.

A SYSTEMATIC VIEW OF THE SCIENCE OF JURISPRUDENCE. 8vo. 18s.

A

Anstey.—THE BLACK POODLE, and other Stories. By F. ANSTEY, Author of 'Vice Versâ.' With Frontispiece by G. Du Maurier and Initial Letters by the Author. Crown 8vo. 6s.

Antinous.—An Historical Romance of the Roman Empire. By GEORGE TAYLOR (Professor HAUSRATH). Translated from the German by J. D. M. Crown 8vo. 6s.

Aristophanes.—THE ACHARNIANS OF ARISTOPHANES. Translated into English Verse by ROBERT YELVERTON TYRRELL, M.A. Dublin. Crown 8vo. 2s. 6d.

Aristotle.—THE WORKS OF.

THE POLITICS, G. Bekker's Greek Text of Books I. III. IV. (VII.) with an English Translation by W. E. BOLLAND, M.A. ; and short Introductory Essays by A. LANG, M.A. Crown 8vo. 7s. 6d.

THE ETHICS; Greek Text, illustrated with Essays and Notes. By Sir ALEXANDER GRANT, Bart. M.A. LL.D. 2 vols. 8vo. 32s.

THE NICOMACHEAN ETHICS, Newly Translated into English. By ROBERT WILLIAMS, Barrister-at-Law. Crown 8vo. 7s. 6d.

Arnold. — WORKS BY THOMAS ARNOLD, D.D. Late Head-master of Rugby School.

INTRODUCTORY LECTURES ON MODERN HISTORY, delivered in 1841 and 1842. 8vo. 7s. 6d.

SERMONS PREACHED MOSTLY IN THE CHAPEL OF RUGBY SCHOOL. 6 vols. crown 8vo. 30s. or separately, 5s. each.

MISCELLANEOUS WORKS. 8vo. 7s. 6d.

Arnold.—A MANUAL OF ENGLISH LITERATURE, Historical and Critical. By THOMAS ARNOLD, M.A. Crown 8vo. 7s. 6d.

Arnott.—THE ELEMENTS OF PHYSICS OR NATURAL PHILOSOPHY. By NEIL ARNOTT, M.D. Edited by A. BAIN, LL.D. and A. S. TAYLOR, M.D. F.R.S. Woodcuts. Crown 8vo. 12s. 6d.

Ashby. — NOTES ON PHYSIOLOGY FOR THE USE OF STUDENTS PREPARING FOR EXAMINATION. With 120 Woodcuts. By HENRY ASHBY, M.D. Lond. Fcp. 8vo. 5s.

Bacon.—THE WORKS AND LIFE OF.

COMPLETE WORKS. Collected and Edited by R. L. ELLIS, M.A. J. SPEDDING, M.A. and D. D. HEATH. 7 vols. 8vo. £3. 13s. 6d.

LETTERS AND LIFE INCLUDING ALL HIS OCCASIONAL WORKS. Collected and Edited, with a Commentary, by J. SPEDDING. 7 vols. 8vo. £4. 4s.

THE ESSAYS; with Annotations. By RICHARD WHATELY, D.D., sometime Archbishop of Dublin. 8vo. 10s. 6d.

THE ESSAYS; with Introduction, Notes, and Index. By E. A. ABBOTT, D.D. 2 vols. fcp. 8vo. price 6s. The Text and Index only, without Introduction and Notes, in 1 vol. fcp. 8vo. price 2s. 6d.

THE PROMUS OF FORMULARIES AND ELEGANCIES, illustrated by Passages from SHAKESPEARE. By Mrs. H. POTT. Preface by E. A. ABBOTT, D.D. 8vo. 16s.

The BADMINTON LIBRARY of Sports and Pastimes, edited by His Grace the DUKE OF BEAUFORT, K.G., assisted by ALFRED E. T. WATSON. Dedicated to H.R.H. the Prince of Wales.

HUNTING. By His Grace the DUKE OF BEAUFORT, K.G., and MOWBRAY MORRIS. With Contributions by the Earl of Suffolk and Berkshire, Rev. E. W. L. Davies, Digby Collins, and Alfred E. T. Watson. With Coloured Frontispiece and 53 Illustrations by J. Sturgess, J. Charlton, and Agnes M. Biddulph. Crown 8vo. 10s. 6d.

FISHING. By. H. CHOLMONDELEY-PENNELL, late H.M. Inspector of Sea Fisheries. With Contributions by the Marquis of Exeter, Henry R. Francis, M.A., Major John P. Traherne, and G. Christopher Davies. Fully Illustrated.

Vol. I. Salmon, Trout, and Grayling. Crown 8vo. 10s. 6d.

Vol. II. Pike and other Coarse Fish. Crown 8vo. 10s. 6d.

Racing { Flat Racing. The EARL OF SUFFOLK and W. G. CRAVEN.
Steeplechasing. A. COVENTRY and A. E. T. WATSON.
[In the press.

Riding and Driving. Riding (including Military Riding and Ladies' Riding) : R. WEIR. Driving : Major DIXON, with an Introduction by E. L. Anderson
[In the press.

⁎ Other volumes in preparation.

Bagehot.—*WORKS BY WALTER BAGEHOT, M.A.*

BIOGRAPHICAL STUDIES. 8vo. 12s.

ECONOMIC STUDIES. 8vo. 10s. 6d.

LITERARY STUDIES. 2 vols. 8vo. Portrait. 28s.

THE POSTULATES OF ENGLISH POLITICAL ECONOMY. Student's Edition. With a Preface by Alfred Marshall, Professor of Political Economy, Cambridge. Crown 8vo. 2s. 6d.

Bagwell.—*IRELAND UNDER THE TUDORS*, with a Succinct Account of the Earlier History. Compiled from the State Papers and other authentic sources. By RICHARD BAGWELL, M.A. Vols. I. and II. From the first invasion of the Northmen to the year 1578. With Maps and Index. 2 vols. 8vo. 32s.

Vol. III., completing the work, is in preparation.

Bailey.—*FESTUS, A POEM.* By PHILIP JAMES BAILEY. Crown 8vo. 12s. 6d.

Bain.—*WORKS BY ALEXANDER BAIN, LL.D.*

MENTAL AND MORAL SCIENCE; a Compendium of Psychology and Ethics. Crown 8vo. 10s. 6d.

THE SENSES AND THE INTELLECT. 8vo. 15s.

THE EMOTIONS AND THE WILL. 8vo. 15s.

PRACTICAL ESSAYS. Crown 8vo. 4s. 6d.

LOGIC, DEDUCTIVE AND INDUCTIVE. PART I. *Deduction*, 4s. PART II. *Induction*, 6s. 6d.

JAMES MILL; a Biography. Crown 8vo. 5s.

JOHN STUART MILL; a Criticism, with Personal Recollections. Crown 8vo. 2s. 6d.

Baker.—*WORKS BY SIR SAMUEL W. BAKER, M.A.*

EIGHT YEARS IN CEYLON. Crown 8vo. Woodcuts. 5s.

THE RIFLE AND THE HOUND IN CEYLON. Crown 8vo. Woodcuts. 5s

Beaconsfield.—*WORKS BY THE EARL OF BEACONSFIELD, K.G.*

NOVELS AND TALES. The Hughenden Edition. With 2 Portraits and 11 Vignettes. 11 vols. Crown 8vo. 42s.

Endymion.	
Lothair.	Henrietta Temple.
Coningsby.	Contarini Fleming, &c.
Sybil.	Alroy, Ixion, &c.
Tancred.	The Young Duke, &c.
Venetia.	Vivian Grey, &c.

NOVELS AND TALES. Cheap Edition, complete in 11 vols. Crown 8vo. 1s. each, sewed; 1s. 6d. each, cloth.

SELECTED SPEECHES. With Introduction and Notes, by T. E. KEBBEL, M.A. 2 vols. 8vo. Portrait, 32s.

THE WIT AND WISDOM OF BENJAMIN DISRAELI, EARL OF BEACONSFIELD. Crown 8vo. 3s. 6d.

THE BEACONSFIELD BIRTHDAY-BOOK. With 2 Portraits and 11 Views of Hughenden Manor and its Surroundings. 18mo. 2s. 6d. cloth, gilt; 4s. 6d. bound.

Becker.—*WORKS BY PROFESSOR BECKER, translated from the German by the Rev. F. METCALF.*

GALLUS; or, Roman Scenes in the Time of Augustus. Post 8vo. 7s. 6d.

CHARICLES; or, Illustrations of the Private Life of the Ancient Greeks. Post 8vo. 7s. 6d.

Bent.—*THE CYCLADES*; or, Life among the Insular Greeks. By J. THEODORE BENT, B.A. Oxon; with Map. Crown 8vo. 12s. 6d.

Boultbee.—*WORKS BY THE REV. T. P BOULTBEE, LL.D.*

A COMMENTARY ON THE 39 ARTICLES of the Church of England. Crown 8vo. 6s.

A HISTORY OF THE CHURCH OF ENGLAND; Pre-Reformation Period. 8vo. 15s.

Bourne.—*WORKS BY JOHN BOURNE, C.E.*

A TREATISE ON THE STEAM ENGINE, in its application to Mines, Mills, Steam Navigation, Railways, and Agriculture. With 37 Plates and 546 Woodcuts. 4to. 42s.

CATECHISM OF THE STEAM ENGINE in its various Applications in the Arts, to which is now added a chapter on Air and Gas Engines, and another devoted to Useful Rules, Tables, and Memoranda. Illustrated by 212 Woodcuts. Crown 8vo. 7s. 6d. [*Continued on next page.*

Bourne. — *Works by John Bourne, C.E.*—continued.

Handbook of the Steam Engine; a Key to the Author's Catechism of the Steam Engine. With 67 Woodcuts. Fcp. 8vo. 9s.

Recent Improvements in the Steam Engine. With 124 Woodcuts. Fcp. 8vo. 6s.

Examples of Steam and Gas Engines, with 54 Plates and 356 Woodcuts. 4to. 70s.

Brabourne.—*Friends and Foes from Fairyland.* By the Right Hon. Lord Brabourne, Author of 'Higgledy-Piggledy,' 'Whispers from Fairyland,' &c. With 20 Illustrations by Linley Sambourne. Crown 8vo. 6s.

Bramston & Leroy.—*Historic Winchester;* England's First Capital. By A. R. Bramston and A. C. Leroy. Cr. 8vo. 6s.

Brande's *Dictionary of Science, Literature, and Art.* Re-edited by the Rev. Sir G. W. Cox, Bart., M.A. 3 vols. medium 8vo. 63s.

Brassey. — *Works by Lady Brassey.*

A Voyage in the 'Sunbeam,' our Home on the Ocean for Eleven Months. With Map and 65 Wood Engravings. Library Edition, 8vo. 21s. Cabinet Edition, crown 8vo. 7s. 6d. School Edition, fcp. 2s. Popular Edition, 4to. 6d.

Sunshine and Storm in the East; or, Cruises to Cyprus and Constantinople. With 2 Maps and 114 Illustrations engraved on Wood. Library Edition, 8vo. 21s. Cabinet Edition, cr. 8vo. 7s. 6d.

In the Trades, the Tropics, and the 'Roaring Forties'; or, Fourteen Thousand Miles in the *Sunbeam* in 1883. With 292 Illustrations engraved on Wood from drawings by R. T. Pritchett, and Eight Maps and Charts. Edition de Luxe, imperial 8vo. £3. 13s. 6d. Library Edition, 8vo. 21s.

Bray. — *Phases of Opinion and Experience during a Long Life:* an Autobiography. By Charles Bray, Author of 'The Philosophy of Necessity' &c. Crown 8vo. 3s. 6d.

Browne.—*An Exposition of the 39 Articles,* Historical and Doctrinal. By E. H. Browne, D.D., Bishop of Winchester. 8vo. 16s.

Buckle.—*Works by Henry Thomas Buckle.*

History of Civilisation in England and France, Spain and Scotland. 3 vols. crown 8vo. 24s.

Miscellaneous and Posthumous Works. A New and Abridged Edition. Edited by Grant Allen. 2 vols. crown 8vo. 21s.

Buckton.—*Works by Mrs. C. M. Buckton.*

Food and Home Cookery; a Course of Instruction in Practical Cookery and Cleaning. With 11 Woodcuts. Crown 8vo. 2s. 6d.

Health in the House: Twenty-five Lectures on Elementary Physiology. With 41 Woodcuts and Diagrams. Crown 8vo. 2s.

Our Dwellings: Healthy and Unhealthy. With 39 Illustrations. Crown 8vo. 3s. 6d.

Bull.—*Works by Thomas Bull, M.D.*

Hints to Mothers on the Management of their Health during the Period of Pregnancy and in the Lying-in Room. Fcp. 8vo. 1s. 6d.

The Maternal Management of Children in Health and Disease. Fcp. 8vo. 1s. 6d.

Cabinet Lawyer, The; a Popular Digest of the Laws of England, Civil, Criminal, and Constitutional. Fcp. 8vo. 9s.

Carlyle. — *Thomas and Jane Welsh Carlyle.*

Thomas Carlyle, a History of the first Forty Years of his Life, 1795-1835 By J. A. Froude, M.A. With 2 Portraits and 4 Illustrations, 2 vols. 8vo. 32s.

Thomas Carlyle, a History of his Life in London: from 1834 to his death in 1881. By James A. Froude, M.A., with Portrait. 2 vols. 8vo. 32s.

Letters and Memorials of Jane Welsh Carlyle. Prepared for publication by Thomas Carlyle, and edited by J. A. Froude, M.A. 3 vols. 8vo. 36s.

Cates. — *A Dictionary of General Biography.* Fourth Edition, with Supplement brought down to the end of 1884. By W. L. R. Cates. 8vo. 28s. cloth; 35s. half-bound russia. The Supplement, 1881-4, 2s. 6d.

GENERAL & SCIENTIFIC BOOKS Published by Messrs. LONGMANS & CO. 5

Chesney.—*Waterloo Lectures;* a Study of the Campaign of 1815. By Col. C. C. Chesney, R.E. 8vo. 10s. 6d.

Cicero.—*The Correspondence of Cicero:* a revised Text, with Notes and Prolegomena.—Vol. I., The Letters to the end of Cicero's Exile. By Robert Y. Tyrrell, M.A., Fellow of Trinity College, Dublin, 12s.

Coats.—*A Manual of Pathology.* By Joseph Coats, M.D. Pathologist to the Western Infirmary and the Sick Children's Hospital, Glasgow. With 339 Illustrations engraved on Wood. 8vo. 31s. 6d.

Colenso.—*The Pentateuch and Book of Joshua Critically Examined.* By J. W. Colenso, D.D., late Bishop of Natal. Crown 8vo. 6s.

Conder.—*A Handbook to the Bible,* or Guide to the Study of the Holy Scriptures derived from Ancient Monuments and Modern Exploration. By F. R. Conder, and Lieut. C. R. Conder, R.E. Post 8vo. 7s. 6d.

Conington. — *Works by John Conington, M.A.*

The Æneid of Virgil. Translated into English Verse. Crown 8vo. 9s.

The Poems of Virgil. Translated into English Prose. Crown 8vo. 9s.

Conybeare & Howson.—*The Life and Epistles of St. Paul.* By the Rev. W. J. Conybeare, M.A., and the Very Rev. J. S. Howson, D.D. Dean of Chester.

Library Edition, with Maps, Plates, and Woodcuts. 2 vols. square crown 8vo. 21s.

Student's Edition, revised and condensed, with 46 Illustrations and Maps. 1 vol. crown 8vo. 7s. 6d.

Cooke. — *Tablets of Anatomy.* By Thomas Cooke, F.R.C.S. Eng. B.A. B.Sc. M.D. Paris. Fourth Edition, being a selection of the Tablets believed to be most useful to Students generally. Post 4to. 7s. 6d.

Cox. — *The First Century of Christianity.* By Homersham Cox, M.A. 8vo. 12s.

Cox.—*Works by the Rev. Sir G. W. Cox, Bart., M.A.*

A General History of Greece: from the Earliest Period to the Death of Alexander the Great; with a Sketch of the History to the Present Time. With 11 Maps and Plans. Crown 8vo. 7s. 6d.

Lives of Greek Statesmen. Vol. I Solon-Themistocles; Vol. II. Ephialtes-Hermokrates. Fcp. 8vo. 2s. 6d. each.

*** For other Works, *see* 'Epochs of History,' p. 24.

Crawford.—*Across the Pampas and the Andes.* By Robert Crawford, M.A. With Map and 7 Illustrations. Crown 8vo. 7s. 6d.

Creighton. — *History of the Papacy during the Reformation.* By the Rev. M. Creighton, M.A. Vols. I. and II. 8vo. 32s.

Crookes. — *Select Methods in Chemical Analysis* (chiefly Inorganic). By William Crookes, F.R.S. V.P.C.S. With 37 Illustrations. 8vo. 24s.

Crozier.—*Civilization and Progress;* being the Outline of a New System of Political, Religious, and Social Philosophy. By J. Beattie Crozier. 8vo. 14s.

Crump.—*A Short Enquiry into the Formation of Political Opinion,* from the Reign of the Great Families to the Advent of Democracy. By Arthur Crump. 8vo. 7s. 6d.

Culley.—*Handbook of Practical Telegraphy.* By R. S. Culley, M. Inst. C.E. Plates and Woodcuts. 8vo. 16s.

Dante.—*The Divine Comedy of Dante Alighieri.* Translated verse for verse from the Original into Terza Rima. By James Innes Minchin. Cr. 8vo. 15s.

Davidson.—*An Introduction to the Study of the New Testament,* Critical, Exegetical, and Theological By the Rev. S. Davidson, D.D. LL.D. Revised Edition. 2 vols. 8vo. 30s.

Davidson.—*The Logic of Definition Explained and Applied.* By William L. Davidson, M.A. Crown 8vo. 6s.

Dead Shot, The, OR *SPORTSMAN'S COMPLETE GUIDE*; a Treatise on the Use of the Gun, with Lessons in the Art of Shooting Game of all kinds, and Wild-Fowl, also Pigeon-Shooting, and Dog-Breaking. By MARKSMAN. With 13 Illustrations. Crown 8vo. 10s. 6d.

Decaisne & Le Maout.—*A GENERAL SYSTEM OF BOTANY*. Translated from the French of E. LE MAOUT, M.D., and J. DECAISNE, by Lady HOOKER; with Additions by Sir J. D. HOOKER, C.B. F.R.S. Imp. 8vo. with 5,500 Woodcuts, 31s. 6d.

Dent.—*ABOVE THE SNOW LINE*: Mountaineering Sketches between 1870 and 1880. By CLINTON DENT, Vice-President of the Alpine Club. With Two Engravings by Edward Whymper and an Illustration by Percy Macquoid. Crown 8vo. 7s. 6d.

D'Eon de Beaumont. — *THE STRANGE CAREER OF THE CHEVALIER D'EON DE BEAUMONT*, Minister Plenipotentiary from France to Great Britain in 1763. By Captain J. BUCHAN TELFER, R.N. F.S.A. F.R.G.S. With 3 Portraits. 8vo. 12s.

De Tocqueville.—*DEMOCRACY IN AMERICA*. By ALEXIS DE TOCQUEVILLE. Translated by H. REEVE, C.B. 2 vols. crown 8vo. 16s.

Dewes.—*THE LIFE AND LETTERS OF ST. PAUL*. By ALFRED DEWES, M.A. LL.D. D.D. Vicar of St. Augustine's, Pendlebury. With 4 Maps. 8vo. 7s. 6d.

Dickinson. — *ON RENAL AND URINARY AFFECTIONS*. By W. HOWSHIP DICKINSON, M.D. Cantab. F.R.C.P. &c. With 12 Plates and 122 Woodcuts. 3 vols. 8vo. £3. 4s. 6d.

** The Three Parts may be had separately: PART I.—*Diabetes*, 10s. 6d. sewed, 12s. cloth. PART II. *Albuminuria*, 20s. sewed, 21s. cloth. PART III.—*Miscellaneous Affections of the Kidneys and Urine*, 30s. sewed, 31s. 6d. cloth.

Dixon.—*RURAL BIRD LIFE*; Essays on Ornithology, with Instructions for Preserving Objects relating to that Science. By CHARLES DIXON. With 45 Woodcuts. Crown 8vo. 5s.

Dowell.—*A HISTORY OF TAXATION AND TAXES IN ENGLAND, FROM THE EARLIEST TIMES TO THE PRESENT DAY*. By STEPHEN DOWELL, Assistant Solicitor of Inland Revenue. 4 vols. 8vo. 48s.

Doyle.—*THE OFFICIAL BARONAGE OF ENGLAND*. By JAMES E. DOYLE. Showing the Succession, Dignities, and Offices of every Peer from 1066 to 1885. Vols. I. to III. With 1,600 Portraits, Shields of Arms, Badges, and Autographs. 3 vols. 4to. £5. 5s. Large Paper Edition, Imperial 4to. £15. 15s.

Dresser.—*JAPAN; ITS ARCHITECTURE, ART, AND ART MANUFACTURES*. By CHRISTOPHER DRESSER, Ph.D. F.L.S. &c. With 202 Illustrations. Square crown 8vo. 31s. 6d.

Dunster. — *HOW TO MAKE THE LAND PAY*; or, Profitable Industries connected with the Land, and suitable to all Occupations, Large or Small. By HENRY P. DUNSTER, M.A. Crown 8vo. 5s.

Eastlake.—*HINTS ON HOUSEHOLD TASTE IN FURNITURE, UPHOLSTERY*, &c. By C. L. EASTLAKE, F.R.I.B.A. With 100 Illustrations. Square crown 8vo. 14s.

Edersheim.—*WORKS BY THE REV. ALFRED EDERSHEIM, D.D.*

THE LIFE AND TIMES OF JESUS THE MESSIAH. 2 vols. 8vo. 42s.

PROPHECY AND HISTORY IN RELATION TO THE MESSIAH: the Warburton Lectures, delivered at Lincoln's Inn Chapel, 1880-1884. 8vo. 12s.

Edwards. — *OUR SEAMARKS*. By E. PRICE EDWARDS. With numerous Illustrations of Lighthouses, &c. engraved on Wood by G. H. Ford. Crown 8vo. 8s. 6d.

Ellicott. — *WORKS BY C. J. ELLICOTT, D.D.*, Bishop of Gloucester and Bristol.

A CRITICAL AND GRAMMATICAL COMMENTARY ON ST. PAUL'S EPISTLES. 8vo. Galatians, 8s. 6d. Ephesians, 8s. 6d. Pastoral Epistles, 10s. 6d. Philippians, Colossians, and Philemon, 10s. 6d. Thessalonians, 7s. 6d. 1. Corinthians.
[*Nearly ready.*]

HISTORICAL LECTURES ON THE LIFE OF OUR LORD JESUS CHRIST. 8vo. 12s.

GENERAL & SCIENTIFIC BOOKS Published by Messrs. LONGMANS & CO. 7

English Worthies. Edited by ANDREW LANG, M.A. Fcp. 8vo. price 2s. 6d. each.

DARWIN. By GRANT ALLEN.
MARLBOROUGH. By GEORGE SAINTSBURY.

The following Volumes are in preparation :—
Steele. By Austin Dobson.
Sir T. More. By J Cotter Morison.
Wellington. By R. Louis Stevenson.
Lord Peterborough. By Walter Besant.
Claverhouse. By Mowbray Morris.
Latimer. By Canon Creighton.
Shaftesbury. By H. D. Traill.
Garrick. By W. H. Pollock.
Admiral Blake. By David Hannay.
Raleigh. By Edmund Gosse.
Ben Jonson. By J. A. Symonds.
Isaak Walton. By Andrew Lang.
Canning. By Frank H. Hill.

Epochs of Ancient History. Edited by the Rev. Sir G. W. COX, Bart. M.A. and C. SANKEY, M.A. 10 vols. fcp. 8vo. 2s. 6d. each. *See* p. 24.

Epochs of Modern History. Edited by C. COLBECK, M.A. 17 vols. fcp. 8vo. 2s. 6d. each. *See* p. 24.

Erichsen.—*WORKS BY JOHN ERIC ERICHSEN, F.R.S.*

THE SCIENCE AND ART OF SURGERY: Being a Treatise on Surgical Injuries, Diseases, and Operations. Illustrated by Engravings on Wood. 2 vols. 8vo. 42s.; or bound in half-russia, 60s.

ON CONCUSSION OF THE SPINE, NERVOUS SHOCKS, and other Obscure Injuries of the Nervous System in their Clinical and Medico-Legal Aspects. Crown 8vo. 10s. 6d.

Evans.—*THE BRONZE IMPLEMENTS, ARMS, AND ORNAMENTS OF GREAT BRITAIN AND IRELAND.* By JOHN EVANS, D.C.L. LL.D. F.R.S. With 540 Illustrations. 8vo. 25s.

Ewald. — *WORKS BY PROFESSOR HEINRICH EWALD,* of Göttingen.

THE ANTIQUITIES OF ISRAEL. Translated from the German by H. S. SOLLY, M.A. 8vo. 12s. 6d.

THE HISTORY OF ISRAEL. Translated from the German. Vols. I.—V. 8vo. 63s. Vol. VI. *Christ and his Times*, 8vo. 16s. Vol. VII. *The Apostolic Age*, 8vo. 21s.

Fairbairn.—*WORKS BY SIR W. FAIRBAIRN, BART, C.E.*

A TREATISE ON MILLS AND MILL-WORK, with 18 Plates and 333 Woodcuts. 1 vol. 8vo. 25s.
USEFUL INFORMATION FOR ENGINEERS. With many Plates and Woodcuts. 3 vols. crown 8vo. 31s. 6d.

Farrar. — *LANGUAGE AND LANGUAGES.* A Revised Edition of *Chapters on Language and Families of Speech.* By F. W FARRAR, D.D. Crown 8vo. 6s.

Fitzwygram. — *HORSES AND STABLES.* By Major-General Sir F. FITZWYGRAM, Bart. With 39 pages of Illustrations. 8vo. 10s. 6d.

Fox.—*THE EARLY HISTORY OF CHARLES JAMES FOX.* By the Right Hon. G. O. TREVELYAN, M.P. Library Edition, 8vo. 18s. Cabinet Edition, cr. 8vo. 6s.

Francis.—*A BOOK ON ANGLING;* or, Treatise on the Art of Fishing in every branch; including full Illustrated Lists of Salmon Flies. By FRANCIS FRANCIS. Post 8vo. Portrait and Plates, 15s.

Freeman.—*THE HISTORICAL GEOGRAPHY OF EUROPE.* By E. A. FREEMAN, D.C.L. With 65 Maps. 2 vols. 8vo. 31s. 6d.

French. — *NINETEEN CENTURIES OF DRINK IN ENGLAND,* a History. By RICHARD VALPY FRENCH, D.C.L. LL.D. F.S.A.; Author of 'The History of Toasting' &c. Crown 8vo. 10s. 6d.

Froude.—*WORKS BY JAMES A. FROUDE, M.A.*

THE HISTORY OF ENGLAND, from the Fall of Wolsey to the Defeat of the Spanish Armada.
Cabinet Edition, 12 vols. cr. 8vo. £3. 12s
Popular Edition, 12 vols. cr. 8vo. £2. 2s.

SHORT STUDIES ON GREAT SUBJECTS. 4 vols. crown 8vo. 24s.

THE ENGLISH IN IRELAND IN THE EIGHTEENTH CENTURY. 3 vols. crown 8vo. 18s.

OCEANA; OR, ENGLAND AND HER COLONIES. With 9 Illustrations. 8vo. 18s.

THOMAS CARLYLE, a History of the first Forty Years of his Life, 1795 to 1835. 2 vols. 8vo. 32s.

THOMAS CARLYLE, a History of His Life in London from 1834 to his death in 1881. By JAMES A. FROUDE, M.A. with Portrait engraved on steel. 2 vols. 8vo. 32s.

Ganot. — *WORKS BY PROFESSOR GANOT.* Translated by E. ATKINSON, Ph.D. F.C.S.

ELEMENTARY TREATISE ON PHYSICS, for the use of Colleges and Schools. With 5 Coloured Plates and 898 Woodcuts. Large crown 8vo. 15s.

NATURAL PHILOSOPHY FOR GENERAL READERS AND YOUNG PERSONS. With 2 Plates and 471 Woodcuts. Crown 8vo. 7s. 6d.

Gardiner. — *WORKS BY SAMUEL RAWSON GARDINER, LL.D.*

HISTORY OF ENGLAND, from the Accession of James I. to the Outbreak of the Civil War, 1603-1642. Cabinet Edition, thoroughly revised. 10 vols. crown 8vo. price 6s. each.

OUTLINE OF ENGLISH HISTORY, B.C. 55-A.D. 1880. With 96 Woodcuts, fcp. 8vo. 2s. 6d.

** For other Works, see 'Epochs of Modern History,' p. 24.

Garrod. — *WORKS BY ALFRED BARING GARROD, M.D. F.R.S.*

A TREATISE ON GOUT AND RHEUMATIC GOUT (RHEUMATOID ARTHRITIS). With 6 Plates, comprising 21 Figures (14 Coloured), and 27 Illustrations engraved on Wood 8vo. 21s.

THE ESSENTIALS OF MATERIA MEDICA AND THERAPEUTICS. New Edition, revised and adapted to the New Edition of the British Pharmacopœia, by NESTOR TIRARD, M.D. Crown 8vo. 12s. 6d.

Garrod.—*AN INTRODUCTION TO THE USE OF THE LARYNGOSCOPE.* By ARCHIBALD G. GARROD, M.A. M.R.C.P. With Illustrations. 8vo. 3s. 6d.

Goethe.—*FAUST.* Translated by T. E. WEBB, LL.D. 8vo. 12s. 6d.

FAUST. A New Translation, chiefly in Blank Verse; with Introduction and Notes. By JAMES ADEY BIRDS, B.A. F.G.S. Crown 8vo. 12s. 6d.

FAUST. The German Text, with an English Introduction and Notes for Students. By ALBERT M. SELSS, M.A. Ph.D. Crown 8vo. 5s.

Goodeve.—*WORKS BY T. M. GOODEVE, M.A.*

PRINCIPLES OF MECHANICS. With 253 Woodcuts. Crown 8vo. 6s.

THE ELEMENTS OF MECHANISM. With 342 Woodcuts. Crown 8vo. 6s.

Grant.—*WORKS BY SIR ALEXANDER GRANT, BART. LL.D. D.C.L. &c.*

THE STORY OF THE UNIVERSITY OF EDINBURGH during its First Three Hundred Years. With numerous Illustrations. 2 vols. 8vo. 36s.

THE ETHICS OF ARISTOTLE. The Greek Text illustrated by Essays and Notes. 2 vols. 8vo. 32s.

Gray. — *ANATOMY, DESCRIPTIVE AND SURGICAL.* By HENRY GRAY, F.R.S. late Lecturer on Anatomy at St. George's Hospital. With 557 large Woodcut Illustrations. Re-edited by T. PICKERING PICK, Surgeon to St. George's Hospital. Royal 8vo. 30s.

Green.—*THE WORKS OF THOMAS HILL GREEN,* late Fellow of Balliol College, and Whyte's Professor of Moral Philosophy in the University of Oxford. Edited by R. L. NETTLESHIP, Fellow of Balliol College, Oxford. In 3 vols. Vol. I.—Philosophical Works. 8vo. 16s.

Greville. — *WORKS BY C. C. F. GREVILLE.* Edited by H. REEVE, C.B.

A JOURNAL OF THE REIGNS OF KING GEORGE IV. AND KING WILLIAM IV. 3 vols. 8vo. 36s.

A JOURNAL OF THE REIGN OF QUEEN VICTORIA, from 1837 to 1852. 3 vols. 8vo. 36s.

Grimston.—*THE HON. ROBERT GRIMSTON:* a Sketch of his Life. By FREDERICK GALE. With Portrait. Crown 8vo. 10s. 6d.

Gwilt.—*AN ENCYCLOPÆDIA OF ARCHITECTURE.* By JOSEPH GWILT, F.S.A. Illustrated with more than 1,100 Engravings on Wood. Revised, with Alterations and Considerable Additions, by WYATT PAPWORTH. 8vo. 52s. 6d.

Grove. — *THE CORRELATION OF PHYSICAL FORCES.* By the Hon. Sir W. R. GROVE, F.R.S. &c. 8vo. 15s.

Halliwell-Phillips.—*OUTLINES OF THE LIFE OF SHAKESPEARE.* By J. O. HALLIWELL-PHILLIPPS, F.R.S. Royal 8vo. 7s. 6d.

Hamilton.—*LIFE OF SIR WILLIAM R. HAMILTON,* Kt. LL.D. D.C.L. M.R.I.A. &c. Including Selections from his Poems, Correspondence, and Miscellaneous Writings. By the Rev. R. P. GRAVES, M.A. (3 vols.) Vols. I. and II. 8vo. 15s. each.

Hartwig.—*WORKS BY DR. G. HARTWIG.*

THE SEA AND ITS LIVING WONDERS. 8vo. with many Illustrations, 10s. 6d.

THE TROPICAL WORLD. With about 200 Illustrations. 8vo. 10s. 6d.

THE POLAR WORLD; a Description of Man and Nature in the Arctic and Antarctic Regions of the Globe. Maps, Plates, and Woodcuts. 8vo. 10s. 6d.

THE ARCTIC REGIONS (extracted from the 'Polar World'). 4to. 6d. sewed.

THE SUBTERRANEAN WORLD. With Maps and Woodcuts. 8vo. 10s. 6d.

THE AERIAL WORLD; a Popular Account of the Phenomena and Life of the Atmosphere. Map, Plates, Woodcuts. 8vo. 10s. 6d.

Harte.—*WORKS BY BRET HARTE.*

IN THE CARQUINEZ WOODS. Fcp. 8vo. 2s. boards; 2s. 6d. cloth.

ON THE FRONTIER. Three Stories. 16mo. 1s.

BY SHORE AND SEDGE. Three Stories. 16mo. 1s.

Hassall. — *WORKS BY ARTHUR HILL HASSALL, M.D.*

THE INHALATION TREATMENT OF DISEASES OF THE ORGANS OF RESPIRATION, including Consumption; with 19 Illustrations of Apparatus. Cr. 8vo. 12s. 6d.

SAN REMO, climatically and medically considered. With 30 Illustrations. Crown 8vo. 5s.

Haughton. — *SIX LECTURES ON PHYSICAL GEOGRAPHY,* delivered in 1876, with some Additions. By the Rev. SAMUEL HAUGHTON, F.R.S. M.D. D.C.L. With 23 Diagrams. 8vo. 15s.

Havelock. — *MEMOIRS OF SIR HENRY HAVELOCK, K.C.B.* By JOHN CLARK MARSHMAN. Crown 8vo. 3s. 6d.

Haward.—*A TREATISE ON ORTHOPÆDIC SURGERY.* By J. WARRINGTON HAWARD, F.R.C.S. Surgeon to St. George's Hospital. With 30 Illustrations engraved on Wood. 8vo. 12s. 6d.

Helmholtz. — *WORKS BY PROFESSOR HELMHOLTZ.*

ON THE SENSATIONS OF TONE AS A PHYSIOLOGICAL BASIS FOR THE THEORY OF MUSIC. Translated by A. J. ELLIS, F.R.S. Royal 8vo. 28s.

POPULAR LECTURES ON SCIENTIFIC SUBJECTS. Translated and edited by EDMUND ATKINSON, Ph.D. F.C.S. With a Preface by Professor TYNDALL, F.R.S. and 68 Woodcuts. 2 vols. Crown 8vo. 15s. or separately, 7s. 6d. each.

Herschel.—*OUTLINES OF ASTRONOMY.* By Sir J. F. W. HERSCHEL, Bart. M.A. With Plates and Diagrams. Square crown 8vo. 12s.

Hewitt. — *WORKS BY GRAILY HEWITT, M.D.*

THE DIAGNOSIS AND TREATMENT OF DISEASES OF WOMEN, INCLUDING THE DIAGNOSIS OF PREGNANCY. New Edition, in great part re-written and much enlarged, with 211 Engravings on Wood, of which 79 are new in this Edition. 8vo. 24s.

THE MECHANICAL SYSTEM OF UTERINE PATHOLOGY. With 31 Life-size Illustrations prepared expressly for this Work. Crown 4to. 7s. 6d.

Hickson. — *IRELAND IN THE SEVENTEENTH CENTURY;* or, The Irish Massacres of 1641-2, their Causes and Results. By MARY HICKSON. With a Preface by J. A. Froude, M.A. 2 vols. 8vo. 28s.

Hiley.—*THE INSPIRATION OF SCRIPTURE:* an Examination into its Meaning, Origin, and Theories thereon. By the Rev. R. W. HILEY, D.D., Vicar of Wighill, Yorkshire. Crown 8vo. 2s. 6d.

Hobart.—*THE MEDICAL LANGUAGE OF ST. LUKE:* a Proof from Internal Evidence that St. Luke's Gospel and the Acts were written by the same person, and that the writer was a Medical Man. By the Rev. W. K. HOBART, LL.D. 8vo. 16s.

Holmes.—*A SYSTEM OF SURGERY,* Theoretical and Practical, in Treatises by various Authors. Edited by TIMOTHY HOLMES, M.A. and J. W. HULKE, F.R.S. 3 vols. royal 8vo. £4. 4s.

Homer.—*THE ILIAD OF HOMER*, Homometrically translated by C. B. CAYLEY. 8vo. 12s. 6d.
THE ILIAD OF HOMER. The Greek Text, with a Verse Translation, by W. C. GREEN, M.A. Vol. I. Books I.–XII. Crown 8vo. 6s.

Hopkins.—*CHRIST THE CONSOLER;* a Book of Comfort for the Sick. By ELLICE HOPKINS. Fcp. 8vo. 2s. 6d.

Horses and Roads; or How to Keep a Horse Sound on His Legs. By FREE-LANCE. Crown 8vo. 6s.

Hort.—*THE NEW PANTHEON*, or an Introduction to the Mythology of the Ancients. By W. J. HORT. 18mo. 2s. 6d.

Howitt.—*VISITS TO REMARKABLE PLACES*, Old Halls, Battle-Fields, Scenes illustrative of Striking Passages in English History and Poetry. By WILLIAM HOWITT. With 80 Illustrations engraved on Wood. Crown 8vo. 7s. 6d.

Howley. — *THE OLD MORALITY, TRACED HISTORICALLY AND APPLIED PRACTICALLY.* By EDWARD HOWLEY, Barrister-at-Law. With Frontispiece, Raffaelle's School at Athens. Crown 8vo. 3s.

Hudson & Gosse.—*THE ROTIFERA OR 'WHEEL-ANIMALCULES.'* By C. T. HUDSON, LL.D. and P. H. GOSSE, F.R.S. With 30 Coloured Plates. In 6 Parts. 4to. 10s. 6d. each. [Pt. 1 *now ready.*

Hullah.—*WORKS BY JOHN HULLAH, LL.D.*
COURSE OF LECTURES ON THE HISTORY OF MODERN MUSIC. 8vo. 8s. 6d.
COURSE OF LECTURES ON THE TRANSITION PERIOD OF MUSICAL HISTORY. 8vo. 10s. 6d.

Hume.—*THE PHILOSOPHICAL WORKS OF DAVID HUME.* Edited by T. H. GREEN, M.A. and the Rev. T. H. GROSE, M.A. 4 vols. 8vo. 56s. Or separately, Essays, 2 vols. 28s. Treatise of Human Nature. 2 vols. 28s.

In the Olden Time.—A Novel. By the Author of 'Mademoiselle Mori.' Crown 8vo. 6s.

Ingelow.—*WORKS BY JEAN INGELOW.*
POETICAL WORKS. Vols. 1 and 2. Fcp. 8vo. 12s. Vol. 3. Fcp. 8vo. 5s.
THE HIGH TIDE ON THE COAST OF LINCOLNSHIRE. With 40 Illustrations, drawn and engraved under the supervision of GEORGE T. ANDREW. Royal 8vo. 10s. 6d. cloth extra, gilt edges.

Jackson.—*AID TO ENGINEERING SOLUTION.* By LOWIS D'A. JACKSON, C.E. With 111 Diagrams and 5 Woodcut Illustrations. 8vo. 21s.

Jameson.—*WORKS BY MRS. JAMESON.*
LEGENDS OF THE SAINTS AND MARTYRS. With 19 Etchings and 187 Woodcuts. 2 vols. 31s. 6d.
LEGENDS OF THE MADONNA, the Virgin Mary as represented in Sacred and Legendary Art. With 27 Etchings and 165 Woodcuts. 1 vol. 21s.
LEGENDS OF THE MONASTIC ORDERS. With 11 Etchings and 88 Woodcuts. 1 vol. 21s.
HISTORY OF THE SAVIOUR, His Types and Precursors. Completed by Lady EASTLAKE. With 13 Etchings and 281 Woodcuts. 2 vols. 42s.

Jeans.—*ENGLAND'S SUPREMACY:* its Sources, Economics, and Dangers. By J. S. JEANS. 8vo. 8s. 6d.

Jefferies. —*RED DEER.* By RICHARD JEFFERIES. Crown 8vo. 4s. 6d.

Johnson.—*THE PATENTEE'S MANUAL;* a Treatise on the Law and Practice of Letters Patent, for the use of Patentees and Inventors. By J. JOHNSON and J. H. JOHNSON. 8vo. 10s. 6d.

Johnston.—*A GENERAL DICTIONARY OF GEOGRAPHY,* Descriptive, Physical, Statistical, and Historical; a complete Gazetteer of the World. By KEITH JOHNSTON. Medium 8vo. 42s.

Jones. — *THE HEALTH OF THE SENSES: SIGHT, HEARING, VOICE, SMELL AND TASTE, SKIN;* with Hints on Health, Diet, Education, Health Resorts of Europe, &c. By H. MACNAUGHTON JONES, M.D. Crown 8vo. 3s. 6d.

Jordan. — *WORKS BY WILLIAM LEIGHTON JORDAN, F.R.G.S.*
THE OCEAN: a Treatise on Ocean Currents and Tides and their Causes. 8vo. 21s.
THE NEW PRINCIPLES OF NATURAL PHILOSOPHY: a Defence and Extension of the Principles established by the Author's treatise on Ocean Currents. With 13 plates. 8vo. 21s.
THE WINDS: an Essay in Illustration of the New Principles of Natural Philosophy. Crown 8vo. 2s.
THE STANDARD OF VALUE. Crown 8vo. 5s.

GENERAL & SCIENTIFIC BOOKS PUBLISHED BY MESSRS. LONGMANS & CO. 11

Jukes.—*WORKS BY ANDREW JUKES.*
THE NEW MAN AND THE ETERNAL LIFE. Crown 8vo. 6s.
THE TYPES OF GENESIS. Crown 8vo. 7s. 6d.
THE SECOND DEATH AND THE RESTITUTION OF ALL THINGS. Crown 8vo. 3s. 6d.
THE MYSTERY OF THE KINGDOM. Crown 8vo. 2s. 6d.

Justinian.— THE INSTITUTES OF JUSTINIAN; Latin Text, chiefly that of Huschke, with English Introduction, Translation, Notes, and Summary. By THOMAS C. SANDARS, M.A. 8vo. 18s.

Kalisch. — *WORKS BY M. M. KALISCH, M.A.*
BIBLE STUDIES. Part I. The Prophecies of Balaam. 8vo. 10s. 6d. Part II. The Book of Jonah. 8vo. 10s. 6d.
COMMENTARY ON THE OLD TESTAMENT; with a New Translation. Vol. I. Genesis, 8vo. 18s. or adapted for the General Reader, 12s. Vol. II. Exodus, 15s. or adapted for the General Reader, 12s. Vol. III. Leviticus, Part I. 15s. or adapted for the General Reader, 8s. Vol. IV. Leviticus, Part II. 15s. or adapted for the General Reader, 8s.
HEBREW GRAMMAR. With Exercises. Part I. 8vo. 12s. 6d. Key, 5s. Part II. 12s. 6d.

Kant.—*WORKS BY EMMANUEL KANT.*
CRITIQUE OF PRACTICAL REASON. Translated by Thomas Kingsmill Abbott, B.D. 8vo. 12s. 6d.
INTRODUCTION TO LOGIC, AND HIS ESSAY ON THE MISTAKEN SUBTILTY OF THE FOUR FIGURES. Translated by Thomas Kingsmill Abbott, B.D. With a few Notes by S. T. Coleridge. 8vo. 6s.

Kerl.—A PRACTICAL TREATISE ON METALLURGY. By Professor KERL. Adapted from the last German Edition by W. Crookes, F.R.S. &c. and E. Röhrig, Ph.D. 3 vols. 8vo. with 625 Woodcuts, £4. 19s.

Killick.—HANDBOOK TO MILL'S SYSTEM OF LOGIC. By the Rev. A. H. KILLICK, M.A. Crown 8vo. 3s. 6d.

Kolbe.—A SHORT TEXT-BOOK OF INORGANIC CHEMISTRY. By Dr. HERMANN KOLBE. Translated from the German by T. S. HUMPIDGE, Ph.D. With a Coloured Table of Spectra and 66 Illustrations. Crown 8vo. 7s. 6d.

Lang.—*WORKS BY ANDREW LANG, M.A. late Fellow of Merton College.*
CUSTOM AND MYTH; Studies of Early Usage and Belief. With 15 Illustrations. Crown 8vo. 7s. 6d.
THE PRINCESS NOBODY: a Tale of Fairyland. After the Drawings by Richard Doyle, printed in colours by Edmund Evans. Post 4to. 5s. boards.

Latham.—*WORKS BY ROBERT G. LATHAM, M.A. M.D.*
A DICTIONARY OF THE ENGLISH LANGUAGE. Founded on the Dictionary of Dr. JOHNSON. Four vols. 4to. £7.
A DICTIONARY OF THE ENGLISH LANGUAGE. Abridged from Dr. Latham's Edition of Johnson's Dictionary. One Volume. Medium 8vo. 14s.
HANDBOOK OF THE ENGLISH LANGUAGE. Crown 8vo. 6s.

Lecky.—*WORKS BY W. E. H. LECKY.*
HISTORY OF ENGLAND IN THE 18TH CENTURY. 4 vols. 8vo. 1700-1784, £3. 12s.
THE HISTORY OF EUROPEAN MORALS FROM AUGUSTUS TO CHARLEMAGNE. 2 vols. crown 8vo. 16s.
HISTORY OF THE RISE AND INFLUENCE OF THE SPIRIT OF RATIONALISM IN EUROPE. 2 vols. crown 8vo. 16s.
LEADERS OF PUBLIC OPINION IN IRELAND. — Swift, Flood, Grattan, O'Connell. Crown 8vo. 7s. 6d.

Lewes.—THE HISTORY OF PHILOSOPHY, from Thales to Comte. By GEORGE HENRY LEWES. 2 vols. 8vo. 32s.

Liddell & Scott.—A GREEK-ENGLISH LEXICON. Compiled by HENRY GEORGE LIDDELL, D.D. Dean of Christ Church; and ROBERT SCOTT, D.D. Dean of Rochester. 4to. 36s.

List.—THE NATIONAL SYSTEM OF POLITICAL ECONOMY. By FRIEDRICH LIST. Translated from the Original German by SAMPSON S. LLOYD, M.P. 8vo. 10s. 6d.

Little.—ON IN-KNEE DISTORTION (Genu Valgum): Its Varieties and Treatment with and without Surgical Operation. By W. J. LITTLE, M.D. Assisted by MUIRHEAD LITTLE, M.R.C.S. With 40 Illustrations. 8vo. 7s. 6d.

Liveing.—WORKS BY ROBERT LIVE-
ING, M.A. and M.D. Cantab.
HANDBOOK ON DISEASES OF THE
SKIN. With especial reference to Diag-
nosis and Treatment. Fcp. 8vo. 5s.
NOTES ON THE TREATMENT OF SKIN
DISEASES. 18mo. 3s.
ELEPHANTIASIS GRÆCORUM, OR
TRUE LEPROSY. Crown 8vo. 4s. 6d.

Lloyd.—A TREATISE ON MAGNET-
ISM, General and Terrestrial. By H.
LLOYD, D.D. D.C.L. 8vo. 10s. 6d.

Lloyd.—THE SCIENCE OF AGRICUL-
TURE. By F. J. LLOYD. 8vo. 12s.

Longman.—WORKS BY WILLIAM
LONGMAN, F.S.A.
LECTURES ON THE HISTORY OF
ENGLAND from the Earliest Times to the
Death of King Edward II. Maps and
Illustrations. 8vo. 15s.
HISTORY OF THE LIFE AND TIMES
OF EDWARD III. With 9 Maps, 8
Plates, and 16 Woodcuts. 2 vols. 8vo. 28s.

Longman.—WORKS BY FREDERICK
W. LONGMAN, Balliol College, Oxon.
CHESS OPENINGS. Fcp. 8vo. 2s. 6d.
FREDERICK THE GREAT AND THE
SEVEN YEARS' WAR. With 2 Coloured
Maps. 8vo. 2s. 6d.
A NEW POCKET DICTIONARY OF
THE GERMAN AND ENGLISH LAN-
GUAGES. Square 18mo. 2s. 6d.

Longman's Magazine. Published
Monthly. Price Sixpence.
Vols. 1-6, 8vo. price 5s. each.

Longmore.—GUNSHOT INJURIES ;
Their History, Characteristic Features,
Complications, and General Treatment.
By Surgeon-General T. LONGMORE, C.B.
F.R.C.S. With 58 Illustrations. 8vo.
price 31s. 6d.

Loudon.—WORKS BY J. C. LOUDON,
F.L.S.
ENCYCLOPÆDIA OF GARDENING ;
the Theory and Practice of Horticulture,
Floriculture, Arboriculture, and Land-
scape Gardening. With 1,000 Woodcuts.
8vo. 21s.
ENCYCLOPÆDIA OF AGRICULTURE ;
the Laying-out, Improvement, and
Management of Landed Property ; the
Cultivation and Economy of the Produc-
tions of Agriculture. With 1,100 Wood-
cuts. 8vo. 21s.
ENCYCLOPÆDIA OF PLANTS ; the
Specific Character, Description, Culture,
History, &c. of all Plants found in Great
Britain. With 12,000 Woodcuts. 8vo. 42s.

Lubbock.—THE ORIGIN OF CIVILI-
ZATION AND THE PRIMITIVE CONDITION
OF MAN. By Sir J. LUBBOCK, Bart.
M.P. F.R.S. 8vo. Woodcuts, 18s.

Lyra Germanica ; Hymns Translated from the German by Miss C.
WINKWORTH. Fcp. 8vo. 5s.

Macalister.— AN INTRODUCTION
TO THE SYSTEMATIC ZOOLOGY AND
MORPHOLOGY OF VERTEBRATE ANI-
MALS. By A. MACALISTER, M.D.
With 28 Diagrams. 8vo. 10s. 6d.

Macaulay.—WORKS AND LIFE OF
LORD MACAULAY.
HISTORY OF ENGLAND FROM THE
ACCESSION OF JAMES THE SECOND:
Student's Edition, 2 vols. crown 8vo. 12s.
People's Edition, 4 vols. crown 8vo. 16s.
Cabinet Edition, 8 vols. post 8vo. 48s.
Library Edition, 5 vols. 8vo. £4.

CRITICAL AND HISTORICAL ESSAYS,
with LAYS of ANCIENT ROME, in 1
volume :
Authorised Edition, crown 8vo. 2s. 6d. or
3s. 6d. gilt edges.
Popular Edition, crown 8vo. 2s. 6d.

CRITICAL AND HISTORICAL ESSAYS :
Student's Edition, 1 vol. crown 8vo. 6s.
People's Edition, 2 vols. crown 8vo. 8s.
Cabinet Edition, 4 vols. post 8vo. 24s.
Library Edition, 3 vols. 8vo. 36s.

ESSAYS which may be had separ-
ately price 6d. each sewed, 1s. each cloth:
Addison and Walpole.
Frederick the Great.
Croker's Boswell's Johnson.
Hallam's Constitutional History.
Warren Hastings. 3d. sewed, 6d. cloth.
The Earl of Chatham (Two Essays).
Ranke and Gladstone.
Milton and Machiavelli.
Lord Bacon.
Lord Clive.
Lord Byron, and The Comic Dramatists of
the Restoration.

The Essay on Warren Hastings annotated
by S. HALES, 1s. 6d.
The Essay on Lord Clive annotated by
H. COURTHOPE-BOWEN, M.A. 2s. 6d.

SPEECHES :
People's Edition, crown 8vo. 3s. 6d.

MISCELLANEOUS WRITINGS :
Library Edition, 2 vols. 8vo. Portrait, 21s.
People's Edition, 1 vol. crown 8vo. 4s. 6d.
[Continued on next page.

GENERAL & SCIENTIFIC BOOKS PUBLISHED BY MESSRS. LONGMANS & CO. 13

Macaulay—*WORKS AND LIFE OF LORD MACAULAY*—*continued.*

LAYS OF ANCIENT ROME, &c.
Illustrated by G. Scharf, fcp. 4to. 10s. 6d.
—————————— Popular Edition, fcp. 4to. 6d. sewed, 1s. cloth.
Illustrated by J. R. Weguelin, crown 8vo. 3s. 6d. cloth extra, gilt edges.
Cabinet Edition, post 8vo. 3s. 6d.
Annotated Edition, fcp. 8vo. 1s. sewed, 1s. 6d. cloth, or 2s. 6d. cloth extra, gilt edges.

SELECTIONS FROM THE WRITINGS OF LORD MACAULAY. Edited, with Occasional Notes, by the Right Hon. G. O. TREVELYAN, M.P. Crown 8vo. 6s.

MISCELLANEOUS WRITINGS AND SPEECHES:
Student's Edition, in ONE VOLUME, crown 8vo. 6s.
Cabinet Edition, including Indian Penal Code, Lays of Ancient Rome, and Miscellaneous Poems, 4 vols. post 8vo. 24s.

THE COMPLETE WORKS OF LORD MACAULAY. Edited by his Sister, Lady TREVELYAN.
Library Edition, with Portrait, 8 vols. demy 8vo. £5. 5s.
Cabinet Editon, 16 vols. post 8vo. £4. 16s.

THE LIFE AND LETTERS OF LORD MACAULAY. By the Right Hon. G. O. TREVELYAN, M.P.
Popular Edition, 1 vol. crown 8vo. 6s.
Cabinet Edition, 2 vols. post 8vo. 12s.
Library Edition, 2 vols. 8vo. with Portrait, 36s.

Macdonald.—*WORKS BY GEORGE MACDONALD, LL.D.*

UNSPOKEN SERMONS. Second Series. Crown 8vo. 7s. 6d.

A BOOK OF STRIFE, IN THE FORM OF THE DIARY OF AN OLD SOUL: Poems. 12mo. 6s.

HAMLET. A Study with the Text of the Folio of 1623. 8vo. 12s.

Macfarren.—*LECTURES ON HARMONY,* delivered at the Royal Institution. By Sir G. A. MACFARREN. 8vo. 12s.

Mackenzie.—*ON THE USE OF THE LARYNGOSCOPE IN DISEASES OF THE THROAT;* with an Appendix on Rhinoscopy. By MORELL MACKENZIE, M.D. Lond. With 47 Woodcut Illustrations. 8vo. 6s.

Macleod.—*WORKS BY HENRY D. MACLEOD, M.A.*

PRINCIPLES OF ECONOMICAL PHILOSOPHY. In 2 vols. Vol. I. 8vo. 15s. Vol. II. PART I. 12s.

THE ELEMENTS OF ECONOMICS. In 2 vols. Vol. I. crown 8vo. 7s. 6d. Vol. II. crown 8vo.

THE ELEMENTS OF BANKING. Crown 8vo. 5s.

THE THEORY AND PRACTICE OF BANKING. Vol. I. 8vo. 12s. Vol. II.

ELEMENTS OF POLITICAL ECONOMY. 8vo. 16s.

Macnamara. — *HIMALAYAN AND SUB-HIMALAYAN DISTRICTS OF BRITISH INDIA,* their Climate, Medical Topography, and Disease Distribution. By F. N. MACNAMARA, M.D. With Map and Fever Chart. 8vo. 21s.

McCulloch. — *THE DICTIONARY OF COMMERCE AND COMMERCIAL NAVIGATION* of the late J. R. MCCULLOCH, of H.M. Stationery Office. Latest Edition, containing the most recent Statistical Information by A. J. WILSON. 1 vol. medium 8vo. with 11 Maps and 30 Charts, price 63s. cloth, or 70s. strongly half-bound in russia.

Mahaffy.—*A HISTORY OF CLASSICAL GREEK LITERATURE.* By the Rev. J. P. MAHAFFY, M.A. Crown 8vo. Vol. I. Poets, 7s. 6d. Vol. II. Prose Writers, 7s. 6d.

Malmesbury. — *MEMOIRS OF AN EX-MINISTER:* an Autobiography. By the Earl of MALMESBURY, G.C.B. Cheap Edition. Crown 8vo. 7s. 6d.

Manning.—*THE TEMPORAL MISSION OF THE HOLY GHOST;* or, Reason and Revelation. By H. E. MANNING, D.D. Cardinal-Archbishop. Crown 8vo. 8s. 6d.

The Maritime Alps and their Seaboard. By the Author of 'Véra,' 'Blue Roses,' &c. With 14 Full-page Illustrations and 15 Woodcuts in the Text. 8vo. 21s.

Martineau—*WORKS BY JAMES MARTINEAU, D.D.*

HOURS OF THOUGHT ON SACRED THINGS. Two Volumes of Sermons. 2 vols. crown 8vo. 7s. 6d. each.

ENDEAVOURS AFTER THE CHRISTIAN LIFE. Discourses. Crown 8vo. 7s. 6d.

Maunder's Treasuries.

BIOGRAPHICAL TREASURY. Reconstructed, revised, and brought down to the year 1882, by W. L. R. CATES. Fcp. 8vo. 6s.

TREASURY OF NATURAL HISTORY; or, Popular Dictionary of Zoology. Fcp. 8vo. with 900 Woodcuts, 6s.

TREASURY OF GEOGRAPHY, Physical, Historical, Descriptive, and Political. With 7 Maps and 16 Plates. Fcp. 8vo. 6s.

HISTORICAL TREASURY: Outlines of Universal History, Separate Histories of all Nations. Revised by the Rev. Sir G. W. COX, Bart. M.A. Fcp. 8vo. 6s.

TREASURY OF KNOWLEDGE AND LIBRARY OF REFERENCE. Comprising an English Dictionary and Grammar, Universal Gazetteer, Classical Dictionary, Chronology, Law Dictionary, &c. Fcp. 8vo. 6s.

SCIENTIFIC AND LITERARY TREASURY: a Popular Encyclopædia of Science, Literature, and Art. Fcp. 8vo. 6s.

THE TREASURY OF BIBLE KNOWLEDGE; being a Dictionary of the Books, Persons, Places, Events, and other matters of which mention is made in Holy Scripture. By the Rev. J. AYRE, M.A. With 5 Maps, 15 Plates, and 300 Woodcuts. Fcp. 8vo. 6s.

THE TREASURY OF BOTANY; or Popular Dictionary of the Vegetable Kingdom. Edited by J. LINDLEY, F.R.S. and T. MOORE, F.L.S. With 274 Woodcuts and 20 Steel Plates. Two Parts, fcp. 8vo. 12s.

Maxwell.—*DON JOHN OF AUSTRIA;* or, Passages from the History of the Sixteenth Century, 1547-1578. By the late Sir WILLIAM STIRLING MAXWELL, Bart. K.T. With numerous Illustrations engraved on Wood. Library Edition. 2 vols. royal 8vo. 42s.

May.—*WORKS BY THE RIGHT HON. SIR THOMAS ERSKINE MAY, K.C.B.*

THE CONSTITUTIONAL HISTORY OF ENGLAND SINCE THE ACCESSION OF GEORGE III. 1760-1870. 3 vols. crown 8vo. 18s.

DEMOCRACY IN EUROPE; a History. 2 vols. 8vo. 32s.

Melville.—*THE NOVELS OF G. J. WHYTE MELVILLE.* 1s. each, sewed; or 1s. 6d. cloth.

The Gladiators.	Holmby House.
The Interpreter.	Kate Coventry.
Good for Nothing.	Digby Grand.
The Queen's Maries.	General Bounce.

Mendelssohn.—*THE LETTERS OF FELIX MENDELSSOHN.* Translated by Lady WALLACE. 2 vols. crown 8vo. 10s.

Merivale.—*WORKS BY THE VERY REV. CHARLES MERIVALE, D.D. Dean of Ely.*

HISTORY OF THE ROMANS UNDER THE EMPIRE. 8 vols. post 8vo. 48s.

THE FALL OF THE ROMAN REPUBLIC: a Short History of the Last Century of the Commonwealth. 12mo. 7s. 6d.

GENERAL HISTORY OF ROME FROM B.C. 753 TO A.D. 476. Crown 8vo. 7s. 6d.

THE ROMAN TRIUMVIRATES. With Maps. Fcp. 8vo. 2s. 6d.

Miles. — *WORKS BY WILLIAM MILES.*

THE HORSE'S FOOT, AND HOW TO KEEP IT SOUND. Imp. 8vo. 12s. 6d.

STABLES AND STABLE FITTINGS. Imp. 8vo. with 13 Plates, 15s.

REMARKS ON HORSES' TEETH, addressed to Purchasers. Post 8vo. 1s. 6d.

PLAIN TREATISE ON HORSE-SHOEING. Post 8vo. Woodcuts, 2s. 6d.

Mill.—*ANALYSIS OF THE PHENOMENA OF THE HUMAN MIND.* By JAMES MILL. With Notes, Illustrative and Critical. 2 vols. 8vo. 28s.

Mill.—*WORKS BY JOHN STUART MILL.*

PRINCIPLES OF POLITICAL ECONOMY. Library Edition, 2 vols. 8vo. 30s. People's Edition, 1 vol. crown 8vo. 5s.

A SYSTEM OF LOGIC, Ratiocinative and Inductive. Library Edition, 2 vols. 8vo. 25s. People's Edition, crown 8vo. 5s.

ON LIBERTY. Crown 8vo. 1s. 4d.

ON REPRESENTATIVE GOVERNMENT. Crown 8vo. 2s.

AUTOBIOGRAPHY, 8vo 7s. 6d.

ESSAYS ON SOME UNSETTLED QUESTIONS OF POLITICAL ECONOMY. 8vo. 6s. 6d.

UTILITARIANISM. 8vo. 5s.

THE SUBJECTION OF WOMEN. Crown 8vo. 6s.

EXAMINATION OF SIR WILLIAM HAMILTON'S PHILOSOPHY. 8vo. 16s.

DISSERTATIONS AND DISCUSSIONS. 4 vols. 8vo. £2. 6s. 6d.

NATURE, THE UTILITY OF RELIGION, AND THEISM. Three Essays. 8vo. 5s.

Miller. — *WORKS BY W. ALLEN MILLER, M.D. LL.D.*

THE ELEMENTS OF CHEMISTRY, Theoretical and Practical. Re-edited, with Additions, by H. MACLEOD, F.C.S. 3 vols. 8vo.
Part I. CHEMICAL PHYSICS, 16s.
Part II. INORGANIC CHEMISTRY, 24s.
Part III. ORGANIC CHEMISTRY, 31s. 6d.

AN INTRODUCTION TO THE STUDY OF INORGANIC CHEMISTRY. With 71 Woodcuts. Fcp. 8vo. 3s. 6d.

Miller. — *READINGS IN SOCIAL ECONOMY.* By Mrs. F. FENWICK MILLER. Crown 8vo. 2s.

Mitchell.—*A MANUAL OF PRACTICAL ASSAYING.* By JOHN MITCHELL, F.C.S. Revised, with the Recent Discoveries incorporated. By W. CROOKES, F.R.S. 8vo. Woodcuts, 31s. 6d.

Modern Novelist's Library (The). Price 2s. each boards, or 2s. 6d. each cloth :—

By the Earl of BEACONSFIELD, K.G.

Lothair.
Coningsby.
Sybil.
Tancred.
Venetia.

Endymion.
Henrietta Temple.
Contarini Fleming, &c.
Alroy, Ixion, &c.
The Young Duke, &c.
Vivian Grey.

By Mrs. OLIPHANT.
In Trust.

By JAMES PAYN.
Thicker than Water.

By BRET HARTE.
In the Carquinez Woods.

By ANTHONY TROLLOPE.
Barchester Towers.
The Warden.

By VARIOUS WRITERS.
The Atelier du Lys. By the Author of 'Mademoiselle Mori.'
Atherstone Priory. By L. N. Comyn.
The Burgomaster's Family. By E. C. W. Van Walrée.
Elsa and her Vulture. By W. Van Hillern.
Mademoiselle Mori. By the Author of 'The Atelier du Lys.'
The Six Sisters of the Valleys. By Rev. W. Bramley-Moore, M.A.
Unawares. By the Author of 'The Rose-Garden.'

Monsell.—*SPIRITUAL SONGS FOR THE SUNDAYS AND HOLIDAYS THROUGHOUT THE YEAR.* By J. S. B. MONSELL, LL.D. Fcp. 8vo. 5s. 18mo. 2s.

Moore.—*LALLA ROOKH.* By THOMAS MOORE. TENNIEL'S Edition, with 68 Woodcut Illustrations. Crown 8vo. 10s. 6d.

Morehead.—*CLINICAL RESEARCHES ON DISEASE IN INDIA.* By CHARLES MOREHEAD, M.D. Surgeon to the Jamsetjee Jeejeebhoy Hospital. 8vo. 21s.

Mozley. — *WORKS BY THE REV. THOMAS MOZLEY, M.A.*

REMINISCENCES CHIEFLY OF ORIEL COLLEGE AND THE OXFORD MOVEMENT. 2 vols. crown 8vo. 18s.

REMINISCENCES CHIEFLY OF TOWNS, VILLAGES, AND SCHOOLS. 2 vols. crown 8vo. 18s.

Mulhall.—*HISTORY OF PRICES SINCE THE YEAR 1850.* By MICHAEL G. MULHALL. Crown 8vo. 6s.

Müller. — *WORKS BY F. MAX MÜLLER, M.A.*

BIOGRAPHICAL ESSAYS. Crown 8vo. 7s. 6d.

SELECTED ESSAYS ON LANGUAGE, MYTHOLOGY AND RELIGION. 2 vols. crown 8vo. 16s.

LECTURES ON THE SCIENCE OF LANGUAGE. 2 vols. crown 8vo. 16s.

INDIA, WHAT CAN IT TEACH US? A Course of Lectures delivered before the University of Cambridge. 8vo. 12s. 6d.

HIBBERT LECTURES ON THE ORIGIN AND GROWTH OF RELIGION, as illustrated by the Religions of India. Crown 8vo. 7s. 6d.

INTRODUCTION TO THE SCIENCE OF RELIGION: Four Lectures delivered at the Royal Institution. Crown 8vo. 7s. 6d.

A SANSKRIT GRAMMAR FOR BEGINNERS, in Devanagari and Roman Letters throughout. Royal 8vo. 7s. 6d.

Murchison.—*WORKS BY CHARLES MURCHISON, M.D. LL.D. &c.*

A TREATISE ON THE CONTINUED FEVERS OF GREAT BRITAIN. Revised by W. CAYLEY, M.D. Physician to the Middlesex Hospital. 8vo. with numerous Illustrations, 25s.

CLINICAL LECTURES ON DISEASES OF THE LIVER, JAUNDICE, AND ABDOMINAL DROPSY. Revised by T. LAUDER BRUNTON, M.D. and Sir JOSEPH FAYRER, M.D. 8vo. with 43 Illustrations, 24s.

16 GENERAL & SCIENTIFIC BOOKS PUBLISHED BY MESSRS. LONGMANS & CO.

Neison.—THE MOON, and the Condition and Configurations of its Surface. By E. NEISON, F.R.A.S. With 26 Maps and 5 Plates. Medium 8vo. 31s. 6d.

Nevile.—WORKS BY GEORGE NEVILE, M.A.
HORSES AND RIDING. With 31 Illustrations. Crown 8vo. 6s.
FARMS AND FARMING. With 13 Illustrations. Crown 8vo. 6s.

Newman.—WORKS BY CARDINAL NEWMAN.
APOLOGIA PRO VITA SUA. Crown 8vo. 6s.
THE IDEA OF A UNIVERSITY DEFINED AND ILLUSTRATED. Crown 8vo. 7s.
HISTORICAL SKETCHES. 3 vols. crown 8vo. 6s. each.
DISCUSSIONS AND ARGUMENTS ON VARIOUS SUBJECTS. Crown 8vo. 6s.
AN ESSAY ON THE DEVELOPMENT OF CHRISTIAN DOCTRINE. Crown 8vo. 6s.
CERTAIN DIFFICULTIES FELT BY ANGLICANS IN CATHOLIC TEACHING CONSIDERED. Vol. 1, crown 8vo. 7s. 6d.; Vol. 2, crown 8vo. 5s. 6d.
THE VIA MEDIA OF THE ANGLICAN CHURCH, ILLUSTRATED IN LECTURES &c. 2 vols. crown 8vo. 6s. each.
ESSAYS, CRITICAL AND HISTORICAL. 2 vols. crown 8vo. 12s.
ESSAYS ON BIBLICAL AND ON ECCLESIASTICAL MIRACLES. Crown 8vo. 6s.
AN ESSAY IN AID OF A GRAMMAR OF ASSENT. 7s. 6d.

New Testament (The) of our Lord and Saviour Jesus Christ. Illustrated with Engravings on Wood after Paintings by the Early Masters chiefly of the Italian School. New and Cheaper Edition. 4to. 21s. cloth extra, or 42s. morocco.

Noble.—THE RUSSIAN REVOLT: its Causes, Condition, and Prospects. By EDMUND NOBLE. Fcp. 8vo. 5s.

Northcott.—LATHES AND TURNING, Simple, Mechanical, and Ornamental. By W. H. NORTHCOTT. With 338 Illustrations. 8vo. 18s.

O'Hagan.—SELECTED SPEECHES AND ARGUMENTS OF THE RIGHT HON. THOMAS BARON O'HAGAN. Edited by GEORGE TEELING. With Portrait. 8vo. 16s.

Oliphant.—MADAM. A Novel. By Mrs. OLIPHANT. Crown 8vo. 3s. 6d.

Overton.—LIFE IN THE ENGLISH CHURCH (1660-1714). By J. H. OVERTON, M.A. Rector of Epworth. 8vo. 14s.

Owen.—THE COMPARATIVE ANATOMY AND PHYSIOLOGY OF THE VERTEBRATE ANIMALS. By Sir RICHARD OWEN, K.C.B. &c. With 1,472 Woodcuts. 3 vols. 8vo. £3. 13s. 6d.

Paget.—WORKS BY SIR JAMES PAGET, BART. F.R.S. D.C.L. &c.
CLINICAL LECTURES AND ESSAYS. Edited by F. HOWARD MARSH, Assistant-Surgeon to St. Bartholomew's Hospital. 8vo. 15s.
LECTURES ON SURGICAL PATHOLOGY. Re-edited by the AUTHOR and W. TURNER, M.B. 8vo. with 131 Woodcuts, 21s.

Pasolini.—MEMOIR OF COUNT GIUSEPPE PASOLINI, LATE PRESIDENT OF THE SENATE OF ITALY. Compiled by his SON. Translated and Abridged by the DOWAGER-COUNTESS OF DALHOUSIE. With Portrait. 8vo. 16s.

Pasteur.—LOUIS PASTEUR, his Life and Labours. By his SON-IN-LAW. Translated from the French by Lady CLAUD HAMILTON. Crown 8vo. 7s. 6d.

Payn.—THE LUCK OF THE DARRELLS: a Novel. By JAMES PAYN, Author of 'By Proxy,' 'Thicker than Water,' &c. Crown 8vo. 3s. 6d.

Pears.—THE FALL OF CONSTANTINOPLE: being the Story of the Fourth Crusade. By EDWIN PEARS, LL.B. Barrister-at-Law, late President of the European Bar at Constantinople, and Knight of the Greek Order of the Saviour. 8vo. 16s.

Peel.—A HIGHLAND GATHERING. By E. LENNOX PEEL. With 31 Illustrations engraved on Wood by E. Whymper. Crown 8vo. 10s. 6d.

Pennell.—'FROM GRAVE TO GAY': a Volume of Selections from the complete Poems of H. CHOLMONDELEY-PENNELL, Author of 'Puck on Pegasus' &c. Fcp. 8vo. 6s.

Pereira.—MATERIA MEDICA AND THERAPEUTICS. By Dr. PEREIRA. Edited by Professor R. BENTLEY, M.R.C.S. F.L.S. and by Professor T. REDWOOD, Ph.D. F.C.S. With 126 Woodcuts, 8vo. 25s.

Perry.—A POPULAR INTRODUCTION TO THE HISTORY OF GREEK AND ROMAN SCULPTURE, designed to Promote the Knowledge and Appreciation of the Remains of Ancient Art. By WALTER C. PERRY. With 268 Illustrations. Square crown 8vo. 31s. 6d.

GENERAL & SCIENTIFIC BOOKS PUBLISHED BY MESSRS. LONGMANS & CO.

Piesse.—THE ART OF PERFUMERY, and the Methods of Obtaining the Odours of Plants; with Instructions for the Manufacture of Perfumes, &c. By G. W. S. PIESSE, Ph.D. F.C.S. With 96 Woodcuts, square crown 8vo. 21s.

Pole.—THE THEORY OF THE MODERN SCIENTIFIC GAME OF WHIST. By W. POLE, F.R.S. Fcp. 8vo. 2s. 6d.

Pontalis.—JOHN DE WITT, GRAND PENSIONARY OF HOLLAND; or, Twenty Years of a Parliamentary Republic. By M. ANTONIN LEFÈVRE PONTALIS. Translated from the French by S. E. and A. Stephenson. 2 vols. 8vo. 36s.

Proctor.—WORKS BY R. A. PROCTOR.

THE SUN; Ruler, Light, Fire, and Life of the Planetary System. With Plates and Woodcuts. Crown 8vo. 14s.

THE ORBS AROUND US; a Series of Essays on the Moon and Planets, Meteors and Comets. With Chart and Diagrams, crown 8vo. 5s.

OTHER WORLDS THAN OURS; The Plurality of Worlds Studied under the Light of Recent Scientific Researches. With 14 Illustrations, crown 8vo. 5s.

THE MOON; her Motions, Aspects, Scenery, and Physical Condition. With Plates, Charts, Woodcuts, and Lunar Photographs, crown 8vo. 10s. 6d.

UNIVERSE OF STARS; Presenting Researches into and New Views respecting the Constitution of the Heavens. With 22 Charts and 22 Diagrams, 8vo. 10s. 6d.

LARGER STAR ATLAS for the Library, in 12 Circular Maps, with Introduction and 2 Index Pages. Folio, 15s. or Maps only, 12s. 6d.

NEW STAR ATLAS for the Library, the School, and the Observatory, in 12 Circular Maps (with 2 Index Plates). Crown 8vo. 5s.

LIGHT SCIENCE FOR LEISURE HOURS; Familiar Essays on Scientific Subjects, Natural Phenomena, &c. 3 vols. crown 8vo. 5s. each.

STUDIES OF VENUS-TRANSITS; an Investigation of the Circumstances of the Transits of Venus in 1874 and 1882. With 7 Diagrams and 10 Plates. 8vo. 5s.

PLEASANT WAYS IN SCIENCE, with numerous Illustrations. Crown 8vo. 6s

MYTHS AND MARVELS OF ASTRONOMY, with numerous Illustrations. Crown 8vo. 6s.

The 'KNOWLEDGE' LIBRARY. Edited by RICHARD A. PROCTOR.

HOW TO PLAY WHIST: WITH THE LAWS AND ETIQUETTE OF WHIST. By R. A. PROCTOR. Crown 8vo. 5s.

HOME WHIST: an Easy Guide to Correct Play. By R. A. PROCTOR. 16mo. 1s.

THE POETRY OF ASTRONOMY. A Series of Familiar Essays. By R. A. PROCTOR. Crown 8vo. 6s.

NATURE STUDIES. Reprinted from Knowledge. By GRANT ALLEN, A. WILSON, T. FOSTER, E. CLODD, and R. A. PROCTOR. Crown 8vo. 6s.

LEISURE READINGS. Reprinted from Knowledge. By E. CLODD, A. WILSON, T. FOSTER, A. C. RUNYARD, and R. A. PROCTOR. Crown 8vo. 6s.

THE STARS IN THEIR SEASONS. An Easy Guide to a Knowledge of the Star Groups, in 12 Large Maps. By R. A. PROCTOR. Imperial 8vo. 5s.

STAR PRIMER. Showing the Starry Sky Week by Week, in 24 Hourly Maps. By R. A. PROCTOR. Crown 4to. 2s. 6d.

THE SEASONS PICTURED IN 48 SUN-VIEWS OF THE EARTH, and 24 Zodiacal Maps, &c. By R. A. PROCTOR. Demy 4to. 5s.

STRENGTH AND HAPPINESS. By R. A. PROCTOR. Crown 8vo. 5s.

ROUGH WAYS MADE SMOOTH. A Series of Familiar Essays on Scientific Subjects. By R. A. PROCTOR. Crown 8vo. 6s.

OUR PLACE AMONG INFINITES. A Series of Essays contrasting our Little Abode in Space and Time with the Infinites Around us. By R. A. PROCTOR. Crown 8vo. 5s.

THE EXPANSE OF HEAVEN. A Series of Essays on the Wonders of the Firmament. By R. A. PROCTOR. Crown 8vo. 5s.

Quain's Elements of Anatomy. The Ninth Edition. Re-edited by ALLEN THOMSON, M.D. LL.D. F.R.S.S. L. & E. EDWARD ALBERT SCHÄFER, F.R.S. and GEORGE DANCER THANE. With upwards of 1,000 Illustrations engraved on Wood, of which many are Coloured. 2 vols. 8vo. 18s. each.

18 GENERAL & SCIENTIFIC BOOKS Published by Messrs. LONGMANS & CO.

Quain.—A DICTIONARY OF MEDICINE. By Various Writers. Edited by R. QUAIN, M.D. F.R.S. &c. With 138 Woodcuts. Medium 8vo. 31s. 6d. cloth, or 40s. half-russia; to be had also in 2 vols. 34s. cloth.

Rawlinson. — THE SEVENTH GREAT ORIENTAL MONARCHY; or, a History of the Sassanians. By G. RAWLINSON, M.A. With Map and 95 Illustrations. 8vo. 28s.

Reader.—WORKS BY EMILY E. READER.
VOICES FROM FLOWER-LAND, in Original Couplets. A Birthday-Book and Language of Flowers. 16mo. 2s. 6d. limp cloth; 3s. 6d. roan, gilt edges, or in vegetable vellum, gilt top.
FAIRY PRINCE FOLLOW-MY-LEAD; or, the MAGIC BRACELET. Illustrated by WM. READER. Cr. 8vo. 5s. gilt edges; or 6s. vegetable vellum, gilt edges.

Reeve. — COOKERY AND HOUSEKEEPING. By Mrs. HENRY REEVE. With 8 Coloured Plates and 37 Woodcuts. Crown 8vo. 7s. 6d.

Rich.—A DICTIONARY OF ROMAN AND GREEK ANTIQUITIES. With 2,000 Woodcuts. By A. RICH, B.A. Cr. 8vo. 7s. 6d.

Rivers. — WORKS BY THOMAS RIVERS.
THE ORCHARD-HOUSE. Crown 8vo. with 25 Woodcuts, 5s.
THE ROSE AMATEUR'S GUIDE. Fcp. 8vo. 4s. 6d.

Robinson. — THE NEW ARCADIA, and other Poems. By A. MARY F. ROBINSON. Crown 8vo. 6s.

Rogers.—WORKS BY HY. ROGERS.
THE ECLIPSE OF FAITH; or, a Visit to a Religious Sceptic. Fcp. 8vo. 5s.
DEFENCE OF THE ECLIPSE OF FAITH. Fcp. 8vo. 3s. 6d.

Roget.—THESAURUS OF ENGLISH WORDS AND PHRASES. By PETER M. ROGET, M.D. Crown 8vo. 10s. 6d.

Ronalds. — THE FLY-FISHER'S ENTOMOLOGY. By ALFRED RONALDS. With 20 Coloured Plates. 8vo. 14s.

Salter.—DENTAL PATHOLOGY AND SURGERY. By S. J. A. SALTER, M.B. F.R.S. With 133 Illustrations. 8vo. 18s.

Schäfer. — THE ESSENTIALS OF HISTOLOGY, DESCRIPTIVE AND PRACTICAL. For the use of Students. By E. A. SCHÄFER, F.R.S. With 281 Illustrations. 8vo. 6s. or Interleaved with Drawing Paper, 8s. 6d.

Schellen. — SPECTRUM ANALYSIS IN ITS APPLICATION TO TERRESTRIAL SUBSTANCES, and the Physical Constitution of the Heavenly Bodies. By the late Dr. H. SCHELLEN. Translated by JANE and CAROLINE LASSELL. Edited, with Notes, by Capt. W. DE W. ABNEY, R.E. Second Edition. With 14 Plates (including Ångström's and Cornu's Maps) and 291 Woodcuts. 8vo. 31s. 6d.

Seebohm.—WORKS BY FREDERIC SEEBOHM.
THE OXFORD REFORMERS—JOHN COLET, ERASMUS, AND THOMAS MORE; a History of their Fellow-Work. 8vo. 14s.
THE ENGLISH VILLAGE COMMUNITY Examined in its Relations to the Manorial and Tribal Systems, &c, 13 Maps and Plates. 8vo. 16s.
THE ERA OF THE PROTESTANT REVOLUTION. With Map. Fcp. 8vo. 2s. 6d.

Sennett. — THE MARINE STEAM ENGINE; a Treatise for the use of Engineering Students and Officers of the Royal Navy. By RICHARD SENNETT, Chief Engineer, Royal Navy. With 244 Illustrations. 8vo. 21s.

Sewell. — STORIES AND TALES. By ELIZABETH M. SEWELL. Cabinet Edition, in Eleven Volumes, crown 8vo. 3s. 6d. each, in cloth extra, with gilt edges:—
Amy Herbert.
The Earl's Daughter.
The Experience of Life.
A Glimpse of the World.
Cleve Hall.
Katharine Ashton.
Margaret Percival.
Laneton Parsonage.
Ursula.
Gertrude.
Ivors.

Shakespeare. — BOWDLER'S FAMILY SHAKESPEARE. Genuine Edition, in 1 vol. medium 8vo. large type, with 36 Woodcuts, 14s. or in 6 vols. fcp. 8vo. 21s.
OUTLINES OF THE LIFE OF SHAKESPEARE. By J. O. HALLIWELL-PHILLIPPS, F.R.S. Royal 8vo. 7s. 6d.

Short.—SKETCH OF THE HISTORY OF THE CHURCH OF ENGLAND TO THE REVOLUTION OF 1688. By T. V. SHORT, D.D. Crown 8vo. 7s. 6d.

Simcox.—A HISTORY OF LATIN LITERATURE. By G. A. SIMCOX, M.A. Fellow of Queen's College, Oxford. 2 vols. 8vo. 32s.

Smith, Rev. Sydney.—*THE WIT AND WISDOM OF THE REV. SYDNEY SMITH.* Crown 8vo. 3s. 6d.

Smith, R. Bosworth. — *CARTHAGE AND THE CARTHAGINIANS.* By R. BOSWORTH SMITH, M.A. Maps, Plans, &c. Crown 8vo. 10s. 6d.

Smith, R. A.—*AIR AND RAIN;* the Beginnings of a Chemical Climatology. By R. A. SMITH, F.R.S. 8vo. 24s.

Smith, James.—*THE VOYAGE AND SHIPWRECK OF ST. PAUL.* By JAMES SMITH, of Jordanhill. With Dissertations on the Life and Writings of St. Luke, and the Ships and Navigation of the Ancients. With numerous Illustrations. Crown 8vo. 7s. 6d.

Smith, T.—*A MANUAL OF OPERATIVE SURGERY ON THE DEAD BODY.* By THOMAS SMITH, Surgeon to St. Bartholomew's Hospital. A New Edition, re-edited by W. J. WALSHAM. With 46 Illustrations. 8vo. 12s.

Smith, H. F.—*THE HANDBOOK FOR MIDWIVES.* By HENRY FLY SMITH, M.B. Oxon. M.R.C.S. late Assistant-Surgeon at the Hospital for Sick Women, Soho Square. With 41 Woodcuts. Crown 8vo. 5s.

Sophocles. — *SOPHOCLIS TRAGŒDIÆ* superstites; recensuit et brevi Annotatione instruxit GULIELMUS LINWOOD, M.A. Ædis Christi apud Oxonienses nuper Alumnus. Editio Quarta, auctior et emendatior. 8vo. 16s.

Southey.—*THE POETICAL WORKS OF ROBERT SOUTHEY,* with the Author's last Corrections and Additions. Medium 8vo. with Portrait, 14s.

Stanley. — *A FAMILIAR HISTORY OF BIRDS.* By E. STANLEY, D.D. Revised and enlarged, with 160 Woodcuts. Crown 8vo. 6s.

Steel.—*A TREATISE ON THE DISEASES OF THE OX;* being a Manual of Bovine Pathology specially adapted for the use of Veterinary Practitioners and Students. By J. H. STEEL, M.R.C.V.S. F.Z.S. With 2 Plates and 116 Woodcuts. 8vo. 15s.

Stephen. — *ESSAYS IN ECCLESIASTICAL BIOGRAPHY.* By the Right Hon. Sir J. STEPHEN, LL.D. Crown 8vo. 7s. 6d.

Stevenson.—*WORKS BY ROBERT LOUIS STEVENSON.*
A CHILD'S GARDEN OF VERSES. Small fcp. 8vo. 5s.
THE DYNAMITER. Fcp. 8vo. 1s. swd. 1s. 6d. cloth.
STRANGE CASE OF DR. JEKYLL AND MR. HYDE. Fcp. 8vo. 1s. sewed; 1s. 6d. cloth.

'Stonehenge.'—*THE DOG IN HEALTH AND DISEASE.* By 'STONEHENGE.' With 78 Wood Engravings. Square crown 8vo. 7s. 6d.
THE GREYHOUND. By 'STONEHENGE.' With 25 Portraits of Greyhounds, &c. Square crown 8vo. 15s.

Stoney. — *THE THEORY OF THE STRESSES ON GIRDERS AND SIMILAR STRUCTURES.* With Practical Observations on the Strength and other Properties of Materials. By BINDON B. STONEY, LL.D. F.R.S. M.I.C.E. New Edition, Revised, with numerous Additions of Graphic Statics, Pillars, Steel, Wind Pressure, Oscillating Stresses, Working Loads, Riveting, Strength and Tests of Material. With 5 Plates, and 143 Illustrations in the Text. Royal 8vo. 36s.

Sully.—*OUTLINES OF PSYCHOLOGY,* with Special Reference to the Theory of Education. By JAMES SULLY, M.A. 8vo. 12s. 6d.

Supernatural Religion; an Inquiry into the Reality of Divine Revelation. Complete Edition, thoroughly revised. 3 vols. 8vo. 36s.

Swinburne. — *PICTURE LOGIC;* an Attempt to Popularise the Science of Reasoning. By A. J. SWINBURNE, B.A. Post 8vo. 5s.

Swinton. — *THE PRINCIPLES AND PRACTICE OF ELECTRIC LIGHTING.* By ALAN A. CAMPBELL SWINTON. With 54 Illustrations engraved on Wood. Crown 8vo. 5s.

Taylor.—*AUTOBIOGRAPHY OF SIR HENRY TAYLOR,* K.C.M.G. 2 vols. 8vo. 32s.

Taylor. — *STUDENT'S MANUAL OF THE HISTORY OF INDIA,* from the Earliest Period to the Present Time. By Colonel MEADOWS TAYLOR, C.S.I. Crown 8vo. 7s. 6d.

Taylor.—*THE COMPLETE WORKS OF BISHOP JEREMY TAYLOR.* With Life by Bishop Heber. Revised and corrected by the Rev. C. P. EDEN. 10 vols. £5. 5s.

Text-Books of Science: a Series of Elementary Works on Science, adapted for the use of Students in Public and Science Schools. Fcp. 8vo. fully illustrated with Woodcuts. *See* p. 23.

'That Very Mab.' Fcp. 8vo. 5s.
*** A Critical and Satirical Romance, dealing with modern theology and philosophy, and social life and character.

Thompson.—*A SYSTEM OF PSYCHOLOGY.* By DANIEL GREENLEAF THOMPSON. 2 vols. 8vo. 36s.

Thomson.—*AN OUTLINE OF THE NECESSARY LAWS OF THOUGHT;* a Treatise on Pure and Applied Logic. By W. THOMSON, D.D. Archbishop of York. Crown 8vo. 6s.

Thomson's Conspectus. New Edition. *ADAPTED TO THE NEW EDITION OF THE BRITISH PHARMACOPŒIA.* By NESTOR TIRARD, M.D. [*In preparation.*

Three in Norway. By Two of THEM. With a Map and 59 Illustrations on Wood from Sketches by the Authors. Crown 8vo. 6s.

Trevelyan. — *WORKS BY THE RIGHT HON. G. O. TREVELYAN, M.P.*

THE LIFE AND LETTERS OF LORD MACAULAY. By the Right Hon. G. O. TREVELYAN, M.P.
LIBRARY EDITION, 2 vols. 8vo. 36s.
CABINET EDITION, 2 vols. crown 8vo. 12s.
POPULAR EDITION, 1 vol. crown 8vo. 6s.

THE EARLY HISTORY OF CHARLES JAMES FOX. Library Edition, 8vo. 18s. Cabinet Edition, crown 8vo. 6s.

Tulloch. — *MOVEMENTS OF RELIGIOUS THOUGHT IN BRITAIN DURING THE NINETEENTH CENTURY:* being the Fifth Series of St. Giles' Lectures. By JOHN TULLOCH, D.D. LL.D. 8vo. 10s. 6d. half-bound, Roxburgh.

Twiss.—*WORKS BY SIR TRAVERS TWISS.*

THE RIGHTS AND DUTIES OF NATIONS, considered as Independent Communities in Time of War. 8vo. 21s.

THE RIGHTS AND DUTIES OF NATIONS IN TIME OF PEACE. 8vo. 15s.

Tyndall. — *WORKS BY JOHN TYNDALL, F.R.S. &c.*

FRAGMENTS OF SCIENCE. 2 vols. crown 8vo. 16s.

HEAT A MODE OF MOTION. Crown 8vo. 12s.

SOUND. With 204 Woodcuts. Crown 8vo. 10s. 6d.

ESSAYS ON THE FLOATING-MATTER OF THE AIR in relation to Putrefaction and Infection. With 24 Woodcuts. Crown 8vo. 7s. 6d.

LECTURES ON LIGHT, delivered in America in 1872 and 1873. With 57 Diagrams. Crown 8vo. 5s.

LESSONS IN ELECTRICITY AT THE ROYAL INSTITUTION, 1875-76. With 58 Woodcuts. Crown 8vo. 2s. 6d.

NOTES OF A COURSE OF SEVEN LECTURES ON ELECTRICAL PHENOMENA AND THEORIES, delivered at the Royal Institution. Crown 8vo. 1s. sewed, 1s. 6d. cloth.

NOTES OF A COURSE OF NINE LECTURES ON LIGHT, delivered at the Royal Institution. Crown 8vo. 1s. sewed, 1s. 6d. cloth.

FARADAY AS A DISCOVERER. Fcp. 8vo. 3s. 6d.

Ure.—*A DICTIONARY OF ARTS, MANUFACTURES, AND MINES.* By Dr. URE. Seventh Edition, re-written and enlarged by R. HUNT, F.R.S. With 2,064 Woodcuts. 4 vols. medium 8vo. £7. 7s.

Verney. — *CHESS ECCENTRICITIES.* Including Four-handed Chess, Chess for Three, Six, or Eight Players, Round Chess for Two, Three, or Four Players, and several different ways of Playing Chess for Two Players. By Major GEORGE HOPE VERNEY. Crown 8vo. 10s. 6d.

Verney.—*COTTIER OWNERS, LITTLE TAKES, AND PEASANT PROPERTIES.* A Reprint of 'Jottings in France, Germany, and Switzerland. By Lady VERNEY. With Additions. Fcp. 8vo. 1s. sewed.

Ville.—*ON ARTIFICIAL MANURES,* their Chemical Selection and Scientific Application to Agriculture. By GEORGES VILLE. Translated and edited by W. CROOKES, F.R.S. With 31 Plates. 8vo. 21s.

Virgil.—*PUBLI VERGILI MARONIS BUCOLICA, GEORGICA, ÆNEIS;* the Works of VIRGIL, Latin Text, with English Commentary and Index. By B. H. KENNEDY, D.D. Crown 8vo. 10s. 6d.

THE ÆNEID OF VIRGIL. Translated into English Verse. By J. CONINGTON, M.A. Crown 8vo. 9s.

THE POEMS OF VIRGIL. Translated into English Prose. By JOHN CONINGTON, M.A. Crown 8vo. 9s.

Walker.— *THE CORRECT CARD;* or, How to Play at Whist; a Whist Catechism. By Major A. CAMPBELL-WALKER, F.R.G.S. Fcp. 8vo. 2s. 6d.

Walpole.—*HISTORY OF ENGLAND FROM THE CONCLUSION OF THE GREAT WAR IN 1815 TO THE YEAR 1841.* By SPENCER WALPOLE. 3 vols. 8vo. £2. 14s.

Watson.—*LECTURES ON THE PRINCIPLES AND PRACTICE OF PHYSIC,* delivered at King's College, London, by Sir THOMAS WATSON, Bart. M.D. With Two Plates. 2 vols. 8vo. 36s.

Watt.—*ECONOMIC ASPECTS OF RECENT LEGISLATION:* the Newmarch Memorial Essay. By WILLIAM WATT, Fellow of the Statistical Society. Cr. 8vo. 4s. 6d.

Watts.—*A DICTIONARY OF CHEMISTRY AND THE ALLIED BRANCHES OF OTHER SCIENCES.* Edited by HENRY WATTS, F.R.S. 9 vols. medium 8vo. £15. 2s. 6d.

Webb.—*THE REV. T. W. WEBB.*

CELESTIAL OBJECTS FOR COMMON TELESCOPES. Map, Plate, Woodcuts. Crown 8vo. 9s.

THE SUN. With 17 Diagrams. Fcp. 8vo. 1s.

Webb. — *THE VEIL OF ISIS:* a Series of Essays on Idealism. By THOMAS W. WEBB, LL.D. 8vo. 10s. 6d.

Wellington.—*LIFE OF THE DUKE OF WELLINGTON.* By the Rev. G. R. GLEIG, M.A. Crown 8vo. Portrait, 6s.

West.—*WORKS BY CHARLES WEST, M.D. &c.* Founder of, and formerly Physician to, the Hospital for Sick Children.

LECTURES ON THE DISEASES OF INFANCY AND CHILDHOOD. 8vo. 18s.

THE MOTHER'S MANUAL OF CHILDREN'S DISEASES. Crown 8vo. 2s. 6d.

Whately.—*WORKS BY R. WHATELY, D.D.*

ELEMENTS OF LOGIC. Crown 8vo. 4s. 6d.

ELEMENTS OF RHETORIC. Crown 8vo. 4s. 6d.

LESSONS ON REASONING. Fcp. 8vo. 1s. 6d.

BACON'S ESSAYS, with Annotations. 8vo. 10s. 6d.

Whately. — *ENGLISH SYNONYMS.* By E. JANE WHATELY. Edited by her Father, R. WHATELY, D.D. Fcp. 8vo. 3s.

White and Riddle.—*A LATIN-ENGLISH DICTIONARY.* By J. T. WHITE, D.D. Oxon. and J. J. E. RIDDLE, M.A. Oxon. Founded on the larger Dictionary of Freund. Royal 8vo. 21s.

White.—*A CONCISE LATIN-ENGLISH DICTIONARY,* for the Use of Advanced Scholars and University Students. By the Rev. J. T. WHITE, D.D. Royal 8vo. 12s.

Wilcocks.—*THE SEA FISHERMAN.* Comprising the Chief Methods of Hook and Line Fishing in the British and other Seas, and Remarks on Nets, Boats, and Boating. By J. C. WILCOCKS. Profusely Illustrated. New and Cheaper Edition, much enlarged, crown 8vo. 6s.

Williams. — *MANUAL OF TELEGRAPHY.* By W. WILLIAMS, Superintendent of Indian Government Telegraphs. Illustrated by 93 Wood Engravings. 8vo. 10s. 6d.

Willich. — *POPULAR TABLES* for giving Information for ascertaining the value of Lifehold, Leasehold, and Church Property, the Public Funds, &c. By CHARLES M. WILLICH. Edited by MONTAGU MARRIOTT. Crown 8vo. 10s.

Wilson.—*A MANUAL OF HEALTH-SCIENCE.* Adapted for Use in Schools and Colleges, and suited to the Requirements of Students preparing for the Examinations in Hygiene of the Science and Art Department, &c. By ANDREW WILSON, F.R.S.E. F.L.S. &c. With 74 Illustrations. Crown 8vo. 2s. 6d.

Witt.—WORKS BY PROF. WITT. Translated from the German by FRANCES YOUNGHUSBAND.

THE TROJAN WAR. With a Preface by the Rev. W. G. RUTHERFORD, M.A. Head-Master of Westminster School. Crown 8vo. 2s.

MYTHS OF HELLAS; or, Greek Tales. Crown 8vo. 3s. 6d.

THE WANDERINGS OF ULYSSES. Crown 8vo. 3s. 6d.

Wood.—WORKS BY REV. J. G. WOOD.

HOMES WITHOUT HANDS; a Description of the Habitations of Animals, classed according to the Principle of Construction. With about 140 Vignettes on Wood. 8vo. 10s. 6d.

INSECTS AT HOME; a Popular Account of British Insects, their Structure, Habits, and Transformations. 8vo. Woodcuts, 10s. 6d.

INSECTS ABROAD; a Popular Account of Foreign Insects, their Structure, Habits, and Transformations. 8vo. Woodcuts, 10s. 6d.

BIBLE ANIMALS; a Description of every Living Creature mentioned in the Scriptures. With 112 Vignettes. 8vo. 10s. 6d.

STRANGE DWELLINGS; a Description of the Habitations of Animals, abridged from 'Homes without Hands.' With Frontispiece and 60 Woodcuts. Crown 8vo. 5s. Popular Edition, 4to. 6d.

HORSE AND MAN: their Mutual Dependence and Duties. With 49 Illustrations. 8vo. 14s.

ILLUSTRATED STABLE MAXIMS. To be hung in Stables for the use of Grooms, Stablemen, and others who are in charge of Horses. On Sheet, 4s.

OUT OF DOORS; a Selection of Original Articles on Practical Natural History. With 6 Illustrations. Crown 8vo. 5s.

COMMON BRITISH INSECTS: BEETLES, MOTHS, AND BUTTERFLIES. Crown 8vo. with 130 Woodcuts, 3s. 6d.

PETLAND REVISITED. With numerous Illustrations, drawn specially by Miss Margery May, engraved on Wood by G. Pearson. Crown 8vo. 7s. 6d.

Wylie.—HISTORY OF ENGLAND UNDER HENRY THE FOURTH. By JAMES HAMILTON WYLIE, M.A. one of Her Majesty's Inspectors of Schools. (2 vols.) Vol. 1, crown 8vo. 10s. 6d.

Wylie.—LABOUR, LEISURE, AND LUXURY; a Contribution to Present Practical Political Economy. By ALEXANDER WYLIE, of Glasgow. Crown 8vo. 6s.

Year's Sport (The). A Review of British Sports and Pastimes for the Year 1885. Edited by A. E. T. WATSON. 8vo. 21s. half-bound.

Youatt.—WORKS BY WILLIAM YOUATT.

THE HORSE. Revised and enlarged by W. WATSON, M.R.C.V.S. 8vo. Woodcuts, 7s. 6d.

THE DOG. Revised and enlarged. 8vo. Woodcuts. 6s.

Zeller.—WORKS BY DR. E. ZELLER.

HISTORY OF ECLECTICISM IN GREEK PHILOSOPHY. Translated by SARAH F. ALLEYNE. Crown 8vo. 10s. 6d.

THE STOICS, EPICUREANS, AND SCEPTICS. Translated by the Rev. O. J. REICHEL, M.A. Crown 8vo. 15s.

SOCRATES AND THE SOCRATIC SCHOOLS. Translated by the Rev. O. J. REICHEL, M.A. Crown 8vo. 10s. 6d.

PLATO AND THE OLDER ACADEMY. Translated by S. FRANCES ALLEYNE and ALFRED GOODWIN, B.A. Crown 8vo. 18s.

THE PRE-SOCRATIC SCHOOLS; a History of Greek Philosophy from the Earliest Period to the time of Socrates. Translated by SARAH F. ALLEYNE. 2 vols. crown 8vo. 30s.

OUTLINES OF THE HISTORY OF GREEK PHILOSOPHY. Translated by S. FRANCES ALLEYNE and EVELYN ABBOTT. Crown 8vo. 10s. 6d.

TEXT-BOOKS OF SCIENCE.

ADAPTED FOR THE USE OF STUDENTS IN PUBLIC AND SCIENCE SCHOOLS.

PHOTOGRAPHY. By Captain W. DE WIVE-LESLIE ABNEY, F.R.S. late Instructor in Chemistry and Photography at the School of Military Engineering, Chatham. With 105 Woodcuts. 3s. 6d.

ON THE STRENGTH OF MATERIALS AND Structures: the Strength of Materials as depending on their quality and as ascertained by Testing Apparatus; the Strength of Structures, as depending on their form and arrangement, and on the materials of which they are composed. By Sir J. ANDERSON, C.E. &c. 3s. 6d.

INTRODUCTION TO THE STUDY OF ORGANIC Chemistry; the Chemistry of Carbon and its Compounds. By HENRY E. ARMSTRONG, Ph.D. F.C.S. With 8 Woodcuts. 3s. 6d.

ELEMENTS OF ASTRONOMY. By R. S. BALL, LL.D. F.R.S. Andrews Professor of Astronomy in the Univ. of Dublin, Royal Astronomer of Ireland. With 136 Figures and Diagrams. 6s.

RAILWAY APPLIANCES. A Description of Details of Railway Construction subsequent to the completion of Earthworks and Masonry, including a short Notice of Railway Rolling Stock. By J. W. BARRY. With 207 Woodcuts. 3s. 6d.

SYSTEMATIC MINERALOGY. By HILARY BAUERMAN, F.G.S. Associate of the Royal School of Mines. With 373 Diagrams. 6s.

DESCRIPTIVE MINERALOGY. By the same Author. With 236 Woodcuts and Diagrams. 6s.

METALS, THEIR PROPERTIES AND TREATment. By C. L. BLOXAM and A. K. HUNTINGTON, Professors in King's College, London. With 130 Wood Engravings. 5s.

PRACTICAL PHYSICS. By R. T. GLAZEBROOK, M.A. F.R.S. and W. N. SHAW, M.A. With 62 Woodcuts. 6s.

PHYSICAL OPTICS. By R. T. GLAZEBROOK, M.A. F.R.S. Fellow and Lecturer of Trin. Coll. Demonstrator of Physics at the Cavendish Laboratory, Cambridge. With 183 Woodcuts of Apparatus, &c. 6s.

THE ART OF ELECTRO-METALLURGY, including all known Processes of Electro-Deposition. By G. GORE, LL.D. F.R.S. With 56 Woodcuts. 6s.

ALGEBRA AND TRIGONOMETRY. By the Rev. WILLIAM NATHANIEL GRIFFIN, B.D. 3s. 6d.

NOTES ON THE ELEMENTS OF ALGEBRA and Trigonometry. With Solutions of the more difficult Questions. By the Rev. W. N. GRIFFIN, B.D. 3s. 6d.

ELECTRICITY AND MAGNETISM. By FLEEMING JENKIN, F.R.SS. L. & E. Professor of Engineering in the University of Edinburgh. 3s. 6d.

THEORY OF HEAT. By J. CLERK MAXWELL, M.A. LL.D. Edin. F.R.SS. L. & E. With 41 Woodcuts. 3s. 6d.

TECHNICAL ARITHMETIC AND MENSURAtion. By CHARLES W. MERRIFIELD, F.R.S. 3s. 6d.

KEY TO MERRIFIELD'S TEXT-BOOK OF Technical Arithmetic and Mensuration. By the Rev. JOHN HUNTER, M.A. formerly Vice-Principal of the National Society's Training College, Battersea. 3s. 6d.

INTRODUCTION TO THE STUDY OF INORganic Chemistry. By WILLIAM ALLEN MILLER, M.D. LL.D. F.R.S. With 71 Woodcuts. 3s. 6d.

TELEGRAPHY. By W. H. PREECE, C.E. and J. SIVEWRIGHT, M.A. With 160 Woodcuts. 5s.

THE STUDY OF ROCKS, an Elementary Text-Book of Petrology. By FRANK RUTLEY, F.G.S. of Her Majesty's Geological Survey. With 6 Plates and 88 Woodcuts. 4s. 6d.

WORKSHOP APPLIANCES, including Descriptions of some of the Gauging and Measuring Instruments—Hand Cutting Tools, Lathes, Drilling, Planing, and other Machine Tools used by Engineers. By C. P. B. SHELLEY, M.I.C.E. With 292 Woodcuts. 4s. 6d.

STRUCTURAL AND PHYSIOLOGICAL BOTANY. By Dr. OTTO WILHELM THOMÉ, Professor of Botany, School of Science and Art, Cologne. Translated by A. W. BENNETT, M.A. B.Sc. F.L.S. With 600 Woodcuts. 6s.

QUANTITATIVE CHEMICAL ANALYSIS. By T. E. THORPE, F.R.S.E. Ph.D. Professor of Chemistry in the Andersonian University, Glasgow. With 88 Woodcuts. 4s. 6d.

MANUAL OF QUALITATIVE ANALYSIS AND Laboratory Practice. By T. E. THORPE, Ph.D. F.R.S.E. Professor of Chemistry in the Andersonian University, Glasgow; and M. M. PATTISON MUIR. 3s. 6d.

INTRODUCTION TO THE STUDY OF CHEMical Philosophy; the Principals of Theoretical and Systematical Chemistry. By WILLIAM A. TILDEN, B.Sc. London, F.C.S. With 5 Woodcuts. 3s. 6d. With Answers to Problems, 4s. 6d.

ELEMENTS OF MACHINE DESIGN; an Introduction to the Principles which determine the Arrangement and Proportion of the Parts of Machine, and a Collection of Rules for Machine Designs. By W. CAWTHORNE UNWIN, B.Sc. Assoc. Inst. C.E. With 325 Woodcuts. 6s.

PLANE AND SOLID GEOMETRY. By the Rev. H. W. WATSON, formerly Fellow of Trinity College, Cambridge. 3s. 6d.

EPOCHS OF HISTORY.

EPOCHS OF ANCIENT HISTORY.

Edited by the Rev. Sir G. W. Cox, Bart. M.A. and by C. Sankey, M.A. 10 Volumes, fcp. 8vo. with Maps, price 2s. 6d. each vol.

THE GRACCHI, MARIUS, AND SULLA. By A. H. BEESLY, M.A. Assistant-Master Marlborough College. With 2 Maps.

THE EARLY ROMAN EMPIRE. From the Assassination of Julius Cæsar to the Assassination of Domitian. By the Rev. W. WOLFE CAPES, M.A. With 2 Coloured Maps.

THE ROMAN EMPIRE OF THE SECOND CENtury, or the Age of the Antonines. By the Rev. W. WOLFE CAPES, M.A. With 2 Coloured Maps.

THE ATHENIAN EMPIRE FROM THE FLIGHT of Xerxes to the Fall of Athens. By the Rev. Sir G. W. Cox, Bart. M.A. Joint-Editor of the Series. With 5 Maps.

THE GREEKS AND THE PERSIANS. By the Rev. Sir G. W. Cox, Bart. M.A. Joint-Editor of the Series. With 4 Coloured Maps.

THE RISE OF THE MACEDONIAN EMPIRE. By ARTHUR M. CURTEIS, M.A. formerly Fellow of Trinity College, Oxford. With 8 Maps.

ROME TO ITS CAPTURE BY THE GAULS. By WILHELM IHNE, Author of 'History of Rome.' With a Coloured Map.

THE ROMAN TRIUMVIRATES. By the Very Rev. CHARLES MERIVALE, D.D. Dean of Ely. With a Coloured Map.

THE SPARTAN AND THEBAN SUPREMACIES. By CHARLES SANKEY, M.A. Joint-Editor of the Series, Assistant-Master in Marlborough College. With 5 Maps.

ROME AND CARTHAGE, THE PUNIC WARS. By R. BOSWORTH SMITH, M.A. Assistant-Master, Harrow School. With 9 Maps and Plans.

EPOCHS OF MODERN HISTORY.

Edited by C. COLBECK, M.A. 17 vols. fcp. 8vo. with Maps, price 2s. 6d. each vol.

THE NORMANS IN EUROPE. By Rev. A. H. JOHNSON, M.A. late Fellow of All Souls College, Oxford; Historical Lecturer to Trinity, St. John's, Pembroke, and Wadham Colleges. With 3 Maps.

THE CRUSADES. By the Rev. Sir G. W. Cox, Bart. M.A. late Scholar of Trinity College, Oxford; Author of the 'Aryan Mythology,' &c. With a Coloured Map.

THE BEGINNING OF THE MIDDLE AGES. By the Very Rev. RICHARD WILLIAM CHURCH, M.A. &c. Dean of St. Paul's and Honorary Fellow of Oriel College, Oxford. With 3 Coloured Maps.

THE EARLY PLANTAGENETS. By the Right Rev. W. STUBBS, D.D. Bishop of Chester. With 2 Coloured Maps.

EDWARD THE THIRD. By the Rev. W. WARBURTON, M.A. late Fellow of All Souls College, Oxford; Her Majesty's Senior Inspector of Schools. With 3 Coloured Maps and 3 Genealogical Tables.

THE HOUSES OF LANCASTER AND YORK; with the Conquest and Loss of France. By JAMES GAIRDNER, of the Public Record Office, Editor of 'The Paston Letters,' &c. With 5 Coloured Maps.

THE ERA OF THE PROTESTANT REVOLUtion. By F. SEEBOHM, Author of 'The Oxford Reformers—Colet, Erasmus, More.' With 4 Coloured Maps and 12 Diagrams on Wood.

THE AGE OF ELIZABETH. By the Rev. M. CREIGHTON, M.A. LL.D. Dixie Professor of Ecclesiastical History in the University of Cambridge. With 5 Maps and 4 Genealogical Tables.

THE FIRST TWO STUARTS AND THE PURItan Revolution, 1603-1660. By SAMUEL RAWSON GARDINER, Author of 'The Thirty Years' War, 1618-1648.' With 4 Coloured Maps.

THE FALL OF THE STUARTS; AND WESTERN Europe from 1678 to 1697. By the Rev. EDWARD HALE, M.A. Assistant-Master at Eton. With 11 Maps and Plans.

THE AGE OF ANNE. By E. E. MORRIS, M.A. of Lincoln College, Oxford; Professor of English, &c. at the University of Melbourne. With 7 Maps and Plans.

THE THIRTY YEARS' WAR, 1618-1648. By SAMUEL RAWSON GARDINER, Fellow of All Souls College. With a Coloured Map.

THE EARLY HANOVERIANS. By E. E. MORRIS, M.A. Professor of English, &c. at the University of Melbourne.

FREDERICK THE GREAT AND THE SEVEN Years' War. By F. W. LONGMAN, of Balliol College, Oxford. With 2 Maps.

THE WAR OF AMERICAN INDEPENDENCE, 1775-1783. By J. M. LUDLOW, Barrister-at-Law. With 4 Coloured Maps.

THE FRENCH REVOLUTION, 1789-1795. By Mrs. S. R. GARDINER, Author of 'The Struggle Against Absolute Monarchy.' With 77 Maps.

THE EPOCH OF REFORM, 1830-1850. By JUSTIN M'CARTHY, M.P. Author of 'A History of Our Own Times.'

www.ingramcontent.com/pod-product-compliance
Lightning Source LLC
Chambersburg PA
CBHW032014220426
43664CB00006B/243